FEEDING THE CITY

D1253724

JOE R. AND TERESA LOZANO LONG SERIES IN
LATIN AMERICAN AND LATINO ART AND CULTURE

1 pound jerked beef
2 tablespoons bacon fat
1 tablespoon butter
1 grated onion
salt to taste
malagueta pepper [originally
   from West Africa]
1½ cups toasted manioc meal

Cut meat into regular-size
pieces, trim off excess fat, and
wash well. Soak overnight in
cold water. Next day, hold under
running cold water and dry on
absorbent paper. Heat bacon fat
and butter and sauté onion. When
onion starts to brown, add pieces
of meat and seasoning and cook
over low flame. Stir with a fork,
adding a few drops of boiling
water from time to time, as
liquid evaporates. When meat is
brown and tender and almost dry,
add salt and chopped pepper and
turn into a heavy mortar to be
pounded until meat is shredded.
Add the manioc meal, a little at
a time, until mixture is of the
consistency of bread crumbs.
Serve immediately.

6 hardboiled eggs
1 onion, chopped
2 cups manioc meal
½ cup butter
salt

Peel eggs and cut into halves,
separating yolks and whites.
Chop yolks. Sauté the onion.
Heat the dry manioc meal in a
heavy shallow pan until it begins
to turn a pale beige, stirring
frequently so that it roasts
evenly. Melt butter and combine
with manioc meal to form a
loose mixture like toasted bread
crumbs. Stir until all the butter
is absorbed. Mix in chopped
yolks, the sautéed onion, and salt
to taste. Garnish with hardboiled
egg whites.

*Adapted from Margarette de
Andrade,* Brazilian Cookery,
Traditional and Modern *(Rio de
Janeiro: Casa do Livro Eldorado,
1975)*

FEEDING THE CITY

From Street Market to Liberal Reform

in Salvador, Brazil, 1780–1860

RICHARD GRAHAM

UNIVERSITY OF TEXAS PRESS ⟡ AUSTIN

First edition, 2010

Requests for permission to reproduce material from this work should be
sent to:
 Permissions
 University of Texas Press
 P.O. Box 7819
 Austin, TX 78713-7819
 www.utpress.utexas.edu/index.php/rp-form

⊛ The paper used in this book meets the minimum requirements of ANSI/NISO
Z39.48-1992 (R1997) (Permanence of Paper).

LIBRARY OF CONGRESS CATALOGING-IN-PUBLICATION DATA

Graham, Richard, 1934–
 Feeding the city : from street market to liberal reform in Salvador, Brazil,
1780–1860 / Richard Graham. — 1st ed.
 p. cm. — (Joe R. and Teresa Lozano Long series in Latin American and
Latino art and culture)
 Includes bibliographical references and index.
 ISBN 978-0-292-72299-6 (cloth : alk. paper) — ISBN 978-0-292-72326-9 (pbk. :
alk. paper)
 1. Produce trade—Brazil—Salvador—History. 2. Salvador (Brazil)—
Government policy. 3. Food supply—Government policy—Salvador (Brazil).
4. Salvador (Brazil)—Social conditions. I. Title.
HD9014.B72G73 2010
381′.41098142—dc22

                                                            2010007680

FOR SANDRA

CONTENTS

LIST OF MAPS AND ILLUSTRATIONS

THE SMALLEST COIN OF THE Portuguese realm was the *vintém*, which could theoretically be divided into twenty *réis*. A thousand *réis* made a *mil-réis* (written 1$000) and a million *réis* constituted a *conto* (1:000$000). The purchasing value of the currency declined considerably over the course of the eighty years covered in this book, so I first converted nominal values of postmortem estates and some other items to 1824 values, as I explain in Appendix A. I then established one particular estate, described in some detail, as a standard to which I compared others. In the notes, however, I indicate both the nominal and real value, the latter in parentheses.

There were many measures used for food, only two of which I use in the text. The *alqueire* in Salvador was equivalent to 36.27 liters; except in some notes and tables where precision is important, I use the word "bushel" instead. The *arroba* weighed 32 pounds, or about 15 kilos.

For names or words in Portuguese within the text, I use modern spelling. In the notes I have cited authors and titles as they appeared in the work used, whether it is a manuscript or has been published.

LITTLE DID I THINK WHEN I received a summer's grant for curriculum development from Global Education Associates' World Order Program that it would eventually lead to a book. The idea was to prepare an undergraduate course that would draw attention to the troubling issues facing the modern world regarding food and its inequitable distribution. As a historian I wanted to explore this question into the past, and as a teacher I wanted to engage my students. I began the course with readings about the present, from protein complementarity to infant mortality, and then moved backward in time, discussing land reform, export economies, and cultural differences, arriving finally at the "conquest" of America, the Columbian exchange, and the Atlantic slave trade as we searched for immediate and long-term causes. I hope my students found this as challenging as did I. Those were the early beginnings of this very different book about food, its producers, its traders, and its meanings.

By luck, I was in the city of Salvador the next summer, on my way to visit my sister in the interior, and decided to revisit a couple of archives. At the city archive, to my amazement, I found the late eighteenth-century manuscript records of licenses granted to street vendors, grocers, butchers, and boatmen, with the names of ordinary people pursuing their business—names that are normally inaccessible to historians. I then learned that at the Bahia state archive a project was underway to prepare a computerized index of postmortem estate inventories. When I presented a short list of names of vendors and shopkeepers, I was surprised to find that some 10 percent of them turned up as principals in these records. Excited by the possibilities, I returned to the University of Texas at Austin at the end of the summer with a new project in mind for further research.

There have been many detours on the journey from those revelatory archival moments to the present book, but they have all offered me the pleasure not only of discovering lives of long-ago people, but also of establishing connections with people alive today who helped me along the way. Archives are useless to the historian without archivists to make their holdings available. At the Bahia state archive I counted especially on the day-to-day assistance of D. Edy Alleluia and Sr. Daniel, who brought bundles and more bundles of documents to the reading room. Mercedes (Mercedinha) Guerra used computer data that she was compiling at that very time to search for the ever-growing lists of names I presented to her, and D. Judite was the key to the separate division housing estate inventories. The director of the archive, Anna Amélia Vieira Nascimento, added to her efficient administration the excited interest of a fellow historian. At the city archive I was greatly helped by Sr. Felisberto. Neusa Esteves shared her archival knowledge at the Santa Casa de Misericórdia.

In the many divisions of the National Archive in Rio de Janeiro I have consistently found the staff conscientious and ready to help. I have had the pleasure of seeing the archive move from the ancient building on the other side of the square to successively more spacious quarters, while the catalog, once held in two large cylindrical cabinets, has been transformed into a sophisticated online instrument. The staff's workload has steadily increased as a transformed history profession turns out dozens of dedicated young researchers. Jaime Antunes da Silva has directed the institution with skill and insight, never forgetting its ultimate purpose to advance knowledge. In the reading room, Sátiro Ferreira Nunes makes the system work and willingly shares his knowledge of how the documents are organized. At the manuscript division in the National Library I was helped by Waldyr Cunha before his retirement and then by Sr. Raimundo. The library and archive of the Instituto Histórico e Geográfico Brasileiro, ably directed by the institute's president, Arno Wehling, offers a quiet place to work as well as a magnificent view of Guanabara Bay. I always benefit from the friendly and effective presence there of librarian Maura Corrêa e Castro.

I long envied Brazilian historians who can be in the classroom today and at an archive tomorrow. For me a visit to an archive meant funding for travel and months of living abroad. Without it, this book would not have been possible. I gratefully acknowledge major support from the Fulbright-Hays Faculty Research Abroad Program, the J. William Fulbright Foreign Scholarship Board, the National Endowment for the Humanities, and the University Research Institute at the University of Texas at Austin. Almost of equal importance are those smaller but essential grants for summer travel that made it possible for me to do research not only in Salvador and Rio de Janeiro but in Lisbon; these grants were made by the university's Institute of Latin American Studies, so ably led in those days by William Glade and Nicholas Shumway.

Other scholars have been unstinting in their help and fellowship. I think especially of João José Reis, who put me in touch with a new generation of historians in Bahia, and of Luis Henrique Dias Tavares, whom I first met as director of the state archive in 1959 when I was doing research on the British presence in Brazil. Guilherme and Lúcia Pereira das Neves in Rio de Janeiro have been the best of companions as we talked about Brazil's past. In North America many have aided this work in one way or another. Members of the Santa Fe Seminar patiently read one chapter after another over a period of some two years. Four colleagues read through an earlier draft of the entire manuscript: B. J. Barickman, William French, Hendrik Kraay, and James Sidbury. I am deeply grateful for their insightful comments. My son Stephen Graham, although wishing I would write a different book, pushed me to pay attention to what I had found on the dynamism of those who worked in the food trade in Salvador. Then there are the anonymous readers contacted by the University of Texas Press who led me to expand on many points and sometimes to search for just the right words to describe what I was finding. Other historians whom I have never met have written about similar trading activity elsewhere in the world, forcing me to look again at the evidence before me. I regret that in order to keep down the length of this book—and on the advice of the publisher—I have removed most of those references. I never intended this book to be a comparative history, but a study of one city and its energetic inhabitants. The comparisons will wait for another time.

I owe more to my wife, Sandra, than I can say. She has been a stimulus to my thinking, a foil to my arguments, and a stern but constructive critic, but most of all a companion in the adventure of discovery. To her I dedicate this book.

FEEDING THE CITY

INTRODUCTION

NO CITY FEEDS ITSELF. Unlike a village or small town, a city depends on a vast array of outsiders to grow or raise food, and most essentially, on people to transport it, and on middlemen and -women to buy and resell it to consumers. Salvador, Brazil—often called Bahia—was a major city in the Americas at the end of the eighteenth century. It invites inquiry not only into such a commercial network, but also into what its workings reveal about the city's social makeup. Street sellers, boatmen, grocers, butchers, cattle dealers, importers; men and women; blacks, mulattos, and whites; slaves, ex-slaves, and free—these are the actors here. Their actions helped forge the city, and their dealings bring its social order, customs, ideologies, and conflicts into relief.

Salvador quintessentially belonged to the Atlantic World, where Europe met Africa in the Americas. This city on the east coast of Bahia province faces an enormous bay, making it one of the few great ports of the South Atlantic. From the rich sugar-, tobacco-, and food-stuff-producing lands surrounding the bay—collectively referred to as the Recôncavo—arrived the goods that fed local people and were exchanged for a great variety of overseas imports in the city's bustling center. Europeans, Africans, people of European and African descent, and a few Indians met in Salvador, establishing tangled links while simultaneously redefining the boundaries that separated them. Governing institutions developed in Europe were here applied to a diverse population and reshaped to fit what must have seemed an exotic place to its Portuguese administrators. People brought up entirely in Brazil argued for or against economic principles or revolutionary doctrines elaborated overseas. Slavery and the slave trade deeply incised the city's social and political being, and its large black population de-

MAP I.1. Brazil and Its Provinces in 1860

cisively influenced local habits, signs, and symbols. Religious beliefs and practices displayed values derived from both Africa and Portugal. By borrowing from and adapting to each other, city dwellers forged a new culture with its own ways of being. In time the city became unique, as different from other Atlantic cities as they were from it.[1]

Salvador played an important role for all of Brazil. It thrived as the commercial entrepôt of the entire captaincy (later province) of Bahia, and its merchants, large and small, also traded far beyond its borders. When gold and diamonds were discovered in Minas Gerais, the initial supply route to that area originated in Salvador. Although its role as capital and principal administrative center diminished after 1763, when the Crown transferred the seat of the Brazilian viceroyalty to Rio de Janeiro, its cadres of civil servants—attached to the governor of the captaincy, to civil, criminal, and church judges, and to fiscal offices—continued to exercise a powerful influence over an extensive region. Until the 1750s Brazil's only High Court sat in Salvador, and it continued to hear cases from all the northern provinces until well into the nineteenth century. Brazil's archbishop had his seat there and made Church policy for the entire country. Much of the city's life nevertheless remains uncharted terrain, still to be mapped.

The diet of Salvador's inhabitants rested on two staples: manioc meal, the major source of calories, and meat. Cattle were driven to the city, but manioc meal came on boats from across a large bay, as did the bulk of the city's fruits and vegetables. Those who were better off also consumed items imported from overseas in larger ships, especially wine and olive oil, but also beer, cheese, wheat flour, and a great variety of high-value, low-volume treats. At the other end of the social spectrum, slaves often had little more than manioc meal and a little dried or salted beef to eat. Africans deeply influenced the cooking methods and spices used in most households, with a liberal use of red palm oil, peppers, coconuts, and peanuts.

As we look at the city as it appeared during the late eighteenth and early nineteenth centuries, the immense variety of its inhabitants, along with their close and multifaceted interconnectedness, is especially striking.[2] Those who distributed and sold food—whether humble street vendors or substantial grocers, butchers or cattle traders, ordinary sailors or captains on boats bringing foodstuffs from across the bay and from ports along the Atlantic coast—were connected to practically everyone in the city. Their occupations were central to urban life but rarely mentioned in the many works on the region that have dealt primarily with sugar planters, international merchants, or slaves, while leaving everybody else unnoticed. People of a middling sort, some better off than others, as well as some very poor and the enslaved, all working hard, filled the city and made it hum. This urban setting allowed the formation of a large intermediary sector of tradespeople with both vertical and horizontal ties to others.

The energy and movement of Salvador's residents display how slave and free, black and white, women and men, the poor and the not-so-poor related to each other, simultaneously exemplifying the laddered ordering of society and challenging our ready notions of how such a society must have worked. Instead of seeing only exploiters and exploited, we find here negotiated encounters along a shifting terrain. As a result, I take particular exception to those who portray blacks, slaves, and women to be, in their essence, just victims, and whites, free persons, and men essentially as oppressors, rather than as persons with multiple concerns and varied relationships, as complex human beings, even if some were privileged and many more severely exploited. Such people occupied social positions along a continuum rather than in sharply separated groups.

In exploring people's lives across a great range of individual experiences, I have looked for specifics, trying to grasp something of the context within which they lived. By focusing on actual practices, a broader notion emerges of how understandings of race shaped behavior or were shaped by law and practice. Similarly, "slave" and "slavery" are terms too blunt to do justice to the variegated experiences they encompassed. There are categories that I, as a historian, impose upon people who did not necessarily think of themselves as belonging to them, but I try to avoid drawing a priori conclusions about individuals from such classifications. In emphasizing particular men and women, and what joined and disjoined them, I look for adjectives rather than labels. To emphasize the particularity of the people who appear here, I often insist on naming them rather than referring to their generic status, even if they surface only once.

The food trade fits within a larger context of concerns that went beyond the question of how food got to people's tables to matters of government responsibility for protecting consumers, the proper place of economic regulation, and debates on what makes a society good and just. At least from medieval times, one of the tasks of city government in most of the Western world had been to ensure adequate and safe food supplies at affordable prices to urban residents. Salvador's city council, following Portuguese precedents, took this responsibility seriously. Attempting to apply a rational order to this task led to the creation in the early 1780s of two publicly owned institutions—a central grains market and a slaughterhouse—that crucially touched on food traders' work. Beginning at that very time, however, some writers and public officials began to criticize the older view of the state and its relationship to the individual, proposing a more freewheeling approach to the economic activity of food traders and less attention to protecting buyers.

A turning point was the year-long war for Brazilian independence from Portugal in 1822–1823, the outcome of which turned on an ultimately successful siege in which boatmen cut off Salvador's food supply. Not only did wartime disruptions themselves cause immediate shifts in many people's lives, disturbing the social order, but the reforms that ensued after independence, inspired by models borrowed from across the Atlantic, had major long-term effects on the activity of those engaged in buying and selling foodstuffs. These liberalizing measures did not succeed in solving the subsistence problems of the great mass of the population, and many of the new policies were resisted, sometimes violently, and gradually watered down or entirely abandoned. The debate on the new philosophy of government can be read as residents reflecting and commenting on themselves and their society, giving voice to their notions regarding its categories and defending values they held dear.

Everyone is daily enmeshed in institutional frameworks with rules that guide behavior, and some of them leave records that provide historians with rich documentary lodes to be explored. Connections between historical actors are often vividly captured in seemingly unlikely documents produced by impersonal government agencies, the actions of which critically impacted thousands of individuals. The institutions that oriented the food trade—the public grains market and slaughterhouse—stand out especially in this account because they influenced the actions of so many. Wills and estate inventories crucially reveal exchanges between people placed in differing social positions, without for a moment casting doubt on the existence or tenacity of such divisions. They form another source on which I rely, especially given the relative absence of diaries and personal letters among Brazilians, and the fact that inheritance law—by forcing the division of goods among legally prescribed heirs—touched even humble households. The opening phrases of last wills and testaments are often formulaic, but from then on they vary enormously and shed much light on affective ties, business connections, and understandings and expectations about others' behavior, as well as details about, for instance, a favorite saint or the testator's past.[3] They speak of friends and the children of friends, of concubines and godchildren, of love and rivalry.

In the first part of this book I write about the people who participated in the food trade, without much attention to alterations over time, whereas the second part is specifically about change and explores the political context within which traders worked. In the initial chapter I describe the physical, social, cultural, and political setting of their lives. The next two chapters discuss street vendors and grocers: Chapter 2 establishes who they were, what they sold, where they sold it, and looks at how they lived—that is, their housing, furnishings, and clothes; Chapter 3 concentrates on their social world—their families, friends, and neighbors—as well as their business contacts and how they fit in as patrons and clients, borrowers and lenders. Chapter 4 focuses on the captains and sailors aboard the boats and ships delivering foodstuffs to Salvador; their wealth or lack of it; their legal status as free, freed, or slaves; the types of craft they sailed; their cargoes; their special skills; and the implications of their geographical mobility. The grains market where all the corn, beans, rice, and manioc meal entering Salvador were required to be placed for sale first is the subject of Chapter 5. After discussing the market's creation and its staff, I turn to the traders themselves—women and men, Africans and Portuguese—before examining the stevedores and porters employed there who successfully struck in early 1837 over newly imposed requirements that they found demeaning. In Chapter 6 I examine the cattle and meat trade and its three nodes: the stockyard, slaughterhouse, and butcher shop. The social positions of those involved and, especially, the tensions that surfaced in their interactions—culminating in a strike of slaughtermen defeated through the use of slaves—are the central points of Chapter 7.

Whereas Part 1 presents close-up portraits of many individual traders and their work, Part 2 broadens the perspective to encompass, first, a major political event—a war—and, then, more broadly still, conflicting ideas on governmental policy regarding the food trade. It begins with Chapter 8, which focuses on Brazil's War of Independence from Portugal (1822–1823), recounting how the crucial issue for both the insurgents and the Portuguese was how to secure food for one's own forces while denying it to the enemy—a demanding and complicated task. In Chapter 9 I turn to the ways by which these events caused a shock to the social system: first by provoking an enormous physical dislocation of residents, and then by weakening notions about hierarchy, even among those at the top, by enhancing the power of ordinary sailors and unsettling the expected ties between slaves and masters. Chapter 10 backtracks chronologically to examine policy prescriptions developed before the war as leaders in Portugal and Brazil slowly moved toward a conviction that releasing the market from government control would benefit everyone. Chapter 11 traces a movement in the opposite direction after the war, as the application of those liberal principles failed to produce abundance and lower prices, leading instead by the 1850s to riot and rebellion.

When I began this project, I expected to find a stable and rigidly hierarchical society firmly glued together by a paternalistic culture in which protection was exchanged for obedience. But, as I focused on individuals, most of whom were far from the top ranks, I found a remarkable stretchiness to social categories, with much nuance, negotiation, and flexibility. Salvador was at one and the same time a city of orders and the locus of competition, rational decision making, fluidity, and opportunity. Nothing was immutable, nor was change unidirectional.

CHAPTER 1

THE CITY ON A BAY

ON THE EASTERN COAST OF BRAZIL and facing westward across a magnificent bay lies the city of Salvador or, to give it its full name, São Salvador da Bahia de Todos os Santos (Holy Savior of the Bay of All Saints). The city's name eloquently recalls the bay as it is its most defining feature. Its shimmering waters could be seen to the west from almost any vantage point in the city, and in 1780 its inhabitants received most of their foodstuffs, except meat, by boat. This enormous bay reaches inland for some 27 miles. It measures 22 miles at its widest point, and 7 miles across at its mouth (see Map 1.1). A traveler in 1809 marveled that in it "the united shipping of the universe might rendezvous without confusion." Because the city sits on a peninsula jutting southward, separating the bay from the Atlantic, its port is protected from ocean storms while its inhabitants enjoy almost constant sea breezes, keeping the temperature relatively mild despite being only 13 degrees south of the equator. Charles Darwin wrote that "no person could imagine anything so beautiful as the ancient town of Bahia; it is fairly embosomed in a luxuriant wood of beautiful trees and situated on a steep bank [that] overlooks the calm waters of the great bay of All Saints."[1] The city's topography and built environment, its social makeup, and its culture provided the setting for the lives of the people I write about in this book and their dealings in the local food trade.

THE CITY

Nothing struck an arriving visitor more immediately than the rugged escarpment separating the "lower city" from the "upper" one. Rising some 200 to 350 feet and broken by numerous crevices, it still impresses anyone viewing the city from the water. In the 1840s an

American visitor admired the two "extended and curving [horizontal] lines of whitened buildings . . . separated by a broad, rich belt of green, itself here and there dotted with houses." An extremely narrow space separated the escarpment's base from the shore, not more than two or three short blocks in width and in many places not even that, although many blocks long and heavily populated.[2] The plateau beyond the high cliff is wider, but gives way to a network of streambeds and marshes (since canalized and drained) out of which rise other stretches of high ground onto which the upper city had gradually spread across a connecting neck of higher land. At this eastern edge of the city, in the words of a visiting Frenchman, lay a "lovely" elongated lake called the Dique, with "cold and limpid" water, surrounded by palm trees. The land beyond it, despite many hills and valleys, gradually declines eastward to the ocean (see Maps 1.2 and 1.3).[3]

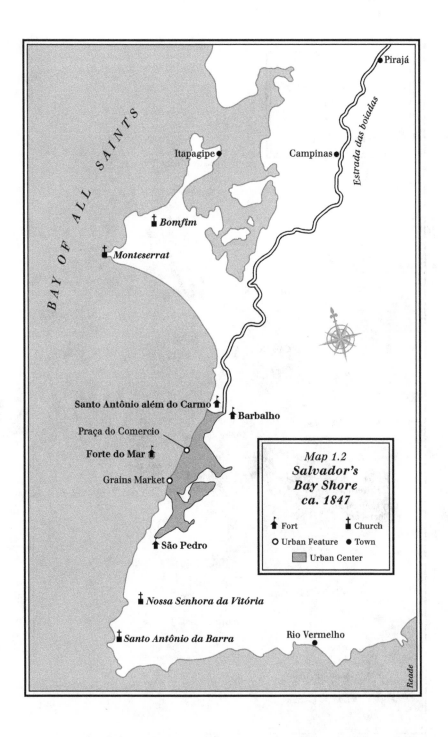

Pirajá

Estrada das boiadas

Itapagipe

Campinas

BAY OF ALL SAINTS

✝ *Bomfim*

✝ *Monteserrat*

Santo Antônio além do Carmo ✝

✝ Barbalho

Praça do Comercio

Forte do Mar ✝

○

Grains Market ○

Map 1.2
Salvador's
Bay Shore
ca. 1847

✝ Fort   ✝ Church
○ Urban Feature ● Town
▨ Urban Center

✝ São Pedro

✝ *Nossa Senhora da Vitória*

✝ *Santo Antônio da Barra*

Rio Vermelho

Reade

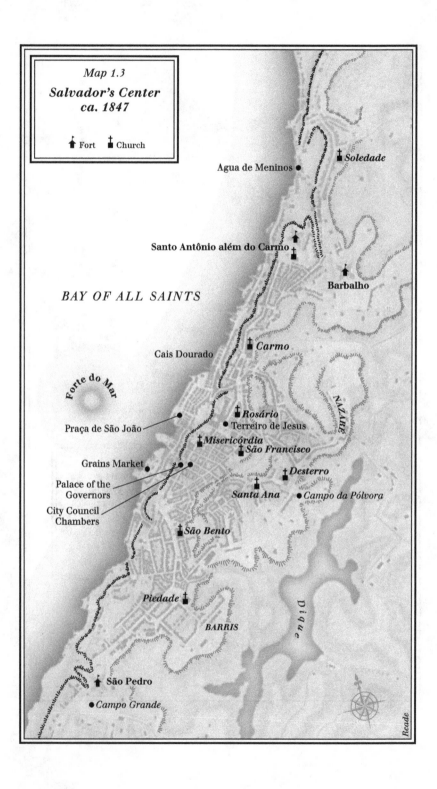

Map 1.3
Salvador's Center
ca. 1847

🚩 Fort   ✝ Church

Soledade

Agua de Meninos ●

Santo Antônio além do Carmo

Barbalho

BAY OF ALL SAINTS

Cais Dourado

Carmo

NAZARÉ

Forte do Mar

Rosário
Terreiro de Jesus

Praça de São João

Misericórdia
São Francisco

Grains Market

Desterro

Palace of the
Governors

Santa Ana

Campo da Pólvora

City Council
Chambers

São Bento

Piedade

Dique

BARRIS

São Pedro

● Campo Grande

Reade

FIGURE 1.1. Panorama of the city, 1861 (see also frontispiece)

The bluff that physically separates the two parts of the city served to divide it socially, an organization of urban space reminiscent of other Portuguese cities around the globe. Describing the lower city with only some exaggeration, a contemporary noted that "all the large merchants reside there with their houses, goods, and offices, as well as all the shopkeepers who live . . . where they have their stores." Canoes and boats were pulled up on its beach to unload foodstuffs brought from across the bay. An intense trade in African slaves turned the lower city into an extended slave market. Wharf-side warehouses with jetties served the export trade in sugar, tobacco, coffee, cotton, and hides, and handled the great bundles, barrels, and casks of merchandise arriving from Europe and even India, including textiles, iron goods, spices, wine, olive oil, and salted codfish. Customers found ship chandlers, hardware stores, watchmakers, suppliers of heavy equipment for the plantations, dry goods stores, toy stores, and insurance company offices—all in the lower city. This was a place of bustle and chatter.[4]

The central part of the upper city housed the governor's residence and offices, the High Court, the city council chambers and jail, the cathedral and the archbishop's residence, the principal monastic institutions, and the fine houses of the wealthy. Although the upper

FIGURE 1.2. The lower city as seen from above, 1860

city was not without its share of narrow, crooked streets, many were wider and certainly less crowded than those in the lower one, with several squares. In 1818 a public garden was created overlooking the bay, providing a place for ladies and gentlemen to enjoy an evening stroll. In colonial times the most prominent people—those whose decisions ultimately affected everyone who traded in food—lived relatively near the headquarters of political and religious institutions, in an area delimited by the Carmelite monastery to the north (Carmo), the Benedictine one to the south (São Bento), and the Franciscan to the east (São Francisco), with the Santa Casa de Misericórdia—the city's most prestigious lay organization—at the center. Most of the prosperous sugar planters maintained houses in this part of town, allowing them to carry on urgent business as well as attend festivities and political celebrations.[5] By the first quarter of the nineteenth century, the upper city was no longer so exclusive, and a sprinkling of cafés, pharmacies, a few inns, and retail stores could be found there. By 1839 it included the Universo Hotel near the Benedictine monastery, with a billiard room over a grog shop. Its decline had begun.[6]

The city eventually grew beyond these early borders. After 1808, with the arrival in Brazil of the Portuguese court fleeing Napoleon's troops and the opening of the former colony's ports to ships from any friendly nation, foreign merchants, especially British ones, moved in. They shunned the lower city, preferring to live in the more appealing, and sanitary, upper one, and they settled in the area south of the center, especially the section of town toward Vitória church (see Map 1.2). The most successful Portuguese merchants had long set the example, and Vitória became an exclusive neighborhood. An American traveler, expressing his prejudices, commented that "on Vitória hill may be found the finest gardens that Bahia affords, the most enchanting walks, and the most ample shade. Here too are the best houses, the best air, the best water, and the best society."[7]

The less affluent middle class residents lived to the north of the central area, reaching to the church of Santo Antônio além do Carmo (Saint Anthony beyond the Carmelites). The neighborhood included grocery stores, tailor shops, the houses of civil servants and professionals, and the town houses of local farmers. Another middle-class neighborhood eventually grew up beyond a valley to the east, around the Santa Ana church, the Desterro nunnery, and the military exercise grounds (Campo da Pólvora), leading to the parish of Nazaré. Further east was a semirural section dotted with small farms and orchards, where an increasing number of people with city occupations lived, served by an occasional general store. From there a road descended southeast to a fishing village, Rio Vermelho, famous as a redoubt of runaway slaves and the delinquent poor.[8]

THE PEOPLE

It is impossible to determine exactly how many people lived in Salvador from the late eighteenth into the middle of the nineteenth century. As a crown official reported with some disgust in 1797, "no one knows for sure because the city council does not have a list of inhabitants." Yet various censuses attempted to count the population, and in a general way we can trace the growth in the city's population from the 39,209 reported in 1780 [1779] to 51,112 in 1807 and 112,641 in 1872.[9] To put these numbers in perspective it is worth noting that Mexico City, with 180,000 inhabitants in 1810, and Havana, with 85,000, consistently outdistanced Salvador. Rio de Janeiro, Buenos Aires, and Santiago overtook it during the period covered here, but

Table 1.1. Origin, Legal Status, and "Color" of the Population of Salvador, 1835

Origin and Legal Status	Number	%	% Slave	% Free	% Mulattos and Blacks	% Whites
Africans						
Slaves	17,325	26.5	26.5		26.5	
Freed	4,615	7.1		7.1	7.1	
Brazilians and Europeans						
Slaves	10,175	15.5	15.5		15.5	
Free and freed mulattos and blacks	14,885	22.7		22.7	22.7	
Free whites	18,500	28.2		28.2		28.2
Total	65,000	100.0	42.0	58.0	71.8	28.2

Source: João José Reis, *Slave Rebellion in Brazil: The Muslim Uprising of 1835 in Bahia*, trans. Arthur Brakel (Baltimore: Johns Hopkins University Press, 1993), p. 6.

Note: Numbers and percentages are estimates.

all other cities in Latin America, including Lima, remained smaller. As for port cities in the United States, the largest one was New York, with just over 33,000 people in 1790.[10]

Contemporaries classified Salvadoreans by their color (black, mulatto, white), their legal status (slave or free), and their place of birth (Africa, Portugal, Brazil). Every one of these categories was represented among those engaged in the food trade. Historian João José Reis has roughly calculated the distribution of the city's population in 1835 by geographic origin, legal status, and "color," as shown in Table 1.1. A provincial president that year was not far wrong when he reported with alarm that "indubitably the class of blacks immensely outnumbers that of whites." A German later said that "everyone who runs, cries, works; everyone who transports and carries is black."[11] It should be remembered, however, that whites were certainly not all well off, and the ranks of the poor included many of them.

With two-fifths of the population made up of slaves, it is not surprising that contemporaries found them everywhere, and slaves figured prominently among those engaged in the food trade. Salvador had long been a major market for imported slaves, especially from around 1580 when its hinterland supplied the bulk of the world's sugar. Even when the Caribbean put up sharp competition in the later seventeenth century, Bahian sugar exports, although not increasing, continued strong, and so did the planters' demand for fresh slaves from Africa. After the Haitian Revolution of 1791 the Brazilian sugar economy boomed again, and slave traders avidly exchanged Brazilian cane brandy and tobacco for still more Africans.[12] Even though in 1831 Brazil officially yielded to international pressure and outlawed slave trading, African slaves continued to be imported into Bahia in large numbers, just not landed on the city's docks. The prohibition on the importation of slaves was only sporadically and inadequately enforced until 1850, when it was definitively forbidden. Estimates of the number imported from 1786 to 1850 (see Table 1.2) should be understood as more suggestive than precise.[13] Besides being the entrepôt

Table 1.2. Estimated Number of Slaves Imported into Bahia, 1786–1850

Dates	Total Imports	Yearly Average
1786–1790	20,300	4,060
1791–1795	34,300	6,860
1796–1800	36,200	7,240
1801–1805	36,300	7,260
1806–1810	39,100	7,720
1811–1815	36,400	7,280
1816–1820	34,300	6,860
1821–1825	23,700	4,740
1826–1830	47,900	9,580
1831–1835	16,700	3,340
1836–1840	15,800	3,160
1841–1845	21,100	4,220
1846–1850	45,000	9,000
Total	407,100	6,263

Source: David Eltis, Economic Growth and the Ending of the Transatlantic Slave Trade (New York: Oxford, 1987), pp. 243–245. These totals were based on work then in progress and subsequently published by David Eltis, Stephen D. Behrendt, David Richardson, and Herbert S. Klein, eds., The Transatlantic Slave Trade: A Database on CD-ROM (Cambridge, Eng.: Cambridge University Press, 1999). Subsequent revisions may increase the numbers in this table; see David Eltis, "The Volume and Structure of the Transatlantic Slave Trade: A Reassessment," William and Mary Quarterly 2nd ser., 58, no. 1 (January 2001): Table 3.

for slaves destined to work the farms and plantations of the interior or be transshipped to other captaincies, Salvador itself was the final destination for many. In a study of hundreds of urban estate inventories dated between 1811 and 1860, one scholar finds the African-born accounting for 62 percent of the city's slaves.[14]

Although I refer to these slaves as "African," they surely did not consider themselves as forming a single group, and their buyers recognized broad ethnic differences among them. Before the 1780s, thousands had come from the Bantu-speaking interior areas of Angola and the Congo, as they would again after 1820. In the interval, though, most came from the lands around the Bight of Benin. They were sometimes called "Mina slaves" because they had been purchased from the area near the fort of Elmina on the Guinea coast or, with equal imprecision, "Guinea slaves." The Yoruba speakers were usually called Nagôs, and those who spoke Gbe\Ewé\Fon were called Jeje. These two groups formed more than half the slaves imported in the last decades of the eighteenth century and the beginning of the nineteenth, although there were a significant number of Hausa, called Ussá, among them too. Salvador at this time received a far greater proportion of its African slaves from a single region than any other slave city of the Atlantic World outside of Brazil.[15] And, as urban slaves, they frequently crossed paths with others from the same area, unlike slaves on scattered plantations. As slaves together in a foreign place, they readily extended the boundaries of their identity, making it more inclusive and finding allies where they once would have seen only enemies.[16] Language formed a distinctive bond, and non-Africans in Bahia sometimes remarked on how slaves conversed with each other without using Portuguese.[17] With the passage of time in a country where they were constantly lumped together as "Africans," some may have even begun to think of themselves as such or to join with the Brazilian-born to adopt a racial and, later still, a class identity.

Ownership of slaves was pervasive. Even former slaves, especially women, owned slaves, not to mention those owned by many people of very modest means who supplemented their meager income by renting out their slaves or allowing them to find their own work.[18] Almost no white household seems to have got along without slaves, not only for their labor but as proof of their owner's social position. It was a sign of "extreme poverty," said a Brazilian lawyer, not to own a slave, and one would suffer "any inconvenience" rather than that.

A tax official questioned the accuracy of a postmortem estate inventory, saying, "It is noteworthy that the deceased did not own a single slave, and it seems absolutely necessary that the executor provide an explanation on this matter."[19]

The city also included a large number of former slaves, many of them African-born, as well as free-born blacks. More than half of the freed Africans were women (as were most of the owners who freed them), and the bulk of freed women were of childbearing age. Their children were born free.[20] As the custom of freeing slaves was of long standing, over the course of two and a half centuries thousands and thousands of non-whites had been born free. Already in 1775 free-born or freed persons of color made up nearly 24 percent of Salvador's population, making all the more credible the estimate in Table 1.1 that by 1835 they accounted for nearly 30 percent.[21]

THE WORK

The city depended on the work of slaves, freedmen and freed women (both Brazilian and African), and the free but poor descendants of Africans. They were essential if others were to live as they thought fit. They carried water from the fourteen public fountains, especially from the two fountains with the best water at the extreme northern and southern edges of the city.[22] They cleaned the houses and public buildings, washed the clothes, and removed the garbage and sewage. They cooked the food and distributed provisions, delivering manioc meal and meat to households and selling fresh fruit and vegetables door-to-door.

Given its topography, the city relied on blacks to transport almost everything. One-fifth of the streets in Salvador were steep streets known as *ladeiras*, indicating the verticality of any locomotion within the city. Moving things between the lower and upper cities presented a particularly daunting challenge. The "rocky escarpment . . . rises almost perpendicularly [with] inaccessible precipices that make going up impractical except by round-about *ladeiras*," so streets from the lower to the upper parts of the city "zigzag . . . along ravines" or "slant across an almost perpendicular bluff." They were all too steep, narrow, and sinuous for wheeled vehicles and proved difficult even for horses and mules, especially when the slightest rain could produce "torrents" that dug deep trenches across them.[23]

Self-hired slaves and freed blacks, most of them African, made the city's commercial life possible. As one resident recalled, "they moved everything: chests, bales, large and small casks, furniture, construction materials." He could have mentioned foodstuffs as well. Using chains or ropes, they would attach heavy barrels, chests, or boxes to a long thick pole and, with some in front and others in the rear, lift the pole onto their shoulders and proceed chanting through the streets. Some bore "huge calluses on their shoulders . . . produced by the pressure of the poles."[24] A Frenchman reported that groups of these men, often from the same region in Africa, worked together, "forming a kind of fraternity"; they "met at the corners of certain streets, awaiting the moment of being hired," appropriating this bit of public space for themselves. Such groups would choose captains to deal with potential customers and summon them for particular jobs. They determined the tasks and how to handle them, and, by setting their own rules, avoided any discipline imposed by others.[25] And it was black people, or at least those at the lower ranks of society, who did the carrying. Persons of higher status refused to carry even a small package through the streets.[26]

CROSSING BOUNDARIES

The variety and complexity of social relations in late eighteenth- and early nineteenth-century Salvador are remarkable. At first glance it appears to have been a typical society of orders with castes, corporations, and brotherhoods layered one atop another or arranged side by side in multiple hierarchies. And indeed, most people seem to have accepted that some, merely by the circumstances of their birth, merited the higher status they enjoyed, and that hierarchical relationships are natural, even immutable. They did not greatly admire upward mobility or speak of equality as a positive good. Yet the paper-thin layers of this society allowed some people to move up or down without challenging the structure's overall legitimacy. Imagine an individual as flowing like water through cracks in limestone strata, without visibly eroding their solidity and only subtly and gradually creating new layers or remaking old ones. Slaves became free without endangering the institution of slavery. Countless persons of African descent occupied positions far above slaves and even poor whites, yet Salvadoreans continued to pay attention to variations of skin color in locating people along a continuum of statuses. For some, newly acquired wealth led to honors, titles, or public offices despite modest beginnings. In any case, the top-down ordering of society could not be rigorously enforced on all individuals toward the bottom, if only because of their sheer numbers. Although the ranking principle sometimes penetrated to the lowest rungs, and did so brutally and without leniency, most of the time it stood out more visibly at higher levels. In the food trade, which is my concern here, the daily transactions between hundreds of participants made it utterly impossible to enforce discipline and deference rigidly. The social structure's flexibility was the secret of its longevity.

The practice of allowing, even encouraging, slaves to find their own work for wages displays the adaptability of the system and the porosity of the boundaries that separated the free from the enslaved. These slaves, known as *ao ganho* (or *ganhadores*), found their own customers and set their own wages, and usually even lived independently. They would turn in a set amount of cash to their owners at regular intervals and keep the surplus, a practice much more common in Brazil than elsewhere in the Atlantic World.[27] This type of arrangement derived from two practical considerations. Relatively few free immigrants came to Salvador compared to other cities of the Atlantic World, and it was generally unprofitable to supervise and administer slaves constantly in an urban setting. For that matter, slave owners in any city would be more likely to rely on persuasion and incentives because so much of the work required skill and enterprise rather than routine physical exertion. In such a setting too much oversight or violence on the part of the owner as a way of enforcing discipline could prove self-defeating.[28]

Yet even when they purchased their freedom, the bargain was one-sided. Manumission was a concession on the part of owners, granted to the obedient and loyal from whom gratitude was to be expected. Still, at the time of a master's death, when a probate judge divided property among the heirs, slaves were generally considered to have the right, although no law required it, to be granted their freedom if they offered a token amount beyond their appraised value.[29] The line between slavery and freedom was blurred and permeable.

Although blacks, whether born free or freed, likely remained poor, not all did. Some African-born former slaves who were engaged in the food trade acquired substantial property and became relatively prosperous. They often bought slaves of their own, sometimes perhaps to display clearly their new status. The African Ignacio José da Silva purchased his freedom and became a baker. According to the will he prepared in 1813, he freed his eight adult slaves and two of their children, but by the time of his death four years later he had acquired some more. Among his slaves he counted two male bakers, one apprentice baker, one female who "sold bread," and another who kneaded bread. His other property included his one-story stone house and, in its walled, tiled patio, his bread-making oven.[30]

Skin color remained an important classificatory element even for those who were born free, but not an essential and determining one. The relative acceptance of mulattos as compared to other areas of the Americas elicited much comment from travelers. They "are received in society and frequently become very competent civil servants whether in administration or the magistracy." Some were ordained as priests and commissioned as officers in the militia.[31] Using partial manuscript censuses and other data from several parishes, historian Anna Amélia Vieira Nascimento has estimated that in 1855 free mulattos accounted for slightly more than a quarter of the city's population; if mulatto slaves and former slaves were included, their proportion reached 29 percent.[32]

Yet Salvador was hardly characterized by racial harmony. Slaves, free Africans, and blacks had every reason to question their lot and push against those of higher rank, who could easily feel threatened by those below. Some Brazilian whites thought all blacks and mulattos, whether slave or free, posed a danger to society. A group of merchants in Salvador, probably Portuguese, reported with alarm in 1814 that "one sees gatherings of blacks in the street at night . . . talking in their tongues about whatever they please." Was their fear justified? Authorities in 1798 linked the appearance of handbills urging a republican revolution and the abolition of slavery to a small group of mulatto soldiers, non-commissioned officers, and artisans, along with some slaves.[33] Black conspiracies, revolts, and rumors of revolts, even if unfounded, peppered the first decades of the nineteenth century.[34]

Whites' fear greatly increased after the January 1835 "Malê" rebellion of Africans, mainly freedmen, led by Muslim teachers and planned to coincide with a major Catholic festival, when others would not be paying attention. The police put it down within hours, perhaps because, provoked by its discovery, the uprising began a day earlier than planned, but the questioning of prisoners revealed unsuspected cohesion among Africans and extensive networks of communication into the countryside. It involved hundreds of blacks, and the authorities prosecuted more than five hundred of them, executing some and sentencing others to hard labor. Outside Haiti, this was the largest black rebellion to occur in the Americas. Not surprisingly, whites were on edge for years afterwards. As a British consul put it in 1847, "the white population are ever kept in a state of alarm by the fear of a rising of the slaves."[35]

In this culture of rank and favor, there was much room for negotiation. Accepting the notion of a social pyramid as fair and normal did not mean a person was content with his or her own position within it, or did not question another's claim to superiority. Those below seized any opportunity to expand the orbit of their self-determination, just as those above tried to augment their decision-making power. Everyone was taken up in a constant process of mutual, if unequal, exchange, adopting varied strategies for coping with day-to-day challenges to one's position. Status was in play and could be lost as well as gained. To protect it required reassertion on an almost daily basis.

Slaves, free blacks, and the poor generally, despite being feared and suffering discrimination and oppression, nonetheless exercised a surprising degree of autonomy. Many found pride, self-respect, and dignity in their work, opening avenues for self-assertion. Some occupations required geographic mobility, with people wandering the city or traversing the bay, free of immediate supervision and able to enjoy a certain independence. Being street vendors, butchers, or sailors required skills and specialized knowledge, trading acumen, an ability to size up those with whom they dealt, a willingness to take risks, and keen business judgment, qualities that could breed self-confidence and resilience. The restrictions present in a hierarchical society floated above those who traded in food; although present and taken for granted, they did not truly impinge on traders' daily lives and the vitality and energy of their entrepreneurship.

Women also found ways to assert themselves, and this was especially true for those engaged in petty trade. By law, all property was held jointly by husband and wife unless there was a specific prenuptial agreement. At the death of a spouse the survivor kept half the estate. Two-thirds of the property belonging to each deceased spouse (eventually four-sixths of the total) had to be divided equally among the children, male and female alike, leaving only the remainder to be willed to a favorite. In terms of property rights guaranteed to women, Brazil stood out when compared to most of Europe and Anglo-America at that time.[36] Women often acted independently. Some remained single and, after reaching their majority, administered their property freely. Some had their own businesses, lived independently, bore children out of wedlock, and headed large households of children and slaves. Women owned male slaves and hired free men, exerting substantial authority. Some dealt with men in their business, bargained with them evenly, and were firmly successful. Still, husbands administered the family's property (short of selling or mortgaging it). Men monopolized the professions and most trades. They exercised civil and military command and received more education than women. Probate judges usually appointed men to be the guardians of children left fatherless, and this happened even when a deceased man had specified in his will that he wished his wife to act in this capacity.[37] So men obviously wielded more clout, but women were far from powerless or ignored.

SACRED WORLDS

Religious practice and performance—Christian, Muslim, and Afro-Brazilian—both gathered people of various stations and fostered distinct and conflictual identities with potentially disruptive and destabilizing effects. The large number of magnificent colonial-era churches in Salvador bear witness to a widespread Christian religiosity. On feast days, with the light of hundreds of candles on silver candlesticks reflecting off the gold-leaf-encrusted walls onto elaborate carved and polished woodwork and the baroque splendor of saints' images, all enhanced by music commissioned from local composers or imported from Europe, worshipers of all classes heard Mass sung.[38] The frequency of Catholic objects in estate inventories reveals the ordinary place of religion in everyday life: rosaries, crucifixes, crosses, and saints' images were common even in extremely modest households. Virtually every household had an *oratório*, a freestanding private altar or a niche in the corner of a room, or, more commonly, a small, upright traveling chest containing the image of Christ or of a saint. An *oratório* could also be an entire chapel: in 1792 Inocêncio José da Costa, a wealthy Portuguese merchant, had been married "in the *oratório* at my piece of land in Barris behind the Piedade church."[39]

Nearly everyone, regardless of class or color, belonged to a lay confraternity, or *irmandade*. These sodalities, devoted to honoring a particular saint, did charitable work, promised a properly attended funeral for the deceased member, and, most important, guaranteed the saying of masses for his or her soul after death. Joaquina Maria de Santana, a poor white street vendor, made a point of noting that she belonged to the very proper confraternity of the Holiest Sacrament in the church of Santa Ana, where she wished to be buried. One mulatto fisherman belonged to eight sodalities. The immensely rich Inocêncio José da Costa also listed his membership in several.[40] Besides the preeminent Santa Casa de Misericórdia (whose tower appears at the upper left in Figure 1.1), particularly prestigious were the Third (or lay) Orders of the Franciscans, Dominicans, and Carmelites. Because property was willed to these orders over time, they became increasingly opulent, able to lend money and rent out property.[41] Since the sixteenth century, sodalities had also provided a means for people of color throughout Brazil—often from particular, though broadly defined, ethnic groups in Africa—to forge solidarity. Like their white counterparts, black and mulatto sodality members venerated a specific saint and performed charitable acts, but these organizations also functioned as mutual aid societies. Several set up funds to purchase the freedom of enslaved members.[42] Sodalities usually had their seat in an established church with a side-chapel dedicated to "their" saint. In one case, however, a black sodality raised enough funds to build its own church, Nossa Senhora do Rosário às Portas do Carmo (Our Lady of the Rosary at the Carmelite Gate—see Fig. 3.1). Over the course of the nineteenth century, these sodalities gradually lost their place as central organizing institutions, at least for freed slaves (see Table 1.3). But, for most of the period examined in this book, they offered everyone the opportunity to extend personal connections beyond the reach of family and neighborhood.

If city residents' behavior did not always conform to the precepts of Christianity as understood then or now, that does not lessen the degree to which they believed in the veracity of Christian teaching, the existence of a spiritual realm, the certainty of an afterlife, the intercessory power of the Virgin Mary and the Catholic saints, and the ultimate power of God to rule men's fate. This placed God at the highest point in an elaborate edifice, with authority flowing downward from him to king and subject, from archbishop to priest and worshiper, from husband to wife and child, and from household head to slave.

But not all of the city's residents were Christian. Well over half of the slaves imported into Salvador sailed from the west coast of Africa, brought from the interior by African captors. Whether Yoruba

Table 1.3. Membership in Sodalities Among Freed Slaves by Period and Gender as Revealed in 482 Estate Inventories

Period	Gender	Belonged	Did Not	Total
1790–1830				
	Male	58	16	74
	Female	66	15	81
	Total	124	31	155
	%	80	20	100
1830–1850				
	Male	19	19	38
	Female	38	28	66
	Total	57	47	104
	%	55	45	100
1850–1890				
	Male	5	123	128
	Female	15	80	95
	Total	20	203	223
	%	9	91	100

Source: Based on Maria Inês Côrtes de Oliveira, O liberto: O seu mundo e os outros (Salvador, 1790–1890), Baianada, no. 7 (São Paulo and Brasília: Corrupia and CNPq, 1988), p. 84.

or Gbe\Ewé\Fon or Hausa, a significant proportion of them were Muslims—the clerics among them more literate in Arabic than many Brazilian masters were in Portuguese. An English missionary in Salvador observed that when being rowed back to his ship from the shore in November 1805, "it was the commencement of the Hegyra and our Mahomedan rowers, dressed in white, were singing hymns all the way to the honour of Mahomet." The testimony presented at the trial of participants in the African rebellion of January 1835 revealed the highly respected place of teachers and religious leaders within this community, men born in Africa who held much authority over their fellow religionists.[43] And it is safe to assume that these Muslims saw themselves and were seen by others as different and separate, with their own dietary rules, their own prayers, their own theology. With the end of the slave trade in 1850, the regular arrival of new Muslim leaders ended, and their influence petered out.

Polytheistic religions, derived especially from Africa, coexisted more easily with Christianity than did monotheistic Islam. Devotion to spirits and spiritual forces—including those of one's real or imagined ancestors, or others associated with natural phenomena such as the sun, moon, trees, rocks, lightning, and thunder—characterized Indian and African peoples and influenced many in Salvador, including whites. Communal ceremonies combined traditions drawn from more than one African ethnicity. Marked by drumming, call-and-response singing, and drawn-out dances, rituals known as *candomblés* culminated in trances as a spirit "descended" and possessed the worshiper, transporting him or her to another level of being. The experience could resolve conflict and restore interpersonal balance, diminish anxiety, lead to a perfect sense of inner peace, decrease stress, or alleviate the fear of death. These ceremonies were directed by priests or, more often, priestesses who commanded the service with authority and great knowledge of the spiritual realm. The beads around their necks, the clothes they wore, even their hairstyles signaled authority, power, and direct access to the spirit world. Leaders were assisted by others: drummers, always male, and spiritual "daughters" and "sons" who gathered herbs, slaughtered sacrificial animals, and performed ritual ceremonies to attract holiness.[44]

Regardless of their particular faiths, religion wove its way through every aspect of daily life for everyone, including street vendors and storekeepers, butchers and bakers. As was true in much of the rest of the world at that time, little conceptual space separated the secular from the holy. Science had yet to make much impact on the worldview of most people, whether educated or not, and folk-Catholicism, folk-Islam, and African-derived polytheism all shared the belief that worshipers could control natural phenomena by appealing for divine intervention. Those who referred to certain practices as "magic" nevertheless accepted the potential efficacy of the occult, attributing its force to the work of the devil and greatly fearing the power of his agents.[45] For protection, virtually everyone carried an amulet or talisman. Catholics, men and women, wore *bentinhos*, described by a British traveler as "printed prayers folded in a small compass and sewn in a silken pad which is ornamented on the outside with a picture of the Virgin or some saint, or embroidered with emblems; they are worn double, one hanging at the back and the other at the breast." Other scapulars, made of gold and bearing a saint's image, were also common among female street vendors.[46] Muslims copied short texts from the Koran, sometimes garbled, and folded these bits of paper into small clay or wooden tubes strung on a necklace. Polytheists wore miniature symbols of their deities worked in silver and attached by a large pin (a *balangandā*) at the waistband of a skirt or made of wood, silver, or gold and worn as necklaces. Blacks especially carried small sewn purses around their neck filled with powdered potions, herbs, and Catholic paraphernalia—prayers, bits of altar stone, consecrated wafers—to ward off evil or secure some desired end.[47] By such means, to borrow from the historian Peter Brown describing another culture, did the people "challenge heaven to come down to those who wore them."[48]

GOVERNING FOR THE PEOPLE

Two government agencies impinged directly on the lives of those engaged in the food business: the city council and the office of the governor-general of the captaincy or president of the subsequent province. In colonial times city council members were elected by and from among the "good men," whom the historian Charles Boxer characterizes as "the respectable—and respected." Contemporaries knew without doubt who fit that description, leaving historians frustrated in their attempt to discover their defining qualities.[49] Not surprisingly 40 percent of the Salvador council members from 1780 to 1821 had close links to the sugar industry, and another 20 percent consisted of international merchants. Workers had no direct voice. After Brazil became independent, a surprisingly broad electorate chose the council members, and the council's composition consequently changed, although the poor still did not take office. One historian has examined the lives of forty-four members who held office between 1840 and 1872. She found that twenty were either doctors or lawyers, seven were civil servants, four were described simply as real estate owners, one was a priest, one a military officer, and only three were merchants, leaving eight whose professions could not be identified.[50]

City councils wielded significant authority. No separation of powers existed in colonial times, and councils were legislative and administrative bodies as well as appellate courts for minor cases. Both before and after Brazil's separation from Portugal, their jurisdiction extended far beyond the urban centers, in effect making them "county" councils. They appointed a number of officers, including tax collectors, inspectors of weights and measures, petty judges who imposed fines for violations of city ordinances, and the personnel of the municipal slaughterhouse. City councils had extensive responsi-

bilities with regard to the food trade, as they were responsible for seeing to it that food was available in sufficient quality at an affordable
price.

The governor or president, appointed from Lisbon or, later, from
Rio de Janeiro, could and often did overrule the council. After independence, national legislation, especially a law of 1828 and a major
constitutional amendment of 1834, weakened city councils to allow
the centrally appointed provincial president even greater power over
the municipality. Few presidents, however, went as far as José Egídio
Gordilho de Barbuda, the Visconde de Camamu, a man of military
background who in 1829 castigated the city council for having said
it would "'comply with [the president's] request'"; he told them that
"the provincial president does not request, but rather orders, and you
shall simply obey his orders." Other governors acted with more cir-
cumspection, perhaps recalling that an unknown assailant had shot
and killed the Visconde de Camamu while still in office.[51] The reality, nevertheless, remained much as he described it. Councils exercised power within the space granted to them by provincial execu-
tives. On the other hand, because provincial presidents often stayed
in office only a few months before being replaced by someone new to
the scene, the city council could exercise autonomy through procras-
tination and perseverance.

The authority of both governor and city council rested ultimately
on their ability to ensure the well-being of "the People." The notion
that those above had a responsibility toward those below was deeply
ingrained in the mentality of Salvador's inhabitants and the authorities. Apart from God, the king or emperor headed the entire edifice,
and he was believed to be as solicitous regarding the welfare of his
people as any father would be for members of his family. In 1807 Salvador's city council captured the prevailing spirit in referring to the
"paternal zeal with which [the ruler] promotes the prosperity of his
loyal vassals." In an independent Brazil, a provincial president later
stressed that he undertook certain measures "so that the Imperial
Government will always appear as the Father of the People [*Pai dos
Povos*]."[52]

For all those who supplied Salvador with food, the city provided
context. Its topography, with a lower and upper city, mirrored its social arrangement. Its visual, built environment shaped their sense

of place. They were ranked and ranked themselves within a strati-
fied world, even as they sought to advance their social position.
More than that, the seemingly neat lines dividing one group from
another were in fact permeable, blurry, always shifting. The status
differences I use here—black/white, rich/poor, Catholic/Muslim/poly-
theistic, African/Brazilian/Portuguese, slave/free, male/female—all
had exceptions that stretched and bent the categories. Flexible relations informed and shaped their culture and were shaped by it. On
the one hand, there was a general understanding of what the rules
were, even if some people regarded them differently, evading or subverting them. Yet there were common customs, common moral assumptions, and common notions about the world that threaded their
way through the whole society. People often differed as to what was
right and just, but on the whole, broadly acknowledged notions about
what was "normal" and "reasonable" tied them together and contributed to cohesion.

Commerce in foodstuffs offers a lens through which we can examine more closely the workings of a ranked society, the connections
and conflicts across strata, the search for identity, the contestation of
place, and the vitality of commercial enterprise. In trade, social divisions become blurred, and interdependence emerges as a constant.
Here is hierarchy in motion: more complex, more nuanced, more contingent on circumstance than any generalization can possibly con-
vey. This commerce is worth examining in some detail.

PART I

GETTING AND SELLING FOOD

CHAPTER 2

FROM STREETS AND DOORWAYS

ANA DE SÃO JOSÉ DA TRINDADE took out a license in 1807 for herself and three of her slaves to sell foodstuffs door-to-door in Salvador or to set up a stall at a corner or square. She died in 1823, and when her will was opened, readers discovered many things that may not have surprised them, but surprise us. That she was illiterate is only to be expected, for she was born in West Africa and brought to Brazil on a slaving ship at an early but unspecified age. Upon arrival in Salvador she was sold as part of a larger group, "in a lot," and put to work selling food on the street for her mistress. She managed eventually to buy her own freedom in exchange for a newly arrived female slave and a substantial sum in cash. She reported that she kept her manumission letter with her at all times. Although, as she said, "I remained unmarried," she had had five children, three sons who had died and two daughters who were still alive. We do not know how old she was at her death, but we know that her granddaughter was already married.[1]

This former slave left a three-story house built of dressed stone with plastered interior walls and glass windows, the ground floor of which she rented out as a store. She owned her land free and clear. She also owned nine slaves, two of whom she still sent out each day to sell food "on the street," including one described as "young and currently pregnant." She conditionally freed one female slave, stipulating that the woman should pay a certain amount to Ana's granddaughter over time to fully secure her freedom. She freed outright another slave, already old, her body covered with open sores. Three of her slaves were children, two of whom she gave to her daughters, freeing the other one. Her rich collection of gold jewelry included crucifixes, scapulars, rosaries—one with seven "Our Fathers" and seventy "Hail Marys"—a reliquary, and many "heavy gold" chains, as well as cuff links and two golden shoe buckles. She also owned a diadem with half-moon mirrors, a pair of earrings set with aquamarines and twelve embedded diamonds, a topaz ring, and a ring with ten small "rose diamonds." Silver objects included a crucifix showing Christ encircled with rays displaying his title and showing the nails with which he was crucified; she also had a silver fork, spoon, and pitcher with saucer. A slave trader who had borrowed money from her and also pawned gold and silver items was still in debt to her at the time she made her will. On the other hand, she "owed no one anything." The total value of her estate was impressive, and I use it as a benchmark in evaluating the wealth of others who appear in this and later chapters. It makes her a middle-class householder. Ana de São José da Trindade had moved from being a slave to being a poor freedwoman and then a woman of property and a slaveowner. She was not alone, for upward mobility was certainly not restricted to whites nor to men.[2]

Grocers, like street vendors, demonstrated entrepreneurial skill in supplying the city of Salvador with food. Most arrived from Portugal with little capital and made their way in a new setting as best they could. Some did poorly. Ana de São José da Trindade probably noticed that many of them had less property than she. Others, however, can be placed in the upper class. Antônio José Pereira Arouca arrived from Portugal at age twenty-two. When his first wife died, after having borne several children, he was in financial straits, owing more than he owned. But by the time of his own death in 1825 he owned a sugar plantation, a manioc farm, a vessel that brought foodstuffs to the city from the southern coast of Bahia, and three large houses in Salvador. Two of them were somehow conjoined. Built on sloping ground in the closely packed lower city, a three-story house faced an interior street and included a dry goods store at ground level. Beneath it was another one, "with a view toward the sea." It included a grocery store "and below it a warehouse with entrance from the sea." His land extended "at the back to the sea and is walled on two sides [and leads to] a stone wharf to resist the waves." The frontage of the property measured only twenty-two feet, but it obviously extended a good distance toward and into the bay, providing valuable direct access from his boat to his stores.[3]

STREET VENDORS

In the absence of a central market place and building—not created until the 1850s and then still deemed seriously inadequate—householders in Salvador routinely relied on street vendors to supply their food.[4] Most of these vendors, in contrast to the owners of general stores, were women, especially women of color. Foreign observers often remarked on Salvador's hawkers and their colorful clothes, attention-getting cries, and exotic goods for sale. Prince Maximilian, of later fame in Mexico, commented in 1860 on the "black people passing through the streets with baskets full of the most splendid fruit, always carrying it for sale as they go." But to those who lived in Salvador, they were simply part of everyday life, hardly worth noticing. They had been present in Salvador for at least two centuries and in Lisbon before that.[5] And in West and Central Africa, women had long dominated trade and were renowned market vendors.[6]

Until 1821 the city required all street vendors to be licensed. There was no charge, and a person could secure such a license for oneself, for one's slaves, or for both. Tellingly, four female slaves took out licenses for themselves. I examined 843 licenses issued in the months of January 1789, 1807, and 1819, accounting for 977 street vendors.[7] The register noted that 106 of those requesting licenses were persons of color, leaving the race of the remainder unspecified. Census data indicate positively that some vendors were white. Although Africans were especially prominent among vendors, there were many creoles—that is, blacks born in Brazil. By adding the 106 persons of color to the 382 slaves for whom their owners secured licenses, I conclude that nearly half of all vendors were black or mulatto (488 of the 977), mostly women. Among the primary licensees, women were more likely than men to be vendors themselves (70 percent of the women compared to 48 percent of the men). Among the 382 slaves who were sent out on the street, only four were men. So for the larger sample of 977 vendors, 866, or 89 percent, were women.

These women worked according to a variety of arrangements. Most often they were self-hired and traded on their own accounts. The slave woman Genoveva paid her mistress 200 réis per day in 1830 (an amount equivalent to the price of three pounds of meat). Many owners rented their slaves to others, who then sent them out with goods for sale. Manoel José Dias lived entirely from the rental

FIGURE 2.1. Female street vendor, ca. 1776–1800

of his three houses and his seven slaves, three females and four males, all engaged in "self-hired selling on the street."[8] Cloistered nuns owned female slaves who sold in this way, and 5 percent of the primary licensees who were women preceded their names with the word "Dona," indicating some claim to status.[9] Some street vendors might specialize in certain products, and others not. Ludovica, for example, "sold milk [only] until 8 o'clock in the morning . . . and Maria only sold fruit 11 days in the month of August and 13 in September . . . and then only 'till mid-day, for from this time on they sell sweets."[10]

A contemporary complained that the streets of Salvador were "jam packed with black female vendors . . . who impede the public's use." Hundreds of them went door-to-door, criss-crossing the street, offering their goods for sale, searching for buyers, although some vendors, like Ludovica, could sell their goods rapidly because they had regular customers waiting to buy from them.[11] The vendors' melodious cries signaled the moment when a housewife would send her house servant, probably a slave woman, out to the street to bargain on price and quality. Today a leisurely Sunday morning stroll with a few stops takes fifty minutes from Santo Antônio além do Carmo south to Campo Grande, covering the principal part of the city as it existed in the late eighteenth century (see Map 1.3). This trajectory does not include moving out to Santa Ana or the neighborhood of Vitória, built up by 1860. There were few paved sidewalks or streets then. Dust or mud predominated. Where it existed, irregular stone paving formed a "V" toward the center of the street "along which flowed the rain water." Rain water and much else: an 1852 traveler described the streets as "irregular, ill-paved, generally narrow, and having a gutter in the middle into which is commonly cast the filth and offal of the adjacent dwellings." Since "the houses are unprovided with water-closets," he added, the alleys served as "temples of Cloacina [Goddess of Sewers]." This is where a street vendor walked, stopping to sell, then rebalancing her load before heading off to another customer.[12]

They typically carried their goods on their heads in baskets or pots, on trays, or, by 1860, in glass-enclosed cases to keep dust and flies away from their goods, but they were not all constantly ambulatory. Those who sold milk had to lug heavy tin milk cans, two of them probably suspended from each end of a pole.[13] It was heavy work. Not surprisingly, then, many vendors displayed their goods on a mat or stand to wait for customers to find them. Prince Maximilian spotted "many young damsels seated in rows by the wall" selling "eatables." At one time sales of fresh meat, fish, and fowl along a posh Vitória boulevard were allowed only "on the heads of vendors" because residents did not want their transit through the streets impeded by shop stalls or mats spread out on the ground.[14] To the despair of those who loved order, sellers even placed their mats at the handsome entryway to the municipal council's chambers, alongside many of the city's beggars. Alternatively, street vendors sometimes

FIGURE 2.2. Male street vendor, 1960

sat on stools or benches behind portable tables, frequently gathering at the same location. Sometimes they placed their small stands right in the street; one vendor who did so had a horse and rider run smack into her, scattering her rice.[15]

By 1799 there were also more permanent wooden structures called *quitandas,* "where many black women congregate[d] to sell every-thing they bring." These were placed at three locations, one in the lower city, one on the central Terreiro de Jesus square, and one by the more southerly São Bento church, where the city council had in 1790 built some stalls for rent to the "female vendors of fish and other edi-bles." Most of the renters were women.[16] Presumably they undertook these fixed costs to be able to have a larger stock and sell items whose weight made it difficult to sell door-to-door. As for the city's motiva-tion, it sought to avoid the "well known inconvenience to the [tran-siting] public" caused by "those who customarily sell victuals and subsistence goods on the streets of the city." But by the mid-1830s the number of booths by the São Bento church had so increased that they were "obstructing the place," leading the city fathers to order those vendors (*quitandeiras*) to retreat to the area that had been originally designated for them. Such an expansion of *quitandas* without any ap-parent diminution in the number of ambulatory hawkers suggests a steady pressure on the part of vendors to gain control over more and more public space.[17]

So vital were vendors to the life of Salvador that, despite the com-plaints of some, most provincial legislators in 1828 rejected a pro-posal that every black who moved about must carry a passport issued either by his or her master, if a slave, or by a public authority, if free. An assemblyman exclaimed that such a law "could not be enforced among us," and immediately introduced an exception on behalf of those who "carry . . . essential foodstuffs." After the Muslim revolt of 1835 a proposed city edict sought to forbid Africans from partici-pating in the food trade (reserving it only for the Brazilian-born), but the provincial chief of police, despite his hostility toward Africans, successfully argued against the measure, saying that it would result in a "rise in prices and mass confusion." Three years later the city council again proposed that no African, slave or free, be permitted to deal in "beans, corn, farinha, etc.," and once again the measure was turned down. Finally, in 1849, a special provincial tax was lev-ied on Africans "who trade," but it apparently had little effect be-cause eight years later, well after the end of the slave trade in 1850, the city council bewailed the fact that Africans "have taken over the business of trading in produce, chickens, suckling pigs, etc."[18] Un-noticed but surely relevant is the fact that besides supplying others with food, vendors were also consumers of goods bought with their earnings.

Table 2.1. Occupations of Freed African Women in the Parish of Santana (Salvador), 1849

Occupations	Number	Percentage
Sellers of foodstuffs		
Greens	33	
Fruit	22	
Fish	2	
Cooked food	14	
Unspecified other produce	5	
Other unspecified foodstuffs	56	
Subtotal	132	78
Sellers of other things		
Unspecified street vendors	5	
Sellers of clothes or shoes	2	
Sellers of unspecified goods (mercadeja)	10	
Subtotal	17	10
Other		
Washerwomen	10	
Domestic servants	3	
Other	7	
Subtotal	20	12
TOTAL	169	100

Source: Calculated from Maria Inês Cortes de Oliveira, "Libertas da freguesia de Santana (1849): Ocupações e jornais," paper distributed at a conference held at the Arquivo Público do Estado da Bahia, Salvador, July 1993 (courtesy of Alexandra Brown). A less precise breakdown, but with more cases, can be found in Cecília Moreira Soares, "As ganhadeiras: Mulher e resistência em Salvador no século XIX," Afro-Ásia, no. 17 (1996): 59.

Vendors sold an enormous variety of things—cloth, ribbons, thread, amulets, shoes, handkerchiefs, dresses—but food was their most prevalent item. In one parish in 1849 almost four-fifths of the gainfully employed freed African women sold foodstuffs (see Table 2.1). Street vendors even marketed basic staples such as manioc meal, beans, dried meat, and salt, although generally they sold more perishable items, including milk and eggs. The sale of fresh meat from the "wooden bowls of black women," provoked city ordinances at first forbidding it but later specifying where vendors could do so.[19] Similarly, the city council, wishing in 1824 either to concentrate the selling of fish at the waterfront or to prevent spoilage by encouraging its rapid sale, required that it be sold elsewhere only by "sellers wandering through the streets of the city for the convenience of its inhabitants, it being forbidden, however, for them to set up stands."[20]

Street vendors were best known for their fresh fruits and vegetables. Among the garden produce were lettuce and other greens, cabbages, okra, green beans, cucumbers, and onions, as well as corn, pumpkins, and yams. With distinctive cries they advertised their seasonal fruit: bananas, oranges, tangerines, limes, mangoes, watermelons, grapes, guavas, papayas, and pineapples. Seen from a window above, their fruit-filled baskets presented "both in form and coloring some of the prettiest pictures of still life that can be imagined."[21]

Vendors peddled cooked food as well, notably lightly grilled meat cut up into bite-size pieces, cooked over a brazier in the street. The city council believed the meat they sold was likely "corrupted." One observer alleged that they used beef that had been pilfered from butcher shops by their soldier-friends, and there is evidence that some of their meat had indeed been stolen. When Francisco, the slave of Rosa Rodrigues, was "caught with a large basket" of stolen fresh meat weighing almost fifty pounds, the men who apprehended him just outside the slaughterhouse concluded, given the small size of her household, that Rosa was probably going to cook and sell it on the street.[22] Street vendors also carried whale meat, which they "brought to market wrapped in banana leaves, ready-cooked," as well as cooked pork, sausages, and grilled fish. Among prepared foods were a large number of dishes unknown to European palates but still found today, such as "carurus, vatapás, pamonha, canjica, . . . acaçá, acarajé, ubobó," dishes that are made from such ingredients as manioc meal, rice, corn, black-eyed peas, dried shrimp, coconuts, and peanuts, prepared with okra, onions, garlic, and tomatoes.[23] These foods were likely cooked in red palm oil with spices of African origin, and—given the blending of the secular and the divine—may have been prepared according to African religious precepts. On the other hand, a characteristic of Bahian cookery now, and probably then, is the intermingling of foods of different origins, scorning none. Portuguese olive oil, African red palm oil, and native American manioc might all be used in the same meal, cooked by the same person. The sellers probably ate this food themselves, and surely one of the advantages of being self-hired, rather than a domestic, was the possibility of determining one's diet and how it would be cooked.[24]

Not only was there great variety overall, but so also for any one vendor, because customers wanted small quantities of several things. Given the perishability of so many items, a vendor would not want a large stock of any one. And if there existed a glut of one product, she would have other things to sell as well. Even the *quitandeiras*, though holding a larger stock than itinerant vendors, were subject to the same considerations.

Street vendors were energetic businesswomen. As Ellena, a hawker, testified about herself, "she retires after dark and gets up early." If the work was hard, however, at least she got to decide where to go, whom to meet, when to rest, and, up to a point, at what rate to work. Her success at selling probably depended less on how much physical energy she expended and more on a savvy choice of streets to wander and the time of day to be there, as well as on her personality. She needed a strong voice with which to call out her wares. Especially the *quitandeiras*, remaining always at the same spot, had to build long-term relationships with customers. All vendors needed good bargaining skills both in purchasing from their suppliers and selling to their buyers. Bargaining required, as it ever does, both a knowledge of its etiquette—only make serious offers—and a keen awareness of the abundance or scarcity of the merchandise at any one moment. In dealing with both suppliers and customers, vendors had to keep mental track of multiple transactions and quickly calculate the required profit, considering as well their time and trouble. They had to be careful in their purchases in order to maintain a good reputation for the quality of items sold, meaning they could not afford to be credulous. Street vendors had to time their sales optimally to avoid deterioration of the merchandise, yet not sell too cheaply. This was all the more important because, insofar as vendors transported the merchandise themselves, it had to be high in value in relation to its bulk and weight, and so likely fragile or perishable. All street vendors had to be vigilant against theft and to protect their goods from rain, sun, and wind. Faced with fierce competition, they had to be satisfied with a slight profit. Their numbers suggest that many were ready to do this work.[25] Still, the exercise of these many skills, the risks involved, and the awareness of having concluded a successful transaction must have given female street vendors the self-confidence, dignity, independence, and dynamism that comes from proficient trading and active participation in a money economy. They were far from hapless victims.

A WAY OF LIFE

Vendors generally wore cool and simple clothes. One who sold bread and corn cakes dressed in a coffee-colored calico skirt with small white polka dots and a white shirt. Another one, who sold boiled yams from a tin box, wore a "white calico skirt, a very old cotton blouse, and a calico cloth wrap." A third woman could be found in a blue calico skirt, a linen blouse, and "cloth from the coast of Africa, already old, with blue and red stripes." A European painter in the 1830s depicted a fish monger with a white blouse off one shoulder, a yellow-flowered skirt, a wrap of African cloth, sandals, and a turban. In the mid-nineteenth century another artist said the slave women "wear a white chemise so loose that it only hangs on one shoulder at a time, wrapping round their waist a striped cloth called 'pano de la [sic] costa': the ground white and striped horizontally with broad blue and pink stripes." He found the result "graceful and becoming . . . always in good taste." The twenty-eight-year-old Prince Maximilian was enchanted with the turban of "white and pale-blue gauze" worn by one vendor. Two other travelers reported on these turbans, one describing them as being of various colors, and the other explaining that the vendors wore "a sort of thick round turban with a cavity in the center on which they deposit their loads which are frequently of immense weight. Their heads are generally shaved or their hair closely cut."[26] Slaves went barefoot, but freed women wore "graceful white sandals" that could be seen thanks to the "very short skirts that allow one to see above the ankles." Ana de São José da Trindade, besides five calico skirts, had more luxurious clothes, but not to wear on the street. She owned two skirts of special cloth, two colored gowns, three crimson velvet belts, three shawls made of cloth imported from Africa, and one half-slip. Rosa Maria da Conceição, another freedwoman, had no relative to whom to bequeath her black and bright-red silk and satin skirts. One historian has suggested that precisely because skin color prevented confusion as to class, authorities did not think it necessary to enforce sumptuary laws in colonial Brazil.[27]

Owning jewelry provided a way, as it did for Ana de São José da Trindade, for vendors to keep and guard their wealth as well as assure its liquidity, aside from its glamour and glitter. The fish monger who modeled for the European painter wore gold earrings and, on her belt, a *balangandá*, a large pin from which hung silver symbols of African spirits and maybe some baubles. In the mid-eighteenth century a foreigner observed that "only with difficulty can you find here the most humble mortal, even among the multitude of black women who sit on the street selling fruit, who does not decorate herself with buckles, bracelets, rings, and buttons of fine gold, many with encrusted precious gems." At the end of the colonial period another traveler described how, "on festival days," he saw black and mulatto women "with their bosom and arms weighed down with golden chains and reliquaries of the same metal." This was still true in the 1850s, when "superb chains of gold" made slave women "look like sultanas."[28]

Many vendors lived like the rest of the free poor and enslaved of the city: crowded into rooms just below street level with small windows that provided little air and barely a glimpse of the feet of passersby. Typically such rented spaces had no dividing walls and only bare ground for floors. Furnishings consisted of woven straw mats, rolled up during the day and spread on the ground at night. Slave women who lived with their masters or mistresses—those who sold sweets, for instance—often occupied windowless rooms on higher floors, but those who lived on their own filled these basement lodgings. When a slave gained her freedom, she soon thought of renting such a room, perhaps sublet from another freed slave. In finding a place to live, she would likely rely on ties of friendship, kinship, or love. According to an 1855 household census, the street vendor Ritta Paula Lisboa lived in a basement alcove with Francisco Lopes Montinho, a carpenter, both of them freed persons. The bulk of street vendors likely lived in such places.[29]

Ana de São José da Trindade lived quite differently, however. Because she had accumulated considerable property, the postmortem inventory of her estate is rich with detail, revealing not only the limits of what was possible for a vendor, but the standard set by the middle class. She lived on the street leading to the Carmo monastery, a prime spot not too far from the city center. Her three-story stone house had glass windows, another sign of affluence, and a rooftop terrace. It was doubtless built contiguously to that of the neighbors, as was typical of the place, and its eighteen-foot frontage was not considered narrow at that time. The list of her furniture began with a small, portable shrine: a jacaranda-wood crucifix set in a darkly painted box made of a lighter soft wood. She left a bed with a headboard and frame of jacaranda, a jacaranda chest with two large and two small drawers, each of which could be locked, a mahogany ark, and a large mahogany trunk with two drawers below. Other furniture included a settee, six cane-bottomed chairs, a small whale-oil lamp with four wicks suitable for the living room, four English paintings with gilded frames and no glass, two rectangular living-room mirrors with gilded frames, and a small brass candlestick. Her dishes consisted of thirty-seven ordinary china plates, a soup tureen with lid, a long serving dish, two china coffee pots (one white, one painted), and two salt shakers. She lived far beyond her beginnings as a slave.[30]

Although Ana de São José da Trindade's property was substantial, probably exceptional, her life story was not unusual in many of its other aspects. Another street vendor, Rosa Maria da Conceição, an illiterate woman from West Africa, purchased her own freedom and took out a license to sell on the street in 1819. She listed not one but four houses in her 1838 will, including the two-story stone one in which she lived, two one-story stone houses (with stone flooring), and a "small rammed-earth one." She and her sick husband, whom she had married in 1804, owned an astonishing total of thirty slaves, although fifteen of them were children. Of the adults, eight were women, all Africans; their occupations are not specified, but at least some of them likely worked as vendors, as did their owner. The Brazilian-born freed woman Maria da Cruz probably began as a vendor, but she moved beyond that. By 1852 she was delivering for sale substantial quantities of manioc meal—far more than anyone alone could carry—to the hospital run by the Santa Casa de Misericórdia. Even after the final end of the slave trade in 1850, she invested in goods shipped on speculation to Africa. She remained illiterate.[31]

Postmortem estate inventories are skewed as samples because they inevitably deal with those who owned property. Yet it is remarkable that of all former slaves who left wills between 1790 and 1850, more than 40 percent possessed urban real estate, albeit most owned only one such property, often built on land for which they paid a perpetual ground-rent. The historians Sheila de Castro Faria and Júnia Ferreira Furtado have amply demonstrated that some freed women elsewhere in Brazil, especially the Africans among them, possessed considerable wealth, countering the common idea that they were universally poor. Female street vendors can certainly not be lumped into the lowest class.[32]

Many, of course, were among the less fortunate, as was the creole slave Florinda, found crying on the street because she feared her mistress would punish her when she got home for not having sold enough. A few vendors may have died wealthy, but most of those with property did not own much. When Benedita Maria Carneiro died, her property consisted of two slaves, some furniture, and some gold and silver objects. Her worth amounted to about one-fifth of Ana de São José da Trindade's. Her property also had to be divided in two (half of it being her husband's part of the joint property), with Benedita's half then divided into three parts for her grandchildren by a former marriage. To make the division, the slaves had to be sold, leaving the widower without the income they would have earned for him "on the street." Other vendors had even less. For most of the freed and free women, one can be sure, selling on the street provided only enough income to survive day-to-day, not enough to acquire slaves of their own or to save for illness and old age.[33]

Illness could prove disastrous or be endured only with great difficulty. Some slaves were abandoned when ill, although certainly many were not, and we know one surgeon presented his bill to a master for "visits I made to the black woman Maria, Nagô, slave . . . during the illness from which she died." Some vendors suffered swollen feet and hernias from carrying heavy loads. Felisberta was "missing two or three teeth from the upper jaw," and Lena was covered in smallpox scars. In 1821 one estate inventory listed an old slave vendor with erysipelas, or St. Anthony's Fire, a painful and highly contagious disease characterized by a high fever and deep red inflammation of the skin and mucous membranes.[34] Sometimes an indigent turned up dead on the street, perhaps the very street on which she had sold door-to-door. The Santa Casa de Misericórdia would use its simplest litter to carry deceased slaves to an ignominious grave in the pauper's field at the Campo da Pólvora; however, a quarter of all church burials were of slaves. To avoid dying without the proper rites and rituals, those who could afford to joined a sodality.[35]

Slave vendors could be pitifully vulnerable to cruel exploitation by their owners, and we should not imagine that former slaves made kinder mistresses than whites. One freed slave, the Yoruba Maria Joaquina de Santa Anna, viciously punished her slave Rosa, also Yoruba, to the extent of swinging a "knife for scaling fish" at her face, cutting off the left side of her upper lip, permanently exposing four teeth and giving her "a frightful appearance." Rosa ran away and hid in the woods, where she was found at death's door for want of food and her festering lip full of maggots. These cruel punishments scandalized the neighbors, and Rosa's screams kept them awake nights. Presumably with the help of others, Rosa got her case heard by a judge of the High Court, before whom Maria Joaquina was charged with the crime of "mutilating a bodily part with a specific function." He sentenced her to cease such punishments and put Rosa up for sale immediately. Instead, on the morning of May 23, 1832, Maria Joaquina, accompanied by her male companion, dragged Rosa off, past the outlying district of Rio Vermelho. They were headed toward a remote spot with the intent, it was said, of having at her freely. They had put a rope around her head like a halter and tied her with straps. But as they passed the seaside chapel of Santa Ana in Rio Vermelho, Rosa managed to wrest herself free and dash into the church, seeking asylum. Undeterred, her captors rushed in after her and violently pulled her away, not hesitating to "commit the sacrilege of leaning on the altar and placing a hand on the Holy Stone." At this point, an officer in the National Guard separated them and removed Rosa to his house, only, he said, to protect the "Chapel's installations." The local police commissioner then asked a justice of the peace to have her value appraised so she could be sold to someone under whose care Rosa's "fortune would be bettered." The judge agreed to do so after getting a doctor to examine her carefully. In his report the doctor noted two other knife wounds on her shoulders in addition to scars of whipping on her "buttocks, back, thighs, arms, and legs." Maria Joaquina was jailed for her public actions "offensive to morality and good customs," but after twenty-eight days in jail she managed to raise funds to post bail. We do not know what happened to Rosa.[36] It may be that Maria Joaquina's low status as a former slave made neighbors and justices more willing to intervene on Rosa's behalf; had Rosa's owner been an upper-class white, her fate might have been ignored. Or perhaps not. Precisely to preserve the institution of slavery, some limits were placed on the behavior of slave owners generally.[37] In this particular case the fact that both slave and mistress were women, and likely street vendors, did not lessen their hostility toward each other, for animosities were not only between black and white, or between men and women. And certainly the life of a vendor was never easy, even if few were as severely mistreated as Rosa.

GROCERS AND THEIR STORES

While vendors walked the streets selling door-to-door in the open air, grocers—the other commercial suppliers of food to the city—worked from their stores. With two or three tall, narrow solid-wooden

FIGURE 2.3. Corner grocery store and street vendors, 1835

doors—and, if on a corner, more still—their shops opened directly onto the street, plunging grocers into the rhythms of urban life. As locals put, they sold "from their outer doors."[38] A separate door led directly to a stairway to the upper floor, frequently the owner's home. The physical unity of the living space and the place of business contributed to a conceptual unity also, so that *casa* could mean (and can still mean) both one's house and one's business.[39] Like street vendors, some grocers outsold others, and a vocabulary developed to distinguish among stores by their size and the volume of goods they stocked. They ranged from the smaller, more makeshift *tendas* to the more substantial *armazens*, with the common *vendas* falling in-between (although the terms were sometimes interchangeable). And while these general stores often sold drinks by the glass, taverns just as often sold foodstuffs.[40]

José Pinto de Almeida's store included a "counter with drawer and key," seventeen "boards that serve as shelves" behind the counter, large and small scales with a number of iron weights, two sets of measures of capacity—some of wood, some of tin—three tin funnels, a wine jar, nine "small and large cups," and a candlestick. Only occasionally did a store counter have glass panels. Many stores also held a shrine with a saint's image.[41]

A general store was a microcosm of the city as entrepôt, displaying goods produced less than an hour's walk from the city center along-side merchandise from far reaches of the world: cinnamon, cloves, ginger, pepper, and tea from Asia; red palm oil and peppers from Africa; bottled beer, wheat flour, butter, cheeses, bacon, and ham from northern Europe and, later, from North America; salt, dry biscuits, sardines, dried codfish, wine, brandy, vinegar, olives, olive oil, raisins, and almonds from Portugal; jerked beef from Uruguay, Argentina, or southern Brazil, and sun-dried meat from the interior of Bahia; sugar, tobacco, rice, beans, corn, and manioc meal, as well as onions and garlic, bacon and lard, sugarcane brandy, coconuts, coffee in the hull or ground, and firewood from the Recôncavo or other Brazilian ports, not to mention fruit, eggs, and live chickens from the city's semirural suburbs and whale oil from the local flenser and refiner. At such a store, buyers also purchased candles, torches, writing paper, pencils, cloth, hardware, rope, brooms, mats, straw hats, fans, chamber pots, tobacco, cigars, needles, cutlery, rough china dishes, toothpicks, and fresh bread, just to mention some of the myriad items for sale. But crucially, all of these stores sold foodstuffs, goods subject to rapid deterioration. Such a store would always be a place where one could buy a drink or, if hungry as two soldiers were, "biscuits and cheese."[42]

Shopkeepers prospered, although some more than others, enough to put most of them in the middle ranks of society. They certainly did not live in wattle-and-daub, thatch-roofed huts as did some of the free poor, nor usually in the sumptuous houses in the Vitória neighborhood owned by a few wholesalers. More typical was Baltazar de Andrade Bastos's place. A dealer in dried meat, he owned a house and land like that of Ana de São José da Trindade near the Carmo church. He rented out the small ground-level store, wide enough only for a door and one window. His living quarters on the upper floors included a "ceilinged front room with three floor-to-ceiling windows with iron balustrade," two bedrooms, one with a ceiling, and a dining room open to the rafters, plus a partial attic with two rooms and a bedroom "with two chest-high glass windows facing toward the front of the house." At the back of the building was a "small patio" with a separate kitchen.[43]

Store owners carefully dressed in keeping with their position. In the 1840s they wore waist-length gray linen or striped cotton jackets, and gray linen or nankeen pants with flaps in front covering the fly. On special days they wore a tie, but only the very rich wore a frock coat. In 1809 an Englishman noted that "the men copy the Europeans in their mode of dress" except on special occasions, when "they wear lace on their linen and have their clothes bedaubed with embroidery." Simply dressed store clerks might ask permission from the owner to wear a tie and vest—that is, to dress above their station.[44] One store owner, wealthy enough to lend money at interest, included in his well-stocked clothes closet two frock coats—a much-used blue one of fine cloth with yellow brocade frogs, and another ordinary black one—as well as an overcoat, a "Scottish" cape with wool lining, three striped jackets of Lille wool, seventeen fine cotton shirts, one pair of serge trousers, four pairs of linen and twill trousers, six vests (two of them made of black velvet and fine cotton, and four "very used" white corduroy ones), twelve handkerchiefs (including seven linen ones and one of silk, "some white and others colored"), thirteen pairs of linen stockings both long and short, and one fine hat with a rounded crown. When he died, his estate totaled three and a half times that of Ana de São José da Trindade.[45]

Among the 475 applicants for store licenses at the beginning of 1789, 1807, and 1819, only 69, or 15 percent, were women.[46] In other sources I found only occasional references to women store owners. Advertisements placed in an early local newspaper referred to a woman who sold drinks, to another who owned an eating house, to one who sold snuff, and to another who had a large store. In 1780 "Bernardina so-and-so," who lived in the outlying district of Rio Vermelho, was fined for not taking out a license for her store and not having her weights and measures inspected. Ninety years later the same rule applied: Maria das Mercês committed a similar infraction.[47] When Ana Joaquina de Jesus and Florinda de Aragão died, the two inventoried estates consisted primarily of general stores, but because of Brazil's joint-property regime, it is impossible to know whether the businesses were primarily their husbands'. In neither case could I find an inventory carried out at the time of their husbands' deaths.[48]

Although Brazilians figured among the owners of general stores, most were Portuguese. Rare indeed was the slave—yes, a slave—born in Africa who owned a small business where he sold beans, rice, and corn on his own account from a rented corner in the lower city. At the time of Brazil's struggle for independence from Portugal the commander of the Portuguese army described the "Commercial Body" of Salvador as being made up of "Europeans," by which he meant his compatriots.[49] An Argentinean stereotyped the Portuguese as hardworking and ambitious, in contrast to the lazy Brazilians, and another foreigner said the Portuguese (not counting those in government or the military) typically arrived poor in Brazil, "but by parsimony and continued exertion directed to one end, that of amassing money, they often obtain their object." For them, Brazil was a place to rise socially.[50] Many Portuguese shopkeepers maintained close ties with their homeland, supporting the Santa Casa de Misericórdia in Lisbon, making separate wills for their property in each country, leaving money to relatives in Portugal, or returning there to die. They were citizens of the Atlantic World, but their connection to Portugal made shopkeepers particularly vulnerable to the xenophobic mob actions of the 1820s and 1830s that followed Brazil's independence.[51]

The energy and self-discipline of store owners were evident. They kept track of inventory, ordering and reordering goods to stock their shelves, while carefully juggling profit and loss. They sought loans and kept records on those to whom they sold on credit. And they stood out by their ability to read and write in a society where few were literate.

Ties of authority and dependence linked shopkeepers to their clerks. Almost all store owners employed at least one, although one grocer stated that he was too poor to do so. It was common for a Portuguese owner to hire a relative, perhaps a nephew, as his cashier. These clerks could also be salaried workers, like the one at Manoel Tavares's establishment. Tavares's widow fired him and closed the store "because it yielded more losses than profit." Owners were said to keep close watch on clerks, even requiring attendance at mass on Sundays and holy days.[52] As a reward for this dependence, some clerks eventually became minor partners in the business, although surely not if they failed to satisfy their boss. The best ones might even inherit the shop, as happened to three clerks of Joaquim José de Oliveira, who owned two stores. The executor described one of them, a Brazilian, as a "relative" of the storekeeper, which may explain his good fortune. Even those who were not related by blood usually lived in the same building as the owner, being housed and fed by him, forming a sort of family.[53]

Slaves could also work as clerks. After Raimundo, who had arrived from Africa in 1815, was put to work clerking, his skill attracted the attention of a Portuguese storekeeper who bought him for the same purpose. In 1823, at the end of the war for independence, his master's allegiance to Portugal meant that the store was confiscated and auctioned off, making Raimundo the property of a third store owner. Finally, in 1828, Raimundo succeeded in purchasing his freedom and set to work, now with a last name of Barros, selling cloth, not just in Salvador but in towns around the bay.[54]

Francisco da Cruz's story is much sadder. A mulatto slave, he claimed to have always been "obedient . . . and faithful" at his job as clerk in his owner's foodstuffs store and that its balance sheets would show that the business "had rendered favorable profits." The master had himself often said that "'no one had a better clerk than he.'" Because of his reputation for fidelity, Francisco was offered credit by others to conduct business ventures on his own, which did well. Then, because of the intrigue of those who were jealous of his success, his master concluded that Francisco's wealth had resulted from his stealing at the store. He then imprisoned Francisco in his private cell and began to torment him, "now putting him in stocks, . . . now limiting his food and feeding him only once a day, now torturing him by shackling his fingers to the point of crushing them and making them swell." Francisco got his case heard by the Criminal Court and was transferred to a public jail, but his master sued for his return. Francisco then appealed directly to the Crown in Portugal, asking that his master sell him or accept a fair sale price for his freedom in compliance with "all the rules of natural law, good reason, and dispositions of positive law." He could afford to buy his freedom, he said, speaking of himself in the third person, "because people who have taken pity on him will lend him the necessary sum." The record does not indicate whether his supplication was successful.[55]

In the 1830s another legal dispute partially revolved around whether Cypriano, a Yoruba slave, had simply "pretended" to be too slow-witted to be a successful store clerk, or whether he had never worked as a clerk. But not only did no one question the claim that an African-born slave could have clerked at a store, but the notion that Cypriano cleverly acted so as to conceal his true abilities or knowledge suggests that contemporaries did not doubt he could have them.[56]

Street vendors and storekeepers formed a complex trading system that linked producers to ultimate consumers. African women and Portuguese men brought with them to Salvador an intensely commercial spirit from across the Atlantic. For most of the period covered here, new waves of immigrants and slaves continued to arrive in

Salvador from overseas, embodying a keen sense for trade and respect for its successful conduct—an expectation and a background that made such work normal and rewarding. Hundreds and hundreds of transactions took place each day in this active, vibrant, and growing economy, creating an air of intense activity throughout the city. A British admiral described the inhabitants of Salvador as being "more active in commerce than those in any other part of Brazil." And it was truly said in 1799 that "commerce is the strongest column sustaining this colony."[57]

CHAPTER 3

CONNECTIONS

AS STREET VENDORS AND STORE OWNERS constructed a citywide community, horizontal ties criss-crossed vertical ones, multiplying their contacts with a broad segment of the population. Business itself meant constructing networks, but those engaged in the food trade were not merely economic creatures. They had a variety of ties to others, pointing in many directions. From these connections they naturally built up solidarity with some and hostility toward others while defining themselves. Families, friendships, neighborhoods, and venues where they frequently gathered provided occasions for sociability and the sharing of cultural backgrounds as well as tense moments that could lead to negotiating compromises or heighten animosities. Even their relationships with borrowers and creditors were personal ones, laced with emotional significance.

FAMILY, FRIENDS, AND NEIGHBORS

Family ties filled the lives of food traders, but formal marriage, although a sign of higher status, was not the usual pattern in Salvador. The proportion of married men and women to those who lived in consensual unions cannot be known, of course, since census takers did not note these latter arrangements. The historian Kátia M. de Queirós Mattoso, who has studied fragmentary manuscript schedules surviving from an 1855 census, concludes that households headed by a man listed as single but which included a single woman of appropriate age, especially one with children and no other man present, amounted to 52 percent of the total. Certainly such unions were a deeply rooted practice in Salvador, as elsewhere in Brazil and Portugal. Foreign travelers commented on them, in one case saying that "marriage is rejected by the majority." Anyway, the less affluent could hardly be expected to undertake expensive Church-sanctioned marriages, the only legal ones, although there were ways to get around such obstacles.[1]

Surely concubinage had its own rules and understandings, but because it operated informally, it remains largely hidden from our gaze. But not always. The children of a concubine—in the probate documents that I examined the word is never used to signify a passing relationship or an adulterous one—had many legal rights, and lawyers, witnesses, and judges spoke favorably of the children's mother as having been "always understood, held, and maintained as a concubine [*sempre havida, theúda, e mantheúda como concubina*]."[2] Evidence from other places in Brazil drawn from civil and ecclesiastical court cases reveals that in these unions almost all the men enjoyed higher status than the women by virtue of class, race, or legal status (free). Marriage was only for equals, although not all equals married. The man could certainly be patronizing, as was one who declared, "I have always remained in the state of bachelorhood and had no children until now and, therefore, I institute as my sole heir Theresa de Jesus with whom I have lived and from whom I have received important services in carrying out her duties, therefore making herself worthy of my gratitude." Portuguese men, most of whom moved to Brazil in their youth, frequently entered into such relationships with women of color, as their wills disclosed. One declared that "at no time was I ever married and, as a bachelor, by my weakness I had repeated carnal copulations with one of my slaves named Francisca and from them I have a daughter whom I had baptized with the name of Josefa, whom I hereby institute as the heir of both parts of my goods." The unequal terms of such a liaison are obvious, but that does not rule out mutual attraction and affection.[3]

Men often explicitly acknowledged the children of such long-term consensual unions as theirs, firmly transforming them into legal heirs. Typical was the case of Bartolomeu Francisco Gomes, a cattle merchant and store owner, who made Epifânia Maria da Conceição, "in whose company I have lived for sixteen years," the executor of his estate and recognized his paternity of her two daughters. When a concubine died, the man might subsequently establish a similar association with another woman, having had children by both and treating the children of both unions as all his. The grocer José Pinto de Almeida lived with Raimunda Veríssiama de Jesus until her death,

and then with Francisca dos Reis Valle, whom he appointed as executor of his estate despite her illiteracy. With Raimunda he had had two
children, and with Francisca, three more. Never did he marry either
of them. José Gomes da Costa declared, "I am a bachelor and I have
always lived in this state; nevertheless I have had some natural children of whom the following are still alive." Here the testator named
the mothers: Florência Maria Ferreira, "a single mulatta," Custódia
Neta, "white, single," and Maria Gomes, her color not specified,
"who is [now] married to Victorino Dias Ferreira."[4] Even without an
official statement, for a man to have treated a woman's children as if
they were his could be used in court to establish his paternity.[5]

The custom was not limited to Portuguese men. João Nunes, a
freed African who himself became a slave trader, listed a number of
his unions over a long period, presumably with consenting women
given that he spoke of them with respect, was careful to name them,
and recognized their children as his, making them his rightful heirs.
With Josefa Gonçalves dos Santos, a West African freed woman, he
had had a daughter Felícia Gonçalves. Both mother and daughter had
died by the time he made his will in 1807, but Felícia had had a daughter, his granddaughter, whose name he knew. With Catarina, who
came from southern Angola, he had a blind daughter named Maria
Nunes. Then he formally married Francisca Ribeira da Cruz, a free
black woman, whether African or not is not stated, who predeceased
him without bearing any children. The last woman mentioned in his
will did not secure the same place in his will as the others: he had
owned a slave, Ana, for whom he had taken out a license as a street
vendor eighteen years earlier. He later granted her freedom, keeping
her letter of manumission along with his own, suggesting either that
they lived as man and wife or that he wished to hold on to her income. After being freed she bore two daughters. He gave Ana and her
daughters virtually nothing and did not acknowledge these children
as his. We do not know whether the two African women with whom
he had earlier lived had been free before he took up with them or
whether, like the vendor Ana, they had been freed by him.[6]

A family controversy erupted regarding a vendor who, according to one version, had once been a general store owner's "publicly
kept and maintained" woman before he married someone else. She
had lived with him openly in his house, and he felt "much cheered"
when she bore a daughter, Máxima, whom "he held in his arms as he
showed her off to his best friends." When Máxima reached marriage-

able age, he found her a husband, gave her a large dowry, and helped her furnish her house. That is Máxima's story. It is unclear whether he continued to maintain Máxima's mother after he legally married another woman and had two sons with her. The other heirs claimed that the vendor, Máxima's mother, had "never" been their father's concubine. They said that she "had had illicit friendships with different men," and that at one time, true, she had managed their father's store for him, "earning two *patacas* [a small amount] per week," but that was all. The judge sided with Máxima, however, ruling that she had been cheated out of her rightful share when the property had been divided.[7]

Wives and concubines played an important part in the lives of store owners, and some of them helped at the store or managed the property. Even Máxima's opponents had to acknowledge that her mother had done so. One wife declared she was "head of household" and held a "power of attorney from her absent husband," a store owner. Men often named their wives as executors of their estate, but few explained their decision as did Felix Ferreira de Santana, a rentier, who stated in his will that his wife would pay all his bills "from whatever moneys there are, for she really knows everything about it as I go over it with her as half-owner of our property."[8] We may speculate that many women had big roles in general stores, helping out as clerks and, when literate and numerate, managing the books and correspondence.

We know little about how store owners felt toward their wives, whether formal or informal. The historian Júnia Ferreira Furtado, having examined ecclesiastical investigations into "sinful" cohabitation, found much evidence of "affectionate ties" between unmarried couples.[9] Francisco Ferreira da Gama, a Portuguese businessman in Salvador, married a poor woman, Vitória Luisa do Rio Gama, with separation of property, a legal contract used when the partners possessed an exceptionally unequal amount of wealth. They remained childless. Although he noted in his will that (aside from an inherited entailed estate in Portugal) "the goods that I possess have all been acquired by me," he acknowledged that he had been married to Vitória for twenty-three years "always with perfect harmony and understanding, with co-operation on her part insofar as possible toward the common good of our household." So, reversing the effect of his marriage contract, he left all his goods to her except the entailed estate, albeit with the stern proviso that if she married again "she will lose this favor" and would merely have usufruct of one-third of his property, while the remainder would go to his brother and sister in equal parts. Although patronizing, he evidently had great confidence in his wife's business sense (if not in her faithful memory of him) as he named her executor for his properties in Salvador, Rio de Janeiro, Lisbon, and Porto. Affection and admiration had grown over time and trumped their originally cautious arrangement.[10]

Love, sex, and family surely occupied as much attention in a street vendor's mind as in anyone's.[11] In 1859 "a large number of black Mina vendors" habitually gathered around the jail in Barbalho, once a fort, and in its central courtyard. There they "spread out their mats . . . next to the grates of the prison [windows]" to sell food to the prisoners and guards, "lingering until 7 at night." An inspector declared this custom constituted an "offense to morals," for they flirted and did much else with the guards, some of whom he found in "less than respectable positions" with the women. A Frenchman described how when black women gathered water at the public fountain, "lovers come there to help [them] draw the water and also carry the jug half way. They stop to talk, offer them flowers, the bushes are near by!"[12]

A fleeting encounter could grow into a loving relationship, one linking a free person to an enslaved one. An 1855 census listed both self-hired slave women and freed women as living with freedmen. A free mulatto paid for the freedom of his enslaved wife, Antonia de Araújo. Another free man borrowed funds from seven friends, including four women, to purchase the freedom of his wife and child. A soldier deserted to join a slave woman. A male slave fled to link up with his love, who had become a freed woman.[13]

A major difference between most shopkeepers and street vendors is that male store owners did not have to provide immediate care for their children, whereas hawkers could be seen on the street "with or without children." The street vendor Ana de São José da Trindade bore five children, and innumerable instances of vendors with children appear in the documents—especially, of course, in the case of slave women, whose children were property and worth recording. Benedita, a young West African slave who sold food on the street, lived with her eight-year-old son Felipe and his little brother, three or four years old. Whether these children resulted from consenting relationships is, of course, unknowable, but the sources show that street vendors often established long-term unions.[14] The flexibility of vending made it possible for self-hired, freed, and free women to work both inside and outside their household.[15] Or a vendor could take her child with her to work, even nursing the baby as she sat, waiting for a customer to pass by. She could ask another to look after her child when needed, counting on friendship and the solidarity of mothers. Eventually children could help their mothers and learn the trade themselves. If a woman's mate had been born in Brazil, their extended family would include his parents, siblings, nieces, and nephews—that is, grandparents, uncles, aunts, and cousins for the children. African partners might have had links to others who had arrived aboard the same slave ship, also forming a kind of family. Each partner probably belonged to at least one sodality, broadening the reach of their ties still further.

From their extended families, children acquired a culture. They presumably took on religious belief, discovered ethnic traditions, heard family stories, learned standards of proper behavior and respectability, witnessed rituals of social interchange, observed patterns of authority, and acquired skills and strategies of survival and resistance. In short, they came to know how to negotiate the sometimes treacherous fields of power and love. The children were enmeshed from the beginning in a larger social universe starting from baptism, so often carried out with named godparents.[16]

The relationship between godparents and child could be especially problematic because it so clearly exposed the interconnection between authority and protection. Godparents were chosen with great care and were meant to be people on whom the child—and, by extension, the parents—could rely for help. In doing so they became clients of a patron and owed him or her their loyalty.[17] One godparent, a cattle merchant, expressed his exasperation that his godchildren did not appreciate his heavy-handed guidance. He declared that he left nothing to them,

to all of whom—to free them from trouble and taxes etc.—I gave during my life and several years ago appropriate gifts and also some sums from my pocket that I placed for each one of them into the Savings Bank [Caixa Econômica] at interest for them, telling them what I did; but their parents, uncles, and they themselves, instead of welcoming this, took the money out to spend right away, etc., etc., and some even criticized me for not going myself to the Bank, saying that I should give them the money directly, even telling me face-to-face that gifts or not, these were their [moneys] and that they wanted them and did not require guardians on this matter!

On the other hand, one African woman who engaged in trade revealed a startling reversal of the usual vertical arrangement of coparent-hood. This ex-slave bequeathed two gold chains to "my goddaughter, the daughter of my former master."[18] Relatives and ritual relatives wound threads of meaning around each person.

As for friends, we may ask, "To whom did a store owner turn when he wished to summon people to testify on his behalf?" In one case the owner of a general store called three friendly witnesses: a French-man, aged twenty-four, engaged in business; a fifty-year-old Portu-guese owner of a commission house who sold slaves; and a tinsmith, born in Salvador, aged twenty-two, with whom the grocer sometimes went hunting. When another storekeeper believed that he had been wronged by an inspector of weights and measures, he called five men as witnesses, three Portuguese and two Brazilians: two were store clerks, one owned a store himself, one "lives from his business," and one, the only mulatto, ran a brothel. Two were married men. These men knew each other, had common interests, and willingly spent their time on behalf of the complainant. We may call them his friends, whom he could call on when needed.[19]

Street vendors gathered at many locations, finding both friends and rivals. They elbowed their way forward at the beach to get the best of the catch from fishermen and the most select fruit where boats docked. They met while competing for manioc meal at the public grains market. The authorities complained about how, not content to remain within the designated locations for food stalls, they also clustered on the steps of the chamber of commerce building, doubt-less chattering, gossiping, joking, or complaining of their lot. A for-eign traveler noted a group of black women "selling fruits . . . in ani-mated conversation," adding that the ones he saw on the streets were "chatting with prodigious loquacity as they walked." What especially impressed him was how they managed to carry on conversations while balancing bundles on their head, sometimes speaking "their native African languages." Prince Maximilian also described "a troop of Negroes and Negresses" who worked "amid much noise and jokes."[20]

Beyond family and friends, store owners and street vendors lived among neighbors, with whom they had face-to-face contact and some-times close association. Residential segregation was by wealth, not by color. Two storekeepers, both born in Portugal—Antônio Teixeira Porto, aged 55 and a widower, and Domingos Alves da Silva, aged 23

FIGURE 3.1. Street vendors at Rosário church, with Carmo in the background, 1860

and a bachelor—lived on the same street in the lower city. They were called as witnesses regarding the theft of a silver lamp stolen from a church. The accused were two other Portuguese: a shoemaker, single, aged 48, described as barefoot (despite his trade), wearing a shirt made of African cloth; and a man who "lived from business," aged 40, dressed in a black jacket and white pants, wearing shoes. To witness a search of their house, the police had summoned the neighbors, all of them male, giving us some notion of who rubbed shoulders with the two store owners: besides a white store clerk, 27, born in the Bahian town of Valença, and a white "businessman," born in Salvador, 46, married, the neighbors included a 50-year-old black man and a 60-year-old mulatto, both born in Salvador, who lived "from buying and selling"; two mulatto tailors, aged 24 and 29, one born across the bay in Cachoeira, the other from the arid region to the north just beyond the border of Sergipe; a mulatto carpenter born in Salvador, aged 40; and a mulatto sailor, born in Salvador, aged 18. Six of the twelve men were white, and, of these, four were born in Portugal. One of the other neighbors was black, the rest mulattos. Three of the eight Brazilians were born outside Salvador, in the surrounding region. Aged between 18 and 60, only three were or had been legally married, although, as we have seen, they likely had long-term female companions. Besides the two store owners, one witness clerked in a store and five others made their living "from business," three were artisans (carpenters or tailors), and one a sailor, besides the shoemaker/thief. None were strictly manual workers without skills or tools. If there were rich merchants on that street, they were not called as witnesses. This was the storekeepers' neighborhood, not counting women, children, or slaves—the social world of petty commerce in the lower city.[21]

Street vendors also lived with a mix of other people. One female street vendor belonged to a storekeeper who also owned a male sedan chair carrier, a male boatman, a male street vendor, two female seamstresses, and a girl learning to be a seamstress; they were in one another's most immediate daily company. The many vendors who lived on their own, both slave and free, had neighbors with other livelihoods. Fragments of the manuscript census carried out in 1855 list those who lived on the centrally located Rua da Ajuda. The first five domiciles, whether houses or rooms we do not know, included these ten people (although the Africans were listed as "free," they could only have been freed):

- First domicile:
  female, 52, single, Gbe, free, street vendor
- Second domicile:
  male, 64, single, Hausa, free, street vendor
  female, 44, single, Hausa, free, street vendor
- Third domicile:
  male, 40, single, Portuguese, free, store owner
  male, 18, single, Portuguese, free, his clerk
  female, 60, single, creole [i.e., Brazilian-born black], free, his
  servant
- Fourth domicile:
  female, 60, single, white [free, of course, probably Brazilian],
  quitandeira
- Fifth domicile:
  male, 34, single, mulatto, free, boatman
  female, 40, single, creole, free, [no occupation listed]
  female, 60, single, creole, free, agregada [i.e., a dependent who
  lived in the household]

These ten, living cheek-by-jowl, included four men and six women ranging in age from 18 to 64; three white, two of whom were Portuguese; and seven persons of color, three of whom were Africans. As to occupations, they included one storekeeper, one clerk, one boatman, and four female street vendors. On another central street "behind the jail," a free creole butcher and two vendors—one a Yoruba with a 12-year-old son and the other a mulatta—were immediate neighbors. Vendors, in short, lived with other relatively poor people, regardless of color and regardless of place of birth. Although some wealthy persons may have lived nearby, the neighbors of street vendors were usually poorer than those of store owners, just as their housing was more precarious.[22] It is nevertheless true that Ana de São José da Trindade, despite being a street vendor, managed to live better than many shopkeepers. A ranked order was daily being undone and then recalled and reinstituted.

WIDER CONTACTS

Beyond families, friends, and neighbors, shopkeepers and street vendors established contacts with a wide community, ranging from the meanest slave to the most respectable householder. Wholesalers in the lower city routinely did business with wealthy import-export merchants, while grocers sold to people of all ranks, including street vendors who bought for resale. Grocers would surely have had their regular customers whom they knew by name and sold to on account. On Sundays and holy days, when most businesses had to close, general stores could legally stay open until noon, as did bakeries. Consequently, they served as gathering places for many, including some whom the authorities considered dangerous or disruptive (see Figure 2.3). The city council found it necessary in 1831 to decree that the owners of those stores in which there were "noisy shouts, illegal gaming, or slaves lingering beyond the time needed to make their purchase" be fined or suffer four days in jail.[23] The frequent repetition of these ordinances indicates they had little if any effect. General stores became meeting places where free and freed persons, regardless of color, mixed with slaves. Certainly the self-hired could meet there any day. These shops welcomed both the orderly and the disorderly, slaves as well as slave owners. They were places for sociable reunions. Nothing suggests that grocers found it awkward to deal with their socially inferior customers.[24]

The practice of hawking and the physical mobility it required drew street vendors into an extensive set of relationships that reached across geographical, social, and cultural boundaries. They wandered the streets or sat at corners where they could talk with water carriers, porters of wine casks, chair-bearers, self-hired slaves, and free and slave passersby, not to mention higher-class customers. Vendors must have met bakers, butchers, city authorities, soldiers, policemen, street urchins, and construction workers. Their suppliers included not only the owners of outlying farms and general stores in the city but the boatmen who brought fresh food and grain from across the bay and the fishermen who disgorged their catch on the beach. Ellena testified that she spent her day selling fish and "hunting up fishermen." The city council claimed that street vendors' association with boatmen unfairly facilitated their business, for it enabled them to get ahead of consumers wishing to purchase directly from suppliers of fruit, legumes, and fish.[25] Vendors would know all or most of these people by name, as well as the names of the domestic servants at the houses where they sold their goods. These encounters formed part of their workday routines.

Not all of the vendors' connections were friendly ones. Soldiers and policemen, although recruited from the same social class as many of the vendors, held the authority to exercise force over them.[26] The worst clashes occurred in negotiations over prices, since soldiers seemed to believe they, and not the vendor, should have the last word on the matter. They sometimes claimed, falsely, that the governor had set prices for such goods and that they were merely demanding that foodstuffs be sold at the regulated price, "arbitrarily [determining] that bananas should be [sold] at ten or a dozen for ten réis, large watermelons for four *vinténs* [80 réis], small ones for two and other foodstuffs in proportion to whatever dictates their desire, . . . their excess reaching the point of taking the said goods by force." Soldiers also insisted that street vendors accept their copper money, despite the fact that supplying merchants refused to accept any of it because of widespread counterfeiting. Accusations that soldiers "mistreated" female street vendors surface as a leitmotif of the era. Their arrogance and disdain did not go unnoticed. A newspaper scathingly reported that when a mounted soldier accidentally trampled a vendor's stand, scattering her goods all about, although unseated himself, he nevertheless calmly remounted his horse and rode off without an apology or backward glance.[27]

Because of their many contacts, shopkeepers and street vendors could consider news as much a part of their stock-in-trade as the goods they sold, although they bartered news for other news rather than selling it for cash. A Portuguese-born shop owner likely kept his countrymen up to date on what was going on. On a single day vendors could exchange information with house servants in the upper-class district of Vitória and boatmen on the shore about to sail to towns in the Recôncavo. Ursulina's food-buying customers included the political prisoners who rioted in 1833 at a prison-fort out in the bay, a place she could only have reached in a rowboat or canoe. It is safe to assume she knew more about their plans for a riot than did the judge who subsequently heard the case against them.[28]

Street vendors were deeply affected by, and sometimes participants in, the 1835 "Muslim" uprising, precisely because they were tied into the larger urban system by their business. The governor learned of the plot through a series of denunciations that began with a vendor. To be sure, the community of street vendors, carriers, and for-hire slaves and freedpersons was awash with rumors, so any one of many may have let something slip. But the documented source of the denunciation was Sabina da Cruz, an African who had had a knock-down drag-out fight with her husband that morning—not their first. He had walked out, taking many of her things with him, and she was still fuming that evening. When she went looking for him, she traced him to a house where they refused her entry because, they said, he was too busy to come out to talk to her. They told her that soon Africans would be masters of the land. She replied that they would all soon be feeling the lash themselves and rushed off to see her friend Guilhermina Rosa de Souza, the wife of a freedman, who had contacts among the whites. Sabina may have been as worried about her husband's safety as she was angry at him, and perhaps hoped her action would stop the movement before he got into trouble. Guilhermina, a freed African and probably a vendor herself, told her white neighbor from whom she rented her rooms about what she had learned, and the news quickly passed up to the president of the province. The authorities reacted swiftly, provoking the rebels to launch their effort prematurely in the middle of the night with disastrous results. If Sabina can be blamed for their quick defeat, other vendors became deeply involved in promoting the revolt: 14 percent of those put on trial were women, most of them street vendors.[29] Still others were negatively affected by it: Teresa Maria de Jesus found herself alone after the authorities deported her husband, a freed African, allegedly for his links to the uprising. Gullible at first—she "trustingly" signed a power-of-attorney in favor of a man who cheated her—she soon learned how to defend herself through pursuing her case in several courts, rallying her friends to testify on her behalf, recovering her property, and getting the man who cheated her put in jail, where he eventually died. Being part of a larger community had its advantages.[30]

PATRONS AND CLIENTS

Most store owners made up the lowest link, aside from the street vendors, in a long chain of commerce and credit. At the other end of the commercial power spectrum were the large-scale merchants, closely allied with the planter class, who engaged in transatlantic trade. Sugar and tobacco exporters, importers of European manufactured goods, major players in the slave trade—these men probably looked down on the bulk of the store owners, while selling them imported food, lending them money, and sometimes owning a shop or two themselves, operated by others.[31] José da Silva Maia's firm, at one time Salvador's leading transatlantic merchant house and a ship owner himself, supplied codfish to José Pinto de Almeida, who owned two groceries where he sold drinks and foodstuffs. Lesser merchants who did not engage in international trade nevertheless built an extensive commercial network into the interior towns of Bahia, especially those around the Recôncavo, and supplied the grocers in Salvador. They also bid for contracts to supply the army and sold large quantities of foodstuffs to institutions such as the hospital of the Santa Casa. Like the big shots, they might also own a retail store. Some store owners engaged in other businesses, as did Manoel Tavares. Besides his grocery, he owned land that he used only to extract firewood, six small boats engaged in sailing across the bay, and slave sailors to operate them. He died in 1816 with an estate worth over two and a half times that of Ana de São José da Trindade's.[32]

Shopkeepers, however, should not be confused with the merchant elite. They focused on small sales and carried a limited inventory. Many, probably most, owners of general stores did not register at the Board of Trade, where a merchant had to have a certain amount of capital or be vouched for by those who did. At the end of the eighteenth century a Portuguese schoolteacher living in Salvador said that although the merchants numbered 164, "there are as well in this city multitudes of businessmen who trade in foodstuffs." At another point he claimed that there were well over 250 general stores in the town. Although store owners were not the wealthiest people, they nevertheless held some prestige. They frequently served as officers in the colonial militia's second regiment or, later, in the National Guard, a position that allowed them to lord it over their clerks, who made up the bulk of the men. Military rank mirrored their social status.[33]

For all the distinctions of status among traders, from the wealthy overseas merchants to the struggling street vendors, they formed an interconnected whole through the transfer of goods and the extension of credit. The Pereira Marinho firm was a leading merchant- and slave-trading house. Its Portuguese founder, Joaquim Pereira Marinho, became a prominent member of Salvador's Santa Casa de Misericórdia, the city's richest sodality and charitable organization, and he left a huge estate at his death in the 1880s.[34] His enormous wealth derived in part from his activity as a money lender at the rate of 2 percent per month; for instance, he financed one man's purchase of a house and land in a city suburb. What matters here, however, is that he supplied other merchants on credit, one of whom was Luiz Manoel da Rocha, a moderately wealthy Portuguese owner of two general stores with capital sufficient to be described by his executor as a *comerciante.* Besides being listed as a creditor in Rocha's postmortem inventory, Pereira Marinho continued to sell salted meat from Rio Grande do Sul on credit to Rocha's estate while in probate.[35]

So what sort of merchant was Rocha? Like Pereira Marinho, he had been born in Portugal. He married, was widowed, and married again. He owned a large food store in the lower city and lived over his smaller shop in an imposing three-story stone house facing a small square in the upper city. Besides the house where he lived, he owned two others immediately next to it, one with a store, presumably rented to someone else. He owned still another ten houses, making a total of thirteen. One sign of his wealth is that his property included two saddle horses, unusual among city dwellers. Typically, however, he owned many slaves; to be precise, twenty-six of them, including one female street vendor. That he brought some of his goods into the city on his two sailing vessels suggests the reach of his business. His enormous downtown store had for sale hundreds of bottles of wine, in addition to many casks, and an astounding 18,000 corks, whereas his smaller one held much smaller quantities of everything, with only 145 bottles of wine. Rocha's extensive debts—passed on to his heirs at his death in 1853—belied all this apparent wealth, although it also speaks to how others understood him to be a good risk. By taking into account what he owed, his real wealth was less than that of Ana de São José da Trindade, the street vendor! Like Pereira Marinho, he was also a creditor, lending money in one case to a widow in the neighboring province of Sergipe whom he mercilessly dunned, and in another case to a borrower in the Recôncavo city of Santo Amaro who lost his house when Rocha foreclosed on the mortgaged property that had been offered as security.[36] Also like Pereira Marinho, he sold goods on credit to others, including Bartolomeu Francisco Gomes, another storekeeper.

Gomes was the natural son of a couple who had lived in the seaside town of Camamu, south of Salvador. Unlike the twice-married Rocha, Gomes never married, but he had two daughters by his longtime companion, Epifânia Maria da Conceição, a literate woman. He named those two, aged twelve and nine, as his heirs. After having earlier been a cattle trader, by 1848, in partnership with his cashier, he owned two general stores in the area north of the Carmelite monastery. The variety of goods in Gomes's stores was as extensive as any, but the amounts were considerably smaller: half a bushel of rice, one bushel of corn, half a bushel of beans, seventy-one pounds of wheat flour, twenty-two pounds of potatoes, twelve pounds of meat. Gomes owned four slaves but no houses, paying rent to a sodality for the house where he lived over one of his stores and to a Portuguese landlord, a dry goods merchant, for his second one. When he died in 1848, his modest estate was worth only a quarter of Ana de São José da Trindade's. Over a period of many months from 1842 to 1845 Gomes purchased from Rocha, always on credit, a wide variety of foodstuffs and other goods. Gomes, of course, also bought supplies on credit from others besides Rocha, just as Pereira Marinho and Rocha leant to many.[37]

That Rocha owned a slave street vendor completes the chain of supply and credit, although free hawkers were perhaps more likely to have bought from Gomes than from Rocha. Sixteen women owed a salted meat wholesaler a substantial total for supplies they had peddled on the street. A man who seems to have lived from lending listed a woman who sold sweets among those in debt to him. For those raised in West Africa, it would not have been strange to receive goods on credit or to borrow goods and cash from others.[38] Occasionally, however, it was the street vendors who lent money to others. I have noted how Ana de São José da Trindade, the African vendor, lent a large sum to a slave trader. She also accepted jewelry from him in pawn. And Joaquina Maria Borges de Sant'Anna, also a street hawker, lent even more to the owner of a dockside warehouse. Although we have no written records as evidence, it is highly probable that vendors generally extended short-term credit to their customers, if for no other reason than that the chronic shortage of small change made it difficult to settle accounts after every transaction. Grocers kept a running account of their sales for later settlement. The city council in 1846 described them as profiteering from the "pennies interest they charge on small loans."[39] So, from Pereira Marinho through Rocha and Gomes to female street vendors and beyond, the goods and credit flowed downwards, and the payments on interest and principal went upward. I assume that Pereira Marinho also owed his suppliers overseas, as did others. British importers were said to go every Saturday to collect something from storekeepers to whom they had advanced goods on credit.[40]

Commerce in Salvador, as in most premodern societies, at least in the Atlantic World, ran principally on credit, not on cash. Banks were nonexistent in Salvador at the beginning of the period studied here and did not become numerous or strong enough to support a major commercial center before the late 1850s. The Santa Casa de Misericórdia, the Desterro nunnery, and other similar institutions lent only on the security of land, principally to sugar planters.[41] So individual merchants or tradesmen did the commercial lending, and it was said in Salvador that those who "sell only for cash, sell little or nothing." If some storekeepers owed much, others could be described principally as money lenders. Loans paid off on time before the death of a borrower do not appear in estate inventories, but these documents nevertheless suggest that virtually everyone who engaged in trade was a borrower, a lender, or both simultaneously. As Antônio José Pinto put it, he "had not a single personal debt" but "I owe for some items to supply [my] foodstuff store."[42] Not uncommonly—it happened elsewhere—debts could exceed the value recovered from auctioning off all the goods of a store. Many estates consisted mainly of paper wealth, requiring the heirs to pursue the debtors. For example, on paper José Pinto de Almeida, who owned a large store in the lower city, was four times as rich as Ana de São José da Trindade. But the value of his estate can be divided into the following categories:

House	1.71 percent
Gold and silver	1.34 percent
Slaves	4.30 percent
Furniture of the store	0.44 percent
Goods for sale	9.24 percent
Cash on hand	3.28 percent
Receivables	79.69 percent
Total	100.00 percent

At the final settlement of this estate almost fifteen years after Almeida's death, the executor noted that many of these loans had never been repaid because "some [debtors] have died, others have gone bankrupt, and others left [the city], leaving no goods." The executor asserted, in his own will, that "I undertook every diligent measure so that the property [of the minors] not be destroyed. . . . I withstood two serious suits that ended by necessary [out of court] settlements." In turn he took debtors to court "from whom I was unable to collect amicably. . . . I paid out of my own property the proven debts owed [by Almeida]. Finally, I supported and [continue to] support the said orphans."[43]

The rate of interest is seldom mentioned in such transactions probably because it had been rolled into the price of the goods in advance. When specified, however, rates were high. In 1781 a local lawyer wrote a friend that if one owned a "smack," one could easily get others to invest in the carrying trade at 18 percent, payable within thirty days of the vessel's return to port. When, in 1795, the governor summoned the city's businessmen to see if they would be willing to lend money to the then-allied British fleet anchored in the bay on its way to South Africa, they replied that it was "much more advantageous for them to invest in [export] goods than to lend [their money] even at an interest rate of 20 percent."[44]

Credit relationships were not simply business ones, but those of clients and patrons. Like most patronage connections in Brazil, they were riven by ambiguity, all the more so since the borrowers were also customers. Although borrowers depended on lenders, lenders also depended on borrowers. Advancing credit to customers required a judgment regarding the borrowers' ability and commitment to repay the loan, but not doing so meant they might well take their business elsewhere. An emotional charge suffused the transaction, and a personal connection made it work. A popular saying today puts it succinctly:

"Better a friend in business than money in one's pocket [*Mais vale um amigo na praça que dinheiro no bolso*]." In 1865 a merchant who dealt in dried meat wrote humbly to a partner of a large firm that had guaranteed his rent, saying somewhat hesitatingly, "*Compadre* and friend: I wish you good health and happiness. Will you do me the favor of lending me the sum of two hundred mil-réis, that is, if it is possible, because I need this sum today to satisfy a creditor of mine. If it is possible, you can send it with my slave. I remain here at your service and with affection." On the other hand, once a connection had been established and goods supplied on credit with some repayments made, the next transaction would surely be easier, take less time, and produce less anxiety for both parties. By definition, however, borrowers wished to expand lines of credit, whereas lenders sought to restrict their risk by limiting the amount owing by any one borrower, while simultaneously making it large enough to attract particular borrowers/customers and solidify their loyalty. In that tension they bargained as best they could, using their social skills, their knowledge of the other's trustworthiness and business acumen, their keen sense of timing, and their ability to persuade, cajole, or threaten, being careful not to overstep the understood boundaries that determined acceptable behavior for client and patron. The borrower, of course, also benefited from the lender's expectation of repeated business because it helped guarantee the quality of the goods in question. Information about potential borrowers was as crucial to lenders then as now. Good ties to notaries—who recorded in their books all legally enforceable obligations to pay, all suits, and all probate inventories and divisions of inherited property—surely proved invaluable to a lender anxious to ascertain the credit worthiness of a borrower. Finally, neither lender nor borrower could afford to make their bond an exclusive one, each preferring to have such links to several people, multiplying the number of patrons and clients. The estate of a wealthy sugar factor and exporter who died in 1814 listed many store owners as debtors, each for relatively small amounts, presumably both because he wanted to spread his risk and the borrowers wished to limit their dependence. The lender-borrower association was never an entirely easy one, and its challenges were present at every link in the chain, from international merchant to street vendor.[45]

Only a few store owners' debts, however, were backed by more than a spoken promise to pay. Some store owners accepted jewelry as pawn to secure their loans, as did street vendors such as Ana de São José da Trindade.[46] All loans resulted from face-to-face transactions that relied on trust and personal knowledge, not on abstract principles of honesty applicable to everyone. Violating the unspoken rules brought condemnation enough and prevented further borrowing from almost anyone. If a storekeeper saw he could not repay his creditors, he would turn his goods over to them and start anew. As John Turnbull, an English businessman, explained, "the laws of debtor and creditor resemble those of Scotland: An insolvent debtor makes a cession of his goods to his creditor and is thenceforth personally free." That is, as another foreigner made even more explicit, "when a bankrupt delivers up his effects, they are sold and divided among his creditors who have no further claim upon him. But if he either neglects or refuses to do this, the law empowers them to seize everything he may possess and in this case they still continue to have a claim on whatever property he may acquire, 'till the whole debt is liquidated." On the other hand, the lender faced still other insecurities, because, short of completed bankruptcy proceedings, it could prove exceedingly difficult to recover money leant to a recalcitrant borrower. A third commentator claimed that to recover a debt of 100$000 "you will easily spend 25$000" in legal and other fees and "lose six months." Nevertheless, many creditors found it worth their while to pursue debtors, and suits for recovery of loans filled the courts and took up the time of bailiffs citing debtors and threatening to have their goods embargoed. Foreclosure for debt was not uncommon.[47]

Auctioning the contents of a store to pay off debts, or for any other reason, had its own publicly performed ritual. The judge, with his scribe present, ordered the bailiff to begin the proceedings:

He did so, loudly saying, "May he who wants to bid on the goods of the food-store of José Pinto de Almeida come before me and I will receive his bid." . . . And accepting this bid he began to announce it, saying in a loud voice "eleven thousand, seven hundred and sixty réis over and above the appraised value of the goods existing in the store; . . . he who would give more come before me and I will receive his bid." There not being a larger bid, he then . . . began to [seek] a larger [final] bid, saying before all present: "Offer more, because I don't find more, if I find more, I'll take more, some little bit, I give you one, I give you two, a larger one, a smaller one, I sell at the market, I auction at the market, and because there is no one to offer more, I hand you the sapling branch." And approaching the bidder he said these final words: "May God give you good value for the goods of the store," . . . and he gave him a green branch as a sign of having won the bidding, and the Judge took it as firm and valid.[48]

Such a proceeding doubtless drew onlookers, even those uninterested in acquiring the property. It demonstrated to a larger public not only the norms of wise business behavior but also the need to render loyalty and deference to those who lent you funds.

Illiterate street vendors did not leave written records of their dealings. When they sold food on credit to householders, these debts could surely prove difficult to collect.[49] When a buyer stiffed a vendor, what recourse did she have? If, however, a vendor failed to pay what she owed, I suspect word spread quickly from supplier to supplier with dire consequences for her. Being at the bottom of the credit ladder had its price.

Vendors, mostly women and mostly black, and shopkeepers, mostly Portuguese men, all interacted with others of distinct social positions. Their financial role mirrored their social one: borrowing from international merchants and lending to street vendors, grocers formed a crucial layer in the pyramid of credit, making practically all traders into lenders and borrowers, patrons and clients. The unrestrained movement of street vendors about the city as they did business broadened their reach, exposed them to other perceptions, and may have given them strength, even power, especially the conceptual ability to counterpoise themselves to dominant groups. Grocers also built connections through and across social ranks, from relationships to slaves—their own and those of others—to ties to wealthy consumers and merchant-suppliers. The formal and informal dealings of grocers and vendors, repeated on a daily basis, widened the scope of their experience through face-to-face encounters across class and ethnic divisions. Yet both vendors and shopkeepers were bounded by understandings of social position, understandings that formed a web—flexible but still present—in which they were caught.

In addition to their business dealings, both shopkeepers and street vendors built extensive networks through family and neighborhood to construct a community—dynamic, flexible, and durable. The surviving evidence allows us only to glimpse something of the dense connections that shopkeepers and street vendors constructed and maintained, not only through business but also through residential proximity, affection, and even love.

CHAPTER 4

"PEOPLE OF THE SEA"

SALVADOR'S PORT FORMED THE HUB of the food trade, with some spokes radiating into the city, and others linking it to points of supply in the hinterland. Sailors, captains, and boat owners connected farmers to the city's grocers and street vendors, making Salvador's inhabitants utterly dependent on them. The bay served as a path for cultural interchange because people on shore daily interacted with those who brought food across the water, with taken-for-granted urban understandings penetrating the interior and vice versa. To a degree, the ranks of those who sailed reflected the shape of society at large, and for these men life was filled with both severe challenges and satisfying rewards.

The bay facing Salvador constituted the city's principal highway of supply, and Salvador relied on waterborne transport for almost all of its food except beef, which transported itself. In no other large Brazilian city, with the possible exception of Belém, was the population so heavily dependent on waterborne traders. The city's location on a relatively narrow peninsula dictated such dependence, but easy accessibility to the bay proved a godsend, water transport being easily the least expensive way of moving goods. Already in 1612 an observer noted that "all movement of these people is on water." In 1775 the governor-general reported that there were 2,148 craft based in the province. Twenty-three years later one of his successors noted that of those operating entirely within the bay, more than a hundred docked at Salvador each week. As for vessels engaged in coastwise trade, they numbered over a thousand arrivals per year. In 1856 the official number of boats and ships based in the area reached 3,441, worked by over 8,500 men (see Table 4.1).[1] Their number created a striking visual effect when seen from the upper city: "thousands of boats that

Table 4.1. Ships and Crews at Salvador, 1856

Type of Vessel	Number	Total Crew	Avg. Crew
Lighters	1,543	3,559	2.3
Bay and Coastal Vessels			
Canoes	1,437	3,578	2.5
Lanchas	274	491	1.8
Barcos	55	135	2.5
Subtotals	1,766	4,204	2.4
Oceangoing Vessels			
Iates	46	172	3.7
Smacks	32	188	5.9
Pinnaces	26	193	7.4
Brigantines	22	80	8.2
Schooners	3	17	5.7
Steamboats	3	40	13.3
Subtotals	132	790	6.0
Totals	3,441	8,553	

Source: Capitania dos Portos da Bahia, Mapa demonstrativo das embarcações nacionais de navegação de longo curso e cabotagem bem como do tráfico dos portos . . . e dos indivíduos que n'elles trabalhão ou se empregão, 31 de dezembro de 1855, in Diogo Tavares (Chefe da Capitania do Porto) para José Maria da Silva Paranhos (Ministro dos Negócios da Marinha), Salvador, 20 de fevereiro de 1857, Arquivo Nacional, Rio de Janeiro, SPE, XM-183.

cross in all directions" creating a "forest of masts." Other observers focused on their cargoes, on all the "tropical fruits and other vegetables . . . brought in small launches or boats from the neighboring coasts," or on "the landing places [where] cluster hundreds of canoes, launches, and various small craft, discharging their loads of fruits and produce."[2] They proved especially important in supplying the city's inhabitants with manioc meal (farinha de mandioca), their major source of calories.

CAPTAINS AND SAILORS

The essential role played by the men who brought food to the city was clear to contemporaries. As a governor explained in 1775 when he was ordered to conduct a general recruitment of personnel for the royal navy, he had limited himself to a minor effort, which he succeeded in carrying out "without the least stirring-up or upset among the people of the sea [*gente do mar*], which I so wish to maintain in quietude, principally those who sail within the bay, because of the dependence on them of all the inhabitants [of the city] for the transport of [our] daily food."[3] Even though documents like this one often lumped them together as "people of the sea," captains and owners should not be confused with ordinary sailors.

Although captains of both smaller and larger vessels were sometimes also owners or part owners, more commonly the captain worked for the owner. As a result, disputes would erupt, as when one owner advanced cash to a captain for the purchase of manioc meal up to a certain price per unit, and the captain, not finding any at that price, bought it anyway.[4] The terms of another contract between owner and captain are sufficiently revealing of rankings and tasks among the crew to merit extended quotation. It was prepared in the town of Caravelas (see Map 4.1) on the southern coast of Bahia in September 1822 during the struggle for Brazilian independence, when insurgent forces were attempting to lay siege to Salvador, blocking off all food shipments:

You go as Captain to the city of Bahia [Salvador] in the said vessel *N. S. da Conceição* which I turn over to you on this occasion loaded with [537½] bushels of manioc meal which I wish you to sell on my account . . . at the best price that can be reached and the condition of the country permits. After having sold the cargo [illegible] as well as your [illegible] for going and coming of 25$000, you will pay Bento José da Costa, helper, for going and coming 14$000, but from this amount you will deduct 2$760 which I already gave him on account, but if he leaves you there you will give him only 7$000 from which you will deduct the said 2$760. You will pay the helper Francisco for going 4$000, entire, because he owes [me] nothing and if he returns you will do whatever you decide for my benefit. You will pay the cook for going 2$000. As for my two slaves give them nothing, but do take every care with them and especially [illegible] if they are sick . . . but do not let them wander on land . . . not even for pleasure, for you know how slaves are. . . . Whatever is left bring it to me with all security and as soon as possible for you know how the times are. Sail far from land as much as you can. . . . God take you and bring you, . . . God being with everyone. And in truth I give you these orders for your instruction alone.[5]

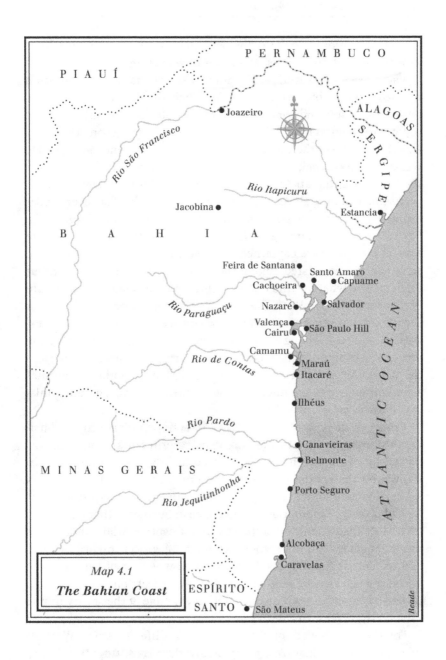

PIAUÍ

PERNAMBUCO

ALAGOAS

SERGIPE

Joazeiro

Rio São Francisco

Rio Itapicuru

Jacobina

Estancia

B   A   H   I   A

Feira de Santana
Santo Amaro
Capuame
Cachoeira
Rio Paraguaçu
Nazaré
Salvador
Valença
Cairu
São Paulo Hill
Camamu
Rio de Contas
Maraú
Itacaré

Ilhéus

Rio Pardo

Canavieiras
Belmonte

MINAS   GERAIS

Porto Seguro

Rio Jequitinhonha

ATLANTIC OCEAN

Alcobaça
Caravelas

Map 4.1
The Bahian Coast

ESPÍRITO
SANTO
São Mateus

Reade

From slave sailor to cook, to "helper," to captain, to owner, the lines of authority, relative status, and kinds of work were clear.

Each vessel, however, was a microcosm of that society, with an operating hierarchy, yes, but one in which the delineation of ranks proved malleable and changing. Many free blacks and mulattos were captains, and so were some slaves.[6] Just as shopkeepers sometimes put slaves in charge of their business, so did João Damaceno Palmeira. He worked the food trade with his small vessel "of which the captain is the black Joaquim, an African, . . . his slave." An 1843 newspaper advertisement listing slaves for sale included one who "has been a boat captain and knows Recôncavo ports." In a list of craft leaving the bay-side town of Maragogipe loaded with foodstuffs during August 1786, a number were captained by slaves; forty years later only one slave captain was listed among those sailing from another spot, but I cannot say whether this change represented a trend.[7] What is sure is that for a slave to be in charge of a vessel meant responsibility for the survival of other workers, for docking safely at the assigned destination, for supervising the loading and unloading, for collecting the proceeds—in short, it meant having authority, even over the free and the white. As was true elsewhere in the Atlantic World, the normal social differences were undone, at least during the voyage, and ranks and statuses criss-crossed.[8]

People of modest means could profitably participate in the business through multiple ownership or short-term rental. One boat was owned by two men, one of whom lived in Salvador and the other in a town on the southern coast of the province from which the vessel carried food to the city. A boat owner in Salvador advertised that he had a vessel "appropriate for Recôncavo business" that he wished to rent or for which he wanted to find a captain who would carry out its business "on the owner's account." A grocer might have several to rent, as did Manuel Tavares, who owned six of various sizes and seven slaves who were sailors. Finally, at least one freed African owned a boat of his own, surely another example of the ability to rise financially, at least to a degree.[9]

For the well-heeled, of course, it was a different story. Wealthy merchants in Salvador often owned outright a large ship or two, and prosperous sugar planters owned smaller vessels to get their product to the port. Something of a merchant's business can be known from the case of Manoel José dos Santos, who owned two smacks:

single-masted sailing vessels typically manned by five or six men. His wife, Rosa Maria de Jesus, had taken out a license for her slave Ursula to sell on the street, so the family had a retail outlet for the goods imported on their boats. Ten of his sixteen slaves were sailors, every one born in Africa. He was especially sought-after by owners of smaller boats and stores in Recôncavo towns when they needed to borrow funds; at the time of his wife's death in 1808, fourteen debtors were listed, some of whom were already under court order to pay up. Manoel's two smacks accounted for 30 percent of his estate, and the total value of his property in 1809 was more than thirteen times that of Ana de São José da Trindade. Not surprisingly, he was among the Portuguese merchants summoned in 1823 to raise money for a then-desperate colonial government and its besieged garrison attempting to prevent Brazil's independence.[10]

Those who actually manned these vessels and the lighters that transferred food from ship to shore came from a very different social stratum. As late as 1856 more than 2,000 of them—that is, nearly a quarter of all the sailors and boatmen based in Salvador—were slaves. Seventy-five years earlier, the governor had reported more generally that half of all sailors were bondsmen, and that on "small vessels only the captain is not a slave" (and, as I have shown, sometimes the captain was also). Occasionally slaves were specifically described in estate inventories as oarsmen or "in lighterage service," but most were described merely as "sailors" or as having a "maritime profession." Young slaves were occasionally inventoried as being in training for such duty.[11] Slave sailors were even forced to work on slaving vessels trafficking to Africa.[12] It was common for slaves who knew how to sail or row a boat to find themselves rented out by their masters to others. Some slaves, however, were self-hired, lived on their own, perhaps with their family, and sought out their own employment.[13]

A large proportion of slave sailors, as was true for slaves in general, were African. In 1805 sixteen slave sailors belonged to a store owner and his partner who together owned fourteen small boats. Five of their slaves were from the west coast of Africa and ten more were from Angola; only one was Brazilian-born. Africans who came from coastal regions doubtless knew the sea well, for some had traveled in dugout canoes even between the west coast of Africa and Angola. They endowed the sea with spiritual significance and even chose the trees from which to make their canoes with attention to their sacred power. When the Portuguese and other Europeans arrived off the coast of Africa, they often employed African crewmen and taught them the use of sails and rigging.[14]

These slaves, like sailors generally, had no easy time of it. They climbed masts, pulled sails, and manned the tiller in rough seas and calm, not to mention repairing the sails, coiling ropes, keeping pulleys clear, pumping bilge water, throwing out nets to catch fish, cooking their food, and keeping watch by night. It was demanding work. Of the sixteen slave sailors mentioned above, five suffered from physical defects probably caused by their work, including swollen feet, an injured groin, and a crooked shin resulting from a blow. One had a tumor on his leg. Like all sailors at the time, these slaves were constantly in contact with tar. It sealed the cracks between the boards of the deck and hull, and was used extensively to preserve wood and rope against the effects of water. It clung to the sailors' feet, hands, and clothing. We now know tar can lead to cancer, and it is labeled a toxic and hazardous substance. The psychological wounds resulting from their slavery can only be guessed at: one of these slaves was a drunk, and another was "addicted to eating dirt," a practice known as geophagy, now understood to be associated with severe vitamin deficiency.[15]

Despite these dangers, sailor-slaves enjoyed certain advantages over other slaves. The many tasks they performed demanded much skill, a source of increased self-respect, pride, and a sense of worth for a job well done. At times of crisis—a storm, a leak, a dragging anchor, a torn sail—rapid, appropriate, and precise action proved crucial. Skill always enhanced the power of a slave vis-à-vis the master because deliberately sloppy work could be used to punish a master for transgressing the customary rules of slave treatment. Like street vendors, slave sailors had contacts with a broad range of people beyond their masters, immediate companions, or family members, in marked contrast to field hands on a sugar plantation. Widening relationships doubtless expanded their mental horizons, suggested alternative ways of coping, and deepened their awareness of the world about them.[16]

Freedmen, free blacks, and free mulattos, as well as poor whites, worked alongside the slaves in sailing these vessels. Over 4,000 of those who worked on the water in 1856 were free but non-white. Like the street vendors, many had bought their freedom and continued their trade. A lucky sailor might, like the young Valentim, have his freedom purchased for him by another, in this case his African mother. Perhaps she was a vendor. A quarter of all the crews in 1856 were white men who shared their work experience with slaves and free blacks. One smack carrying manioc meal from the province of Sergipe to Salvador sailed with an extra large crew of fourteen: two African slaves, one mulatto slave, one African freedman, seven free men born in Sergipe (no race stated), and two from Portugal, plus the Portuguese captain-owner.[17]

THE BOATS

What kinds of vessels did these sailors man? The bottoms that brought food to the city fall into three categories by size, and so also by where they came from, what they carried, and the number in their crew. The most numerous were sailing dugouts, smaller versions of which can still be seen today plying the waters of the bay and its tributary rivers, and even going out to sea for short distances. In 1775 a census taker counted 1,392 of them, and in 1856 there were 1,437. They typically measured between 23 and 72 feet in length, and more than a yard in width. An 1850s inventory listed a canoe that measured 54 feet in length and a yard in width. They could be poled or rowed in shallow waters, but they usually had one or two triangular lateen sails attached by one side to the mast and at one point to a rope held by the sailor. They "look[ed] like huge birds." Wide boards placed on the side as a kind of temporary keel provided stability in a strong wind. Designed with a tiller, they were known for their shallow draft, maneuverability, and speed, all of which made them highly desirable for trade. In 1816 one given as part of a dowry was valued at between a third and a half of the cost of a prime slave.[18] Canoes could be sailed by one person alone, although they usually had two and sometimes three sailors (see Table 4.1).

It took two or three skilled sailors to man a vessel of another sort much used in the food business, with ribbed hulls, and stretchers, bracing, and exterior planks laid side-by-side, not overlapping but carefully caulked. These boats' "round bottoms" minimized their draft to never more than 3 feet, and they often entered port at high tide and careened on the beach at low tide. They were not longer than the biggest canoes, but deeper and wider, their width roughly equal to one-third their length.[19] They too used lateen sails, but quadrangular ones with a boom holding the lower edge. They could sail sharply into the wind, giving them "the speed of an arrow," an important consid-

FIGURE 4.1. Sailboat with provisions, 1835

eration when sailing northward to the city from the southern coast of Bahia, where the prevailing wind, except in winter, is from the north or northeast.[20] Despite marked variations in size, ranging from 20 to 120 tons, the shape of the prow, or the existence or not of a castle or tower, three words for this type of vessel were used interchangeably, sometimes in the same document to refer to the same craft: *saveiro* (also called by later observers *saveiro-da-Bahia* to distinguish it from the lighters used in Rio de Janeiro), *lancha*, and *barco* (or *barca* or *barco-do-recôncavo*). *Alvarengas*, that is, lighters, had the same kind of hull but depended primarily on oars and poles rather than sails and were used for loading and unloading cargo from oceangoing ships; frustratingly for historians, they too were sometimes called *saveiros* by contemporaries. I will refer to all of them as "boats."[21]

A more complex set of ranks and relationships were found on ships such as square-rigged smacks, brigantines, sloops, *iates* (with two masts and quadrangular lateen sails), two- or three-masted merchant ships called *galeras*, top-sail schooners, and so-called corvettes, most of them locally made. They typically required a larger crew of about six. These vessels brought staples in great volume to Salvador from

Brazilian ports. They could also be equipped for transatlantic sailing, and many arrived with slaves, manufactured goods, and specialty foodstuffs imported from Africa, Europe, or Asia. Their tonnages ranged as low as 56, so the essential difference between them and other vessels was the shape of their deep keels, which prevented them from docking at most ports and forced them to rely on lighters for unloading and loading.[22] In Salvador they typically anchored "parallel to the Forte do Mar," unlike the "boats [that] at high tide anchor next to land" (see Map 1.3).[23] Of those engaged in the food trade, smacks were the most frequently mentioned, and brigantines the next.

THE CARGOES

Sailors and captains were responsible for cargoes that varied according to the size of the vessel and its origin. The speedy canoes transported principally perishables and items not likely to be damaged by salt spray or rain, especially fresh vegetables, fruit, fish, or chickens, although goods were protected from the elements with canvas or thatch. Other vessels crossing the bay or plying the coast brought in other staples, such as on the "large smacks . . . that continually enter and leave every day," described in 1781 as being "loaded with corn, beans, manioc meal, cases of sugar, dried meat, dried or salted fish," and by a governor in 1798—specifically referring both to larger ships and to boats—as carrying "cases of sugar, manioc meal, rice, beans, corn, salted fish, lumber, mangrove bark for tanneries, . . . cotton, coffee, and other foodstuffs," as well as tiles, bricks, and red clay pots.[24]

Manioc meal, the city's principal staple, accounted for the largest share of foodstuff cargoes. It derives from the elongated tuberous roots of the manioc or cassava plant, a slender shrub native to tropical America that typically grows about five to seven feet high, does not require rich soil, and is exceptionally resistant to drought. It is unrivaled in its production of edible calories per land area planted. Cultivation of manioc is relatively easy, and, if the soil is well drained, the roots can be left in the ground for up to two years after reaching maturity, enabling the farmer to choose the right moment to prepare it for sale. The meal itself has no "germ" to spoil and can be stored in a dry place for months on end.[25] There are several varieties of manioc. One called *aipim* in Bahia and *yuca* in the Caribbean can be soaked, peeled, cooked, and eaten immediately, somewhat like potatoes. But the roots of the most significant one in Salvador's food trade contain a poison, hydrocyanic (or prussic) acid, which must first be removed. The Indians had learned how to do so long before the Portuguese arrived, and the latter quickly adopted the technique for themselves. Rural folk took the roots, up to three feet long and six inches in diameter, scraped off their woody skin with a specially designed knife, and grated them on a small studded cylinder turned at high speed by means of a pulley. The motive force was usually human, although occasionally animal or water power was used. Once grated, the meal was squeezed in a large "screw or lever press" to expel its smelly liquid and, with it, most of the acid. A worker then dried the meal over a large tile or copper grill about four feet in diameter, being careful, while stirring with a wooden spatula, to keep moving the meal from the coolest to the hottest part. This process removes the last of the noxious acid. Once dry, careful sifting produced various grades of meal, the finest resembling a slightly tan wheat flour and the coarsest reminiscent of sawdust.[26] The resulting meal has a remarkably high starch content, but very little protein and few if any vitamins.

Everyone in Salvador ate manioc meal. The multiple ways in which it can be used in cooking makes it easy to understand why residents consumed it in large quantities. It could even be used to make bread, especially if mixed with wheat flour, but its principal function was as a thickener to any broth in order to prepare a gravy or heavy sauce, such as the cooking liquid from beans. When properly seasoned, another tasty staple of the Bahian diet was and is *pirão*, made by gradually adding manioc meal to hot stock and carefully stirring over heat until it reaches the consistency of thick porridge. "Everyone here eats manioc meal and this in all forms, especially . . . *pirão*," commented a medical student in the 1880s. Children's gruel was made from manioc meal, and it was added to coffee with hot milk at breakfast. It was also a major ingredient in *cuscuz*, a steamed savory or sweet side dish. Bananas were rolled in manioc meal before being eaten. By toasting the meal and adding onions, spices, hardboiled eggs, and some olives, cooks turned out *farofa*, an accompaniment to meat dishes.[27] It is not too surprising that, according to a 1799 account, people in Bahia, when offered bread, asked for manioc meal to eat with it, and the house of an extremely wealthy man in the elegant district of Vitória had a special room just to store it. Only a few consumed wheat flour.[28]

For at least a century the standard daily ration of manioc meal for slaves, soldiers, sailors, prisoners, employees, and pensioners was one-

Table 4.2. Average Amount of Manioc Meal at the Grains Market by Decade, 1780s–1840s

Decade	Yearly Average (in alqueires)	Decade	Yearly Average (in alqueires)
1780s	252,735	1820s	373,327
1790s	286,369	1830s	414,304
1800s	304,025	1840s	406,046
1810s	356,869		

Source: Amounts calculated from Appendix B.
Note: Alqueires are roughly equivalent to bushels.

fortieth of a bushel, or 0.907 liters, an amount weighing about one and a quarter pounds.[29] This made it roughly equivalent to rations of other grains used elsewhere.[30] This much meal supplied between 2,000 and 2,500 calories, which is more or less the daily requirement of a working adult male in the tropics.[31] But manioc meal was also used as a standard of value or means of exchange, so contemporary figures do not always represent the actual handing over of so much meal, or, if they do, it was expected that some of the meal would then be sold or used to support a family. One table of troop payments indicated the monetary value of a "ration" of meal precisely in order to calculate how much cash each soldier should receive.[32] Certainly not every prisoner, soldier, or slave actually received their daily ration, and those in charge were sometimes accused of siphoning off some of it to sell, pocketing the proceeds.[33]

It is impossible to know exactly how much manioc meal the city of Salvador consumed because the only registry, kept by the central grains market, did not distinguish between what was transshipped to other places and what was sold locally. Its records show that the registered volume rose from approximately 253,000 bushels per year in the 1780s to 406,000 by the 1840s (see Table 4.2), but the population also increased. Even if all of it were consumed within the city, the amount handled at the grains market fell from 0.646 to 0.531 liters per person per day, considerably less than the standard 0.907. Per capita data, however, assigns the same weight to infant children, women, and the aged as to able-bodied men, so these figures may not be radically inconsistent with those on rations presented above.[34]

FIGURE 4.2. Sailboats docked in Nazaré before sailing to Salvador, 1860

Vessels carrying manioc meal sailed principally from areas along the southern and southwestern edges of the Recôncavo, where the soil was relatively sandy and manioc plants flourished (see Map 1.1). On Saturdays in the market town of Nazaré, some 10,000 to 12,000 bushels changed hands. The townships of Jaguaripe and Nazaré together provided 43 percent of Salvador's manioc meal.[35] Salvador's foodshed, however, extended well beyond the Recôncavo. First, the towns stretching southward along the Atlantic coast as far as Camamu and the small towns bordering its large bay were supply points from which small boats easily sailed to the city (see Map 4.1). Sailing from any of the ports farther south along the coast to São Mateus required a larger vessel, a good portion of the sailing being in the open sea. Still other supply points lay to the north in the province of Sergipe, just beyond the border with Bahia. Finally, at times of particular demand, crews brought food from much farther away, from Rio de Janeiro, Santos, and especially from the province of Santa Catarina, where abundant supplies of manioc meal were secured and invariably transported only on ships with a prominent keel (see Map I.1).

How much manioc meal could a vessel carry? Since manioc meal had to be kept dry, canoes were used only in exceptional circumstances. Despite the confusing and overlapping terminology, *barcos* were usually larger than *lanchas,* and *lanchas* larger than *saveiros.* Of the manioc meal transported to Salvador from Jaguaripe during two months in 1826, *barcos* transported on average 503 bushels, whereas *lanchas* averaged only 92. Yet one *lancha* transported 400 bushels. Smacks and *iates* were still larger, often carrying over 1,000 bushels and sometimes even 2,000, 3,000, or 4,500. A brigantine was even bigger: one of them disgorged 7,850 bushels in Salvador.[36] Unloading such large quantities required onshore stevedores, but captains expected their crews to help. Their vigorous and coordinated activity created a bustling commotion in port.

EXPERIENCES

The people of the sea developed distinct skills and cultural understandings that tell us much about their lives, their ranks, and their influence on others. Those who manned the vessels supplying Salvador were notable for many kinds of expertise, the first being their knowledge of the best routes to take. Canoes and boats carrying food to the city reached Salvador not only from across the bay but from several coastal ports to the south by finding their way behind islands and hugging the coast for only short distances between such points of protection. From Maraú, for instance—which is about 80 miles from Salvador as measured in a straight line—and from any point in the large bay facing Camamu, it was an easy reach along a short bight to a large island, behind which one could, to quote a source from 1628, "sail along a dead river" past Cairu and Valença, other food-producing areas, to a point just north of São Paulo Hill. Sailing from there across another small open stretch to the southern tip of Itaparica Island allowed a boat to join all those others coming downriver from Nazaré and Jaguaripe (see Map 1.1). In good weather they sailed directly from there to the city, but, if need be, they crossed what was called in 1781 the "false bar," entering the sound behind Itaparica and emerging at the northern point of the island, within sight of the city across its marvelously protected bay.[37] Although this long route increased the travel time, it enabled small vessels to escape high winds and dangerous storms. It was not risk free, however. The passage was narrow, and the rushing water of a lowering tide often led to wrecks. At best, only "small, three-masted vessels peculiar to this locality," measuring up to 40 feet in length, could manage it, although in time of war

FIGURE 4.3. Sailboats unloading provisions at a Salvador beach, 1960

at least one schooner was ordered to choose this route. In 1842 a *iate* was suspected of surreptitiously using it when leaving the area.[38]

Sailors on all vessels kept a sharp eye for changes in the wind. Even within Salvador's bay all danger was not past. During the fall and winter months, from mid-March onward, sailors faced frequent squalls and strong gusts of wind that could suddenly change direction by as much as 270 degrees. These seasonal storms prevented the arrival of boats in Salvador both from across the bay and from southern ports; in earlier times, before the 1785 creation of a public grains market and warehouse, the result had been "sudden . . . great scarcities" of food in the city. After 1816, smaller vessels put in at the Itapagipe cove just north of the city (see Map 1.2) and reached the docks through a newly built canal. At any season the city's escarpment broke the wind, but also made it that much more unpredictable. For larger ships coming from southern Brazil or from overseas, the unmarked and shifting sandbars at the entrance to the bay posed another danger.[39] Water transport posed challenges for all the "people of the sea."

Social distinctions may have blurred as crews on board shared each other's company for a long time. Boatmen calculated it would

take twenty-four hours in normal weather to reach Salvador from Camamu. Ships from Rio de Janeiro took five days in good weather and
much, much longer if winds were contrary.[40] Surely as they worked
together there built up a camaraderie regardless of race or legal status, knowing that the effective work of each one ensured the safety
of all. And some must have slept while others kept watch, a show of
trust.

Sailors and captains enjoyed a necessary geographical mobility,
meaning that people of color moved throughout the Recôncavo and
up and down the Bahian coast, meeting land-bound slaves, other
blacks and mulattos, poor whites, and better-off boat owners wherever they went. In conversation they reinforced commonalities, related their experiences, questioned their own previous assumptions,
exchanged ideas, and shared knowledge.

And sailors carried news. Thanks to them, information about
events across the Atlantic, in other parts of Brazil, or in the city or
countryside spread rapidly throughout the region. When any ship
from overseas sailed into the harbor, it was met by oarsmen on lighters and canoe-men selling fresh fruit and vegetables. They inevitably exchanged information with sailors on board, who then also met
the dock workers and stevedores. Visiting sailors tarried in town for
days or weeks while goods were unloaded and reloaded, and the ship
repaired and provisioned. Presumably they drank and entertained
themselves at general stores while chatting with the locals, including street vendors, and so touching still another, urban news system.
Facts about the French Revolution circulated extensively in Salvador,
and political developments in the Caribbean were much discussed, as
was true elsewhere in the Americas. In the bay-side town of São Francisco do Conde slave owners reported in 1816 that the spirit of insur-
rection was widespread among slaves, "fomented especially by those
of the city [Salvador] where ideas of liberty have been communicated
by black sailors coming from São Domingos [Haiti]."[41]

An inquiry into the Africans' Muslim-led revolt of 1835 revealed,
in the words of the provincial president, that "in several places of the
Recôncavo and even . . . in Valença there are indications that the in-
surrection extended its branches to various parts of the province with
which the insurgents maintained communication and [passed on] in-
telligence." Sailors were the means through which such coordination
most likely occurred, establishing a covert web of communication
through the overt network of commerce. Later testimony revealed

that Muslim boatmen gathered with their coreligionists for ritual meals in Salvador, and that one slave boatman actively participated in the rebellion. A freed African who owned a boat was accused, along with his wife, of participating in the movement because the police found signs of Muslim worship and writing in his home. But surely the greatest role these and other sailors played in the events of 1835 was simply through the contacts they forged while conducting their daily work. Fourteen years later a newly alarmed chief of police in Rio de Janeiro alleged that Africans in Salvador still "corresponded" with the Africans in Rio shipped there after the uprising and did so through "ciphered writings." It may be, however, that such written communication, if it existed, had more to do with religion than re-volt. Shortly after the end of the slave trade in 1850, English Quakers on an antislavery mission to Rio de Janeiro learned that a group of Yoruba-speaking freedmen had hired a ship to take them back to Africa and planned to stop first in Salvador, doubtless because they had remained in contact with people there who would join them in the venture. These Africans clearly had maintained relationships across hundreds of miles, and sailors must have played a crucial part in their communication by carrying and delivering messages and news.[42]

By transmitting as well as creating standards of behavior, endowing their experiences with meaning, the people of the sea played a crucial role in the cultural and even political life of Salvador, well beyond physically sustaining its inhabitants. Working on the water meant geographical mobility and contact with a great variety of people that broadened experience and fostered self-confidence. Regardless of the types of craft they sailed, how many men formed each crew, and the size of the cargoes transported, these men established communica-tive links not soon forgotten.

The ambiguity of hierarchy is evident among them. At first glance we have it clearly presented: owners told boat captains what to trans-port and set the destination; captains commanded the helpers be-cause they were paid, and the slaves because they were slaves. On closer inspection, however, we discover that slaves occasionally be-came captains with authority over white helpers, and freed blacks ac-quired their own small boats. A slave who captained a boat was still a slave, but he was much else as well, for he had major responsibilities and exercised authority even over the free. Sailors suffered from the unremitting and dangerous work, but it could also lead to solidarity with others regardless of color or legal status. Whether slave or free, their skills were crucial to the enterprise, fostering self-confidence and pride in the quality of their work. Certainly they had to cooperate actively for the good of all.

CHAPTER 5

THE GRAINS MARKET

SAILORS, CAPTAINS, AND BOAT OWNERS met stevedores and porters, petty traders and large merchants at Salvador's bay-side grains market (see Map 1.3). Unlike the street vendors who had to jostle each other to purchase the vegetables, fruits, fish, and chickens arriving on boats at every beach and quay, men and women at the publicly administered grains market bent to specific institutional rules enforced by a small bureaucracy at a single location. Unlike grocery stores, the grains market centered on just four staples: rice, beans, corn, and, especially, manioc meal. Various kinds of people rubbed shoulders here and, by crossing paths with each other, blurred, if only in this setting and for a brief time, the social boundaries that separated them. This proximity created both the chance of friction between them and the possibility of alliance and common action.

THE MARKET

Until 1785 most vessels carrying manioc meal, having anchored near the beach, sold to those who came out in rowboats or lighters. Someone who wanted to buy only a week's supply found it nearly impossible to manage. Besides having to rent a rowboat, one would "risk losing the male or female slave by falling overboard, as well as the money and the bag." The quality of the meal received did not always match the sample, and measuring was not carried out in the presence of buyers, only of their slaves. So it was principally owners of grocery stores and wholesalers who bought, doing so in large quantities. In times of scarcity the governor ordered militiamen to distribute meal equitably; instead, the sergeants parceled out extra-large quantities to the bigwigs and sold the rest on board or at their own shops at outrageous prices, shrugging off the objections of city council officers and leaving "the poor to return home without the least amount of manioc meal for feeding their families."[1]

At a time when, as a local teacher of Greek later put it, the "hungry people [of the city] were in a desperate *phrénesis*," Governor Rodrigo José de Menezes e Castro—after personally visiting the supplying areas of the Recôncavo and giving the matter "much thought"—took action to ameliorate the situation. Publicly he maintained that he was inspired by the "lack of essential food that the People have confronted for some time," but to the Crown he added that the shortage had been caused by "monopolists," and he wished to avoid "disorder" aboard the boats.[2] He modeled his solution on the Terreiro de Trigo of Lisbon, founded in the sixteenth century, which operated as a central market where all the wheat entering the city was required to come first, making supplies visible to all and allowing the quality of each to be compared.[3] The governor also took account of complaints from producers and boat captains who brought meal to the city. Instead of unloading at once and leaving someone else in charge of selling what they had brought while they returned for another load, they had to spend several days at anchor awaiting buyers. While on board the meal could be spoiled by rain and humidity, satisfying no one. On days when winds were unfavorable, no vessels arrived, leaving the city short even in times of plenty. So in 1785 Governor Menezes created the public grains market.* It had the additional advantage of allowing officials to keep track of available supplies.[4]

Governor Menezes held to the Enlightenment principle that rational solutions could be found for most problems and that government could help find them. In the three years he had served as governor of Minas Gerais before coming to Bahia in 1784, he had displayed a boldly innovative (if sometimes violent) spirit by building roads, encouraging a renewed search for gold, and ordering intensified attacks on the Indians. He also discarded the colonial formula according to which all manufactured goods should be supplied by the mother country, forcefully proposing instead the creation of an iron foundry. In Bahia he directed enormous energy toward urban improvements.

---

*It was called the *celeiro público*. *Celeiro* has more in common etymologically with the English word "cellar"—that is, a storage place—than with "granary," but it functioned as a market. Manioc meal does not derive from a grain, but because of its parallelism with wheat flour contemporaries referred to it as if it did—hence, "a grains market."

He constructed a retaining wall to protect the lower city from land-slides, built a slaughterhouse, and established a leprosarium. A near contemporary who believed in laissez-faire and was critical of Menezes's actions, declared that he had acted out of "a piety and zeal more religious than based on good policy." But an enthusiastically applauding city council asked the Queen to keep him on as governor in Salvador.[5]

Finding a place for the market was not easy. Building it from scratch was out of the question, although Menezes likely had that in mind as a long-range solution. Instead he took over the ground-floor warehouse of the Navy Yard, just south of the commercial center of town in the lower city and across the street from its main church. Figure 1.1 shows this church about two-thirds of the way from left to right, on the lower level of the city; the grains market is in the fore-ground, on the waterfront. The yard had a small, C-shaped dock that allowed two or three midsize boats to enter and safely unload.[6] Mene-zes ordered rows of wooden bins built in the former warehouse, each holding 500 bushels of manioc meal (over 18,000 liters), and the prepa-ration of numerous chests for smaller amounts up to 250 bushels. The aisles between the bins were wide enough so that those who brought in only a sack or two (typically a sack held two or three bushels) could place them there without interfering with customers and stevedores as they moved about. Menezes added a balcony at one end to allow the staff to oversee the entire space. The overall size of the market is not explicitly stated in the sources, but years later, when holders of bins and chests were identified, they numbered eighty-seven. The full floor above the market had at one time provided sleeping quarters for navy officers, but they preferred to find rooms in the upper city, so it became the naval hospital. Apparently only in the mid-nineteenth century did anyone object to this arrangement on the grounds of pub-lic health, despite the fact that at that time and presumably earlier, "patients and nurses seemingly on purpose throw their trash and dirty water onto the patio [below]" in front of the grains market.[7]

At this market the various participants in the meal trade met face-to-face. The granary's first days in September 1785 proved tu-multuous. Crowds gathered to seek their supplies, and the press was so great that allegedly some shoeless slaves had their feet broken. A week after it opened, however, the governor judged it to be such a success that he decided to add beans, rice, and corn to manioc meal as items arriving by water that could be sold only there. Over time manioc meal accounted for 87 percent of its business.[8]

The institutional structure of the market gained importance not only because it was the place where the "people of the sea" met the traders, but because it set the rules governing their exchanges. Its regulations were straightforward. The market remained open "from sunup to sunset" even on those days during which the Church proscribed commerce, manioc meal being essential "for daily sustenance." A small tax was levied on every bushel to finance the market's operation, with any surplus revenue designated for the newly created leprosarium. The tax applied to all specified provisions brought by sea—whether ultimately intended for the city's consumption, for transshipment to other ports of the bay, or for export outside the captaincy—even if the owners chose to sell their load in the old way, from their boat. If they wished to use the marketplace, they received a key for a bin, or more than one for a large load.[9]

According to the statutes, the administrator had to be a businessman of noted honesty, who would visit the market twice a day, morning and afternoon. Appointed for only one year at a time, he received no payment for his service "because, being a man of wealth and honor, it can be assumed that he will be satisfied with the glory that obtains to every good patriot in serving the public." Yet he also enjoyed much power, for he could order the arrest of captains or those who, "whether within the market or where manioc meal is unloaded and carried, make riot or create disorder." One writer accused these administrators of exercising a "despotic authority."[10]

The caliber of administrators envisaged by Governor Menezes may be judged by his first appointee: Inocêncio José da Costa, the prosperous Portuguese merchant who kept his own chapel for the saying of mass. He belonged to the most prestigious lay orders in Salvador, and was both a brother in the Santa Casa de Misericórdia and a member of the Order of Christ. His brother sat on the High Court. Inocêncio married the daughter of a marshal related to Portuguese nobility, and when she died, he persuaded the Church (by what means we do not know) to permit him to marry her sister, and then his second wife's daughter by her previous marriage. Thrice married and widowed, he had no children. He wished to be buried alongside his three wives, "especially" the third one. Governor Menezes did not expect to attract such a man by a salary, but only by added prestige and authority.[11]

Other market administrators came from similar backgrounds. Adriano de Araújo Braga, an international merchant and slave trader, served from 1796 through 1799. When he died in 1816, his property included partnerships that owned three vessels: a large ship (*navio*), a brigantine which he had named for himself as "Emperor Adrian," and a smack. The smack had recently arrived from Angola with seventy-five slaves, eleven of whom had soon died. Its equipment included neck irons, fetters, and a large number of water casks. Braga owned four houses in the city, land in manioc-rich Nazaré, and sixteen adult slaves, seven men and nine women, all from Africa, as well as their four Brazilian-born children.[12]

José da Silva Maia, a sugar factor, served as market administrator from 1802 to 1803. One of Braga's partners in the ownership of the "Emperor Adrian," he possessed his own smack and a smaller boat. His property included an extraordinarily large dry goods store, thirteen male slaves (including several porters or stevedores and two sailors) and eight female slaves (four seamstresses, two laundresses, a lace maker, and a cook), not counting the slave children. When he died in 1809, he was building a wharf-side warehouse.[13]

The governor appointed Francisco Dias Coelho as administrator in 1806. The following year, in partnership with the governor, Coelho unloaded 932 slaves at the very docks of the grains market. Among other interests, he exported tobacco and financed the cattle trade. Both Maia and Coelho were ranked among the city's leading importers in 1798.[14] Administrators, during the colonial period at least, were drawn from the top ranks of the Portuguese merchant class.

Marketplace staff members received salaries. The scribe kept records on all the meal brought into and sent out from the market, comparing his figures with the ship manifests carried by the captains and reporting the weekly data to the governor (or, later, to the provincial president). A treasurer kept the books on the tax collected, on other fees paid, and on the market's expenditures. Boatmen directly and invariably confronted the overseers. One stood at the dock-side door of the market, placing a chalk mark on each sack of meal, beans, rice, or corn brought in, noting their number and ownership. Another went about in a small canoe checking the supplies aboard those boats whose captains sold directly to consumers in the old way or who intended to sail to other ports, making sure they paid the tax. Later, a third overseer, inside the market, kept tabs on its activities and maintained order among traders and customers. Together the overseers opened and closed the market doors, kept the place clean, and made sure the first persons to arrive were first served. These overseers may have been Portuguese, for in 1799 one of them received permission from the Crown to extend his leave in Portugal. Finally a bailiff was charged with enforcement.[15]

Boatmen both colluded and clashed with the staff. They sometimes bribed the officials "with heavy sums" to avoid paying the tax. As the city council put it, "it is well known that [those] vessels that arrive . . . and remain [docked] overnight have no manioc meal left in the morning." Captains allegedly presented manifests that understated the cargo so they could sell part of it elsewhere before turning up in Salvador, a maneuver managed either by bribing officials in manioc-rich Nazaré or by fooling them by covering their real cargo with bananas. In 1834, the administrator of the market proposed an elaborate system whereby captains would have to bring specially verified documents from the authorities in the food-exporting points of the province to establish how much they carried; the president of the province must have sighed as he wrote on the margin "such measures are useless."[16]

If they sometimes bribed their way, captains and traders had grievances of their own against the administrators, either for being too strict or not strict enough. Adriano de Araújo Braga was said to be a man of honor who dismissed dishonest staff members, but he also cracked down on those traders whom he accused of hoarding. Francisco Dias Coelho, it was claimed, had "invented" new and "execrable" fees for various services that multiplied the charges per bushel by four or five times. He appointed a *compadre* as treasurer and allowed the overseers free rein to accept bribes and even promoted those who did, provoking dissatisfaction among honest traders.[17]

TRADERS

Boat people encountered various sorts of traders at the grains market. Some were Portuguese-born merchants living in Salvador. In the 1840s they found themselves the target of hostility from a Brazilian-born businessman who had managed to get himself named as market administrator. João Pereira de Araújo França shared the widespread xenophobia of his time, and in March 1842 he simply forbade any Portuguese from selling at the grains market, arguing that they engaged in coastwise shipping, forbidden to foreigners by law. From that he deduced they "should not trade even on a wholesale basis with the cereal foodstuffs of this country and much less in retail at the grains market, competing with Brazilians." When the Portuguese merchants, feeling victimized, protested that they were not the owners of the vessels, but only of the manioc meal they transported, and that a series of treaties had guaranteed them the right to engage in commerce freely within Brazil, França retorted that those treaties contained nothing about "retail selling of essential foodstuffs . . . produced in this country, nor [that] they could sell them at a public agency." He later preachily denounced "the immoderation with which they behaved there, associating with individuals of both sexes known for their immorality, to which must be added their contact with workers at the Navy Yard." The Portuguese traders took their case to the provincial legislature, the provincial president, and then the Portuguese consul; he referred it to the Portuguese embassy in Rio de Janeiro, which took it up with the Brazilian foreign minister, who referred the matter to the minister of empire, who turned for advice to the Crown's counsel. This last authority concluded that França's actions were "illegal and patently impolitic and odious, suggested by these erroneous notions of false patriotism that have done so much harm to Brazil and so impede its progress and prosperity." He also noted that the administrator, "going beyond the functions of his position, took on that of interpreter and enforcer of treaties, something that surely is not within his competence." But the bureaucrats persisted in passing the issue on to someone else or asked for more information, sometimes leaving their position before receiving a reply. The record ends almost three years after the initial incident without saying whether these particular merchants ever regained the right to trade at the grains market, although Portuguese citizens were openly trading there by 1857.[18]

One of those persecuted Portuguese traders was Antônio de Oliveira. Born in the city of Oporto, he had come to Brazil in 1811. When he made his will in 1849, he lived in a four-story house in the lower city just down the street from his large store, next to a dock where he anchored his lighter. At that time he held an unusual amount of cash in Spanish, Portuguese, and Brazilian silver and gold coins, but when he died six years later he left little cash, most of his income consisting of rents from real estate investments. Judging from his property, a trader at the grains market could have been a merchant of some wealth who had probably never spent a full day by the bin he rented there. His expulsion from the floor did not plunge him into penury.[19]

Many other traders were freed Africans, men and women who, like the Portuguese, bought and sold manioc meal, negotiated prices, and arranged for delivery to their customers. At the time the market was created, it was said that "black women, commonly called *ganha-deiras*, buy foodstuffs off the boats to resell, hoarding them to keep up the price and selling them little by little." If they were hoarding the food, they had to be confident the price would rise, and doing so probably required coming to an agreement with others so they could together corner the bulk of the trade. We can wonder whether the accusation derived from fact or prejudice. Yet certainly African women continued to be active in this trade. Sometimes they, like their male counterparts, hired a boat, as some of them did in 1836, going across the bay to buy stocks directly from the producers, bringing back "two, three, or four sacks." Several would travel in one vessel, and once they arrived at the grains market, the bags would be passed from one to another and "disappear," making it hard for market personnel to identify who should pay the tax.[20]

The tax was far from being such a trader's only expense. She had to pay transport costs both for her stock and herself. She had to feed herself during the days she was away and, if she had children, arrange for someone to take care of them during her absence. Sometimes bribes had to be paid. To turn a profit, she had to purchase meal in the Recôncavo for substantially less than she sold it for in Salvador. All this required capital which she had either accumulated in earlier transactions or borrowed. Perhaps she paid the boatman only after selling her load. Practice and business savvy went into a successful operation. African women likely brought the necessary skills with them because in many places in Africa women customarily went out from their village into the country to purchase farm products. White merchants in the Recôncavo town of Nazaré complained in 1858 that freed Africans, whether women or men they do not say, not only came over from Salvador, but went along interior roads to buy manioc meal directly from the farmers, many of whom were black or mulatto, bypassing the whites altogether. In their complaint they implied a racial solidarity between people of color who produced the manioc meal or brought it on horses to Nazaré, and the African freedmen and women who purchased it for resale in Salvador. I suspect the allegation says more about the conspiratorial and racial preconceptions of the whites than about reality. Probably these Africans were simply smart and energetic traders who did not need to appeal to any affinities with producers to be successful.[21]

França, the anti-Portuguese market administrator, prudishly determined that women traders should be separated from the men, assign-
ing separate aisles to them. Caetana Maria had friends among important shippers in Nazaré who protested this action, but França pointed
out that Caetana Maria could still sell at the market if she stayed on
the women's side. According to França, his measure met with "general applause among those who are not bad," although his definition
of "bad" remains unclear. Whether this separation continued after
his tenure I cannot say. In 1857 45 percent of the traders were women:
39 out of 87. Although they presumably handled less manioc meal
than did the men, for decades on end they held their ground against
major male traders at the grains market, evidence of their resolve.[22]

Rank mattered in the relationship between traders of whatever sort
and the administrators. França did not target only the Portuguese-
born or women, but anyone who did not show him sufficient respect.
In 1844, in an effort to control the allocation of bins and chests, he
summoned several traders to his office. One of them sent word that
he had no business to do with França. França went downstairs among
the bins to speak to him, but the man retorted "with arrogance keeping his hat on although I was not wearing one." França ordered him
expelled, denying him permission to sell. The fellow had not "remembered on that occasion that he had a wife and children," said
França in reply to an inquiry from the provincial president. The poor
man then returned to the market "armed with a club and proceeded
to sell from his sack," so França ordered him arrested and sent under
guard to the president, who had him tried. The sources do not indicate the final outcome, but a deferential stance was obviously the
safer one before the moralizing and haughty França.[23] Yet, if hierarchy had to be enforced in this way, it cannot be said to have been a
taken-for-granted and unspoken rule. The ousted trader obviously did
not buy into it. Even if he ended up in jail, he may have boasted of his
refusal to comply.

Besides the traders, there were their clerks. Many traders did not
remain personally at the market, but relied instead on others whom
they put in charge of selling the meal. In 1808 these clerks were described as "poverty-stricken whites, mulattos, and blacks without
credit or goods" who do this "in order to secure their scarce daily
bread," and as "people of lowly origins and status, many of them mulattos and blacks." The very words used reveal current notions of
rank and place. In the 1850s it was said that Portuguese merchants

put "various Africans, their protégés," in charge of bins, and they would buy up entire boatloads "as soon as they arrive," leaving no manioc meal to be purchased by minor traders. In this way the Portuguese allegedly could set whatever price they wanted. Although the complainants posed as defenders of the consumer, their allegation also reveals possible friction among traders. Proximity did not erase differences or rivalries.[24]

Traders in manioc meal even assigned slaves to handle their goods at the market. One market administrator set out to end this practice in the 1830s, saying that, although no regulation forbade it, it was not proper that slaves be placed as clerks, "discouraging free persons from taking up and occupying such positions." It is unclear whether he was assuming a proto-abolitionist stance, whether he was principally responding to demands of free workers to be rid of slave competitors, or whether he was acknowledging complaints lodged by small-time traders against those with slaves who could afford to go out for another boatload of meal instead of waiting themselves to sell what they had brought. Two days later, when the administrator discovered two slaves selling manioc meal against his orders, he had it transferred into sacks and set aside until the owner returned. To this "the said slaves objected, and so I ordered them arrested." In the 1840s França repeated these orders, again determining that owners should not leave their slaves in charge of selling. The practice could not be tolerated since, as he put it, it would mean he would have "to come to an understanding" with them—that is, he would have to deal with enslaved inferiors as if they had the status of free persons, reducing his own position.[25]

LIFTING AND LUGGING

The most numerous participants in the market were the black men, especially African, who did the physical work. They were the stevedores and porters who carried the sacks of manioc meal from boat to bin and then to grocery stores or other customers in the city. We have no exact count of their number, but the quantity of manioc meal they handled per year ranged roughly from 250,000 to 400,000 bushels—that is, from 700 to 1,000 for every single day of the year (see Table 4.2)—so they were certainly numerous.

Many were slaves. In 1808, complainants alleged that administrators had, for the last eleven years, transformed their personal slaves into "a private company for unloading at the grains market, not allowing outside stevedores to enter the marketplace, physically striking anybody who turned up with that in mind, and holding back [even] those [slaves] who belonged to the owner of the goods for 10 or 15 minutes." Boatmen and traders insisted that this move doubled the cost of unloading. The slaves allegedly stole meal, and a boat captain had no way to complain because, if he did, said another witness, the market overseer could make him suffer by deliberately leaving some bags without chalk marks in order to charge him with fraudulently avoiding the tax. In this way slaves exerted some power over free traders, perhaps even over white men. Such complaints not only reveal the underlying tensions between boatmen and marketplace bureaucrats, but underscore the large role of slaves in the business.[26]

Self-hired slaves and freedmen, again mostly African, transported the big bags of manioc meal to the stores. Like other porters, they formed crews, wharf-side groupings available for hire. Headed by a captain chosen from among themselves—and whose position was celebrated by elaborate rituals on taking up the post—these workers turned to him to find their clients, assign tasks, and adjudicate disputes. In 1860 Prince Maximilian noticed that "hard by the Navy Yard [that is, the grains market] is the grand place of rendezvous of the noted Bahian porters [who] are let out to hire by their owners." He romantically described their songs as "improvised upon a melody that runs throughout; and, though for the most part they treat of manioc meal or cane brandy, yet they often throw a very remarkable light upon the relations of master and slave and upon the treatment received, mingled sometimes with lament for the free home on the other side of the broad ocean."[27]

Stevedores and porters were not afraid to assert themselves when threatened. In the frenzied effort of the white community in 1835 to regain authority over Africans—responsible for that year's great Muslim revolt in January—the provincial legislature passed a law in June to organize a registry of oarsmen, stevedores, and porters, who would now be assigned to specific crews under the control of appointed captains. Only in April of the next year, however, did the provincial president issue the necessary regulations. They called for each such worker, whether slave or freed, to wear a copper bracelet on his right wrist with a tag specifying his registration number and the crew to which he belonged. The captains, free men, would wear a black leather strap across their chests from shoulder to belt on which would be attached a brass plate with the number of their crew. Each parish would also have an inspector, a "Brazilian citizen of good conduct who knows how to read and write," who would register the workers, appoint the captains, carry out a weekly inspection, and impose disciplinary measures. A worker would be subject to a daily fee (whether he had secured work that day or not), one-third of which went to the captain of his crew and two-thirds to the inspector. Oarsmen and longshoremen would be organized with one crew per docking area, and their captains would "always remain on land" to control the work. Lighters were to have posted on their stern the registry number of the oarsman in charge.[28] Enforcement actually began almost a year later, in March 1837, in the parish of Conceição da Praia, where the grains market stood.

The result was immediate and shocking: no workers turned up "whether on land or sea." The justice of the peace reported that even the customs house had no lighters at its disposal. The work stoppage created "a terrible upset in commerce and despair among those who need to transport what they require for their own food." This, he added, "cannot go on. . . . Because of this terrible state I am pressured by the carriers from Nazaré and Maragogipe, now arriving at this city, to take the necessary measures so they can unload their meal or else they will be forced to return with it." Another justice of the peace reported that all the lighters were tied up at the quay and only some "dinghies of small vessels" were in use. When he tried to persuade the men to return to work, they refused. More startling, "except for fifteen, all those registered in the two land crews have disappeared." What was probably considered even worse, "the disobedient blacks . . . are insulting the [appointed] inspectors and captains." The provincial president had to admit that "there is no law that obliges someone to pursue this or that means of earning a livelihood, so . . . those registered may cease to be porters." He ordered the personnel of the Navy Yard to unload the meal from some vessels and then suspended enforcement of the law while he referred the entire matter to the provincial legislature. The lawmakers, in their turn, buried the question in committee. The strike had been successful.[29]

Their action revealed a solidarity and organization among porters, stevedores, and lighter crews at the grains market, and also their confidence in their importance to the functioning of trade. The black leather strap with brass plate, although surely designed by whites to lend status to the black captains, had served instead to distance them from workers accustomed to choosing their own leaders from among themselves without regard to distinctions between slave and freed—distinctions imposed on them by whites. On the other hand, lumping the freed with the slaves by requiring them all to wear copper bracelets (reminiscent of handcuffs?) may have been a central objection for some. All of them wanted most of all to preserve their autonomy. Twenty years later, when the city council again attempted to regiment porters, the effort again failed because of workers' reluctance to wear metal tags around their necks. They did not strike for higher wages or better working conditions, but for autonomy and, apparently, for recognition of their corporate position within a society of orders. Their notions of social place had to be recognized and respected.[30]

In 1850 many men of color who worked the lighters nevertheless suffered a devastating blow. With the overseas slave trade ending, and planters ardently wishing to force urban slaves and freed Africans into rural work, the city council persuaded the provincial president to approve a petition from a group who proposed to run the entire lighterage business and exclude from it all slaves and all Africans, whether slave or free. The British consul referred to these exclusions as throwing 750 Africans out of work, many of whom had become free by "paying large sums to their [former] owners." Thirty some years later it had become accepted lore that in 1850 four brothers, the Cardosos, who jointly owned a warehouse and wharf, had bought sixty lighters, presumably from those now disqualified from using them, and turned them over to free-born Brazilians of unspecified race, asking them to pay "only when they could." Whether this is how it really happened the contemporary documents do not say. The provincial president at the time, who had been the police chief in 1835 and bore a great hostility toward Africans, emphasized that by these and similar measures slaves would be funneled into work on the sugar plantations and prevented from concentrating at the capital. He also boasted that he had ended "the disagreeable spectacle of a multitude of half-naked Africans gathered at the docks and on small vessels which presented a sad notion of our civilization to any foreigner who disembarked here for the first time." A subsequent president complained in 1857 that the measure had decreased competition, raised the cost of lighterage, and encouraged an emigration of Africans back to Africa, resulting in a labor shortage. Yet already by 1853 the anniversary of the 1850 measure on lighterage had become the occasion for a celebration on behalf of "free" labor, and it persisted as an annual affair at least until 1879. It is sadly ironic that a step that so harshly affected those who, as the consul noted, were already free, was touted as a proto-abolitionist step.[31]

LINKAGES

The closely integrated system of food supply, connecting captains and storekeepers, transportation and retailing, slaves on boats and slaves on streets, meant that many individuals played more than one role in the food trade. Manoel Carlos Gomes, a grocer who lived on the steep street leading up to the Misericórdia, took out a license for his slave Ana to sell on the streets in 1789. He also owned a manioc farm on Itaparica Island. His rural property included a "building in which manioc meal is prepared, with rammed-earth walls and a tile roof, and the grinding wheel for manioc with its accoutrements." He was also the proprietor of a "large mahogany canoe" and a large boat with two new sails. He produced the meal, transported it to the city, sold it in his store, and presumably on the street at the hand of his vendor-slave Ana.[32] Then there are links among Manoel José da Silva, his wife, Joana, and Antônio José Dias Lopes. Lopes was one of the major import-export merchants in Salvador summoned to join several others constrained to raise money for the Portuguese side during Brazil's war of independence in 1823. In 1814 he leant money to Manoel, the owner of both a canoe and a boat engaged in transporting food across the bay. Manoel married the widow Joana Maria da Conceição, a woman of color who, before their marriage, had taken out a license to sell on the street. This threesome captures the multiple ties between and among major international merchants, cross-bay traffickers in food, and street vendors.[33]

When fully extended, the network of trade involved an even larger number of people. It included the manioc producer who sold meal to a village merchant in a Recôncavo town; the merchant who offered it to the boat captain, who transported it to the city; a trader at the grains market who bought the meal from the boat owner and sold it to a grocer; the porter who lugged it to a store, quite likely in the upper city; and the grocer who advanced it to a street vendor, possibly a freed woman, to sell to the consumer. This was a complex and vibrant commercial system. And, as in most such systems, those within it understood each other on various matters and mutually accepted certain rules and practices, even if sometimes contesting them.

While people at the grains market can be separated into categories by gender, race, ethnicity, and legal status, they all met under the same roof. The sailors and captains on the bay were all men, whereas both men and women traded at the market and made deals with owners of general stores, mostly men, and with street vendors, mostly women. Slaves (many self-hired), freedmen, and free blacks worked together as they unloaded the sacks of meal from boats or ships, emptied the meal into bins, resacked the meal for buyers, and bore it off to the stores. Although all those who worked at the market encountered a place of order and regulation to which the documents mostly speak, it was surely also a place of disorder, laughter, fun, and repartee. Those who worked in this territory full-time knew each other, and no matter how acrimonious their relationships may have sometimes become, they likely viewed those from outside as not one of them. The people at this center of a trading network differed from the street vendors on one side and boatmen on the other, both of whom had wider experiences and contacts and the potential for a greater variety of alliances. One can also assume a greater solidarity among those who worked together at the grains market day after day.

The market was also a contentious place. Administrators and staff clashed with boatmen and traders. African women energetically competed with Portuguese-born merchants. Clerks, even slaves, bargained sharply with white customers. Defiance of authority was signaled by deliberately refraining from doffing a hat. Stevedores and porters successfully resisted efforts to limit their autonomy, demanding respect and the right to choose their own leaders. Proximity did not necessarily signify harmony.

CHAPTER 6

THE CATTLE AND MEAT TRADE

BEEF WAS THE MAJOR SOURCE of animal protein for residents of Salvador. Not that they shunned pork, fish, whale meat, chicken, or eggs, but they hoped to eat red meat daily. The city consumed 350 to 600 head of cattle per week in the late eighteenth and early nineteenth centuries.[1] Although this number is moderate on a per capita basis, the symbolic importance of beef in this society must not be underestimated. A dearth of meat stood for danger and insecurity. City authorities took seriously their responsibility to ensure its supply at an affordable price, and the subject occupied a great deal of their time, not to mention the reams of paper used to keep track of the cattle and meat trade. In assuming this responsibility the city council drew on ancient law and counted on the backing of the colonial governor and other royal representatives.[2] In the 1780s, reflecting the Portuguese government's new enthusiasm for rational organization, the city's control of the business extended still further and became more systematic. An examination of the physical arrangements and legal provisions of the meat business reveals a vigorous commercial network of central importance to the life of Salvador.

PUBLIC CONTROL

The city's cattle came first of all from the arid interior of the province, especially the northwest, from the town of Jacobina and from along the middle São Francisco River, but also from the area directly north of Salvador along the Itapicuru River and from Sergipe (see Map 4.1). Secondarily, but importantly, cattle were driven from more distant places, especially from the provinces of Piauí and Goiás.[3] These are far-off points: 200 miles to Salvador just from the town of Jacobina, a principal gathering place because of its extensive pastures, and at least 600 miles from ranches in Goiás.

Every Wednesday in colonial times a "great Cattle Fair" was held at Capuame (present-day Dias d'Ávila), a town of some 300 houses in 1785, about 30 miles from Salvador (see Map 1.1). All cattle destined for the Recôncavo region were legally required to pass through it, even those going not to the city but to plantations or villages in the district. The Cattle Fair superintendent, a public employee, lived in a building set aside as a registry. The site also included a place for drovers to eat and sleep. The corrals, built as a stockade with heavy posts sunk vertically into the ground side by side, were numerous enough to keep each owner's cattle separate. From this stockyard, cattle were driven down the Estrada das Boiadas (Cattle-Drive Road) to the city slaughterhouses, and from there the beef was delivered to the butchers (see Map 1.2).[4]

Until the 1780s the city council auctioned off the right to use the publicly owned butcher shops in each section of town, no other ones being allowed, and the successful bidders were then entitled to buy cattle at the fair, process them at their slaughterhouses, and in this way hold—aside from the ranchers themselves—a monopoly on both the wholesale and retail meat trade. In exchange, these traders had to sell their meat at or below a price set by the council.[5] Occasionally no bids were tendered, and the council itself ordered the cattle bought and slaughtered at its own expense. More commonly just a few cattle dealers offered bids. Then a single man bid up all the city's butcher shops and created, it was said, a false scarcity to pressure the city council into raising the allowed maximum price of meat.[6]

In early 1783 the city council debated likely reasons for meat's continual short supply. Although some argued that the causes were beyond control and could be traced principally to the "severe droughts" in the interior, others blamed the cattle dealers who, they said, created artificial shortages. In September the council discovered, to its dismay, that there were only enough cattle in the city for two days' consumption. At this point they raised the maximum price of meat, resulting, said the council, in an increase in the number of head brought to market. Widespread dissatisfaction continued, and complaints poured into the governor general's office.[7]

In response, in March 1784 the new governor, the same Rodrigo José de Menezes e Castro who would create the public grains market the following year, laid out a general "Plan . . . for the Administration of the Cattle Trade" that radically altered the old system. Although maintaining ranchers' right to bring or send their cattle to slaughter, the plan gave the city council firm control over all other segments of the trade—that is, over the cattle dealers, the slaughtering business, and the butchers. Instead of allowing anyone to bid for every aspect, traders were now restricted to the trade between the Cattle Fair and a publicly administered slaughterhouse. Moreover, rather than granting the right to trade to the highest bidder, the council would handpick eight to twelve men whom they judged to be trustworthy and financially secure enough to pay for the cattle they bought. A new central slaughterhouse would be constructed and run directly by the council through a public employee, its administrator. Although ranchers and traders were free to hire their own slaughtermen, the council provided workers through labor contractors to those who wished them, setting a fee for this work to be paid by the cattle owners. No employee was allowed to be financially interested in the trade. Independent butchers, not the cattle merchants, now bid for the right to operate the publicly owned butcher shops, where they sold on their own account twenty pounds of meat from each animal they butchered, being responsible to the owner of the cattle for the rest. The city not only provided the butchers with their shops but with "iron scales with copper pans, . . . [appropriate] weights, and a machete," charging them a weekly rental fee. The butchers were, in effect, licensed to conduct a public enterprise on behalf of the city council. Under the new system, since the council would no longer receive the money that used to be bid for the right to monopolize the business, it collected a tax on each head, paid by the cattle owners, be they ranchers or traders.[8]

Menezes's plan meant greater system and order and sought to protect consumers by strengthening public control of the business. The appointed Cattle Fair superintendent and the slaughterhouse administrator, acting in concert, now oversaw the entire operation. No one could legally trade in cattle or meat after the animals had left the fair until the meat was sold to the ultimate consumer at the butcher shops. To prevent such trading, the drover who brought the cattle from the fair had to present a manifest stating their number prepared by its superintendent and delivered to the slaughterhouse administrator; the latter, in turn, had to send a similar document to each butcher shop indicating ownership of the meat and its quantity. These rules continued in force until the early 1820s.[9]

The entire business revolved around three organizational nodes where participants in the trade encountered each other. First was the gathering point at the fair and, much later, at a public pasture near the city. The slaughterhouse from which the quarters of beef were distributed to the butchers formed a second important locale, revealing the social landscape in Salvador. Last were the butcher shops themselves where consumers made their purchases.

THE CATTLE FAIR

The superintendent at the Cattle Fair had multiple responsibilities, including supervising several staff members. Charged with "watching over the fair, avoiding all the disorders, monopolies, and frauds that usually spread in such places," he had to be a strongman, imposing his will on an unruly population. It was up to him to prevent surreptitious trading outside the confines of the fair, even ordering the arrest of those who violated the rules, and he had to do so within a volatile social setting. It was considered an appropriate qualification for someone who wanted to be Cattle Fair superintendent that he had previously "apprehended and dispersed the runaway blacks of this city [Salvador] who had formed a maroon community." One superintendent supposedly exercised "despotic authority," putting free men into stocks and imposing other "torments." On the other hand, he had to be a person of some social standing: a man with a mulatta mother and whose alleged father refused to recognize him as his son would not do.[10]

The Cattle Fair had one major drawback: its location. Set up at Capuame in the early seventeenth century at a time when most of the cattle came from the area directly north of the city, between it and the lower São Francisco River, by the late eighteenth century the bulk of the supply came from the west and northwest. Drovers from these directions found the most convenient location for trading cattle to be a town that came to be named Feira de Santana. The old restrictions remained in place, however, and in 1818 the city council reiterated its prohibition against trading anywhere except at the Capuame Fair and ordered that "all those who purchase cattle at the fair called Santana must without exception bring such cattle to the Capuame Fair, register them, and bring the customary manifest." But the rule was about to expire. As early as the next year a petitioner referred to the "unregulated market at Santana." The War of Independence

(1822–1823) and the ensuing liberal reforms meant the end of the publicly administered Cattle Fair. By 1824 Feira de Santana was the seat of a fair held every Tuesday that attracted 3,000 to 4,000 people. It was easily the most important one in the province, and in 1855 it was still the source of the city's cattle "on a large scale." It continues to be so today.[11]

With the end of a publicly controlled Cattle Fair, the city bought a large pasture, something long advocated, relatively near the slaughterhouse. Before the 1820s the cattle, once purchased by a dealer at the fair, were driven 30 miles into the city along a dusty road, or one so muddy and slippery as to be impractical in the rainy season, stopping at no pastures or watering holes along the way and arriving at the slaughterhouse exhausted, hungry, thirsty, and often sick, remaining in corrals, watered but unfed, until slaughtered.[12] The new pasture was located at a place suitably named Campina (meadow), about 4 miles from the slaughterhouse. Only the cattle needed for each day's slaughter would be moved out of it. The following year the council ordered fences and cattle pens, with tile-roofed houses for the "drovers' lodgings," but two years later little had been done, and it complained about the pasture's shabby state. Finally, in 1826, the council proudly announced that the Campina pasture was ready. It was still in use as late as the 1860s, although by this time one observer described it as "rather a hospital and cemetery for animals than a regular stopping place," as it lacked adequate grass and water.[13]

All this means that by the 1820s the first node of the cattle business had been split in two: a privately run market where cattle were bought and sold, open to any self-declared cattle dealer, and a publicly administered pasture, supposedly free of any trading, where municipal controls could be reasserted. Still, in 1829, it was said that the pasture had also become a gathering spot for those who sought to entice cattle owners to sell illegally to them on the black market. The pasture's administrator was then required to send a manifest with each departing herd to the slaughterhouse personnel so they could verify that the tax had been paid and no head had been sold to illegal butcher shops along the way.[14]

Not all cattle came by land. With the passage of time and the introduction of larger vessels on the bay, more and more cattle arrived by boat. At first such a route was illegal because cattle so transported had obviously come from the west, and not from the Capuame Fair to the north. In 1807 the governor denounced boat owners for engaging in this trade. But later on, after Capuame had been abandoned and trade rules liberalized, this water route became perfectly acceptable, and in 1830 it appears that 40 percent of the city's cattle landed on the beach, arriving in lots of 23, 24, and even 50. In 1833 the city council designated a particular wharf, Agua de Meninos, for their landing, and from there they would go to the pasture. As happened with so many regulations, people soon disobeyed, bringing cattle in through other landing places and selling beef clandestinely outside the regulated channels, without paying the required taxes.[15]

By the 1840s, after several decades of urban growth, the route that cattle took from the pasture to the slaughterhouse passed along many city blocks. At the front of each herd went a cowhand blowing a horn, typically long and picturesque, drawn from an old steer and twisted in shape, to lead the cattle and to warn passersby to clear the streets. Behind the herd came the other drovers, urging the animals forward and sometimes creating a small stampede as some attempted to gore those ahead of them. A cloud of dust hung over the neighborhood long after the herd of longhorns had passed. The provincial police chief, responding to citizen complaints, sought to limit the danger to pedestrians posed by this practice. He insisted that at least along the last stretch the cattle should be driven only between midnight and 5:00 a.m. When the objecting city council insisted that the danger was minimal since "the blowing of the horn" provided adequate warning, the police chief replied that his measure would avoid "startled surprise, bruises, injuries and deaths" and certainly the warning horn of the herdsman did not adequately protect "cripples, children, or the deaf." The president of the province approved the new rule, and the city then blamed him for the ensuing scarcity of meat.[16]

THE SLAUGHTERHOUSE

The second node of the cattle and meat trade was the slaughterhouse. At first, when the new plan for the meat trade was put in place in 1784, the city had rented properties for slaughtering cattle at four locations, properties that belonged to a few cattle traders who were now deprived of their control of the entire business. These installations were distant from each other, at each end of town, badly built, and so situated that the newly appointed slaughterhouse administrator could not "prevent fraud." The city councilmen pressed the governor for a new establishment, "large enough and worthy of being called a slaughterhouse, . . . seeing that this city is so noble and populous." Governor Menezes responded by providing the wherewithal to build a new one, inaugurated on Easter Saturday, 1789, with the presence of several city officials. On what was then the northern edge of the city toward the supplying region, it was located up from a small stream and along the road that ran from the district of Soledade toward the Barbalho Fort (see Map 1.3).[17]

To understand the human effort expended in its operation, it is worth sketching a somewhat detailed physical description of the facility. In 1799 a Portuguese man described it as better than any other slaughterhouse, "not only in other towns and cities of Portuguese America but even in Portugal itself, including the capital." As many as twenty ranchers or merchants could bring in cattle at once "without fear of mixing them up." A writer in 1818 shared this opinion and described the place as "well finished, with all the [necessary] installations." At its center a yard under a tiled roof made space for the slaughtering and skinning. Next to it was an enclosed room where the quarters hung while they bled, a weighing room with its scales and desk, and a third large room, "surrounded with hooks" and full of divisions so that the quarters belonging to each owner were kept separate and in order. The slaughterhouse included small offices for the administrator, the scribe, and other officials, and space where cattle owners or their cowhands could hang their hammocks and spend the night. Some of the installation was paved with flagstones and some with bricks (which were easier to clean), but some remained unpaved, which allowed ant hills to emerge in the middle of the room where carcasses hung. When they graveled this area, it only made it harder to clean. The stone pillars that held up the roof were eventually lined with lumber to prevent the damage steers might cause.[18]

The passage of time led to either the objective deterioration of the slaughterhouse or altered perceptions about its salubriousness—or both. Although earlier the slaughtering yard was described as so well drained that when it rained "not one drop remained at any spot but washes the grounds," by the late 1820s the pump was broken that provided water "for the daily washing of the slaughterhouse to avoid the putrefaction that comes from stagnant blood," and twenty years later the city hoped to dig a new well for the purpose or draw water from nearby properties.[19] Slaughtermen cast the detritus into a "ditch or canal" built at a sufficient incline, it was said in 1818, to make it all slide into a nearby public property where people gathered it for fertilizer. As the city expanded, enveloping the slaughterhouse, neighbors complained of the smell, all the more so, one may suppose, because of the growing belief, based on the latest scientific literature, that disease resulted not so much from God's will as from environmental conditions, especially from so-called miasmas or bad air. In 1843 the slaughterhouse administrator thought the smell inevitable, "since blood and feces are placed where there is insufficient drainage for them to reach the river." This despite the city council having insisted with his predecessor that "under no circumstances" should manure remain there because this had made it "entirely filthy and intolerable, [putting at risk] not only the neatness that should characterize your department but also the health of employees and even the vicinity." Even in the best of circumstances the establishment attracted numerous large black vultures, described by a traveler as "hovering over the slaughterhouse."[20]

Cattle often sickened and died at the slaughterhouse. At the time of the pre-Lenten festival of 1824, a newspaper reported that meat from so many sick cattle was mixed up with good meat and sent off to butcher shops in the normal way that even the black street vendors refused to buy it for resale. The city council responded the very next day by ordering an investigation into the matter. Two weeks later it directed the administrator never, under any circumstances, to allow the slaughter of cattle that appeared ill, because citizens "are not able to know the failing themselves and . . . trust in the good faith of your office." Three years later it instructed him to hold all the head for twenty-four hours before slaughter so he could observe the state of their health, but then, for reasons that are not specified but can probably be explained by the desire of owners to sell as soon as possible, the council revoked the order. In 1830 the council assured the provincial president that the administrator had received firm instructions not to approve the slaughter of any cattle that appeared ill. The administrator reported that a "doctor" did random checks on the cattle and on the quality of the meat. Complaints about its lack of healthfulness continued to surface as a regular theme in correspondence.[21]

How properly and legally to dispose of cattle that died from natural causes posed a constant problem. At times their number reached 600 per year, almost 12 per week. At first, when a steer or cow died at the corral, the slaughterhouse administrator was required to verify that none of its meat was sold to the public but, rather, "carried on horses and thrown, along with the offal, into the sea, . . . only salvaging the hide." That was in 1801. In 1816 the carcasses were placed in a locked room overnight and buried the next morning in a cemetery with a properly notarized document drawn up to avoid quarrels between owners and those handling the cattle. The cemetery consisted of a small plot next door to the slaughterhouse.[22] The administrator explained in 1829 that he could not find anyone willing to do the burying except "an old black to whom strength is lacking to open up a deep pit, so the carcasses are buried near the surface." In 1837 the council decided that such cattle would be burnt, but a few weeks later, for reasons that seem obvious, they rescinded that instruction. Later councilmen repeated that carcasses were buried at an insufficient depth, and a committee, noting that dogs dug them up, recommended that a fence be built around the burial ground.[23]

The slaughterhouse administrator, like the Cattle Fair superintendent, had heavy responsibilities, especially to make sure that no skullduggery was practiced either against the owners of the cattle or by them. When the Cattle Fair superintendent reported that a man had disobeyed city ordinances by purchasing cattle after leaving the fair, it was up to the slaughterhouse administrator to seize the respective cattle and sell the meat below market price as a punishment. According to the original plan, no trading was to take place at the slaughterhouse, and the meat remained the property of the registered owner of the cattle until sold to the consumer. Not all administrators succeeded in enforcing this rule, and the writer of a letter to a newspaper editor claimed that "abuses and negligence" at the slaughterhouse allowed buying and selling to take place under the administrator's very nose, "reducing the slaughterhouse from a place only for slaughtering cattle into a market square or fair where the principal food of the people is sold in order to be resold."[24]

Major patronage attached to the position of administrator. This much power encouraged accusations of malfeasance. In 1798 the administrator, Pedro Francisco de Castro, was accused of being an interested party in the meat trade. He allegedly leant money to traders and put his own money directly at risk in buying cattle at the fair and in the nearby hinterland. The city council suspended him, pending an investigation, but later reinstated him. In 1802 the council finally dismissed him outright, but the new governor—a major cattle owner himself—inquired into the matter and forwarded the documents to the Crown. Although the reply took four years, once again Castro regained his post.[25] By 1812 a new administrator was in place: Antônio de Araújo Santos, who lived not far from the slaughterhouse. After at least seventeen years of service, Santos became ill in January 1829, and, at his request, his son substituted for him. When the father died three months later, the son learned with dismay that the city council had named Miguel de Souza Requião as successor. Requião had served as the slaughterhouse scribe for eleven years, and the council now appointed him administrator "for life." He still held this position in 1855.[26]

Others did the hard physical work. First were the four corral men, or *corraleiros*, hired by the city to handle the cattle for those ranchers or traders who did not have their own employees for the work. They drove the cattle from pasture to slaughterhouse every day to make sure they were ready for slaughter in the mornings, and they returned at the end of the day with any that had not been needed. Because they were held responsible for the cattle until the beef had been taken away to the butcher shops and the hides and offal delivered to buyers, they had to be constantly alert as to what was happening.[27]

Next were the slaughtermen. In the early days of the institution each of the four corral men took charge of ten slaughtermen. By the 1850s the slaughtermen worked under the direction of a captain, or *capataz*, who bid for the labor contract. By this time the number of workers had decreased to twenty, although the number of cattle had greatly increased. There were never eighty or one hundred workers, as one contemporary claimed.[28]

They first lassoed the cow or steer, tied it to one of several upright posts, drove a knife into its jugular vein, and dragged the carcass under a horizontal bar to which they raised it, gutting it and leaving it to hang until "well bled." They then skinned and quartered it, taking the quarters to a building where they hung each quarter on an iron hook long enough "to dry out"—that is, for the blood to completely drain (in the tropics meat had to be consumed soon to avoid spoilage with no time for curing). They also removed "the blood, filth, and other leftovers." On average, a slaughterman handled eight to ten head per week. It was heavy, dirty, smelly work, most commonly done by blacks, many of them freed Africans. In 1857, however, as part of a renewed effort to rid the city of Africans and force them to seek work on sugar plantations, regulations specified that slaughtering should be done "with the exclusion of Africans when Brazilians are available." Given the difficulty of the work and the low pay, this provision may have proved irrelevant. Although a lowly position, slaughtering cattle required courage and skill, and workers could take pride in the swiftness with which they felled an ox or the perfection of the hide they removed. If they did it badly, the owners complained that the hides "were good for nothing except making glue."[29]

Slaughtermen sometimes seized the chance to steal meat. The administrator despairingly wrote in 1830 that although he ordered the arrest of those whom he caught doing so, "since they are soon freed and newly admitted by the labor contractor, they continue to steal." When a rancher caught "the black Venancio, a slaughterhouse employee, . . . stealing meat," Venancio let out "an atrocious insult," and the rancher complained directly to the city council. The council ordered the administrator "not to allow said black Venancio to enter the slaughterhouse on any pretext," and to "have the scribe read this order out-loud to all the workers." Whether that did the council or ranchers much good is doubtful. In 1848 an anonymous but perceptive observer noted that since the city was unwilling to pay slaughtermen more than a miserable sum, "it's clear that only by becoming skilled thieves can they subject themselves to such unpleasant work at such a ridiculous salary." The writer went on to say that they stole "enormous pieces of meat from every ox they kill and skin . . . even in front of the cattle owner or his agent who, not having anyone to whom he can appeal, suffers in resignation."[30]

Outsiders sometimes set their slaves to do the stealing. In 1816 the administrator, alerted by Manuel de Souza Lima—a man engaged in transporting quarters from the slaughterhouse to the legal butcher shops—went to the slaughterhouse himself in the evening "after the Ave Maria [the tolling of the angelus at sunset]," posting Souza Lima and the cattle trader João Simões Coimbra "at different points." They found the gate "ajar" and the gatekeeper inside, just as two blacks ran away. They managed to catch one of them with "two [sic] quarters of beef in a big basket." He identified himself as José, a Nagô slave of Francisco de Andrade. The administrator then discovered the involvement of others. A slave at the neighboring leper's hospital accused a free black woman, Andreza de Menezes, "who lives by selling meat by the piece at her street stall," of paying Felix de Araújo, a free mulatto, to steal meat. On being alerted, the administrator headed toward town, and, sure enough, on the steep street leading down from the Carmelite monastery, he caught up with two Jege women, Maria and Quitéria, both slaves of Andreza de Menezes, carrying fresh meat cut into pieces that they were taking to their stall on the Baixa dos

Sapateiros street. The practice continued, and in 1829 the slaughter-house administrator caught "the black Francisco, slave of Rosa Rodri-gues, leaving the corral with a basket of stolen meat weighing over 50 pounds."[31]

Always present at the slaughterhouse were the tripe women. Al-though frustratingly absent from the sources, contemporaries knew their worth, and a special room had been set aside for them in the original design of the building. The city council set the maximum price for the cow's head, tongue, intestines, liver, and heart—parts that could be sold at only two places in the city. Using the stomachs of the cattle, but surely also the liver, kidneys, lungs, hearts, and in-testines, the tripe women supplied the poorer classes. As soon as the cattle were killed they would set to work on the offal. When beef was stolen from the slaughterhouse, suspicion fell, first of all, on them. Like the slaughtermen, they were perceived as dangerous because they wielded knives.[32] But in their ordinary daily lives, they were probably sharp businesswomen like the city's other street vendors. They too had to find consumers for their product and, price controls not withstanding, bargain for the best deals.

Given the city's topography, it is not surprising that the quarters were delivered from slaughterhouse to butcher shops not in carts, but on the backs of horses or mules. In 1790 it was alleged that meat "rot-ted . . . in the sun, in the rain, and [spoiled] as a result of contact with the bodies of these horses and even more from the disgusting falls of the horses in the mud and filth" of the streets. The council ordered conductors of these quarters to put hides over the horses before load-ing the meat in order to protect the meat from the horses' "sweat and dirt," and cover the meat with oilcloths, clean linen, or cotton cloths to shield it from the sun and rain.[33]

At the slaughterhouse the quarters were "marked" to indicate to which butcher shop each one should go. Those responsible for their transport were to be "instructed on the butcher shop marks so as not to deliver [the meat] to the wrong one." It is unclear how they made this mark, whether with ink or by branding. The quarters were weighed both at the slaughterhouse and the butcher shops, leaving deliverymen to make up any disparity. They carried with them a note specifying the correct weight. Some of these deliverymen worked for someone else, but others were themselves the owners of the horses they led and even became prominent small businessmen.[34]

THE BUTCHER SHOPS

The final stage of the meat trade took place at the butcher shops. The meat belonging to the traders and ranchers was supposed to be assigned to these publicly owned shops according to the number of head each owner had brought out of the Cattle Fair, although one rancher complained that they were assigned "arbitrarily" according to the influence of the "interested party." Ranchers spoke bitterly about how dealers used various shenanigans to secure shops for themselves to the detriment of the ranchers. Eventually lots were drawn to see whose meat would go to which butcher shop.[35]

In colonial and early nineteenth-century Brazil, as was once true elsewhere, people thought shops that sold similar goods should be next to each other so that shoppers could readily compare price and quality. In the case of butcher shops the city council further argued that such a measure would facilitate official inspections to protect the consumer. In 1799 the bulk of the publicly owned butcher shops were located at two spots: there were seventeen at the back of the city council building's ground floor, and eight in the lower city, a few blocks north of the grains market. Some years later the council building's seventeen shops had all been closed, while seven had been set up at a location toward the north, in the Santo Antônio além do Carmo district, and another seven had moved south next to the São Bento church, where there had been a privately owned slaughterhouse before 1784 (see Map 1.3).[36] Under the more liberal regime in post-independence Brazil, butcher shops could be opened all over town.

At butcher shops, as the 1784 plan made clear, the meat still belonged to the rancher or cattle dealer, and the shop itself was public property. The right to sell on their own account twenty pounds of meat from each head of cattle made the business sufficiently profitable to attract butchers who submitted bids each year at Easter time. Then, every Friday they presented receipts to the slaughterhouse administrator proving that they had paid the rancher or trader what they owed for the meat sold that week. Every Saturday morning they appeared at the city council offices with the tax money deducted from what they had paid the owners.[37]

Their honesty was often questioned. Some butchers, although legally licensed, nevertheless sold meat that had not come from the public slaughterhouse but had been acquired from other ranchers or illegal merchants, cheating the system. And there were those who surreptitiously sold meat outside the officially sanctioned shops; it was said that black marketeers typically sold "rotten" meat. The "falsification of weights" provoked "not infrequent complaints," reaching the ears of a provincial president who particularly deplored the practice, he said, because of its impact on the poor.[38]

Getting food from distant producers to urban consumers was a complex business. In the case of cattle and meat, many, many actors worked hard to make it happen. The drovers who brought the cattle to the Cattle Fair and later to the municipally owned pasture were only the first links in a long chain of people who transported, distributed, and sold meat. The slaughterhouse presented a scene of constant motion as the cattle were killed, skinned, bled, and quartered, all while keeping the ownership of the meat, tripe, and hides clearly identified and getting rid of the blood, feces, and other waste. Moving the meat to the butcher shops in a city defined by its steep streets required additional effort and coordination. The butchers then sold the meat to householders or their servant-slaves, finally producing an income that went back up the chain of commerce, eventually to the rancher. As many were involved in the business, many were the occasions for rivalry, conflict, and jockeying for position.

CHAPTER 7

CONTENTION

THE WORK OF SUPPLYING MEAT to Salvador reveals some of the cross-hatched tensions that permeated this society, as well as the way social distinctions could blur and alliances form. By and large, cattle merchants, butchers, and those who transported beef within the city shared a roughly equivalent social position. Some middlemen in the cattle and meat trade were mulattos, summoned along with their white counterparts to enforce its rules and yet, like them, sometimes described as mere creatures of the tanners and hide exporters. In contrast, free black workers at the slaughterhouse were badly paid and perceived as dangerous to society—even as violent revolutionaries. They sometimes struck for better wages. City dwellers considered all cattle drovers from the interior as brutish and wild, requiring constant vigilance, but alliances occasionally developed between the drovers and the urban-based cattle merchants.

WEALTH AND STATUS

How did Salvador's cattle dealers and butchers fit into the social order? Most of them belonged in the same general income bracket as Ana de São José da Trindade, although none of those I found were African or freed slaves, as she was. Their prestige was low, and in 1802 João Simões Coimbra, a mulatto militia colonel, considered it "indecorous to his dignity to trade in meat himself," and hired someone else who, for a small fee, acted on his behalf. This may have been a widespread practice among cattle traders, for in the 1830s the slaughterhouse administrator declared that "the names under which cattle arrive . . . are fictitious." In 1809 the city council disparagingly referred to "the multiplicity of indigent buyers who, abandoning the arts and trades in which they were employed, gather tumultuously" to buy cattle at the fair. If they bought, they were not indigent, but the opprobrium social leaders so often heaped upon middlemen in the food trade fell especially upon these cattle dealers. One governor urged the city council to be alert to such traders "who will not fail to think up some shady deal."[1]

On the other hand, cattle dealers did have some property and a degree of respectability. To prove that someone was unqualified to be a licensed dealer, it was enough to allege that he was related to gypsies, rented his house, and "does not own a foot of land on which to raise cattle." Some traders managed to move up a bit, as did Bartolomeu Francisco Gomes, who was labeled a cattle merchant in 1839 when he was summoned as a witness in an investigation at the slaughterhouse. When he died in 1848, however, he owned two general stores where he resold meat bought from another businessman. Even so, he probably did not enjoy a high standing among his mostly Portuguese fellow shopkeepers because he was one of the few grocers who had been born in Brazil and was of illegitimate birth.[2]

Cattle merchants depended heavily on others wealthier than they. Regardless of their own resources, all licensed traders had to present the names of guarantors who would stand surety for their debts to ranchers. A guarantor was required to either have real property with a value equal to fifteen times that of Ana de São José da Trindade's total estate or be deemed a credit-worthy merchant as attested by sworn statements from other businessmen.[3] Tanners and hide merchants either lent money to the cattle dealers or offered guarantees of their solvency. (Hides represented 11 percent of Bahia's exports during the period 1796–1811, reaching 22 percent in 1802.) In exchange for this financial backing, the traders sold the hides to their underwriters for somewhat less than the going price. The entire arrangement, it was said, made the traders "slaves of the guarantors," who could "arbitrarily set the price of hides."[4]

As for the butchers, the city council described them as being "of the lowest class [pessoas da última classe da plebe]." Yet there were distinctions of wealth among them: of twenty butchers who bid for shops within the city proper in 1805, eight successfully bid for more than one shop, and some for as many as five.[5] Despite the butchers' own precarious social standing, or because of it, they do not seem to have shared some of the elite's racialist obsessions even in the 1830s, noticeably a time of social unease. Their shops were instead a favorite gathering spot for idling slaves, some of whom had been sent there to purchase meat and lingered to chat with others.[6]

Several butchers accumulated nearly as much wealth as Ana de São José da Trindade. Jacinto Vieira Rios, who ran only one butcher shop in 1805, owned two one-story houses when he died at the end of 1817. He possessed no slaves, an unusual circumstance for a small businessman. Having married legally, he left a son and two single daughters, and it was to his two daughters that he willed the third of the estate that he could legally dispose of, perhaps as a substitute dowry. Besides the houses he owned, his property included nothing else except a considerable amount of clothing, such as an olive-colored coat, three white shirts, eight well-worn but high-quality vests—some fustian, others of satin or cambric—three pairs of twilled-cotton pants, plus underwear and a cocked hat, "all of it old and used." Before funeral and other final expenses, his estate's value amounted to just slightly less than that of Ana de São José da Trindade's.[7]

A butcher could have other businesses, as did Alexandre Gomes de Brito. He ran four butcher shops in 1805, and five twenty years later. He also delivered meat from the slaughterhouse to other butchers. A mulatto, Brito lived at a good location facing the Pelourinho Square, albeit in a rented house, and possessed a single-story stone house of his own quite near the slaughterhouse, on lands belonging to the Carmelite monastery. There he stabled the horses he used in the meat-delivery business and provided living quarters for some of his slaves, including two Jege women who sold fresh fruits and vegetables at their stand. He also owned two male street vendors and three housemaids, all of whom were African and one of whom had a five-year-old son. He seems to have sought respectability by becoming an officer in the militia and legally marrying a free black woman. He died in 1826, owing more than he owned. His daughter married another butcher who carried on that part of the business.[8]

Most of those who transported beef from slaughterhouse to butcher shop were, like Brito, men of only modest wealth, but at least one of them, João Simões Coimbra, was undeniably well off. Coimbra, who at one time camouflaged his role as a cattle dealer and later helped catch thieves at the slaughterhouse, exemplifies the possibility of successfully moving between sectors of the trade, in this case from trading cattle to the meat-delivery business. Of legitimate birth, born in the neighborhood of the slaughterhouse, he was a mulatto. In 1809 Coimbra "live[d] from trading in cattle" and during several months in the mid-1820s he supplied meat from his cattle to Brito's butcher shop. As late as 1839, when the city council summoned a meeting of dealers to deliberate on the reasons for a dwindling supply of meat, Coimbra was among them. But by the time he died in 1860, he no longer bought and sold cattle but dealt exclusively in transporting meat from the public slaughterhouse to the butcher shops. By that time he owned a stable, sixty mules, and an equivalent number of sumpter-saddles (padded wooden frames) to hold the beef. He had invested in several plots of land and drew income from extensive orchards with orange, banana, and coconut trees, from his manioc fields and equipment for making meal, and from the sale of corn, beans, okra, and hay. He owned sixty-four slaves and rented them out or used them on his land, in his stable, and for his meat transport business. Coimbra even leant money to the slaughterhouse administrator. The value of his estate was almost sixteen times that of the middle-class Ana de São José da Trindade. His superior officer in the militia described him as "willing, agile, obedient, ready, zealous for work, true, honorable, and of good habits," and his designated heir said Coimbra's property had derived from "his excessive and persevering work, [a property] that he did not consume nor waste." He had become a highly prosperous and independent businessman.[9]

Brito and Coimbra—both of whom eventually invested in the meat delivery business—were good friends. At a time when Coimbra dealt in cattle and Brito was only a butcher, Coimbra wrote his friend saying that, in lieu of sending a receipt for the 200$000 in cash that Brito had remitted, they would settle up the following day because he, Coimbra, was about to go out. Then he added, "Yesterday, when I returned from my mother's house at night, I found a present. . . . Many, many thanks for remembering me." At another time, Coimbra asked Brito to advance him the amount that he would be owing by the end of the week so he, Coimbra, could send it to the interior to pay for cattle.[10] Although butchering, dealing in livestock, and delivering meat to butchers suggest distinct occupations, the people involved formed part of a single community with shared beliefs and equivalent notions of the good and proper, not usually considering themselves as being in opposition to each other.

TENSIONS

The cattle and meat trade also produced much serious conflict, exposing fault lines that did divide the city. The three nodes of the business—the Cattle Fair, slaughterhouse, and butcher shops—each provoked particular forms of hostility and friction, revealing the interplay of people's differing levels of wealth, different skin colors, and different legal statuses.

The Cattle Fair at Capuame was a turbulent place where "innumerable people" of different classes, varied races, and contrasting backgrounds met, far from their homes and free of many constraining social ties. The drovers, hailing from distant points, probably did not know each other. Toughened as they were by their experience in traversing miles and miles across a harsh landscape, they were known to assert themselves through violence, doubtless acting according to rules to which I have no access. Some city folk accused them of "habitual indolence and laziness, which are superabundant in our country for lack of good repressive laws." Worse still, city dwellers thought of them as "fearless thugs lacking obedience" and as "fugitives from justice."[11] To control them, the city council paid the salaries of two militiamen drawn from the surrounding district, supplying them with horses. The subsequent nongovernmental cattle market at Feira de Santana was also described as a place where "horse rustlers, runaway slaves, and vagabonds" gather to provoke "constant disorder, thievery, and murders." These comments may say as much about the prejudices of the observers as about the objective qualities of the observed, but they point to social tension.[12]

The pasture at Campina, like the earlier Cattle Fair, was hardly thought of as a peaceful place. In 1829 the council asked the governor to place a guard of three men at the pasture to help its administrator enforce his authority. Two years later the administrator explained, "this is a point where a large number of backwoodsmen and drovers congregate, men whose indomitable character cannot yet be regulated by moral authority and gentle laws, an effect of a civilization which they do not have." "Civilization" had apparently still not arrived a quarter of a century later when, in 1858, the city council stressed the need for a police presence at the pasture "to avoid any clashes that almost always develop when the cattle drovers arrive." Continuing social differences perpetuated prejudices.[13]

Besides the friction among drovers, and between them and the authorities, the owners of the cattle, whether ranchers or traders, had their own reasons to clash with the city-appointed Cattle Fair superintendent. Although legally charged with impartially enforcing the regulations as a disinterested party, some superintendents bought and sold on their own account, competing with dealers. Some used their authority to pressure each cattle owner to sell them a head or two below market value, or looked the other way when one party or another committed fraud.[14]

Traders could respond by using to their advantage the seething social conflict visible at the fair. An example survives in documents originating from a complaint filed in 1806 by some twenty locals in Capuame who accused the superintendent of having ordered the assassination of André Corcino da Silva, a mulatto. "The henchmen whom [the superintendent] had charged with doing it left him for dead with many knife and cudgel wounds," but Silva survived and could name his attackers. The superintendent, they added, had regularly threatened to jail "the poor" and left them "disquieted." That was one version of the story. The superintendent replied that the signers of the complaint were "men of the lowest class [da ínfima plebe], suspicious, given to lying, mulattos, mixed-breeds [cabras], blacks, vagrants . . . who occupy themselves only in gaming, taverns, and other vices, without obedience or respect for officers of the law." He did, he said, arrest a "little mulatto [um mulatinho]" (a disparaging diminutive), but then Silva's friends "freed him in open resistance, riot, and mutiny." In the course of the mêlée, Silva was injured, "I know not by whom, while I was inside my house." Then a third point of view was introduced into the story, although in the superintendent's own words: what's worse, he said, a certain cattle merchant, "because I forbade him from doing certain things within my purview, conspires against me, [and has] bought witnesses, [and] conspired against my honor to the point of taking me to court with the unjust pretext that I had ordered the resister killed." To further the case, added the superintendent, this cattle dealer "keeps the witnesses at his house, sustaining and maintaining them, spending his money on the court case against me, treating the injured, and even giving money to the witnesses during the delays of ten or twelve days." These witnesses may have been drovers who needed to be sustained if they stayed in town or they may have been peasants from the area. Some were probably villagers. When a quarrel erupted between a trader and the superintendent, the trader could, by throwing his weight behind the poor, bring into the open the class and racial tensions present all the time.[15]

Cattle dealers also clashed with ranchers for the simple reason that ranchers wished to sell dear and traders to buy cheap. As a group, traders held the better hand because ranchers, often keen to sell their cattle and return to their land as soon as possible, were willing to settle for a lower price than they could have got themselves by taking their cattle into the city. Dealers, moreover, in the normal course of affairs, in effect borrowed from ranchers, paying for the cattle not when they took possession but only months later. Brito, the cattle dealer, went to the fair carrying money "in silver" to pay for cattle previously bought. Sometimes dealers failed to pay. One governor, a rancher himself, became incensed to learn that a livestock dealer in debt to a rancher had gone bankrupt along with his backer. When the city council did nothing, the governor ordered the arrest of the entire body, including the presiding royal judge, and demanded they sequester the remaining goods of both dealer and guarantor and make up any difference owed to the rancher by using funds from city coffers or from their own pockets.[16] In addition, dealers knew how to use class advantages, for ranchers "ordinarily do not know how to read or write." Dealers allegedly did everything they could to discourage ranchers from bringing in their own cattle to market.[17]

Ranchers who nevertheless did so encountered slaughtermen and tripe women whose loyalty lay with the cattle traders. The women, allegedly at the traders' urging, sometimes refused to buy the ranchers' offal, insisting on dealing only with traders, as happened in 1797. More evidence emerges from the following 1839 incident. At a time when the head of the city council believed cattle merchants were holding cattle back from market to force up the price of meat, he went personally to the slaughterhouse and had forty head arbitrarily seized and slaughtered. He succeeded in disposing of the offal of only fourteen, and for nine of these he did so only by turning it back to the owner of the cattle. For the other five cases he set the price unusually low. There were no takers at all for the remaining tripe, "although some tripe women were present and the administrator urged them to buy. . . . From which we concluded [the women] were conniving with the cattle dealers and their agents." To remain a client of a particular merchant regularly present at the slaughterhouse doubtless had its cost for the tripe women, including a diminution of their independence, but the relationship offered real security. The same was true of the slaughtermen, who could also be loyal clients of traders. As an official explained in 1809, the traders had their "protected dependents [fâmulos] and so are more faithfully served than the rancher, unknown to these servants." The rungs of clientage linked the lowliest workers to the traders, just as the traders depended on tanners and hide merchants; in both cases, the rancher fell outside the urban patronage chain, relatively isolated.[18]

If traders counted on those who bankrolled them, they clashed bitterly and successfully at one time with others who, although rich enough to have financed them many times over, chose instead to compete with them. In the 1830s, when most of the colonial regulations of the trade had been lifted, scarcity still provoked complaints about the quantity and price of meat. In 1836 a group of wealthy businessmen formed a company proposing to run both the slaughterhouse and the public butcher shops, guaranteeing that they would supply the city with at least a minimum amount of cattle and sell the meat for no more than an agreed-upon price, allowing others to bring in their cattle too, provided the company's meat sold first. They proposed to reinstitute features of the business as it had existed before 1784 and privatize it. The council accepted the company's proposal in late December 1836, a move that threatened the entire business of the regular cattle dealers.[19]

Five major merchants joined to form the new company. We know something about two of them. Everything about Manoel José dos Reis spelled capable, trustworthy, upright. Born in Portugal, he made his money as a builder in Brazil and owned substantial real estate when he died thirty-five years after joining the meat supply company. He had been the principal investor in the newly created local branch of the Bank of Brazil, opened at the beginning of 1817. His son later became a lawyer. His wife, Maria Constança da Purificação Pereira, was the daughter of a military officer. She had died less than three months before the contract for the meat business was signed, leaving two children, one still nursing. As Reis explained in his 1864 will, his children had been so young and, as "I had to leave each morning to work in my business, I had no choice but to seek someone to raise them and care for my house. To this end I bought and later freed the mulatta Eufêmia Maria da Conceição who always served as their mother until the time of their weddings," which she attended and helped prepare. He carefully specified the modest furniture and clothes that belonged to her, and granted her the service of an African slave woman and the usufruct of four contiguous one-story houses. He was a prosperous man of upright bourgeois behavior. No wonder the city trusted him and relied on him to fulfill the meat supply contract.[20]

Antônio Pedroso de Albuquerque was another partner in the company. Born in Rio Grande do Sul, he became a prominent international merchant, money lender, and slave trader in Salvador by the 1820s; he was still engaged in these activities in the 1830s and 1840s, long after the slave trade had been formally outlawed. He foreclosed on several mortgaged plantations in the Recôncavo, and so entered the province's landowning elite. In the 1850s he built a cotton mill on one of these estates. Sometime before 1836 he married into a prosperous Bahian family, and his wife inherited an imposing urban residence where, in the late 1850s, they entertained the emperor on a visit to the city. Their son married the daughter of one of Bahia's leading politicians. By the time of his death in 1878, Pedroso de Albuquerque had amassed an enormous fortune, leaving an estate that included 6 sugar plantations, 477 slaves, and 39 urban properties, including a house near the slaughterhouse. Although his hard-driving deals and slave trading may have made him suspect in some quarters, it would be hard to question his business sense or doubt the likelihood that an enterprise that he backed would be successful.[21]

Yet the meat company, because it threatened those who had previously controlled the cattle business, encountered difficulties almost as soon as it began operations. Its opponents turned to direct action. In mid-January 1837, just a month into the contract period, the city council urgently asked the provincial president to provide a guard to protect the company's cattle. Two weeks later a company employee reported the steers belonging to the company were dying at an unusual rate. The city council suspected skullduggery on the part of "enemies of the contract," and the provincial president ordered the National Guard to assist the justice of the peace in investigating the case in the district through which the cattle were driven. These measures proved useless, and the council reported in mid-February that a "gang of outlaws" operating there "lie in wait solely to destroy" the company's cattle. A few months later the city council charged that through "occult machinations" the company's opponents at the slaughterhouse and at Feira de Santana were "suborning the drovers with money to increase the mortality rate (it is said) by introducing iron needles [into the cattle] that kill without leaving a trace." In this way dealers and drovers worked together against rich outsiders.[22]

The company had to contend with other, less direct but equally effective measures taken by those whose interests it had damaged. The butchers employed by the company, allegedly bribed by its "enemies," either siphoned off meat to be sold clandestinely themselves or sold it to cronies who then resold it. The retaliating dealers also connived to bid up the price of cattle at the fair in order to ruin the company. Finally, company directors discovered to their chagrin what others in the trade knew well: the roads were "impassable," especially on the steep parts and across the rivers.[23] Nothing was easy.

At first the company put up a brave front and claimed that its work was already, by March, "a benefit to public health." When the provincial president alleged a shortage of fresh meat, the city council denied it, saying this was simply the claim of the company's opponents, "traffickers in meat" who used to enjoy "the base and scandalous profit they derived from the People's sweat." By August 1837, however, the council admitted that the company could not supply the agreed-upon quantity of meat. The firm appealed to the contractual clause regarding "pestilence and flood" to escape its obligations. Although the company "seemed to possess to an eminent degree the principal base of commercial credit," it failed to live up to the terms of the contract. The legal control of the meat trade reverted to the council, and its financial control to traders. Their tactics had worked.[24]

The traders, not being clients of these wealthy men and not entangled in credit relationships with them, felt free to push back, despite their modest backgrounds. Because the company men and the traders did not deal with each other on a regular basis, they had not rehearsed how to conduct their encounters. The dealers could not get their way by using the ancient tools of dependents and subordinates in a hierarchical and paternalistic society, and so turned instead to violence, even if practiced only surreptitiously.[25]

Friction also emerged between owners of the cattle, whether ranchers or traders, and the butchers who sold their meat to consumers. Butchers were sometimes accused of delaying their weekly payments to the owners of the meat.[26] The owners, not the butchers, set the initial price for which meat was to be sold. "On Saturdays, before selling a single pound, [the butchers] will make public the price of the meat, calling it out in a loud voice or having it called out by their agents 'for such a price is sold each *arroba*.'" During any day, however, the butchers were entitled to lower the price to make sure no meat was left over, and it was up to them to report to the cattle owner what they had actually sold it for. It was easy for them to lie. "A goodly portion of meat for which the people paid 1$280 is reported as [sold for] 960 réis," with butchers pocketing the difference.[27]

Conflict also played out at the slaughterhouse. The slaughtermen tried on several occasions to raise their wages, but the competition from slaves defeated them. In 1826 the administrator accused workers of "colluding" to increase their wages, forcing his hand. Either he would "capitulate, granting them the absurd benefits that they have proposed or [he would] leave the city without meat." The city council then temporarily took over the hiring of the workers directly, although where they found men willing to work is not said.[28] Three years later the administrator had more reason to complain. When the going rate for the work was 80 réis per head slaughtered, the labor contractor announced that his workers would only do it for 200. The administrator put him off, but after several months of fruitlessly searching for alternatives, he reported that the slaughtermen had agreed to 120 réis per head, and he went along. Then some ranchers and cattle merchants declared they could get the work done for 110, but this turned out to be a false promise. In October 1830 only eight workers showed up: "All the others failed to appear, being unwilling to work for less than 120 réis per head." The result was that, as the administrator explained, "only a little meat [will be] available for sale to the city's consumers." The administrator then appealed once again to the cattle dealers "to do the favor of sending their slaves for this work." A few complied, but not enough. After a fortnight only two slaughtermen were willing to work. The administrator sent one of his staff to find the others, but they would not come. "Not one steer has yet been killed for lack of workers, . . . Tomorrow there will be no meat in the city." The council caved in, telling him that the next day he should "do the slaughtering by whatever means is in your reach, paying something more for the slaughter, just as long as there is meat furnished to the city."[29] This, I believe, is Brazil's first strike for better wages, a capitalistic notion, in contrast to the subsequent work stoppage of boatmen and dock workers for the restoration of their corporate autonomy. In the very act of striking for better wages, entering into conflict with employers, they forged a class.

The workers' success was short-lived. The next day João Simões Coimbra, the cattle dealer and later beef transporter, offered his slaves "for free" to do the slaughtering. He then succeeded in recruiting replacement workers, presumably threatening that otherwise they would not have any work at all. A few days later the city council announced that it would pay 87 instead of 80 réis. Whether their offer was accepted is not clear, but conflict between free and slave workers led to knife fights.[30] In the end the strike was broken: slave owners rented their slaves to do the slaughtering, leaving free workers no choice but to accept a low wage. By 1845 the pay per head ranged between 70 and 80 réis, and a local newspaper cited 80 réis in 1848, the same amount as in 1809, when the currency had been worth four times as much! For so little, they continued to slaughter, clean, skin, and quarter; to remove the mess; to move the beef onto scales and then hang it on hooks; and to dispose of any cattle that died from disease.[31]

Because of their race, ethnicity, class, and particular trade, slaughtermen and tripe women were always suspected of being willing to use violence. Daily covered in blood, they looked the part. From the time of the slaughterhouse's creation, the governor posted one lieutenant, two non-commissioned officers, and four soldiers there specifically to halt disorders among workers, and a police presence continued long afterward. In 1799 it was said that, armed as they were, slaughterhouse workers "would just as soon kill a man as bring down an ox."[32] The 1835 "Malê" revolt focused general attention on the supposed danger posed by blacks, especially, of course, by Africans. In its wake investigators arrested six meat cutters on suspicion of involvement. Four were slaves, the others freedmen, and all were Africans. A few months later the slaughterhouse administrator nervously reported that workers there, "numbering thirty or forty, are largely Africans who use in their work two or three knives each, as well as iron lances, axes, and long prods, not to mention a considerable number of tripe women, also in large part African, who use knives as well for their work." He shared the "mistrust with which such people are justly held" and feared that the slaughterhouse would become "a place where they may arm themselves for any assault." The provincial president, who also feared blacks, quickly responded, sending three soldiers to "remain at the slaughterhouse during all the slaughtering." Three years later the administrator still believed he needed an armed guard since "some of those employed in the meat trade show little respect," and "a great number of individuals gather at this public institution, and some are armed with knives used in the slaughtering."[33] Nothing in the sources tells us whether black, mostly African slaughtermen felt as hostile toward whites as some whites believed. Yet if people come to see themselves as mirrored in how others see them, it is quite possible that they, enraged at their helplessness in the face of exploitation, might think of turning on those who were better off.

Anxiety surfaced at every turn as each participant in the cattle and meat business contended with others. Cattle traders daily had to keep a watchful eye over the slaughtermen who might otherwise steal from them. They then had to sell the hides below market price to the fellow who had financed the venture. They coped as best they could, but when faced with a major and specific danger, they took direct action against the wealthy men who in 1837 threatened to displace them entirely. A butcher was under the thumb of the cattle merchants as a group, even if not under the same one week to week. At the same time, some butchers got ahead of others by illegally securing meat of better quality from traders who connived in a surreptitious trade. A butcher also had to be on the lookout for cheating by those who delivered beef to him. At the Cattle Fair or at the public Campina pasture, the bargaining was not only about money but about status and prestige. In both places deference was exchanged for protection, or the unspoken social bargain was broken. The participants simultaneously measured the weight of cattle, observed each other's skin color, and calculated the degree of someone's "civilization."

Throughout the cattle and meat trade, racial markers intertwined with social distinctions in the complex and amorphous way they still do in Brazil. Although the black and mostly African slaughtermen were close to the bottom of the social scale, they were freedmen or freeborn. They were proud of that, and not about to ignore the distinction between themselves and slaves, or at least those slaves sent by their masters to break a strike at the slaughterhouse. Traders, butchers, and the transporters of beef could be white or mulatto; many of them viewed the mostly black slaughtermen with a mixture of contempt and fear. Dealers sought respectability and social recognition by marrying in church, becoming militia officers, and purchasing real estate and slaves, yet city councilmen were quick to refer to their color or lowly social rank, even as they relied on them to supply the meat considered so essential to the city's survival. A leitmotif resounding through the city council's actions was the tendency to disparage others or accuse them of being someone else's creature. The very detail and extension of all the regulations of the trade implied a low regard for the honesty and good will of people generally.

Given the nature of the sources I have used—government documents—it is not surprising that officials are less often the object of criticism. A butcher doubtless feared having his meat and butcher shop inspected at any moment by a city official, whose corruptibility had to be subtly and accurately assessed. We can easily imagine the favoritism witnessed daily, or the lazy performance of duty that slowed the bureaucracy of the meat trade and caused financial loss to others. As is often said in Brazil, "The law is for your enemies." The power exercised by superintendents and administrators probably explains why these men sought these positions in the first place. I would guess that such officeholders were sometimes arbitrary in their actions, as often happens with those who are powerful within a limited sphere, but are themselves relatively powerless in larger society.

Friction permeated the trade. Men, and sometimes women, wrangled with each other, driven partly by financial interest and partly by their differing points of view. To dampen the volatility, Salvadoreans relied on the inculcated notions of patron-client exchange, where protection was offered, and loyalty and deference received. Before their financial backers, traders almost surely hid any resentment they felt at the tanners' demand that hides be sold to them at a lower price than the prevailing one. And tripe women were smart enough to know that it would pay off in the long run to show loyalty to the traders who were regularly present, no matter the immediate cost. In this way Salvadoreans managed to contain daily conflict well enough. But how would they deal with outright war?

PART II

CHANGED RULES: REFORM AND RESISTANCE

CHAPTER 8

"THE TRUE ENEMY IS HUNGER":
THE SIEGE OF SALVADOR

FOR MORE THAN TWELVE MONTHS in 1822–1823, those struggling to free Brazil from Portuguese control laid siege to Salvador, where a Portuguese army was ensconced. The effort to cut off Salvador's supply of food finally succeeded, and the Portuguese army, along with many merchants, set sail for Europe. Before examining the alternatives that local people faced, and the crucial political role they played in the high drama of bringing about this major political transformation, it is important to understand the war's course. That task hinges on a close examination of the siege itself—never studied in detail before.

INDEPENDENCE

The military phase of Brazil's struggle for independence from Portugal took place almost entirely in Bahia, even though the initial spark came from outside the province and can be traced back fourteen years.[1] Portugal's prince-regent, later crowned João VI, arrived in Brazil in 1808, driven from Europe by Napoleon's army. He did not merely set up a court-in-exile, but installed the complete apparatus of his government, transforming Brazil from a mere colony into a seat of empire. By opening the ports of Brazil to the trade of friendly nations, especially Britain, the new administration ended the monopoly of overseas commerce by Portuguese merchant houses and removed a defining characteristic of the previous colonial relation. The judicial system was reorganized, and appeals no longer went to Lisbon. João lifted the prohibition on manufacturing, encouraged agriculture, and created a national bank—all signaling Brazil's new, noncolonial position. Once the French were out of Portugal and a new international order had been established, he elevated Brazil to the legal status of a kingdom equal to Portugal, choosing to remain in Brazil to be crowned king of both countries when his mother died in 1816.

A quickly quashed republican revolution in Pernambuco the following year led João VI to doubt the loyalty of Brazilians in general, even though those who defeated that chimerical movement were almost entirely Brazilian. He soon ordered the transfer of several battalions of veterans of the peninsular war in Europe to Brazilian cities. The 12th Battalion, commanded by Luís Inácio Madeira de Melo, was posted to Salvador. With the arrival of Portuguese troops, many Brazilians perceived increasing discrimination, and tensions mounted.[2]

Meanwhile, in Portugal dissatisfaction with the absence of the king was slowly surfacing. In August 1820 a revolt broke out demanding his return. Although its instigators were Portuguese army officers, they had linked up with both the civilian liberals who wished to transform the absolutist monarchy into a constitutional one and with merchants who longed to reestablish the Portuguese monopoly over trade to Brazil, the lack of which they blamed for greatly depressing the Portuguese economy. With the revolutionaries' easy victory in Portugal, they immediately summoned a Cortes, the ancient parliament that had not met for more than a century. It would be elected not by estates, as in the past, but through a reasonably democratic process, and charged with creating a constitutional framework for a monarchical government. Although the Cortes included representatives chosen in Brazil, the first Brazilians did not arrive until eight months after deliberations began in January 1821.

The Cortes's majority soon overplayed its hand and, in a series of moves, managed to offend most Brazilians. It immediately summoned the king to Lisbon, leaving João to face the reality that unless he complied, Portugal would declare its own independence. He departed, leaving his son Pedro as prince-regent in Brazil. The Cortes rejected this arrangement, doubting the loyalty of Brazilians toward whom some members expressed outright contempt, referring to the alarming "heterogeneity of castes" in Brazil and the mixture there of "blacks, mulattos, and creole whites." Most Portuguese politicians saw no reason to treat Brazilian provinces differently from those in Portugal, where they took central authority for granted in a now unitary liberal government. Even some Brazilian delegates wanted to see the province of Rio de Janeiro stripped of its special place, for its predominance since 1808 had never sat well in the northern provinces.

The Cortes voted to abolish the separate Kingdom of Brazil altogether and bend all provinces to Lisbon's rule without even a viceroy as go-between. In October the Cortes instructed João VI to order Pedro to leave Brazil and return to Europe, an order that arrived in Brazil in December 1821.[3]

Alert to the danger, Brazilian leaders in Minas Gerais and São Paulo added their voices to those of leaders in Rio de Janeiro, demanding that Pedro remain as prince-regent in Brazil and exercise executive power from the Brazilian capital. Encouraged by this support, on January 9, 1822, Pedro authorized a delegation of Brazilian leaders to announce to the people that "I will stay." This defiant declaration, by which he ostensibly disobeyed an order from his father, the king, proved a turning point, pushing Brazil toward complete independence.

Three days later, as Portuguese troops in Rio de Janeiro prepared to reimpose their will, they found themselves surrounded by as many as 10,000 militiamen and hastily armed civilians who had managed to secure several artillery pieces. The Portuguese troops, numbering almost 2,000, well trained and disciplined, could probably have won any battle against the Brazilians, but at an enormous cost in lives and goodwill. Instead they surrendered. Within a month, they had left Rio de Janeiro for Portugal, escorted as far as Pernambuco by ships loyal to Pedro. When a new contingent of 1,200 Portuguese troops arrived off the coast of Rio de Janeiro, Pedro's forces kept them from landing, urging them to join the fledgling Brazilian Army. Some 894 men did just that.[4]

Pedro moved quickly to assert his authority. He decreed that no law from Portugal should be obeyed in Brazil unless sanctioned by him, and that all local governing boards swear allegiance to him. Seeking to attract support from elsewhere in Brazil, he convoked a constituent congress for Brazil itself, clearly understanding that such a measure would win over those who, even if wanting to be ruled from within Brazil, had been attracted to the constitutionalism of the Portuguese revolution. The Cortes played into Pedro's hands in March and April 1822 by considering a proposal that would once again require Brazilians to trade only with Portugal, and would close Brazilian ports to commerce with other nations. Pedro pointed out that those in the Cortes who would legislate in this way for Brazil "knew it only in maps." When news came back that the Cortes had canceled the validity of his every measure, the positions of Pedro and the Cortes were joined. On September 7, 1822, Pedro declared Brazil independent. In December he accepted a crown as Emperor Pedro I of Brazil.

DIVISIONS IN BAHIA

Not all of these actions met with approval throughout Brazil, and most notably not in Bahia.[5] Earlier, on February 10, 1821, the military garrison in Salvador, in allegiance with their fellow officers in Portugal, had declared for the constitutionalist revolution and deposed the governor, replacing him with a governing committee made up mostly of the Portuguese-born, including several merchants. Many Brazilians were unhappy. A Portuguese bureaucrat in Salvador noted the diffusion of "chimerical ideas of independence" and the spread of a "political epidemic," so much so that he returned to Portugal.[6] The governing committee remained firm in its liberal, pro-Portuguese purpose and organized an election in September for representatives to the constitution-writing Cortes in Lisbon. But sensing the precariousness of their position, they requested additional troops from Portugal. In response, the Cortes sent out an expeditionary force dubbed the Constitutional Legion that arrived in Salvador in August 1821 with 1,137 soldiers and officers, along with the customary accompaniment of wives, children, and servants.[7] This unit's purpose was clear, since it was obviously not intended to defend Bahia against foreign invasion.

Military force in Salvador at this time fell into three categories. The rank-and-file of the regular army regiments long present in Brazil were entirely recruited from within the province, and some four-fifths of its officers were Brazilian. Enlisted men were typically poor men of color, and the officers were linked to major slave-owning families. Then came the two entirely Portuguese units: the 12th Battalion that had come in 1817 and the newly arrived Constitutional Legion. A third category consisted of four militia units recruited from among civilians: men who held regular jobs but donned uniforms and trained on Sundays without pay. One unit consisted of the wealthier merchants and their clerks, mostly Portuguese by birth. A second unit was described in 1799 as being for "owners of general stores and taverns, artisans, and other qualities of white men," including both Brazilians and Portuguese, probably more of the latter. Finally there were two regiments, one for mulattos and another for free blacks, the so-called Henriques, named for a black soldier who had fought against the Dutch in the seventeenth century.[8] We have already met João Simões Coimbra, a colonel in the mulatto militia, who traded in cattle and later invested in the business of transporting beef to butcher shops. Not only Brazilian-born free blacks, such as Luiz Gomes de Oliveira, a literate silk maker, but freed Africans such as Felipe Francisco Serra, José Simões, and Manoel Bomfim, were in the Henriques, and some Africans even reached command positions. Among the possessions left at her death in 1823 by the African street vendor Ana de São José da Trindade was an "old uniform" belonging to a mulatto militiaman, unnamed. Who had once worn it? The father of one or more of her children? Or one of her two sons who predeceased her?[9]

In early February 1822 the city of Salvador cracked in two. In keeping with instructions received from Lisbon, an election was held for a provisional governing board. Much to the chagrin of the Portuguese-leaning committee that had been in charge since the military action the year before, all but one of the winning candidates were Brazilian. A major crisis erupted from a dispute over the board's appointment of a military governor for the province: either the Brazilian officer who had led that revolt a year earlier or the Portuguese-born Inácio Luís Madeira de Melo, commander of the 12th Battalion, who had also supported the coup. Both men had legal claims to the post. An unsuccessful effort to find a compromise lasted through the night of February 18, but Madeira would not give in. At dawn, fighting broke out between the Portuguese and Brazilian forces. Some one hundred people died, including an abbess who vainly sought to deny entrance to Portuguese troops who claimed shots had been fired from the abbey. Whether because of such violence, their battle-tested experience in Europe, their greater discipline and organization, or their advanced planning, the Portuguese won easily and coerced the provisional governing board into making Madeira the military governor. The board continued to be officially in charge of the city's civil matters, formally loyal to the Portuguese king. Madeira, however, frequently clashed with its members and did not trust them. In the aftermath of the battle in Salvador, a majority of the army's Brazilian segments and many black and mulatto militiamen left the city for the Recôncavo.[10]

The constitutional, liberal-conservative question now gave way to a nationalist, anticolonial one. As recounted by a French naval captain, most Portuguese merchants, store owners, and their clerks rejoiced at Madeira's victory. They lit candles in their windows to show their joy and celebrated loudly, "even as Brazilians buried their dead." Anger increased on both sides, although some Portuguese sided with the Brazilians.[11]

A decidedly hostile mood toward the Cortes predominated in the rural districts of the Recôncavo. Sugar exports had boomed in previous years not only because competition from Haiti had been eliminated by its revolution at a time when Cuban exports were only beginning, but also because the opening of Brazilian ports to international trade had enabled direct exports to northern Europe, leading to higher profits for planters. They strongly opposed efforts by the Cortes to reimpose the old colonial practice of awarding Portuguese merchant houses the exclusive right to control this export trade. Some planters, moreover, were decidedly conservative in their political attitudes and may have feared the Portuguese Cortes would be tempted to abolish slavery in Brazil, as had been done in Portugal long before. One planter had earlier bemoaned the "revolutionary plague" sweeping through Europe.[12] Having a monarch or prince-regent resident in Brazil would clearly make him more sensitive to planters' concerns than would be an elected parliament sitting in far-away Portugal.

On June 25, 1822, the town of Cachoeira (see Map 1.1), led by prominent sugar planters, declared for Pedro as regent, although still professing ultimate loyalty to João VI. Four days later another major town of the Recôncavo, Santo Amaro, followed Cachoeira's example, and by the end of the month so had São Francisco do Conde and Maragogipe, soon to be joined by Jaguaripe. The sugar and tobacco regions, along with some of the food-supplying sectors of the Recôncavo, threw in their lot with Prince Pedro. In September, as Pedro declared Brazil independent, the leaders of various interior towns arranged to work in concert and formally established a revolutionary government seated in Cachoeira, naming it the Interim Provincial Council. Little radicalism characterized their actions, however. From the beginning they justified what they did on the grounds that both the city and the Recôncavo were in a "deplorable state of fermentation," and they wished only to prevent "anarchic excesses." The slaves would remain slaves.[13]

Towns along the southern coast of Bahia were much less willing to sever their ties to the city of Salvador. Camamu (see Map 4.1) openly voted to side with the Portuguese and had to be brought into the revolutionary fold by the Jaguaripe militia. Farther south, in today's Itacaré, the county council formally supported Pedro but surreptitiously continued to deal with Salvador. Only in late November 1822 did the county council in Porto Seguro overcome the resistance of the Crown judge and another member of the local government in order to support Pedro. Eventually all of the Bahian districts except Salvador sent representatives to the Interim Provincial Council, although not all residents endorsed this action, and many boatmen continued to provision Salvador.[14]

Both sides perceived the strategic importance of Bahia. The Portuguese saw it as a rich colony, understanding that if the province stayed on their side, it would encourage the other northern provinces to remain loyal as well and prevent easy communication between them and Rio de Janeiro. Pedro's advisers, recognizing the same facts, were determined to prevent that from happening. Without Bahia, the independence of any part of Brazil would have been in doubt, and, certainly, the new country would have lacked any semblance of unity unless much reduced in size. These perceptions resulted in an intensely fought confrontation, requiring a vast mobilization of Brazilian men and resources over more than twelve months, from late June 1822 to July 1823, and an equally determined effort by the Portuguese government to hold on to Bahia.

Town leaders in the Recôncavo who opted to ally themselves with Prince Pedro, knowing what they had to fear, quickly sought help from Rio de Janeiro. Pedro, even before declaring Brazil independent, dispatched Pierre Labatut, a Frenchman who had fought in Europe and then in Colombia, along with 260 soldiers and 38 officers to head the insurgent army. Along with him went materiel for forces to be raised locally: 5,000 rifles, 500 carbines, 500 pistols, 2,000 lances, and 500 sabers, as well as 6 cannons. Labatut landed in Alagoas, to the north of Bahia, in late August, but only moved into Bahia in October after securing additional men from Pernambuco and removing from power the pro-Portuguese faction in Sergipe, in this way protecting his rear. Rebels based in Cachoeira had, in the interim, mobilized the militia of every interior town and launched a vigorous recruitment effort. Meanwhile Madeira had received more reinforcements. With these forces facing each other, it was obvious, as a perspicacious emissary from the Rio de Janeiro government had noted even earlier, that the Cachoeira group "has enough forces to defend itself from any attack," but "lacks the resources needed to attack and drive out the Portuguese."[15] Given this stalemate, the Brazilian side decided to lay siege to the city.

FEEDING THE INSURGENT TROOPS

For Salvador the war turned on the supply of food. The challenge was to make sure one's own side had food and the other did not—something that commanding officers on both sides knew well. The insurgents had a triple problem. First, they needed to feed their troops, who eventually numbered some 11,000. Second, most of these soldiers had been drawn away from their ordinary occupations: producing and transporting food. Third, the insurgents had to succor a vast number of refugees who had abandoned the city of Salvador either from ideological preference or for fear of greater hunger if they stayed there. Revolutionary leaders noted with alarm the "increase of consumers in this province." They quickly acted to secure supplies and sent orders to all loyal towns to cooperate. But they took no chances. Nazaré loomed as an obvious target for both sides because of its huge production of manioc meal. On August 20, 1822, a battalion of volunteers from Cachoeira marched in and took control of the town. At the beginning of October the insurrectionaries set up a centralized food supply agency with major responsibility for gathering and distributing cattle and manioc meal to the armed men. At first they tried to get their food supplies "by gift and loan or by cash purchase," but later only cash worked. Insurgents found their funds limited, and at least one vessel's captain complained that he had not been paid for the "65 bushels of meal" he had delivered.[16]

Bahians considered fresh meat essential, and its lack a disaster. Troubling, then, was word from Nazaré in October 1822 that "the merchants who deal here in this item [cattle] are mostly Europeans [Portuguese] . . . who have ceased arranging for their cattle to come from the hinterland." Insurgent leaders responded to such reports by sending a military officer and forty men westward, beyond Feira de Santana, to round up cattle and confiscate any belonging to uncooperative Portuguese ranchers. Insurgent leaders later ordered every sugar planter in São Francisco do Conde and Santo Amaro to contribute one ox each, regardless of whether or not it was being used to haul cane or drive the mill. They also requisitioned many herds from ranches owned by religious orders, and from the Conde da Ponte, who owned huge estates.[17]

Despite such efforts, there were never enough cattle, and this heightened anxiety. On November 6 a first lieutenant in charge of a small fort reported, "I only have two head to furnish this garrison." Two days later he referred to "the last head I have to feed the garrison." On the twelfth he wrote, "I only have cattle for two days because, of those I received, I sent half to [another garrison] and I kept mainly small yearlings, of which we need two for one day's consumption." By mid-December, with the troops under his command numbering 1,000, another garrison commander reported their "terrible desperation," exclaiming, "I don't know how I should act. . . . They complain against me, and with reason, saying that everywhere else troops get a pound-and-a-half of meat and we give them only one, without the supplement of beans, bacon, or rice, and this always late and sometimes not even that." He added, "I don't know how it is possible to impose military law on men who lack all food." He understood that the lack of adequate food can quickly undermine any soldier's morale.[18]

Scarcity of manioc meal dominated the correspondence among insurgent officers. "Our greatest need [is] manioc meal for the sustenance of the troops. . . . I plead with you to exert all diligence in supplying this need by delivering meal," said one officer, adding that "certainly the troops cannot be disciplined when they are dying of hunger." Feeding the army commanded by General Labatut became the highest priority after he appeared on the scene in October 1822 and set up his general headquarters at Engenho Novo, not far north of Salvador (see Map 1.1). Key points served as gathering places for food supplies to be shipped in boats across the northern part of the bay if they could not come on water from farther south.[19]

The insurgents set to work assembling their own small fleet of armed vessels to accompany boats laden with manioc meal and rice from the southwestern quadrant of the bay to army locations. The revolutionary council complained that some "owners of boats used in commerce . . . have hidden [them] so they will not be used in serving the public cause of Brazil." Needing boats "to carry . . . foodstuffs," they ordered them seized "along with their respective crews of captains and sailors." Similar orders went out to another officer to confiscate boats or canoes and use them to ship manioc meal "either to Cotegipe [inlet] directly if the enemy boats allow it" or to a certain sugar mill, to be sent from there to Acupe. The search for boats still missed some: as late as June 1823 one was found belonging to a "Portuguese man, an enemy of Brazil," now commandeered for the patriot cause along with his "three black slave sailors."[20] What surfaces in the documents, of course, are these cases of individuals who refused to cooperate. The fact that army and militia units, despite occasional crises, did receive food over a period of several months indicates that their food supply system worked well.

STARVING OUT THE PORTUGUESE

Just as important as securing food for the Brazilian troops was preventing the Portuguese from getting any. Sieges, an ancient military tactic, may culminate in storming the ramparts, but their essential device is the cutting off of the enemy's food supply. As no city feeds itself, cities are prime targets: Jericho, Numantia, Jaén, Orléans, Tenochtitlán, Vienna, Yorktown, just to mention a few well-known targets of sieges in the Western world before 1822. Cutting off the food supply costs no lives among the besiegers and can be extremely effective. Salvador was especially susceptible because it sits on a peninsula, and the immediately surrounding area did not produce much food. Its supplies had to be brought from across the bay or, in the case of beef, from many miles inland.

The easiest task was to block cattle drives into the city. In July 1822 rebel forces, especially the black Henriques militia, cut off Salvador's cattle supply by occupying the high ground at Pirajá, north of the Campina pasture (see Map 1.2). A few days later the city council admitted that of four cattle drives coming from the north and headed for the Cattle Fair at Capuame, two had been "seized by armed forces from the Recôncavo," and the other two had turned back. No cattle had arrived at the slaughterhouse, leaving the city without fresh meat.[21] It was no accident that General Labatut, on entering the province in October, had immediately occupied Capuame.

For the insurgents, exerting control over shipping within the bay proved more difficult than intercepting cattle drives, but still feasible. Although some one hundred vessels coming from Recôncavo ports customarily docked at Salvador every week, most came from just a few locations. They could be watched. The patriot leaders knew that persuasion would not be enough and posted a garrison at Jaguaripe because of its crucial importance. That town "required the greatest security to deprive the enemy from receiving from it manioc meal and [other] victuals." Cutting off bay-side traffic was the major key to the eventual insurgent success. As a French naval officer put it, writing from Salvador in July 1822,

The true enemy that threatens Bahia [city] is hunger—a scourge that became inevitable by virtue of the arrangement of the surrounding population. This city . . . receives hardly any sustenance from the northern provinces except some cattle herds. All the rest comes from the other side of the bay. The aggressor who either spreads land forces out in the field or simply stations a few ships at a small number of chosen points in the bay will command all the resources of Bahia. A blockade at the entrance to the bay would maximize the city's suffering.[22]

Ah, but blocking the entrance from the Atlantic was precisely the insurmountable problem. The rebel forces had no navy capable of mounting a blockade. Although they could stop vessels sailing from Recôncavo towns, they could not completely prevent boatmen based in towns along the southern coast of Bahia from reaching the city. In October 1822 the governing board in Salvador noted that although many towns had formally proclaimed for Pedro, "nevertheless some of those towns have continued to send foodstuffs to this city, unlike what happens in the Recôncavo where commerce and communication are entirely intercepted." For their part the Brazilian side lamented that an officer in their own militia had been found to be in contact with Salvador, "to which he has recently dispatched a boat with foodstuffs." In late November the officer in charge of supplies for the Portuguese naval squadron reported that some food was still arriving in Salvador:

all the ports from the Rio da Prata [Uruguay] to Pernambuco are forbidden to allow vessels to leave for this port and, as a consequence, there will be a [complete] lack here of meal, dried meat, and other essential foodstuffs. This has not happened as yet not only because we were abundantly supplied earlier but also because in the last few days some smacks with these items have entered from Porto Seguro, Alcobaça, Caravelas, São Mateus, and even Rio Grande [do Sul], having left those ports with passports for Pernambuco or Rio de Janeiro, signing commitments, and posting bonds.[23]

Still, the insurgents proved successful in two ways. They organized an elaborate and efficient method for securing food supplies for themselves, both manioc meal and meat, without apparently alienating most food producers, despite recruiting many of them into the armed camp.[24] And just as important, they had cut off the bulk of the foodstuffs going to the Portuguese. By preventing almost all food from crossing the bay, and by greatly reducing the supply that boatmen could bring from along the coast, they had created great scarcity in the city.

HUNGER IN THE CITY

Madeira, the Portuguese commander in Salvador, no less than the insurgent captains, recognized the struggle over food as decisive. He faced a greater difficulty, however, because of his distance from Portugal, the only certain supply source for his army and the civilians they protected. It took an average of seven weeks for a one-way transatlantic crossing, although under unusual circumstances westbound ships could sail it in as few as four weeks.[25]

The threat to Salvador was evident. In April 1822, well before Cachoeira and its neighboring towns had declared their allegiance to Prince Pedro, Madeira predicted that the Rio de Janeiro government might send ships "to blockade this port to prevent the city from receiving foodstuffs that come from other parts of the province." Civilians also knew the danger. As one woman in Salvador wrote her husband a couple of days after Cachoeira had declared its allegiance to Pedro, "soon there will be neither manioc meal nor meat. God save us!"[26]

Anyone could see, as an official had earlier noted, that Itaparica Island was strategically located for controlling traffic from "the towns of Cachoeira, Maragogipe, [Santiago do] Iguape, and other places in this Recôncavo." At the end of July 1822, Madeira ordered an attack and landing at the far southern tip of the island facing the narrows. But the officer in charge of the offensive described how his men had been repulsed, despite their numerical superiority, by "the completely invisible enemy" who "attacked from all sides [while] we saw nothing but woods." His men faced "a volley so heavy and so accurate that it was impossible to try disembarking." A similar attempt in January 1823, with a much larger force, met with a similar defeat.[27]

By early October 1822 the civilian authorities in Salvador understood their desperate situation. The enemy had advanced to the outlying suburbs of the city, and the towns of the Recôncavo, Itaparica Island, and the immediate northern coast "remain separated from this capital." Sergipe, moreover, "from which this capital has received some cattle—which no longer comes from the interior—and even some corn and other items for the people's sustenance, is now unstable." For those in Lisbon they spelled it out: "If the great shipments of manioc meal from the [southerly] Porto Seguro area are intercepted, this city will suffer greatly, as it is already denied the meal that Nazaré once furnished."[28]

When a naval squadron with twelve ships arrived from Portugal at the end of October, Madeira and Portuguese civilians breathed more easily. The siege could now be broken. Squadron commander João Felix Pereira de Campos, however, was surprised to learn on his arrival that "all the peoples of the Bahian Recôncavo have declared themselves against our cause, limiting our possession to the city and port." Dismayed at the "urgent necessity for victuals in which we find ourselves, . . . given that we lack the succor of other provinces on which we counted," he took immediate measures to repair the situation and reported that he had posted two warships to the north and another to the south "in order . . . to make every coastal vessel carrying food from port to port come to this port." But his ships succeeded only minimally in this mission, perhaps because the boatmen transported so much of the food in shallow-draft vessels that hugged the coast, out of reach of the Portuguese warships. Still, in early December a spy in Salvador reported to a Brazilian officer that a frigate, cruising off the coast, had forced several smacks, including those headed for Pernambuco, to dock at the Salvador grains market "with manioc meal, rice, and beans."[29]

Critics heaped blame on Campos for the continuing dearth. The naval squadron had been in Bahia only five days when he received a petition with 655 signatures urging him to blockade the ports of Rio de Janeiro, Pernambuco, and Alagoas so that "all the products of various ports in those provinces—not being able to enter their capitals—will come to our market." And they issued a dark threat: "The lack of bread has been the origin of thousands of revolutions." Campos calmly replied that his primary task was to secure the city as a beachhead for other expeditions, and he could not abandon Salvador to blockade other ports. Citizens were sure they knew better—and perhaps they did. A city newspaper asked,

> Why not send a warship to Caravelas to punish half a dozen evil men there and allow poor producers of manioc to sell it and bring it

here? . . . And more: Can we not open communication with Nazaré with 800 sailors and soldiers? The enemy forces worth attention are all located between Pirajá and Feira [de Santana] and will disperse when they lack the foodstuffs [that come] from Nazaré and Maragogipe.

From the civilian point of view, however, Campos did nothing.[30]

By February 1823 the situation had worsened further. Campos bewailed the "privations resulting from the lack of victuals. . . . All foodstuffs are at a peak in cost and some are totally lacking, such as legumes and rice." The city's civilian provisional governing board also stressed the shortage of manioc meal, "that essential foodstuff for the sustenance of the people." Madeira declared that "the last places (Prado and São Mateus) from where some manioc meal still came, have been obliged to revolt," and "the lack and high price of victuals is every day more excessive. . . . The people already suffer. . . . They will not suffer less with the dearth of dried meat which for some time has not arrived." He may have been exaggerating, for a civilian complained that same month that "we have only salted food to eat (although there is plenty of this); what we lack is fresh meat and manioc meal."[31]

The arrival of reinforcements offered both a blessing and a curse for the Portuguese camp. Madeira kept insisting he needed more soldiers, and the Lisbon government sent them, but this only increased the need for food. In mid-July 1822 he had 1,600 men; by August, 2,400. At the end of October the naval squadron arrived with major army reinforcements, bringing the total number of soldiers and sailors in Salvador to 4,285, not counting Portuguese militiamen there already. By mid-February the regular army alone numbered 4,222. Some 2,000 more soldiers arrived in April 1823. Although alarmed by the arrival of Portuguese reinforcements, the insurgents recognized "this augments the number of consumers [in the city]."[32]

At the same time, the flight of urban residents to the hinterland continued, lessening the civilian demand for food in the city. Already by late August 1822, only one member of the city council remained in town, and when Madeira summoned the previous year's members, none turned up. The civil government authorities exclaimed that "the emigration of the locals to the Recôncavo has been extraordinary." Madeira reported in early 1823 that the personnel of "almost entire civilian government departments" had left. Still, some legal matters proceeded in the normal way. When the street vendor Ana de São José da Trindade died in March 1823, her will was opened, and the inventory of her goods carried out without evident deviation from the usual practice. As well, officials proceeded with a postmortem inventory of at least one large estate despite the war, excepting a property in Sergipe, left for later settlement because communication was cut off.[33]

The Brazilian military also faced difficulties and mounting discouragement. Labatut's troops, despite having turned back all Portuguese offensives, were several times themselves repulsed as they attempted to penetrate the city's defenses. Malaria and other diseases had spread among insurgent soldiers. In mid-April 1823 the Interim Provincial Council in Cachoeira acknowledged privately that "the outcome of the war is uncertain" and that supplies "whether monetary or of food" were running low. "We are at the same time the besiegers and the besieged."[34]

FINAL DAYS

Everyone recognized that if Salvador were to face a determined external blockade, the Portuguese could not hold out. Brazilian preparations for closing the port had been long underway. As soon as Pedro declared Brazil independent in September 1822, his chief minister began to form a Brazilian Navy and successfully recruited Thomas Cochrane, famous for daring naval exploits during Britain's war with Napoleon and now serving the Chilean navy to head the effort. He arrived in Rio de Janeiro in mid-March 1823 and set to work fashioning a workable naval force: equipping his ships, establishing rapport with the British officers who had come to Brazil to join the cause, and training his multilingual crews. By the beginning of May his small fleet was off the coast of Bahia near Salvador. Pedro's government made sure to dispatch supply ships to Cochrane's fleet loaded with ship's biscuits (hard tack), manioc meal, and vegetables and alerted the patriot forces in Bahia of Cochrane's arrival and of his fleet's need for food. The insurgent leaders put two sugar planters, experienced in managing people and goods, in charge of gathering "hogs, suckling pigs, sheep, hens, and young roosters" for the purpose, setting up a supply facility at the port of Valença.[35]

The outcome of the war now would depend on control of the Atlantic coast. After an inconclusive first encounter with the Portuguese

squadron, Cochrane determined to use his two fastest and most agile ships to blockade Salvador, avoiding a full-scale battle. He seized
some fifteen merchant vessels heading for the city, including at least
one from Portugal and a U.S. ship transporting rice and wheat flour.
By mid-June merchants in Salvador reported that six vessels "laden
with provisions," expected from Buenos Aires, had not arrived, nor
had ships from Europe, not to mention "some vessels from Maranhão
[and] six smacks that went to get manioc meal at southern ports," as
well as the "foreign ones that frequently come here." They assumed
Cochrane had seized them and knew for sure that he had captured a
brigantine "with rice, meal, and other foodstuffs."[36] With this news,
the steady flight of civilians from Salvador became a raging flood, an
"emigration that . . . already exceeds ten thousand people." They had
all left to escape "the hunger and misery that oppressed them."[37]

The Portuguese held on for as long as they did not only because
they had fewer mouths to feed, but also because, despite Cochrane's
presence, they were not yet completely cut off from food supplies.
The Portuguese government had not abandoned its squadron and
army and continued to send supplies, although irregularly and sometimes irrationally: evading Cochrane's blockade, one ship arrived
from Lisbon in early June with 161 large casks of wine, eight casks
of olive oil, 47 barrels of salted beef, 313 barrels of pork, 120 small
barrels of dried cod, 250 bags of beans, and 3,720 bushels of salt, but
without any "biscuits or flour which, besides being an essential food
[item], is the one for which we are experiencing the greatest lack,"
wrote the exasperated naval commander. The Lisbon government
also dispatched less eccentric cargoes, and Portuguese merchant
ships brought some foodstuff.[38] Presumably so did ships from northern Europe and North America, for captains of foreign ships knew
that if they eluded Cochrane's vigilance, they could get good prices
for the food they transported.

The crucial point, however, is that some boats from Brazilian ports
along the Atlantic coast, attracted by high prices, continued to evade
the embargo imposed by Cochrane in early May 1823 and were able to
bring manioc meal and other foodstuffs to Salvador. A large shipment
of dried meat arrived from Rio Grande do Sul on May 27, and the city
council referred in early June to "the smacks with meal recently arrived." Until mid-June 1823 one captain of a smack, forty-nine years
old, along with its owner, thirty-one, both born in Portugal, traveled
in and out of Salvador to a port in Sergipe, with occasional trips south
even to São Mateus, a port long believed to have been completely

dominated by the patriot side. Whether the smack returned with food is not stated, but seems almost certain, given that these destinations were among the normal supply points for Salvador, and other motives for their trips are unlikely. Portuguese authorities, writing as late as June 10, reported their spirits lifted "and hope revived by the successive arrival of various vessels laden with manioc meal and other foodstuffs." One of these smacks alone carried 3,000 bushels. As one of the Brazilians in charge of the war effort subsequently noted matter-of-factly, "There were repeated accusations regarding the introduction of victuals into the besieged city."[39] The siege had not provoked a famine, and the city's residents did not have to eat rats.

The intensifying crisis over food nevertheless stirred sharp dissension among leaders in the Portuguese camp. With an enemy fleet offshore, Madeira felt justified in declaring martial law on May 9, ending all pretense at liberalism. He deposed the elected provisional governing board and the existing city council, and installed new bodies in their place made up entirely of Portuguese merchants.[40] But then Madeira and naval commander Campos had a falling out over the course to follow, with each accusing the other of needless inaction. Madeira exclaimed, "What a disgrace that we are now blockaded, having a squadron larger than that of our enemies!" Over 229 petitioners charged Campos with cowardice,

for he watches in cold blood as armed canoes capture vessels full of manioc meal, the principal food of the people, right within this port, he creates difficulties and hampers the departure of other vessels who try to get foodstuffs wherever they can be got, and, rather than encouraging them or better yet protecting them, he tries to dissuade them, emphatically asking them 'Where do you think you are going? You won't make it in time. Etc.' So it is the chief himself who has blockaded us within this port.

But when Madeira attempted to depose Campos, the naval officers backed Campos and refused to sail without him.[41]

Disagreements fostered confusion at all levels of government. Even the city council, newly appointed by Madeira, found its traditional authority over the food supply seriously eroded precisely because of him. The council complained about the

confusion and disorder at the public grains market: . . . The administrator and scribe do not take orders from this Council, . . . only obeying [the new provisional governing board] and the military governor. The Naval Supply Officer also gives orders there. The Army quartermaster does as he pleases when he pleases in removing manioc meal, to the detriment of the people. And on these occasions sacks go missing in the hands of monopolists."[42]

Lines of authority blurred, and the city council could no longer demonstrate its care for the people.

As evacuation became ever more likely, provisions for a lengthy overseas voyage had to be laid in and belts tightened still further. Soldiers and sailors went on half rations. When Campos warned that he could not battle Cochrane because civil authorities had not supplied the necessary food, even the new governing board replied defiantly: "this board does not have the ability to perform miracles in order to find food within a blockaded and besieged military stronghold." Madeira later explained that "the lack of food had reached the ultimate extremity; the troops were suffering much; the foodstuffs we had in our deposits were barely enough to sustain [us] on a long trip." Finally, with their soldiers and sailors already on half rations, and local loyalties wavering as civilians competed with the military for depleted food stores, Madeira and Campos, with few objections from their officers, set the departure date for July 1, recognizing that every day's delay meant less food for the voyage. Pulling out became the urgent task.[43]

The day of departure must have been one of furious activity and inevitable disorder. Ninety vessels sailed out of the bay in the early morning of July 2, including forty-five warships and transports of various sizes, including thirteen men-of-war, with some 5,504 troops. Traveling with the fleet went merchant ships carrying civilians: 133 civil servants and businessmen with their families and servants, and the officers' families. Supplies soon ran short.[44] In their haste and confusion they left behind an essential fifty barrels of ship's biscuit, twenty-eight of wheat flour, one of manioc meal, and more than thirty oxen brought by boat from the southern coast of the province. Some departing vessels had only two-thirds rations and others only half, and no special food for the sick. Cochrane, who captured several merchant vessels and turned them back to Salvador, could crow, "We have starved the enemy out of Bahia."[45]

Victorious Brazilian patriots entered the city on the heels of the Portuguese departure, and by noon they had raised their flags on the city's principal towers. The supply lines for troops already stationed just outside the city, numbering 9,515 men—including Labatut's army and the militiamen—were stretched just a bit farther to come up with food for these arriving soldiers. The patriot commissariat based in Cachoeira had, since its creation at the beginning of October 1822, purchased 11,647 head of cattle, 42,652 bushels of manioc meal, 934 bushels of beans, 1,418 bushels of rice, 2,475 bushels of corn, 2,352 pounds of bacon, and "many" chickens to be distributed to the troops at various garrisons. Its efficiency proved decisive.[46]

Civilians returned to the city they had fled during the war. Street vendors, slaughtermen, and butchers once again had work to do in the city. Captains and crews arrived with manioc meal, rice, corn, and beans to be unloaded at the grains market by stevedores, slave and free. The huge disruptions in the region still limited arrivals, and the market's supply of manioc meal during all of 1823, despite the market's resumption of operations in July, amounted to only 35 percent of the average amount for the three years before the war. Three weeks after entering the city, the newly reinstalled authorities took measures to prevent a monopolization of the meat trade, signaling the return of a normal cattle supply to the slaughterhouse. Store owners who returned to Salvador found their stocks of food, wine, and olive oil sacked. They had to start anew, under a radically altered political regime.[47]

The victory in Salvador assured Brazilian independence, formally concluded by treaty with Portugal in 1825. Both sides came to understand anew the crucial truth that armies march on their stomachs. Cochrane has justly been credited for completing the circle in May 1823. More important, however, was the insurgents' success in drastically diminishing the city's food supply during those many months, starting in July 1822. This is not to minimize other aspects of the struggle. Because Madeira failed to concentrate his forces to secure Itaparica Island right at the beginning, he could not command the waterborne traffic in the Recôncavo. By engaging the Portuguese in several battles, the Brazilian armed forces prevented them from making serious gains on the ground. But the siege of Salvador proved the key to victory. The war had centered on food.

CHAPTER 9

A TREMOR IN THE SOCIAL ORDER

THE INDEPENDENCE WAR IN BAHIA sent shocks along the fault lines of Salvador's society, causing undeniable upheaval. Had it continued for years, the result might well have been a radically reshaped social order, but it lasted long enough for underlying tensions to surface. No one could fail to notice the precarious position of those at the top. Authority no longer remained openly unquestioned, and those with wealth and political power proved unable to fulfill their paternalistic role. Working people took on unprecedented roles. Slaves glimpsed possible freedom, and certainly gained leverage. The war ended before the old ways collapsed, but its effects were deeply felt. Victory depended not on generals or viscounts, but on common people—especially on the boatmen who had always transported manioc meal to Salvador and on the choices they now made. Although the consequences were international and broad, the dispute was intensely local and particular, depending on the actions of people too often overlooked in previous accounts.

DISRUPTION

The sheer weight of physical dislocation and the general upset of war led to altered perceptions of others and oneself. No one escaped the war's disturbance. Those involved in the food trade were the most directly engaged in the siege and can be considered here, group by group. Most large Portuguese merchants of Salvador had an ambivalent relationship with officer Madeira, torn between their business interests and loyalty toward the Crown. They supported Madeira's initial effort to defeat the Brazilians and enthusiastically welcomed the idea of reimposing a monopoly of colonial trade in their hands.

At the beginning of the struggle they provided abundant foodstuffs to the Portuguese troops. Even near the end, and on the same day Madeira declared martial law in May 1823, thirty-three merchants, all of them Portuguese, gathered to advise him on raising funds, replacing the previous treasury office. Seven of them were among the twenty largest import merchants in Salvador as measured by their customs payments. Six more were major slave traders, and one other expected a brigantine to arrive from Mozambique at that very time. Another supplied 762 pounds of sugar to the Santa Casa de Misericórdia in one month during 1821. Two others had direct connections to the internal food business: one owned two smacks and a number of slave sailors and had earlier lent money to manioc farmers in Nazaré. Another owned a large boat and lent money to a female street vendor. I assume the remaining seventeen were of the same general sort.[1]

Yet Madeira expressed disappointment regarding the efficacy of this body and the loyalty of Portuguese merchants and store owners, later complaining that "the greater part" of the Portuguese-born had "nothing more in sight than their private interests." Scores had left for Portugal long before the final evacuation of the city by the troops in 1823. A local biweekly paper reported in late 1822 that "capitalists have sent much money to Lisbon. With departing ships go many emigrants whose lack is felt and whose wealth is taken out of commerce." On one ship alone had gone 270 *contos* in cash, nearly seven times the entire estate of Ana de São José da Trindade. But other Portuguese merchants, said a navy man—creditors of people in the hinterland or with "other ties that bind them to the land," perhaps concubines and children—"resolved to follow the fate of the province come what may." These hunkered down and waited.[2]

Joaquim José de Oliveira portrays the ambivalence felt by those at the peak of the Portuguese merchant community. Born in Portugal, he was among the thirty-three individuals summoned by Madeira to oversee fundraising for the cause, but when Madeira left Brazil, he stayed behind. What were his interests? Four years earlier he had taken out a license for his boat and owned seven sailor-slaves when he died in 1831, indicating his probable involvement in the food trade. He owned an enormous list of properties, among them a *casa nobre*, or virtual palace, in which he lived. Besides his coastwise shipping business, he was a builder, constructing a series of identical houses all lined up near his own mansion. His slaves included two quarrymen, four stonemasons, and three carpenters. He lent money to both Brazilians and Portuguese. His Brazilian debtors alone owed him twice as much as the entire value of Ana de São José da Trindade's property. The records on the value of his real estate have not survived. He had no children, and he freed all his slaves at his death, thirty-five men and nine women, along with their children. But he was not a generous man. He had married a woman in Salvador in 1812 who had signed a prenuptial contract calling for the separation of their goods. In his will he stressed that she had "brought nothing whatsoever into this consortium," and although he named her as executrix of his estate, she received, aside from a bit of cash, property only in usufruct. In 1823, despite his service to Madeira, he preferred to shift his loyalty to the new nation. Brazilian authorities understood they could not blame him for Madeira's actions.[3]

Some merchants saw the war as a chance for immediate advantage. Store owners and traders at the public grains market, although reduced in number because of scarcity, found new opportunities for great profit. Naval commander Campos became furious when he discovered at the end of January 1823 that a North American ship carrying a cargo of beans was preparing to leave Salvador, having found no buyers, and that other American ships planned to do the same: "[Local] dealers in these items, facing the high price at which, they say, this cargo has been offered, fear that later on there will be competition and the price will fall. For dread of the loss they would then face, they refuse to buy. They do not feel—indeed they are indifferent to—the calamity to come from a general famine and perhaps even imagine the advantageous profits to be made once the goods they hoard reach an infinitely high price."[4]

When Cochrane appeared offshore in May, the problem became much worse. City councilmen, hand-picked by Madeira, accused merchants of "scandalous abuse" in buying large "portions of manioc meal, beans, rice, and corn in order to resell them to the people, resulting in the absolute absence of these items from the public grains market while they hold them secretly in their places of business." The council decreed that these items could not be sold in quantity "on the public streets or at the doors of [business] houses," but only in small portions and even then only by licensed persons, although the licenses would be issued "gratis." Those who stocked in larger quantities in their houses or businesses had three days to bring them to the grains market. The councillors invited "citizens to denounce these middlemen in order to terminate such abuses" but, to their chagrin, found that "denouncers had entered the houses of citizens, seizing foodstuffs without legal authorization." The council belatedly explained that those having knowledge of hoarding should first come before it to fulfill the proper requirements, before any confiscation could be ordered. The situation demanded bold action. When a ship arrived from Portugal with "some foodstuffs," Madeira immediately placed sentries aboard it "so the food does not go astray privately."[5]

Less prosperous participants in the food trade, along with the bulk of the city's population, suffered great physical dislocation. If no civilian oarsmen, stevedores, and sailors, if no Navy Yard workers could be found in the city, where had they gone, and with whom did they go? Although the sources refer to the departure of people of some means, that great segment of the population engaged in petty trade, especially those in the business of retailing food, had also left the city, many of them on foot, heading for interior towns. During the night of May 16, shortly after the imposition of martial law, a Brazilian store owner, himself the son of a Portuguese man who owned two grocery stores, found his way, accompanied by more than twenty others probably of the same middling sort as he, through the reefs toward the south of the port "with water up to my navel," reaching the peninsula's point and then walking north along the Atlantic-side beach to reach the insurgent outpost in Rio Vermelho. This outpost was commanded, he said, by "a black man of much courage and daring," suggesting his own new patriotism. It's clear he did not secure the papers that would normally have been required when moving to a new place to establish residence. The civilian governing board expressed shock that even those who might have had money to lend to the Portuguese forces had left the city "without passports."[6] Certainly, during the war, few people any longer obeyed the regulations of the grain or meat trade. Individuals instead turned their houses into granaries or butcher shops whenever they managed to secure some quantity of manioc meal or a cow.[7] We may imagine that many of those who fled the city, perhaps most of the whites, had relatives, friends, or business contacts in the interior, even if distant ones, on whom they could impose no matter how crowded the quarters. Regardless of color, those with skills, such as blacksmiths, stonemasons, bakers, or barbers, could surely find employment among other émigrés.

The clerks at stores with no food to sell, the slaughtermen and butchers who had nothing to slaughter or hang up for sale at their doors, and most of the workers at the public grains market which had only a few bags of manioc meal to load, unload, and measure out—all these unemployed food-trade workers must have seen at some point that the Portuguese army was doomed to fail. If they remained in the city, they faced hunger, perhaps even starvation. Since Portuguese soldiers and sailors, and even officers, had deserted to the patriot camp, why should civilians stay behind?[8] They probably acted not out of ideology or patriotism, but from a rational choice to avoid hunger. To be sure, the able-bodied men among them would likely have been recruited into the insurrectionary army—there is no word that the Portuguese wanted potentially disloyal Brazilians in *their* ranks—but I suspect the choice was clear nevertheless. Anyone who left the city would eat, and, after all, outright military encounters had proven relatively rare.

The question of the street vendors is more problematic. Insofar as they sold fruits and vegetables produced in backyard gardens and semirural bottomlands near the city, they would still have had something to sell, but what could they have bought? Without manioc meal or meat to eat, they surely chose to exit well before Cochrane's blockade. For all these people it must have been both a disruptive and an instructive period, even if understood as temporary; it altered not only their relationships to each other but their notions of how the world works and how power is exercised.

What about slaves? Their fate can be distinguished according to both their relationship with their owner and the type of owner. The self-hired ones, many of whom were street vendors and porters, were in the same category as the free and freed, making their own decisions on whether to leave or stay, just as they chose where to live and what to do daily. Slaves belonging to a Portuguese master preparing to leave for Lisbon would probably have been sold early on, or, failing that, their owner would have lumped their loss together with that of his other property and abandoned them—that is, freeing them to find their way out of the city. If this hypothetical Portuguese slave owner, like Joaquim José de Oliveira, expected to stay on to the bitter end and remain in Brazil after Madeira's army had left, then he would likely have tried to preserve his property as much as possible, feeding his slaves as best he could. As for Brazilian owners, they would probably have taken their enslaved domestics or skilled workers with them to the Recôncavo, although the unsettled conditions might have encouraged slaves to flee during such a trek. One master instructed his slave to meet him at a designated place in the interior. Instead, the slave joined the ranks of the Brazilian Army. It is doubtful that there is any validity to the report by a British visitor that slaves were left "dying on the street" or locked up to die in town houses.[9]

One group did suffer egregious harm. As had long been the case, and despite the war, urban slaves and free blacks occasionally gathered in secluded wooded areas around the city. The major purpose of their gatherings might have been religious or merely to have the opportunity to meet and enjoy the company of others and to prepare their own food entirely in their own way.[10] Two such gatherings took place in November 1822: one near the high point of Pirajá, about five miles north of the center of the city, and the other near Itapoã, about ten miles northeast. According to General Labatut, these men and women, armed with bows-and-arrows and machetes and carrying flags, attacked the Brazilian forces at Pirajá, supposedly acting at the command of Madeira. Just a few days earlier Madeira's own battle-hardened army of 2,000 veterans had been defeated in an attack on Pirajá, so if these runaways really acted at his command, he can only have meant it as a suicide mission, perhaps designed to eliminate them from his territory. But I have found no document from the Portuguese side acknowledging any participation or even knowledge of this event. Given Madeira's low view of slaves and blacks in general, it seems unlikely that the stimulus came from him. In March 1822 he expressed alarm at the rumor spread among the slaves that the Cortes had decreed the end of slavery. He feared this would make Brazil another Haiti. In July he bemoaned the "insane" actions of the insurgent leaders in "arming blacks and mulattos." More likely, the slaves had simply armed themselves as protection against any possible police raid, and the newly arrived General Labatut, a Frenchman, misunderstood their purpose. Labatut's men captured fifty-one of the men and twenty of the women. He ordered the men executed, and the women whipped, justifying such harsh action by noting that it would prevent other slaves from enlisting under the Portuguese flag, for such "hordes united with our Portuguese enemies would be able to sustain a long war." Slave holders on the Brazilian side took a different view and condemned his action of "barbarously mowing down 52 [sic] blacks." They may have been disturbed by his barbarity, but no doubt they were also worried about such a loss of property. Whether the women in this group were street vendors in the city cannot be known, but is quite possible.[11]

CRACKS IN THE PYRAMID

The disruption of war and escalating racial tensions contributed to weakening the commonplace assumption that some were entitled, even destined, to rule, and threw into question older notions about slavery and freedom. The change could be seen even at the top. Revolutionary forces in Portugal had dared to challenge the absolute rule of the hereditary king. Even though João VI had appointed Pedro as Regent of Brazil, João subsequently signed the order issued by the Cortes demanding Pedro's return to Portugal; the son then disobeyed the father. As a contemporary noted, Pedro had moved "against Divine Right by not obeying the King, against Natural Law by not submitting to the wishes of his father, and against the Law of Nations by acting against the interests of the Portuguese Crown."[12] Planters in the Recôncavo then chose to side with the prince, ignoring orders from the Crown and becoming complicit in Pedro's crime. Army and militia had split along lines of national origin and ignored military discipline. The Brazilians committed what amounted to treason.

The threat of hunger made subversion ever more acceptable. When Madeira declared martial law in early May 1823, he noted, as justification, the "propagation of incendiary papers" and "open talk" tending toward "undermining public peace." His puppet city council echoed his view, saying that his action had been necessary not only because of the enemy's interception of all food, leaving the city in a "pitiful state," but also because "the scarcity . . . had stimulated some people of turbulent spirit to post inflammatory manuscript hand-bills on three successive days against those authorities and against the military commander." Madeira set up military courts to judge those who threatened his government, but his actions do not seem to have made much difference. Three weeks later he acknowledged that, although there had been a republican faction in the city for a long time, "this party could make no progress" as long as the people were satisfied and "the troops were regularly paid." With changed circumstances, "this party has taken advantage of the moment to provoke disorder." He later explained his decision to abandon Salvador by pointing to the "giant steps taken by sedition through various means." The principle of authority had been frontally challenged.[13]

One challenge came specifically from blacks and mulattos. Their militias played a prominent part among those who left the city in February 1822. It was the black Henriques who first occupied Pirajá in July, cutting off Salvador from its supply of cattle. Henriques in the siege eventually numbered 1,100. Other men of color formed the bulk of rural militiamen and army enlisted men arrayed against the Portuguese. Their common experience of armed service away from home must have changed them. Moving from a familiar to an unfamiliar world widened their perspective, challenged their usual expectations, and altered how they saw themselves and others. Some rose to become leaders, and the circle of personal connections expanded for all of them. Frequent revolts of men in the armed forces punctuated the immediate postwar period, something unheard of before 1822. In 1824 an army unit heavily made up of black and mulatto soldiers mutinied when ordered to another province. The war brought to the surface currents that earlier had remained submerged, now roiling society. Privileged whites now felt increasingly uneasy as the ethos that had protected them wore thin.[14]

The slave system itself suffered blows. Some slaves escaped their masters by joining military units whose commanders, like others before them, asked few questions, glad to have additional men under their command. One irate owner sought permission from the insurgent government to seize his Brazilian-born slave—"very black with an earring in one ear, large eyes, round face, good legs and feet"—who, "like many slaves, fled to join the Army." João Angola, whose name says he was African, joined up with a Brazilian unit that was later sent to Rio de Janeiro, where, according to rumor, João became the personal servant to one of its officers. Plácido da Silva, once a slave in Salvador, perhaps engaged in the food trade, served under Labatut and eventually formally secured his freedom from the government in Rio de Janeiro, along with others in similar circumstances—the government having compensated their former masters.[15]

As slaves became more overtly recalcitrant, slave owners warned of revolt. Some measure of their sense of lessening control is the effort undertaken by the revolutionary government, just five weeks after its victory, ordering all officials to search out runaway slaves and all landowners to verify that none hid on their properties. The order's preamble asserted that it acted to "prevent the grave damages that result both to private persons and to all the Province generally from the dispersion of slaves who wander away from their masters in the villages, woods, and [other] places of the Recôncavo." Many of these now-former slaves probably came from the city, the location most disturbed by the war, where so many of them had once worked the food trade. In 1825 a newspaper article complained about the proliferation of maroon communities around the city. Ostensibly, the effort to re-impose authority worked, but it is clear from the subsequent record of revolts and insubordination that the slave system would never again be as firmly in place in Bahia as it had been in colonial times. Slavery nevertheless persisted in Brazil for another sixty-five years, in contrast with those slave-owning areas of Spanish America where the slave system was much more significantly undermined by the widespread independence wars that lasted for many years on end.[16]

BOAT CAPTAINS AND SAILOR SLAVES

The shredding effects of the war are further revealed in the choices made by a pivotal group that included captains and crews, including slaves, who sailed canoes, smacks, and other boats in Bahia. Their numbers roughly measure their importance. Of some 8,513 crewmen in 1856, nearly three-quarters were black or mulatto, and roughly a quarter were slaves (see Table 9.1). The success of the siege depended on men like these, and on their cooperation with the Brazilian forces. Because they were so vital in provisioning the city, they faced choices with profound ramifications. What did they decide?

Those who sailed within the bay to supply Brazilian forces confronted dangerous challenges posed by the Portuguese. A Brazilian commander reported in mid-November 1822 that for the previous three days "various gunboats and among them the big one" had been cruising off the mouths of the Paraguaçu and Jaguaripe rivers at the northern and southern tips of Itaparica Island, "chasing the boats that sail there, which have made them flee. [The gunboats] cannot have another purpose but to cut off the transport of manioc meal to the Army." Another officer noted the Portuguese tactic "is causing us much damage by the lack of manioc meal which we are feeling." In early December two Portuguese vessels attacked a boat loaded with manioc meal, and its captain, rather than let the enemy have the food, courageously loosened a board below deck and sank it, winning much praise (how he or his crew lived to tell is not explained). As late as mid-June 1823 the Portuguese "posted small boats at the various channels of our inland sea, cutting off communication between villages and the transport of food to the Army."[17]

It is startling how many boats outside the bay, along the Atlantic coast, avoided Salvador, obeying the revolutionaries. Those who crewed such boats gave up a highly lucrative market in besieged Salvador to supply food to the impoverished insurgents. Yes, a trickle of food reached the city, enabling the Portuguese to stay as long as they did. "Smacks with manioc meal" still arrived in Salvador until the end, despite the insurgents' prohibitions, and it is about these that we have the most records.[18] But contemporaries knew that the manioc meal of the region principally fed Brazilian armed forces, not the Portuguese.

The revolutionary government in Cachoeira attempted to end the traffic altogether by imposing a requirement that captains of every boat leaving a food-supplying town carry an official document indicating the boat's cargo and supposed destination, and to return with the same document countersigned by the authorities at the receiving port. The rebel leaders, faced in March 1823 with the reality of ongoing evasions of their previous orders, decided to issue new and more stringent regulations regarding trade. The new rules were clear enough: "Henceforth no one may deal in victuals of any sort within the province without a license and passport issued by this Council, which will be valid for two months." A few days later they elaborated, saying that those transporting foodstuffs by boat would have to secure from a local judge a manifest declaring not only the shipment's origin and destination, but also "the name of the vessel, its captain, and all persons aboard and, lastly, the victuals transported with their quantity and quality," presenting upon return a proof of having fulfilled the shipment's declared purpose. These measures provoked such confusion and outcry that the council found itself forced to admit that its previous orders "have not been completely understood." Those regulations had not been intended to restrict anyone from buying "manioc meal, corn, and rice in small quantities for their own use," but only from buying large amounts, they said. Judges should determine an appropriate ration "in relation to the size of each person's family." Nor was anyone to buy chickens, hogs, or other animals "for trade"; the council did not specify their number because, for these items, "it is easy to judge if [the purchase] is or is not for trade." Soon the council recognized that it had still not retreated far enough: "Experience having shown that the orders . . . have not led to the desired goals," it revoked many of them, so that buyers of victuals could consume them and "trade them without . . . licenses . . . or passports," although boatmen would still need to carry a document "specifying the exact quantity of the purchased victuals that they wish to transport," returning with a signed declaration that the load had been sold at the designated destination.[19] These documents probably resembled

Table 9.1. Race and Legal Status of Crews at Salvador by Type of Vessel, 1856 (Number and Percentage)

| | Bay and Coastal Vessels | | | | | | | | | |
| | Canoes | | Boats | | Lighters | | Oceangoing Vessels | | Totals | |
Race	No.	%	No.	%	No.	%	No.	%	No.	%
Blacks										
Free	701	19.6	111	17.7	804	22.6	84	11.2	1,700	20.0
Slave	750	21.0	106	16.9	1,035	29.1	165	22.0	2,056	24.2
Total Blacks	1,451	40.6	217	34.7	1,839	51.7	249	33.2	3,756	44.1
Mulattos										
Free	939	26.2	147	23.5	1,139	32.0	110	14.7	2,335	27.4
Slave	30	0.8	11	1.8	38	1.1	3	0.4	82	1.0
Total Mulattos	969	27.1	158	25.2	1,177	33.1	113	15.1	2,417	28.4
Indians										
Free	48	1.3	74	11.8	0	0.0	20	2.7	142	1.7
Slave	0	0.0	0	0.0	0	0.0	0	0.0	0	0.0
Total Indians	48	1.3	74	11.8	0	0.0	20	2.7	142	1.7

Subtotals	2,468	69.0	449	71.7	3,016	84.7	382	50.9	6,315	
Whites										
Free	1,110	31.0	177	28.3	543	15.3	368	49.1	2,198	25.8
Slave	0	0.0	0	0.0	0	0.0	0	0.0	0	0.0
Total Whites	1,110	31.0	177	28.3	543	15.3	368	49.1	2,198	25.8
Total	3,578	100.0	626	100.0	3,559	100.0	750	100.0	8,513	100.0
Legal Status										
Free	2,798	78.2	509	81.3	2,486	69.9	582	77.6	6,375	74.9
Slave	780	21.8	117	18.7	1,073	30.1	168	22.4	2,138	25.1
Total	3,578	100.0	626	100.0	3,559	100.0	750	100.0	8,513	100.0

Source: Capitania dos Portos da Bahia, Mapa demonstrativo das embarcações nacionais de navegação de longo curso e cabotagem bem como do tráfico dos portos . . . e dos indivíduos que n'elles trabalhão ou se empregão, 31 de dezembro de 1855, in Diogo Tavares (Chefe da Capitania do Porto) para José Maria da Silva Paranhos (Ministro dos Negócios da Marinha), Salvador, 20 de fevereiro de 1857, Arquivo Nacional, Rio de Janeiro, SPE, XM-183.

the "passport" issued in São Francisco do Conde in the Recôncavo to a man born in Portugal but who had lived for eighteen years "in this vast and pleasant Empire of Brazil" and swore allegiance to it. Sailing within the bay, he went to Nazaré, he said, referring to himself in the third person, "with his boat called 'Brasileira' . . . to buy manioc meal and foodstuffs" for delivery to the revolutionary forces. But having arrived in Nazaré "shielded by his passport," he was nevertheless jailed. He secured his freedom only after the authorities in Nazaré checked with the captain who had issued the document and verified the truth of his statements. This particular "passport" consisted of an inch-wide strip of paper with the man's name, that of his boat, and the purpose of his trip.[20]

Why did some captains sail to Salvador while most did not? The factors that encouraged most to side with the insurgents is a crucial point for understanding the war. But, first, how did some manage to trade with the besieged city? The system attempted by the Brazilian authorities of issuing passports and having them countersigned at receiving points counted on the honesty, good will, and political loyalty of local authorities. This became especially complicated if these officers were divided in their opinion. In Itacaré, following common practice, the two local justices (*juizes ordinários*) took turns each month. During September 1822 the judge granted licenses for "boats laden with manioc meal to sail to the city," and did so until the very last day of the month. The judge who took over on October 1 not only "forbade the departure of two boats with the same cargo and same destination [but also] began to jail all those captains who had gone to sell meal in the City after 25 August, the day of [Pedro's] acclamation [here]." The person who reported these events concluded that "these said boat captains . . . are not guilty, the guilty one is that judge . . . who issued the authorizations."[21]

A boatman might forge the required countersignature, and rebel forces were alert to that possibility. Manoel de Aguiar Silva, a Portuguese who lived in Cairu, was identified as being "contrary to our cause." He "left for Bahia [city] with his boat before the glorious day of Acclamation of His Highness," but returned with a document signed by the sergeant-major in command of Pirajuía (a rebel settlement on the shore just across from the western side of Itaparica Island), purporting to establish that he had turned over all his cargo at that insurgent place. He was stopped at the fort on São Paulo Hill and sent to Valença to have his papers evaluated. But "the signature of that sergeant-major is not recognized here and, therefore, [its validity] remains in doubt." Manoel remained under house arrest until it could be verified. Forgery was likely. When the Portuguese authorities in Salvador asked the city council of far-southern São Mateus to "promote the export of manioc meal to this city where those who bring it will not only find high prices but all the protection they need," what protections could they offer? Surely help with forging a signature would be one of them.[22]

A boat captain could persuade an official to certify falsely that the load had been properly delivered, making the manifest appear perfectly legal when he returned to his home port for another load. Captains might unload part of their cargo in Salvador either before or after stopping at a port on the patriot side and obtaining the necessary signature. To secure this help, a captain might call upon ties of friendship or family—or he might offer a share of the profit. Although the Portuguese in Salvador announced publicly that those who brought manioc meal to Salvador would find "high prices," they complained among themselves that the cost of foodstuff in the city had reached an "exorbitant" level. This meant hefty sums for those who dared supply it, and substantial bribes to those who facilitated it. That is why the Portuguese could say, referring to ports on the southern coast of Bahia, that "some of those towns have continued to send us foodstuffs."[23]

Despite these powerful incentives, supplying the Portuguese proved more the exception than the rule for boat people in the region. The fact that some vessels were hidden, and the Interim Provincial Council in Cachoeira had to order them seized "along with their respective crews of captains and sailors," only means that most did not need to be taken by force.[24] Many owners, probably most—whether from calculation for the future, patriotic feeling, or fear that they would be caught—decided to take the Brazilian side and volunteered their boats. Ignoring the temptation to make an enormous sum of money, most boat people cooperated with the insurgents, denying food to the Portuguese and eventually forcing their withdrawal. If they had done the opposite, the war might have had a very different outcome. Instead, the majority of boat captains and their crews preferred to supply the Brazilians. Their support turned the war into a Brazilian victory.

Slaves also played a part. Captains who considered helping the Portuguese must have weighed the advantages versus the risks, as would any businessman. What was the risk of being caught by the Brazilian officials and having their boat and slaves sequestered? In weighing the danger of being exposed, a major factor was the size and nature of the crew. The more numerous and less reliable they were, the more likely a boat violating the Brazilian-imposed embargo would be denounced to the insurgent authorities. A canoe that could be manned by one person, or maybe two, could easily get away with it. But for a larger boat to trade successfully with Salvador from any Atlantic coast town required that several people on board participate in the subterfuge, a complication that could escalate still further for anyone in charge of a larger craft, say a smack. Slaves aboard consequently gained bargaining power if the captain traded with the enemy. Could they be counted on to keep their mouths shut?

Slave sailors were surely aware not only of the general instability of the times but of circumstances specifically affecting them. General Labatut sought to form a battalion of former slaves, freed by planters for the sake of the cause, and had ventured the idea of actively persuading masters to free their slaves so they could serve on the Brazilian side. He had done this publicly, stirring rumors among slaves that those who volunteered would be freed—they "speak of nothing else."[25] They could expect to be warmly welcomed in the rebel army. Labatut had even confiscated slaves from Portuguese landowners and enlisted them in his army with the implied promise of eventual freedom. Any owner of a vessel found trading with Salvador would surely have had his vessel seized for service on the insurgent side, as happened with the "Portuguese man, an enemy of Brazil," whose boat was taken along with "three black slave sailors."[26] Such a move left his sailor-slaves in an ambiguous position, for who was their legal master now? They could logically conclude that they were closer to freedom. So as they sailed to and from Salvador, did it not occur to them to throw a spanner in the works? Or did not the captain fear as much? Slaves may well have influenced a captain's decision to side with the Brazilians.

The Portuguese allegedly offered freedom to the slaves who sailed their patrol boats. It is important to distinguish here between what Brazilian masters feared from what actually happened. War disrupted everything, creating a widespread panic among the propertied. A sugar planter believed the Portuguese would "foment an African" uprising, enlarge their forces with "slaves whose freedom they will proclaim," and "go through the land destroying properties, . . . stealing what they find, taking possession of foodstuffs." Authorities in Nazaré alleged that Portuguese-born food merchants there were spreading the rumor among slaves that when the Portuguese forces landed in the district, they would free those slaves who helped them. "The slaves show signs of desiring such a perfidious outcome by their zeal in asking for political news." These reports tell us as much about the mental state of masters as about that of slaves, and very little about the Portuguese. I have not found any records from the Portuguese side to confirm this allegation, but the patriots in Nazaré firmly believed that Madeira had staffed his "boats with slaves, arming a large portion of them, freeing them or promising them freedom."[27] Of course, he used slave sailors, for slaves accounted for a quarter or more of all crews that docked in Salvador.

If, in fact, they were freed or promised freedom, or if whites believed this to be the case, the slaves on the Brazilian side would have had considerable clout to affect events, even if only by an implied threat to join the enemy. It could no longer be taken for granted that slaves would obey their masters. Even before the war began, the French consul had reported that "ideas of liberty continue to ferment among slaves"; although they "do not yet ask for freedom," they act "with independence."[28]

The war had a powerfully disruptive effect on the entire society of Salvador. Large merchants engaged in the import trade at first supported the Portuguese cause, but some of them later had second thoughts. Store owners fled to the interior in search of sustenance. Street vendors, butchers, and bakers surely followed. Some slaves did the same, even joining the Brazilian army, while still others gathered in maroon communities. The "people of the sea," so central to Salvador's food supply system, had to make difficult choices, deciding whether to obey the insurgents or make a killing in the city. Everyone became more fervently aware of an identity linked to their place of birth. Race became more intensely felt, as whites feared blacks in general and slaves in particular—even as they relied on them in the armed forces. The old certainties about social place wavered, and so did the paternalistic ethos that had held this society of ranks together. People of modest means, even slaves, understood the power they exercised at this defining moment, acting to defeat the Portuguese and making a major, and until now unrecognized, contribution to the transition from colony to independent nation.

CHAPTER 10

MEAT, MANIOC, AND ADAM SMITH

BEYOND THE DAY-TO-DAY BEHAVIOR OF those engaged in the food trade, and beyond the devastating and specific impact on them of a many-months-long war, there are questions about the government's role in regulating the economy, about ideology, and about notions of justice and equity that directly affected those traders and the wider consuming public. As merchants and political leaders argued about rules for supplying essential provisions, their debates, both before and after the war, exposed differing views on the nature of a good society, on ethical behavior, and on the appropriate role of government. Having begun this book by concentrating on the traders, here I broaden the reach of my concern to encompass the polity.

By the end of the eighteenth century a number of Salvadoreans were questioning the validity of inherited paternalist values as they applied to the role of government. Up to that point the king had been seen as the ultimate protector of the public from rapacious middlemen, and governors and city councilmen were understood as his deputies in this task. Gradually some turned to a new liberal philosophy, one that urged government authorities to refrain from setting restrictions on self-reliant individuals in their business transactions, leaving consumers to fend for themselves. This ideological shift occurred by fits and starts. The novel paradigm at first attracted only intellectuals and a few bureaucrats schooled in political economy. But eventually city councilmen—abetted by the demands of cattle dealers, grocers, boatmen, and other merchants large and small—became converts. Governors, journalists, and traders were all swept up in the debate as specific liberal measures were discussed, implemented, forgotten or rescinded, and then reimposed. I here explore the outlines of the older, conservative viewpoint before turning to a discussion of economic liberalism up to the 1820s.

PATERNALISM

Paternalism formed the webbing that held in place the pieces of a hierarchical social structure. As late as 1810 Prince-Regent João, even as he explained an economically liberal measure to the "People," said it would be "a new proof not only of the love I bear toward you as a good *father*, but also that . . . the interests of my subjects, always present to my eyes, deserve the attention of my *paternal* care."[1] As good fathers, he and others in analogous positions also had to discipline and punish. Grown men and women were imagined as children before them. Yet central to the father's role was the expectation that the poorest and weakest would be protected from exploitation because, to maintain a ranked order, it must be seen as just. Such behavior, or the expectation and approval of such behavior, was woven through the very texture of society. The operative law on city councils in the Portuguese empire, as was true in Spanish America, stated that city councillors had a duty to do everything possible so that "inhabitants may live well," and royal governors justified a measure by saying it would lead to "the common benefit of the people of this city."[2] Deviations from the ideal were no doubt all too frequent, and it is easy today to dismiss as hypocrisy the rationale then presented for certain governmental actions; nonetheless, the taken-for-granted notion of what good government meant included not only benevolence and mercy, but also a sheltering stance on behalf of common people to protect them from any abuse. Paternalism was joined at the hip to hierarchy.

These understandings provided a powerful incentive for municipal officials to ensure that the populace received an adequate supply of unspoiled food at an accessible price. They did this not by providing it, but by making and enforcing rules for the suppliers who did. People understood that an unregulated food market opened the way for the devious, the unscrupulous, the greedy, and the oppressive, and, if left to their own devices, all those who traded in food would be tempted even to cause a famine if they could profit from it. Although all businesspeople by the very nature of their activity had profit as their only goal, the food trade required special supervision because life itself depended on the items traded. The malfeasance of those who bought food to resell injured not just consumers, but society itself. These views, derived from ancient traditions in Europe, had deep roots in Brazilian culture.[3] They were unquestioned at first, later challenged, but continued to resonate in Salvador until the 1860s at least.

There were two prongs to authorities' efforts to protect the people in the matter of food. One was to control price, the other to exert constant vigilance over those engaged in four interrelated activities: (1) forestallers, who intercepted and bought up foodstuffs before they reached the public markets; (2) regraters, who bought foodstuffs not for their own use or even to transport elsewhere but to resell in smaller amounts in the same market at a profit; (3) engrossers or wholesalers, who bought large quantities, allegedly with the aim of cornering the market; and (4) hoarders, who caused artificial scarcities and awaited rising prices with which to gouge the hungry buyers. The label "monopolist" was applied to all who would place their private gain above the common good. Trade, according to a widespread belief, was a zero-sum game: If one person gained, another must necessarily have lost, for merchants did not create wealth but only extracted it from others. The ideal situation would be for consumers and producers to be in direct, face-to-face contact; failing that, there should be only one trader between them.[4]

The forestallers were the most frequent targets of government and public opprobrium because they stood between the producer and the consumer, and their activity arguably led to high prices.* They usually did only what we today might expect of any middleman, but it was then widely believed that producers would sell directly to consumers, and at a lower price, if only middlemen did not deliberately scheme to prevent it.[5] The Philippine Code, issued in 1603 to reiterate and organize previous legislation, applied not only to Portugal but to all of its colonies; it specifically forbade the purchase of "wheat, flour, rye, barley or corn" for resale, the advancing of money to farmers for these grains, or actions to forestall them. In 1704 a law extended these prohibitions to the trade in manioc meal within Brazil, and the same rules applied to meat.[6]

*It is striking that the very word "forestaller," once a common term in English, is listed in the *Oxford English Dictionary* as obsolete except in history, whereas the Portuguese word *atravessador*—literally, "one who cuts across a street, a road, or a river," but used figuratively to mean "someone who intercepts trade"—is still much used in Brazil.

Hoarding to provoke higher prices, cornering the market, monopolizing supply, or conspiring with others to do so were all deemed to be the natural aim of middlemen in general—if they could get away with it. Governor Rodrigo José de Menezes justified the creation of the public grains market in 1785 by noting that traders "have exerted their ambition to hoard [manioc meal, rice, corn, and beans] in their own business houses, . . . so that the price should not falter, selling little by little." It was also to curtail the activity of such public enemies that he issued new regulations placing control of the cattle and meat business firmly in the hands of the city council.[7]

The other major way in which city authorities in colonial times sought to protect consumers was by setting and enforcing price controls on foodstuffs. Western Europeans had long done so, at least at times of dearth, and the practice went back to the eighth century in England, where it had not fallen out of favor until the late eighteenth, remaining on the books until the 1830s. Price controls did not end in Boston until 1797, and were widespread in Spanish America.[8] The instructions given to the very first captain-general of Brazil (1549) included the provision that he should "decide the prices that [merchandise] could honestly be worth [for] sale or exchange." The Philippine Code placed the responsibility for setting maximum prices on foodstuffs squarely on the shoulders of city council members. It did, however, exempt bread, wine, and olive oil from such controls, although at times of scarcity city councils were entitled, even encouraged, to impose controls on these items as well. The code said nothing about exempting meat, and in Brazil the exemption for bread did not extend to manioc meal. Indeed in 1701 the governor of Bahia insisted that the city council vigorously enforce price controls on it. A few years later the king ordered that no bail be allowed for those arrested for "publicly selling meat . . . at a price higher than that set by the [city] council." So the two principal items of food in Salvador remained subject to official price controls until the end of the eighteenth century.[9]

PROTECTION APPLIED

The prohibition against the nefarious activities of middlemen and the establishment of price controls worked in tandem. If successfully enforced, price controls discouraged middlemen from attempting their shenanigans because the advantage would be small if any. Better yet, if consumers bought directly from producers, price controls would not be necessary because third parties would not be able to line their own pockets by interfering in the trade.

The records are replete with accusations against forestallers and *forminas* (a local word of uncertain and flexible meaning) who allegedly interfered with trade or sold for prices above the official maximum. Any operator who traded outside the legal channels was called a *formina*, whether the item exchanged was manioc meal or cattle and meat, but it most often applied to these last two. In the most general use, *forminas* referred to those who traded in cattle after leaving the Capuame Fair, especially to traders who then surreptitiously sold the meat at retail, taking advantage of its scarcity to sell at prices above those set by the council.[10] Boaventura Soares "turns up on the roads from the Fair . . . where cattle drives pass and sometimes buys eight to twelve head and takes them to the backyard of the house he rents [that is, he does not even own it], and there he slaughters them and sells the meat by the piece," without using scales. Declaring that cattle had died on their way from the fair to the slaughterhouse was a favorite dodge. At one time dealers claimed that 200 head had died in a period of two weeks.[11]

Aside from cattle dealers, butchers were most often accused of shady dealings. Much effort was spent in trying to control their many "horrible outrages." They charged consumers more than the legally authorized maximum price, probably claiming at first that they had none for sale. Or they "remove[d] the marbled meat to sell on the black market above the regulated price, leaving the lean and bad for the people." They used a butcher's thumb and "scandalously stole" from the public when weighing meat. To stymie this practice, the city in 1821 placed public scales at principal butcher shop locations so customers could check the weight of purchased meat. But there was worse: the city council's legal officer reported that "meat called 'turned,' which is often rotten, is sold in the afternoon." The council responded to such news by issuing a new ordinance stating that "Whereas this body has learned that many butcher shops sell meat to the People even at night . . . and often even when it is rotten, . . . [we] hereby order that henceforth no butcher shop may remain open after 2 p.m.," a logical reaction in a tropical climate without refrigeration. The enterprise and energy of butchers required regulation.[12]

Other measures aimed to protect the public from unscrupulous grocers. Casks or barrels of wine and other drinks had to bear the seal of city authorities "to avoid mixing the liquors," although it was said that store owners often "had seals made with the Council's arms" and then "affixed said seals themselves." City officials clamped down on stores selling spoiled food and insisted that scoops, pans, measuring cups, and scales must be "always clean and neat."[13] Twice a year a storekeeper had to take his weights and measures to the city inspector to be checked for accuracy, a requirement they found irritating and onerous. In the case of meat, fish, or drinks sold in small amounts, the inspection was required every two months on the grounds that these measures wore out more easily than others. When store owners complained about the inconvenience, the city council self-righteously replied that these complainers, "who lack probity, are always seeking to cheat the public, and the officials of this Council, who care for the public good, are then resisted and pestered by suits and demands."[14] Stores had to be licensed annually, paying a fee to the city council, with heavy fines levied on those who failed to present their licenses. Store owners constantly faced officials ready to enforce city ordinances and had to size up whether it might be useful to offer a bribe.[15]

Street vendors, whether slave or free, took out licenses every year, although they were granted free of charge. City ordinances minutely specified the maximum prices of everything they sold, including lettuce, eggplant, grapes, large and small mangoes, large and small jack fruits, four varieties of bananas, and various sweets. It required the mostly illiterate street vendors to "have with them a list of the set prices of the foodstuffs they sell," and they were fined if they failed to carry their licenses and "all these papers" with them. If a vendor sold items to be weighed or measured instead of counted, she must have with her the necessary calibrated instruments and have them checked for accuracy twice a year. This easily added four or more pounds to her load. Fines levied against street vendors for not having their license, for selling above the maximum set price, or for violating other regulations amounted to 10 to 15 percent of the city's revenue.[16] Street vendors were good for city finances.

Boatmen arriving in Salvador with provisions for sale confronted an extensive bureaucratic apparatus designed to protect consumers, but which the captains deemed unfriendly, hypocritical, and certainly open to abuse. In 1801 boat owners from Camamu lodged multiple complaints with the governor about how city officials treated them and the "irritations and persecutions" they encountered. Even while at Itaparica Island awaiting high tide before moving on to Salvador, municipal bureaucrats confronted them and demanded they present papers that could only be secured in the city. By such "assaults," they said, the fine collectors "sucked their substance," for they had no choice but to "leave the money there and shut up." Once they reached Salvador, they were accused and fined for anything officials could dream up, some "for not having measures aboard even if they are not bringing merchandise that requires measuring, . . . still others because, for example, arriving in March or April for the first time in the year, they had not had their measures checked in January." They were then arrested and taken to the judge's office while "their boats' sails and rudders are placed on land." If on the way, "because of ignorance or rusticity or in order to avoid the rigors of the collector's unleashed greed," they paid the arresting officer, they were immediately released. When they complained to the city council, they were told to appeal in court, but, they said, "the poor boatman cannot remain in the city pursuing suits." They acknowledged that if complaints mounted, the city sometimes dismissed the officer in question, but "the poor dispossessed [person] cannot recover his loss." City officials saw things differently, accusing boatmen of systematically "forestalling and regrating foodstuffs."[17]

All these rules—so bothersome to boatmen, vendors, grocers, butchers, cattle traders, and just about anyone engaged in the food trade, and so often an excuse for official harassment, if not bribery—had as their rationale the need to shelter consumers from grasping businesspeople. The stated intention of the police power was to maintain order by protecting the health and welfare of the people, because part of the government's duty was to foster a just system.[18] A large segment of the population, both poor and not so poor, relied on the state for this minimum protection. Hierarchy, deference, and inequality, when accompanied by a shielding benevolence, seemed more appealing than the raw competition offered by the system's critics. Belief in the virtue of such protection was so strong that it left an after-image etched into the collective retina and lasting long after a new liberal philosophy became widespread.

LIBERALISM

In the late eighteenth century many began to question the logic of these protections. A contrary belief in the virtues of economic liberalism formed part of a great transformation occurring throughout the

Atlantic World. Governments should cease to interfere in the economy, obstacles to trade should be removed, and price controls lifted. Such convictions flowed from Enlightenment principles of universalism, rationalism, and, especially, from a belief in the need to free individuals from the coercive action of the state. Political elites in Portugal and Brazil felt the pull of these transforming ideas coming from the world centers of economic power that they hoped to emulate.

Pressure on the Salvador City Council toward liberalization came from two directions. The boatmen, cattle merchants, store owners, and other food sellers avid for profit pushed from below, while the agents of central government, seeking general economic growth, pushed from above. The first stirrings of a new direction in the Portuguese world regarding price controls and other regulations may be traced to a royal order issued in 1765. Although applicable to Lisbon alone—whether because the measure was seen as an experiment or because of the Crown's conceit that Lisbon was the only city that mattered—its preamble perfectly captures the thrust of the new policy. It began by noting "the public harm that results from price controls and the fines levied by municipal petty judges." In populous places "only the multiplicity of vendors, . . . the competition of these vendors, and the resulting abundance can regulate and moderate the price of edibles. [But] fear of price controls and fines has . . . impeded a great number of sellers of provisions . . . from bringing foodstuffs to the city." The text concluded, "as soon as that fear ceases by [granting] liberty to each one . . . to sell at his price, . . . the number of these foodstuff sellers will necessarily grow and, with their competition and the abundance of victuals, prices will diminish to the common benefit of my people." Noting all this, the king ordered "all price controls be lifted . . . on all foodstuffs sold in this city of Lisbon . . . so that everyone who transports, brings, and introduces them may freely sell [them] for the prices agreed upon by the buyers." Not just grain and bread, wine and oil, but all foodstuffs were now exempted from any price control in Lisbon.[19]

This watershed change doubtless drew inspiration from policies being adopted in France, where books and articles attacking price and other controls on the grain trade had become widespread enough to influence public policy. The economist François Quesnay (1694–1774) and his adepts touted the notion that private property and the right to dispose of it as one wishes derived from natural law. Eventually finding the argument persuasive, the French government in 1763 and

1764 allowed anyone to deal in grain and even to stockpile it, charging whatever a buyer would pay. The measure's unabashed purpose was to protect producers rather than consumers, and these measures met with popular outrage. The government finally gave way, reversing course in the early 1770s, only to adopt other liberalizing policies a few years later.[20]

It was in 1764 that Adam Smith (1723–1790), a professor of philosophy and ethics at Edinburgh University, arrived in France for a two-year stay. There he came to know Quesnay and engaged in active discourse with his group. In his earlier lectures Smith had already explored the implications of natural law, private property, and humans' propensity to look out for themselves as a guide to economic behavior. Stimulated by his new contacts, Smith devoted himself to deepening that analysis on returning to Scotland. He excelled at breaking every economic activity down into its component parts and evaluating the weight of each. He discarded the French notion that agriculture was the basic source of national wealth, arguing instead that wealth derived from every business activity, whether of farmers, merchants, industrialists, or workers. He maintained that if everyone were allowed to do what came naturally, pursuing their self-interest, society's wealth would unavoidably grow and so increase the well-being of every individual. The unhindered workings of the market system in which everyone was free to exchange their labor or goods for the labor or goods they desired from others would inevitably produce this result. The state should not attempt to control an individual's use of private property. Government had, rather, the duty to make sure each person enjoyed the freedom to pursue his or her own interest without infringing on the rights of others to do the same. On the other hand, monopolies and combinations—whether of employers or workers, producers or merchants—should be forbidden, and Smith wrote telling passages condemning businessmen for attempting to form them. His resulting book, *An Inquiry into the Nature and Causes of the Wealth of Nations*, published in 1776, sent ripples throughout western Europe. His ideas directly influenced many individuals in the Portuguese world.[21]

One of those inspired by Adam Smith's work was the Portuguese Rodrigo de Souza Coutinho, later Conde de Linhares (1755–1812), who helped shape the destiny of Portugal and Brazil. As a young man he asked a friend coming from England to bring him a copy of *The Wealth of Nations* just two years after its publication, and he often cited it in his correspondence. After a long stint as Portuguese ambassador to the court of Sardinia-Piedmont in Turin, Souza Coutinho was recalled to Lisbon in 1796 as colonial secretary. In 1801 he was chosen to head up the royal treasury as well. He increasingly veered away from mercantilism and its proponents' view that the sole purpose of colonies was to aid the mother country in securing a favorable balance of trade and that colonies should never be allowed to compete with metropolitan producers. He argued instead that development of any part of the empire would strengthen Portugal itself. As he vigorously pressed for reform, he managed to create a number of powerful enemies. In 1803, in face of Napoleon's pressure on Portugal, Souza Coutinho recommended the Crown move to Brazil, a proposal that created such a firestorm of opposition, especially among influential francophiles at court, that Prince-Regent João removed him from the cabinet. In 1807, however, as Napoleon prepared to invade Portugal, Souza Coutinho was hastily recalled to oversee the transfer of the government to Rio de Janeiro. In Brazil, as secretary of war and foreign relations, he had a free hand to push through the liberalizing changes he deemed essential, beginning with foreign trade, now opened to all nations.[22] An example of Souza Coutinho's specific ideas is his 1798 instruction to the viceroy in Rio de Janeiro saying that "the full and free circulation of all foodstuffs and the security of a market where prices depend only on demand are the best means of achieving a reliable abundance." Two years later he qualified his views in the case of mines and forests, saying they needed to be regulated and not turned over to "private interests," but he stressed that "in these cases and only in them" does public utility require "a notable exception to the general principles of political economy." In 1811, now in Brazil, he referred to the "great, beautiful, and simple system of liberty," and called for "the removal of all obstacles that oppose the natural level which results from free competition, . . . leaving each one to decide the best employment of his activity." He sponsored the first Portuguese translation of *The Wealth of Nations*. He repeatedly encouraged several liberalizing measures regarding the food trade and specifically applied them to Salvador.[23]

José da Silva Lisboa (1756–1835), a native of Salvador, became a major protagonist of Adam Smith's ideas in Brazil. At age seventeen he had been sent to Coimbra University in Portugal, where he studied law and observed the implementation of several major fiscal and administrative reforms. Returning to Salvador to practice law and teach school, he revealed his keen interest in economic matters by preparing a lengthy report on the entire captaincy for his former mentor in Portugal.[24] In 1797 he made a brief trip to Portugal, delivering to a publisher the manuscript for his seven-volume treatise on European maritime, tariff, and commercial law, a work that revealed his wide knowledge of the practices of other countries as well as the legal traditions of his own. In 1804 his highly influential *Principles of Political Economy* (*Princípios de economia política*) appeared, specifically designed to introduce Portuguese and Brazilian readers to the ideas of Adam Smith, doing so only a year after Jean-Baptiste Say had published his equally effective *Treatise on Political Economy* (*Traité d'économie politique*) in France. When the Portuguese government-in-exile stopped briefly in Salvador in January 1808, Souza Coutinho arranged for Prince-Regent João to appoint Silva Lisboa as the first professor of "economic science" in a course to be created under his direction in Rio de Janeiro. Although Silva Lisboa moved to Rio, he decided to produce an appropriate textbook instead of teaching this course. He also complained that the salary offered did not exceed that of a grammar school teacher and amounted to only half the earnings of a professor of mineralogy, "a science that, although very useful, has no comparison to economic science, which Adam Smith, the great master of *The Wealth of Nations*, considers appropriate to legislators and men of State." Many years later he received the title of baron and then viscount Cairu. Souza Coutinho commissioned Silva Lisboa's son to prepare the Portuguese translation of *The Wealth of Nations*, published in 1811.[25]

JOSÉ DA SILVA RIBEIRO

Souza Coutinho and Silva Lisboa were only the most prominent of those whose liberal economic views affected the food trade in this corner of the Atlantic World.[26] Adam Smith's work directly influenced two individuals closely tied to Salvador's economy, José da Silva Ribeiro and João Rodrigues de Brito. Ribeiro played a major role in the growing debate as a mouthpiece for disgruntled participants in the food trade. He owned a wharf-side warehouse that supplied the navy with rice and beans, and allegedly enriched himself from the trade in manioc meal. He became treasurer of the public grains market in 1796. He believed firmly in laissez faire and advocated it whenever he could. Each person—he obviously was not thinking of slaves—should have "the free use of what is his" and be free to dispose of his or her goods "at the greatest possible profit at the time and place where they are sought. This is the common interest."[27]

Ribeiro especially focused on what he saw as the plight of cattle dealers and traders in manioc meal. He later claimed that he had persuaded governor Fernando José de Portugal to remove the price cap on manioc meal temporarily "as an experiment" in 1795, an act that was later approved in Lisbon and made permanent. Whether or not he exerted such influence, he certainly maintained close links to those traders and some years later spoke for them to protest increased charges at the grains market.[28]

In March 1797 a group of cattle traders interested in ending price controls on beef presented a long petition to the Salvador City Council. Ribeiro had penned it. At fourteen manuscript pages it is a treatise on economic liberalism that, twice quoting Adam Smith with page citations to the French edition, insisted that the public welfare was best served by protecting individual interests, a maxim "as obvious as the very principles of mathematics." The old system was not working because price controls prevented sufficient quantities of meat from reaching the legal market, being sold instead surreptitiously by black-marketeers at inflated prices. Only the rich could afford it, leaving the poor no better off than if the legal price were higher but meat more abundant. Open competition and market freedom would solve these problems. Almost plagiarizing Adam Smith, Ribeiro's disquisition compared a fear of middlemen to the

terror that in earlier less enlightened times was felt toward the power of magic. Those unfortunate ones who were [then] accused of magic and witchcraft were as innocent of the evils attributed to them as are those today who are called forestallers and monopolists. The law that . . . ended prosecutions of witches removed from the evildoer the right to gratify his malice by accusing his neighbor of an imaginary crime. This law put an end to this terror by suppressing its cause. Such would doubtless be the effect of a measure that granted unlimited freedom for commerce in meat.[29]

Not everyone was persuaded. The city council, in forwarding this petition to the governor, denied that freedom of prices in essential foodstuffs had produced any advantage.[30] The governor, however, sided with the cattle merchants against the city council and ordered it to lift price controls on meat. The council did so, but would not rest. It argued that the price of meat "rises daily" because traders abused their "freedom," which "is not adaptable in this city. . . . Ten or twelve men take advantage, running freely to satisfy their insatiable greed, while the people moan."[31]

Then, in January 1798, Ribeiro organized an effort by "victualers and foodstuffs carriers" to have price controls lifted on *all* foodstuffs. In the "Representation" he wrote for these boatmen, grain traders, and some street vendors he argued that it was absurd to free prices on manioc meal and meat and not on other foods. Certainly "corn, beans, rice, fruit, roots, and every victual should be considered essential." He admitted that price controls had been imposed originally to protect the poor, but maintained they had become "a scourge, . . . a cause of greater penury and costliness." Municipally appointed petty judges, acting arbitrarily, decided on the correct price of fruits, root vegetables, and other foods, setting prices even for different size fruits and inconsistently imposing on some equivalent items a lower price than on others. The present judge "has set the price of rice and beans at 1$600 [per bushel], although it arrives [here] at a cost of 2$000 or more." He had, outrageously, ordered "the bailiff to block the doors of the public grains market" until he had his way. All this principally benefited the tax farmers who "split the fines with the judges, their benefactors." Goods priced too low were snatched up "in a few minutes by the black female regraters who soon grab everything to later re-sell," while other sellers stopped coming to the market, preferring "to sell furtively to whomsoever will pay more." The customer had no option than to buy from the "black women."[32]

The petition worked. In mid-November 1799 the governor informed the city council that Souza Coutinho, the Portuguese colonial secretary, had ordered the Lisbon rules of 1765 extended to Salvador: "To benefit the victual sellers and street vendors all price controls and resulting fines on all foodstuffs sold in this city and its jurisdiction shall cease, so that any person who transports, carries, or introduces them [into the city] may sell them freely for the prices that they may settle on with the buyers."[33]

Characteristically, the city council did not welcome these orders. They maintained that Ribeiro was a "monopolist" who had rapidly enriched himself through his official post at the public grains market and was well-known for perturbing the council's sessions with unfounded complaints, "taking the part of peddlers, as he was once one of them." He often made "exotic" demands, for instance, "that cane brandy be classified as a foodstuff to be freed from price controls." Nevertheless, after much foot-dragging, the council in 1801 claimed liberalization as its own idea. It embraced the system "that the most civilized and polished cities . . . have adopted, a practice that consists in removing price controls of essential foodstuffs, leaving the price free. . . . as has been done in the capital city of the Kingdom."[34]

JOÃO RODRIGUES DE BRITO

An ardent proponent of a liberal system—who directly confronted the issue of forestalling—was João Rodrigues de Brito, a Portuguese-born judge who sat on Bahia's High Court and was intimately connected to local sugar planters and merchants. He lived at the very center of Salvador, not far from the governor's residence and city hall. A friend of José da Silva Lisboa, he commented on a draft of his *Principles of Political Economy*. He had read widely on the subject and could cite by chapter and verse works by Adam Smith, Jean-Baptiste Say, and many other European economists. When, in early 1807, the colonial secretary in Portugal asked the governor of Bahia to consult the Salvador city council as to what obstacles blocked the further prosperity of the colony, the council solicited the opinion of various persons, including Brito. In reply, he wrote an extraordinary essay of some eighty printed pages that so closely followed Adam Smith's argument, and applied it so directly to the food trade and institutions examined in this book, that it merits specific comment.

In his thundering declaration of economic liberalism, Brito attacked the remaining paternalism of the government. Public officials, he said, had failed "to perceive that truth so loudly proclaimed by the economists, that there is nothing better than the private judgment of every citizen who can regularly see what is best for himself in the exercise of his industry. What is best for each one is what is best for the public, the interest of the latter being nothing more than the sum of the interests of the former." Freedom was needed—the freedom "to plant whatever they please, . . . to [sell] at any place or along any road and by any person whom they wish to hire (all without onus or the minimum formality), to prefer any buyer who offers the most, and, finally, to sell whenever they wish."[35]

The main thrust of Brito's treatise was to argue, as had Ribeiro, that freedom should specifically be granted to those whom others called regraters and forestallers. There was nothing sinister or even mysterious about what these merchants did, being "nothing more than small businessmen who offer their services between the producer and the consumer with benefit to both in the hope of some gain, which is the recompense for their labor and the risk and immobilization of their capital." Their work "cannot be a hindrance to the farmer nor to the consumer, because [the reliance on them] is purely voluntary. The farmer always has the freedom to take his goods to the consumer's door and the latter to buy them directly." If the farmer does otherwise, "it is because that suits his interest." Both farmers and consumers benefited because "the greater production that results . . . spreads abundance everywhere and with it a better price."[36] He zeroed in especially on the two central features of Rodrigo José de Menezes's 1780s reforms, the public grains market and the central slaughterhouse.

He condemned the requirement that no manioc meal, rice, corn, or beans be sold anywhere unless first put up for sale at the grains market. He pointed out that traders had to endure not only the expenses of a trip and the tying up of their capital, but also "the loss of their time, . . . the fee that is demanded supposedly for the expenses of the bins (which they did not wish to have) and the rental of sacks, and the labor expenses of unloading. . . . This mass of burdens . . . is equivalent to robbery," but with a difference. If a boatman/trader were actually robbed of ten coins out a hundred, he "soon returns to gain another hundred," guarding them with "more caution." But if he is "obliged by the regulations to receive only ninety coins net, he loses interest, convinced that there is no cautious act that can be effective against the tax collectors who rely on public force." Not only does he not return, but he spreads "dismay everywhere, discouraging those who might undertake similar enterprises." Such restrictions on commercial freedom were bound to have a deleterious effect on the supply and price of food.[37]

Brito equally criticized the rules restricting the trade in cattle and meat. Even the city council, he said, recognized that "there are some lines of business that . . . require middlemen." They authorized dealers, "but only under restrictions and cautions adopted in order to prevent the producers from being defrauded," limiting their number to "no more than eight or a dozen persons," requiring guarantors and licenses. "These clauses and restrictions, however, destroy all the effects of the remedy. Forestallers are only useful when their number is indefinite, without any limitation, because it is the very competition of some that prevents others from becoming rich through exorbitant gain, something that is prevented when any citizen can compete to participate in those gains, freely entering into the same business." He concluded that the policy "gravely injures both the ranchers, who are obliged to sell their cattle for less than their value for lack of competition among buyers, and the city's consumers, who must necessarily pay more for the meat they buy, for lack of competition among sellers."[38]

Then he turned his ire on the public slaughterhouse and butcher shops. According to the rules, "the rancher is . . . deprived of his freedom to sell wherever he wishes and through his [own] agents." Not only is his drover "obliged to place all his cattle into the [slaughterhouse's] corrals," but "even then . . . the poor man is obliged to turn his goods over to someone else to administer." The cattle owner does not have "the right to choose the butcher shops where he wishes to sell his meat nor the butchers who will sell it." Given this setup, "Where is the [butcher's] incentive?" If butchers "competed before the cattle owners, the matter would be righted. . . . He who best served the owner would be preferred." Such an altered practice, Brito argued, would encourage ranching and increase production, leading to greater abundance and lower prices.[39] No one else in Salvador laid out the liberal position with such detail and clarity, and certainly not regarding the food trade.

Governor Conde da Ponte, who had been appointed in 1805, well before Souza Coutinho had returned to power in Portugal, forwarded Brito's report to Lisbon, but in his covering letter he rejected all of it. He began with an ad hominem attack on Portuguese merchants, saying that those who wished less regulation of commerce were only those who wanted "absolute liberty for fraud and deceit," mainly new arrivals from Portugal "little favored in their own country and ambitious to better their fortune . . . precipitously." Then he went further, taking on liberal theory itself and defending mercantilism. Although acknowledging that "the arbitrary principles . . . of modern economists" condemned "all brakes or restrictions . . . on commerce, even colonial commerce, I cannot but feel contrarywise, knowing that colonial establishments like this one have as their principal (I should say only) purpose the interest and utility of the metropolis." As for Brito's specific suggestions regarding the commerce in foodstuffs, not a word.[40] The governor's letter, dated in late August 1807, would not have arrived in Lisbon with Brito's treatise any sooner than mid-October. By then the Lisbon authorities, more concerned with the French threat to Portuguese sovereignty than with colonial affairs, and with Souza Coutinho once again in the cabinet, were preparing for the worst.

At the end of November the Portuguese court and government, forced out of Europe by Napoleon's invading army, fled Lisbon for Brazil, touching briefly at Salvador in January 1808 on the way to Rio de Janeiro. Faced with the obvious necessity of altering the previous system limiting all Brazilian overseas trade to Portugal (now in the hands of the French), met by some Brazilian sugar planters and export merchants anxious to resume shipments to Europe, and probably aware of Silva Lisboa's views on the subject, Prince-Regent João opened the ports of Brazil to trade with all friendly nations. By this single stroke he abolished the colonial system so trenchantly defended a few months earlier by the Conde da Ponte.[41]

POLICY

Meanwhile aspects of the earlier paternalistic impulse continued to drive stated public policy, aided by critics of reform. Ribeiro's success in getting the governor to lift price controls was a first step toward liberalizing the food economy, but ending the prohibition against forestallers and regraters as Brito urged was something else again. Although liberal theory simultaneously attacked price controls and restrictions on the middleman/forestaller, policy makers did not always understand that the two issues had common roots and could not be separated. Even the 1765 Lisbon law ending price controls called for the authorities to "extirpate monopolies and forestalling activities." To the same end in Salvador in 1801, regulations forbade purchases of large quantities of manioc meal before a certain time of day to allow consumers to buy directly from producers or their agents first. A few years later the governor's office commented favorably on a petition claiming that although the law forbade "forestalling, . . . the forestallers are so fearless and energetic that . . . they forestall everything that comes from outside, buying in order to resell to the people and even going out to meet the vessels [before] they arrive." Policy makers' views on middlemen remained a mixture of the old paternalism and the new liberalism.[42]

But even the removal of price controls came only by fits and starts.

At first, the course of action seemed firmly set toward economic liberalism. We have seen how Fernando José de Portugal (governor from April 1788 to September 1801), responding to instructions from Souza Coutinho, took up Ribeiro's cause and lifted price controls on manioc meal (in 1795), then on meat (1797), and finally on all food-stuffs (1799–1801), allowing businessmen to charge whatever the traffic would bear, a policy embodied in an 1801 city ordinance. Marcos de Noronha e Brito, the eighth Conde dos Arcos, governor of Bahia from September 1810 to January 1818, remained deeply ambivalent. He first sought to protect consumers, strongly criticizing those who "buy foodstuffs wholesale [em grosso] with the sinister goal of resell-ing them." But in 1812 he thought "unlimited freedom [is the] only and safest rule that man has found until now to promote the welfare of all and any type of commerce." Three years later he reiterated that price controls harmed both the ranchers and the public, yet in 1816 he seemed ignorant of earlier decisions and approved—but only as an "exception"—the freeing of the price of meat. The following year he agreed that, since the crisis had passed, "this business should return to its ancient way, not allowing anyone to slaughter freely or sell for a higher price . . . than earlier set." Price controls on meat were still in place as late as 1820, no one acknowledging that an earlier mea-sure had removed them.[43] The weekly newspaper of the Portuguese community, which consisted mainly of storekeepers and other mer-chant-middlemen, referred favorably in 1813 to "the new economic system of which Adam Smith is the author," but acknowledged that "old prejudices" had presented some obstacles to its implementation. Selfish people, to protect their particular privileges, "struggle to re-instate the old system."[44] Ambivalence toward liberalism persisted to the end of the colonial period, and when it came to actual practice, neither the advocates of paternalism nor of liberalism were free from the taint of the other. Decisions depended on contingencies, not on adherence to dogma.

It is perhaps not coincidental that the initial spread of liberal thought and practice occurred during the same period as the creation of a more systematic order in the food trade as set up by Rodrigo José de Menezes, governor from 1784 to 1788. In organizing the central grains market and slaughterhouse, he imposed new rules on both traders in manioc meal and cattle dealers and butchers. It may have been precisely these reforms, in strengthening the role of the state in the economy, that stimulated a reaction on the part of cattle traders, boatmen, and store owners as they demanded greater freedom. And the resistance of city councillors to liberal reforms may have resulted not only from their concern for the welfare of consumers, but also from their realization that such reforms would mean the loss of one of their principal attributes—the regulation of the food trade—and with it the loss of significant municipal income derived from the fines and vendors' license fees. With liberalism, their role in this trade would be reduced to checking and verifying weights and measures. Regardless of motive, the council's arguments resonated among urban residents. The new approach remained contested well after the Independence War altered Brazil's political system.

Adam Smith's influence can be found permeating not only abstract arguments on behalf of liberalism in Portugal and Salvador, but also the rationale for specific policies on the trade in manioc meal, meat, and other foodstuffs. By 1820 even those who opposed liberalization did not find these proposals outlandish or unheard of, as they would have in earlier times. And whether we examine the statements of colonial secretary Souza Coutinho or local lawyer Silva Lisboa, of a High Court judge–cum–sugar planter like Brito or of a perennial gadfly and small-time food merchant such as Ribeiro, we find that their weighty arguments drew heavily on Smith.

"THE PEOPLE DO NOT LIVE BY THEORIES"

PUTTING ECONOMIC LIBERALISM INTO PRACTICE after independence proved more difficult than the theoreticians could have imagined. As Salvador authorities dealt with the trade in foodstuffs from the 1820s to the 1860s, they veered back and forth from laissez faire policies to those on behalf of protecting consumers, changing direction more than once. Food traders and reformers argued that unfettered individual initiative would lead to competition, abundance, and lower prices, while many Salvadoreans saw the removal of price controls on food and the end of restrictions on traders as opening the way for profiteering by a few and hunger for the many. These people looked back with longing on a regime that, although not perfect, had provided certain predictable protections for urban residents. Policy makers were caught in the middle. They could not simultaneously guarantee the individual freedom of sellers and still obey the older imperative to maintain a protective stance toward buyers. Governing agencies, like elites generally, were often at loggerheads. Even when liberals won victories, they confronted challenging local conditions that forced them to back down. Salvador proved a crucible within which competing ideologies clashed, and food sellers and the food trade were the objects of discord.

DEBATING IDEOLOGY

Policy debates were heated, with individual freedom and economic liberalism on one side and the paternalistic-hierarchic impulse on the other. The new Brazilian constitution specifically guaranteed the right of property and said no type of industry or commerce could be forbidden.[1] But what did that mean? The argument, as it played out in the elaboration of concrete measures, revealed abundant reasons for hostility toward economic liberalism. Three issues provoked particularly heated dispute: the number and, especially, the locations of butcher shops; the place of middlemen in the food trade generally; and, most important, price controls.

The constant tension between the two competing policy prescriptions can be perceived in a debate over the seemingly trivial question of where butcher shops should be located. Already in 1821 a city council spokesman alleged that it was difficult to inspect the quality of meat sold and the weights used or to avoid a black market because too many shops had been authorized by the colonial government, and they were scattered all about town. Butcher shops should be "reconcentrated" on the ground floor of the council chambers, "where they once existed." In 1824, a year after driving the Portuguese forces out of Salvador, the city council enacted a broadly liberal reform of the meat business, allowing butcher shops to be set up by anyone and placed anywhere. The councillors then proudly pointed to the "multiplicity of butcher shops" that had sprung up "where buyers may choose meat and buy at the price they like." But, then, two years later, they thought again, noting that the new policies, far from producing the expected results, had "facilitated abuses by . . . a multiplicity of visibly unnecessary butcher shops scattered at some distance and, consequently, by the insuperable difficulty of [carrying out] the necessary inspections in this most important branch of municipal government." Reversing course, council members decreed that butcher shops must now be located in just four places, in addition to one shop in each of five outlying parishes, and that no meat could be sold outside these butcher shops. Subsequent councils adopted a decidedly liberal stance in 1828 and 1829, but reversed course again in 1833. They reinforced their conservative position in 1839 when they condemned the "traffickers in meat who . . . sacrifice . . . the health of their fellow citizens [by] selling them rotten meat in butcher shops that open sometimes here, sometimes there, to escape police vigilance."[2] These zigzagging policy moves demonstrate the difficulties of reconciling freedom of commerce with the desire to protect consumers. This argument ostensibly centered on the difficulty of enforcing sanitary measures, but one can sense an underlying doubt as to any butcher's motives. "Badly intentioned people" put "meat up for sale from cattle that have died from sickness, opening a shop only to close it immediately after having committed this act of scandalous immorality."[3]

"Abuse," "badly intentioned people," "scandalous immorality," "traffickers," are all phrases suggesting a continuing repugnance toward
middlemen in general.

A second source of controversy centered on the forestallers, the in-
termediaries between producers and consumers. They, like butchers,
continued to be the targets of public opprobrium. The city council
frequently received written accusations like the one that said "monopolists and cattle dealers" were ready to "commit every sort of
malfeasance," selling meat "for an excessively higher price than that
for which the cattle were bought." Those who traded in manioc meal
were equally conniving: the city council decried the fact that "there
exist companies of certain men, known as 'guerrillas,' who assault
all the [arriving] boats, whether foreign or domestic, and, through
this criminal forestalling action are able to hold in their hands all
foodstuffs at the price they choose." Some notion of the general attitude can be gleaned from an action in 1830 taken in a nearby town
whose council proposed to imprison those "forestallers and monopolists who buy manioc meal wholesale or even retail in order to resell
to the public." In 1825 an author describing Cachoeira, another town
across the bay from Salvador, said it was a gathering point for "the
odious swarm of moneyed but inhuman monopolists and forestalling
regraters of essential foodstuffs, . . . societal blood-suckers who . . .
sell to the people for four what they bought for one." Emotions ran
high, and middlemen were the targets.[4]

Before pursuing these ideological divisions further, it is worth asking, Who were these forestallers who allegedly profited so much from
liberal reforms? What class of people did they represent? The answer
remains contradictory. Pedro do Espírito Santo, a wealthy merchant-
planter, owned two sugar mills with large cane plantations, at least
170 slaves, many manioc fields—and plenty of cattle. In 1828 the
slaughterhouse administrator accused him of "purposefully removing his competitors from the market by buying up their herds so that
only he would have cattle to sell this week on his terms." The price
of meat then skyrocketed, despite the overall abundance of cattle at
this season, because Espírito Santo severely limited the number of
head he sent to the slaughterhouse. The administrator railed against
him and the "sordid greed and ambition of monopolists and forestallers [who] adopt any means of promoting hunger in order to wrench
an illicit profit, using the weapon of the People's need for basic food."
In response, the city council ordered the administrator to seize from

Espírito Santo's herd 160 head that day to slaughter and distribute to the butcher shops. When Espírito Santo protested, describing himself as someone who "is accustomed to buying large herds and feeding them in his pastures which are very good, in order to send them to the city," the council used his very words against him as proof of his true occupation as a "monopolist." Eleven years later Espírito Santo was back. The official in charge of the city-owned pasture at Campina reported that he had heard vague allegations that at a place called Santo Antonio "cattle were being kept back in order to create a scarcity or total lack of an essential foodstuff." So he went in search of this place and met drovers who told him where the cattle were being held and that "they belonged to Pedro do Espírito Santo." So it is not surprising that the city council described forestallers as well off—that is, "quite wealthy people [already, who] only think of adding to their wealth through the suffering of other members [of] the social community."[5]

Maybe forestallers, however, were people of a very different class. In the early 1840s the city council identified "the forestallers of essential foodstuffs" as "African regraters." One alleged "band of forestallers" included "the dark mulatta [cabra] Custodia so-and-so and, what's worse, two daring Yoruba Africans, Ignacio and Manuel Joaquim, who, instead of being deported as they should have been, treat the authorities with the greatest rudeness and disrespect as they board boats and go beyond the sea-fort to meet vessels that come from outside the bay carrying legumes, so that when they drop anchor all their cargo has already been sold."[6]

"Forestaller" could mean a mulatta and two African men, or an owner of several sugar mills whose estate was valued at forty-three times that of Ana de São José da Trindade, the prosperous street vendor. One difference is that the blacks traded manioc meal, while Espírito Santo dealt in cattle. As well, the two views regarding the status of forestallers are not necessarily contradictory, since the phrase "quite wealthy" might be applied to a person of decidedly modest means if he or she was an African who was expected to be dirt poor or enslaved. It is likely that many petty traders were held in disrepute precisely because they were small-time actors who were hard to identify and yet seemed to be everywhere.[7] It is also worth noting that one of the objections cited above to the Yoruba traders in manioc meal was that they were "daring" and treated the authorities with "rudeness and disrespect." Worry about authority probably colored the viewpoint of many of those who decried the new economic liberalism.

The issue provoking the most heated controversy after independence, as it had before, centered on price controls. Formally abolished in Salvador at the end of the eighteenth century, those controls had seeped back into colonial practice, largely because of the rotation of governors without institutional memories and the continuing desire of the city council to impose them. With Brazil still part of the Portuguese empire, the Lisbon Cortes in 1821, "considering that only the free competition of buyers and sellers can produce abundance," extinguished all price controls on foodstuffs sold anywhere in the Portuguese dominions.[8] In 1823 the Constituent and Legislative Assembly of newly independent Brazil voted that all the laws that had been in effect up to that time, even if issued by the Cortes, would be made part of Brazilian legislation unless subsequently altered, specifically mentioning the continuing validity of that 1821 measure on prices. The national law on city governance issued five years later included the provision that city councils throughout Brazil must "absolutely abstain from setting prices on any foodstuff or placing any other restriction on the full liberty [to trade] which belongs to owners." So the general thrust of legislation moved toward ending all controls on prices, for the national political elite in the 1820s and early 1830s were enamored of liberal dogma.[9]

How did traders fare? With independence and a shift toward liberalism, opportunities for making a living increased significantly. In 1830 there were some 130 to 140 butchers in town—that is, almost four times more than in colonial days. Six years later the council declared that "this city counts over 300 butcher shops," a rate of growth far exceeding that of the city's population.[10] In March 1822 the city council abolished the requirement that street vendors take out licenses, although maintaining them at that time for "those who sell any foodstuffs from their open door"; that is, for storekeepers. Street vendors must have enjoyed the greater freedom from official supervision.[11]

CONSERVATIVE REACTION

In the 1830s city leaders unambiguously identified economic liberalism as a threat to public welfare. The logic of political economists did not sway them. Legislation stamped with this philosophy granted "limitless freedom" to the cattle merchants, who controlled "a necessary and important commodity" and were "without the least doubt, in possession of an exclusive monopoly." The city council did not know what they could legally do to escape "the lasso which fell into the hands of a half dozen individuals," and councillors strongly condemned the "fine theories" that "make licit every type of commerce and industry." Now "all [the city's] cattle are bought by forestallers at the rancher's gate, who pass them on progressively to other owners, and such trafficking does not cease even within the city limits." Hoarding was a logical result. "We see here . . . a vigorous rule against the principles of political economy according to which he profits most who sells most. In the present case, he profits most who sells least." They expressed nostalgia for "former times under the absolutist regime, [when] such monopolies were remedied by sending soldiers to the interior to drive the cattle." Similar protests rained down on the authorities "against the unlimited freedom of commerce in manioc meal and fresh meat."[12] Limitations on the role of the state were immoral—or at least amoral—and the public deserved more of its chiefs. In early 1833 the provincial president himself, fully aware that the law forbade "price controls on foodstuffs," maintained that it "does seem that without violating the law one could limit the abuses that weigh down on consumers and especially on the poorest classes." He complained to his superior in Rio that the liberalizing 1828 law had pushed the price of foodstuffs, especially the essential ones, to excessive levels, reflected in "surfacing popular discontent."[13] Reaction was in the wind.

Price controls seemed absolutely necessary. The results predicted by liberal theory did not materialize, and city residents throughout the 1820s witnessed constant rises in the prices of foodstuffs from year to year. We know the devaluation of the currency accounts for some of the increase. A particular cause of unease was the widely counterfeited copper coinage, which many store owners refused to accept. Meanwhile, the ills of the Brazilian sugar economy, faced with the rising competition of Cuban cane producers, lowered incomes. Salvador still confronted the endemic problems of inadequate transportation in the region combined with a growing urban population, not to mention periodic scarcities produced by drought or flood. Perceptions, however, matter more than reality or may be said to constitute the only meaningful reality, and voices rose blaming the new liberal policies for the high cost of food.

High prices fueled political unrest. The threat of disorder in turn stimulated hoarding, leading to still higher prices, and city leaders clearly perceived the connection. They did not hesitate to forcefully intervene at times of disturbance. On one occasion, because "of the present political crisis in the province," the city council rushed to assure supplies of meat by purchasing cattle on its own account. But their actions were not enough. A relatively minor revolt and the panic it caused forced up the price of manioc meal by a third in the course of six weeks.[14]

Insurgents promised to pay more attention to food issues than the incumbents were doing. We "will undertake measures so that there will be an abundance of victuals" and "take care to sidetrack and punish the forestallers of essential foodstuffs." Another federalist movement declared that revolution would be "the only way to make manioc meal cheaper." The provincial president acknowledged that "the lack and marked high cost of manioc meal continues, and the People groan and cry out against this scourge." A veteran of the Independence War chimed in, saying, "the patience of the People has a limit; . . . the good family father suffers from this misery and hunger."[15] Constant political upheaval contrasted with centuries of colonial rule when governmental restrictions on businessmen to protect consumers went hand-in-hand with authoritarian political rule. At least that is how it seemed to many contemporaries, and economic liberalism fell increasingly into disfavor.

The debate reached its pitch by the mid-1830s. When the centrally appointed provincial president pressed the councilmen on the reason for the rising price of meat, they saw an opening to push their case. They had no legal authorization to set maximum prices, they explained, much as they wished to do so. It "is notorious" that governments control the prices of subsistence goods "even in the freest and most constitutional countries," recognizing that "the price of essential foodstuffs" cannot follow the "general economic rule" because no matter how expensive they get, people must buy them in order to survive. "The council confesses that it finds it repugnant to consider something that constitutes an urgent and highest public need as someone's private property."[16] They apparently saw through Adam Smith's construction of reality and did not believe market forces were part of nature.

"The city is in crisis," declared the council in mid-September 1837. Some means would have to be found to prevent people from taking the law into their own hands, "committing some outrage impelled by their need." Public tranquility teetered. The councillors proposed to reenact price controls on meat and drew up a draft ordinance stating that "for ranchers, the price [of meat] is free of controls at the market; to cattle traders and [other] private persons, however, it is forbidden to sell meat for more than 2$560 an *arroba*." When they forwarded this text to the acting provincial president, it provoked a furious exchange. Not surprisingly, he vetoed the proposed ordinance, saying it would directly contradict the 1828 law on municipal government, not to mention the constitution. In reply, the council stressed that, according to their proposal, they still allowed ranchers to set their own prices, but he would have none of it. Dealers, he argued, were entitled to the same protection as ranchers. The councillors refused to budge. Only price controls could keep "the People from desperation."[17]

City councillors then drew unexpected support from higher-ups because of a new government in Rio de Janeiro. When a Conservative Party ministry took over, it adopted measures that turned back the clock on a series of liberal political reforms ranging from jury trials to elected justices of the peace. The acting provincial president in Bahia sensed immediately the meaning of this change. On October 16, 1837, aware of the seething discontent in Salvador and faced with the stirrings of a food riot, he gave way, authorizing the council to set a limit on the price of meat. Since councillors feared that the lack of meat "could lead the People to desperation," and since they maintained there was no other solution but to set a price limit, he had decided, for the interim, "to consent, even if just to remove this pretext for disorder from the perturbers of public tranquility." It would be, he stressed, only an experiment. The council acted immediately, announcing publicly that many of the old colonial-era practices would be restored, even limiting butcher shops to public ones, auctioned off to the highest bidder. And they set a maximum price for meat.[18]

But they were too late. Three weeks later, on November 7, a major revolt erupted in the city. Initially its leaders declared that "Bahia is entirely and completely separated from the 'Central Government of Rio de Janeiro,' and is considered a free and independent state," but they then had second thoughts and declared they would rejoin the Brazilian empire once the prince and heir apparent reached the age of majority in 1844. The movement—despite this confused talk of secession and protest against the newly installed Conservative prime minister, who had, as they said, taken the place of a "Brazilian Liberal"—actually pushed in some conservative directions, demanding the return of several features of the old regime.[19] Historians once saw it as a predominantly "regionalist" revolt against the central government and associated it with federalism, a supposedly liberal goal. More recently they have noted that local autonomy does not necessarily translate into individual freedom or a market economy, and they have paid more attention to the insurgents' social program. Brazilian-born free blacks, mulattos, and poor whites played a major role in shaping the revolt's direction, and the movement responded to their plight and the distress of poor consumers. In its earliest manifesto the revolutionary junta declared, "Bahia knows the mistaken policies of the administration . . . regarding hunger."[20]

Although this revolt was put down after five months, in March 1838, government paternalism was once again in vogue. The restored legalist government approved a city ordinance issued in May that repeated the exact wording attempted by the earlier city council, stating that "to ranchers . . . the price is free at the market; to cattle dealers, however, and [other] private persons it is forbidden to sell for more than 2$880 per *arroba*." Consolidating the postcolonial state required some compromises with the values of the old regime. Price controls on meat remained in effect and were not formally removed until decades later. The era of unfettered liberalism was ending. The city council later captured the tone of the times when it asserted that its ordinances were "principally elaborated on behalf of the indigent class," and expressed repulsion at "the scandalous spirit of black-marketeering, of sordid profits, of depraved behavior that resists the execution of laws and threatens to destroy our social state." Some people continued to insist on the validity of liberalism, but their voices were muted and almost invariably resisted by city officials. In the mid-1840s the council described protesters as "a caste of traffickers" who, "torturing all the rules of hermeneutics," base themselves on "the exceedingly ample and unlimited understanding [they] deduce from the Constitution." These self-interested critics maintained that the constitution was violated by "*any* measure designed to protect the great mass of consumers from the scandalous speculations and thievery they commit in the shadow of commercial freedom."[21]

THE BATTLE OVER MANIOC MEAL

In the 1840s friction developed between the city council and the owners of general stores regarding where manioc meal could be sold, leading in the next decade to a major social clash over contrasting views of the good and the just. Liberals made little progress at first, but then got the city council to move toward their side, only to face widespread outrage as a result.

The roots of the controversy go back to the end of the colonial period. It is worth recalling that from 1785, boatmen had to deliver their manioc meal, corn, rice, and beans to the public grains market, and only there, so the public and the authorities would have a clear notion of the available supply, and consumers could purchase small quantities as they needed, comparing quality and price between sellers. Grocers and street vendors could purchase their supplies only after individual consumers had had a chance to buy for their household needs. As the city council members themselves later recognized, with the increased population and expanding urban area, people often preferred to buy somewhere closer to home or "even at night."[22]

The old rules remained in place after the Independence War, but by 1826 the city council believed that regraters and hoarders were subverting the original 1785 effort to prevent "monopolies" at the grains market. Some were even selling contraband grains and had not paid the tax, in a parallel and illegal second grains market, contradicting the "beneficial aim" of having all grains sold at one place to foster transparency in the trade. So in the same year that they tried to restrict the number of butcher shops, they limited the stocks of manioc meal that could be held at stores to one bushel, later raised to four, and required that sales from these stores be always in small quantities, not to exceed a tenth of a bushel (about three and a half liters) at a time. During a time of unrest in 1833, councillors limited even this allowance to stores only in more distant parts of town, while those close to the grains market were forbidden to sell any manioc meal at all. By the early 1840s, city inspectors were pursuing violators and forcing those found hoarding manioc meal "with the evil purpose of pushing up the price" to return their stock to the market.[23] On this matter the general principle among city councilmen remained as it had been in colonial times: in order to protect the consumer, government had the right and duty to restrict the freedom of commerce in manioc meal. The grains market linked producers and consumers more directly, in contrast to secret deals between intermediary merchants and the boatmen.

Shopkeepers naturally opposed these limitations on their businesses, while the city council insisted on them. In 1842 store owners finally succeeded in getting the provincial legislature to revoke the old rules, but the provincial president vetoed that bill. Three years later they were at it again, presenting a petition to the president signed by thirty-two customers who complained that they could not get their household's meal at the stores.[24] The city council countered with a strident denunciation of store owners. "For a long time the greed of this city's storekeepers has aimed at the total annihilation of the public grains market so that they could, free of it, monopolize the trade for meal. . . . The name of the People and the interests of the indigent classes are always invoked in these representations," but it was really the grocers, it said, who promoted these petitions. If they had their way, "the public market will never again gather in one place all meal so [buyers] can judge its value." Even if manioc meal were still unloaded there, "it will be quickly carried off to such stores" where it will be sold as "agreed upon by the guerrillas (for such exclusive companies carry out all the trade in foodstuffs of Salvador) . . . at an exorbitant price hidden in [hundreds of] small sales. This will give such storekeepers an excessive profit." In contrast, the existing regulations allowed a customer to buy as little as $\frac{1}{32}$ of a bushel at the public market, serving the poorest householder very well. As for the argument that the grains market was too far away or did not sell at night, "it is not the mission of those in charge of the People's government to encourage indolence and the lack of foresight regarding the means of subsistence by providing [it] at [the customers'] door at a very high price instead of at a place a few steps away [where] they could find it more cheaply." The market encouraged "competition of sellers, a competition that can never be found in a store where it takes place only among buyers." The grains market was "the last remaining work of the old wisdom that succored the poor," and ending it "would be the last blow [derived] from the terrible application . . . of economic theories."[25] So the arguments, pro and con, were clearly put. Who would win?

With the fate of the public grains market in doubt, in 1847 the provincial president named a commission to consider whether the market should be maintained. Their report was ambivalent. It concluded that, indeed, the market served a useful purpose "for those engaged in the petty commerce of buying meal [in the towns of the Recôncavo] for sale in this city" by providing them with "a good storage place" for their goods. But the larger ships engaged in coastwise shipping should no longer be required to use it instead of unloading where they pleased, since they wanted to linger in port as little time as possible.

To avoid such delay, many of them bypassed Salvador altogether. The commission concluded that large-volume merchants should be entitled to unload manioc meal directly to their warehouses.[26]

Nothing came of the commission's report at the time, but in 1849 the grocers managed to persuade a newly elected city council, by what means one can only imagine, to reverse their long-held course and adopt a firmly liberal position, completely abolishing the old rules. The council granted permission to sell manioc meal in all stores with only one restriction: such stores must be located on squares where competitors could also set up shop, and buyers could compare prices. The administrator of the grains market complained bitterly, saying that "a lot of persons, store owners in the upper city and others who in various places resell it," had rushed onto the boats "and bought up all the large amounts that were aboard and unloaded them to their stores, leaving only a few small remainders" for the grains market. As a consequence, he said, the price shot up by 55 percent. The now-liberal city council denied the price had risen and then said that, well, if it had, that was because of the "huge storm that day." They claimed that "everyone praised the said measure," concluding that "freedom is the soul of commerce. Any imposed restrictions are fetters that deny it all progress, all prosperity." Storekeepers did not crow publicly, but they must have cheered their success at last.[27]

Advocates of the older system refused to give up. The conflict came to a head once again when the city faced a dire shortage of manioc meal in late 1856, caused by a severe drought and the previous year's cholera epidemic.[28] Reacting to loud and widespread complaints that store owners were hoarding it, the council reversed its 1849 decision and, in January 1857, ruled that all meal entering the city must again be sold first at the grains market, and only there, so that everyone could see how much was on hand. They then rationed the amount that could be sold to any one buyer and banned "forestallers," including street vendors, from buying directly from boats anchored in the bay. Strikingly, they here emphasized transparency without trying to set a maximum price.[29]

All city ordinances had to be approved by the provincial legislature, although the usual practice was to put them into force provisionally until the legislature met. In this case, even though it was not scheduled to meet until October, the provincial president persuaded the city to suspend enforcement until then. They reluctantly did so, but only as a test, they said, pointing to "history" and the success of the grains market in curtailing monopolies in past times of scarcity, "ever since the governorship of Sir Rodrigo [José de Menezes]." The president, João Lins Vieira Cansansão de Sinimbu (1810–1907) was a dyed-in-the-wool economic liberal who had spent several years in Europe working on his doctorate at the progressive University of Jena and was married to the daughter of a British-German businessman whom he had met in Dresden. When the legislature met, it took no action on the matter, perhaps because Sinimbu had briefed them on his views. City councillors wrote him again in November, noting that there was abundant manioc meal in the interior, yet the price in the city continued to rise. They blamed the grocers.[30]

In late January 1858, with the drought intensifying and prices once again shooting up, the council reissued the previous year's ordinance, arguing that since the legislature had not turned them down, its validity was assured. Not only did it repeat that all manioc meal must be sold at the grains market, but required that all stocks currently held at the stores should be turned in to the market within twenty days. The price of manioc meal immediately fell by 24 percent.[31]

Sinimbu saw things differently. He sent the council a long letter presenting in detail his liberal economic principles. He accused the council members of not sufficiently committing themselves to the "examination of economic matters." He asserted that their power "does not extend to obliging the producer to send his products to a place where he cannot sell them as he wishes." When they ignored him, he declared their decision invalid and ordered the provincial chief of police to guarantee storekeepers their right to sell manioc meal and block the city inspectors from doing their work.[32]

His act invited urban outrage. On February 25 the council sent the president a stinging rebuke, stating their legal right to issue the ordinance and accusing him of malfeasance and usurpation of authority. His response was swift. He suspended most of its members from office for a period of 160 days, charging them on a technicality of "failing to carry out a legally issued order from another [public] employee," and then summoned their substitutes. A deposed council member proclaimed that "the People do not live by theories, they live by reality! When they know that . . . the lack of foodstuffs [results from] a monopoly formed by some soulless men . . . they cannot help but curse them. And the target on which they then fire is the government because the government has as its most important duty to promote . . . the well-being of the governed." Handbills appeared on walls in protest, some even threatening the president's life.[33]

On Sunday, three days later, things turned nasty. A crowd gathered in the square in front of the governor's palace to protest an apparently unrelated matter—the president's protection of a French order of nuns accused of abusing their power to administer a retreat house for young women—and the area was filled by midafternoon. (The governor's palace is the large building at the upper center of Figure 1.1.) The British consul described those present as "composed exclusively of the lower orders," and the chief of police alleged there was not "a single man of any importance" in the crowd, but a contemporary illustrator portrayed several men with top hats. Aside from one street vendor whose food stand went crashing in the subsequent mêlée, all those pictured were men. The crowd soon forgot the nuns and switched to demands for better and cheaper food, accusing the president of siding with the greedy storekeepers against the starving people. They shouted rhyming slogans about manioc meal and fresh meat. They stormed the council building, which also faced the square, and climbed its tower, ringing the bell, an ancient means of summoning people at times of crisis. Returning to the front of the governor's palace, the crowd became ugly. Stones began to fly. When they broke windows in the palace—a building Sinimbu had spent much effort to remodel—troops were called out, some from the cavalry. Soldiers on foot with fixed bayonets worked alongside the mounted officers in dispersing the crowd. By 7 p.m. they had succeeded.[34]

The next morning protesters were back, this time to impede the formal seating of the new council members. By occupying city hall and taking possession of the space that symbolized decision making, they insisted on the legitimacy of their demands. The council chair called on soldiers to expel the crowd from the chambers. More violent confrontations took place on the square outside, and fifty-three participants in the fracas ended up in jail, including fifteen slaves and three other men of color, which suggests that most of those imprisoned were white. Others, probably persons of color, were summarily drafted into the navy.[35]

Sinimbu and the storekeepers appeared victorious. The newly seated council members moved immediately to revoke the controversial ordinance and allow storekeepers to stock as much manioc meal as they wished. Sinimbu promised a few palliative measures

FIGURE 11.1. City council chambers, Salvador, ca. 1860

within the limits of his authority "to minimize the evil of which the people complain," and then turned for advice to the Commercial Association, made up of merchants, a third of them foreigners, mostly British. Not surprisingly, they favored liberalism and backed him up. The long-term solution to high prices was to stimulate "open and free competition," which was "the greatest enemy of monopoly." The current crisis was the result of drought, and "all the restrictive measures that can be imagined will not make one manioc plant grow or bring one grain of meal" to market. That is what Sinimbu wanted to hear, but his actions hardly made him popular. More threats on his life were made after the riot, and when he was presiding over a parade in March, a shot rang out, the bullet just missing him. Whether it was fired by one of the soldiers on parade or by a spectator was never established. When Sinimbu left for Rio de Janeiro in June, he was escorted to the ship by an armed guard to ensure his safety.[36]

Presidents came and presidents went, but the people of Salvador remained. As soon as Sinimbu left to take up a seat in the senate, the original members of the city council reassumed their posts and reissued their controversial ordinance. The provincial vice president, a local man, presented it for approval to the legislative assembly. The council repeated their case, alleging that the trade in manioc meal had fallen into the hands of three or four individuals who formed "a calculatingly planned and applied monopoly," agreeing on prices of "purchase and of sale." These men, "not content with reasonable profits, customarily speculate on the needs of people from whom they aim to suck the last substance." In a not too subtle jab at Sinimbu's hectoring condescension, they added that those who considered only commercial freedom had not sufficiently committed themselves to "the examination of our market's circumstances." The legislature approved the measure, agreeing that the root cause of scarcity and high prices was hoarding by merchants.[37]

The prestige of the grains market had nevertheless been diminished, and as the drought eased, so did the controversy. By the end of 1860 the city had designated several additional locations besides the market where manioc meal could be legally purchased. The next year members of a new city council once again leaned toward economic liberalism and completely freed the trade in meal, allowing merchants to store as much of it as they wished and to sell it wherever they wished. Consequently, a few big businessmen gained control of the trade. About this time a city committee described the old marketplace as "a pigsty; the floor is filthy [and] covered in mud so that in some places the bricks are entirely hidden." In 1866 the public grains market permanently closed its doors. In 1878, during one of the most blistering droughts ever experienced in northeastern Brazil, the old public grains market was recalled with nostalgia as "the only secure, regular, and speedy means of always knowing at a particular moment . . . the real supply of meal in the market."[38]

Economic liberalism made only hesitant progress in Salvador. In the 1820s, with Brazil newly independent, national laws embodied its principles, although in practice its advocates in Salvador enjoyed only moderate success. In the 1830s a reaction set in as people noted that prices soared while competition among sellers remained anemic. Twenty years later people understood the liberal champion Sinimbu to be taking sides against the people, especially against the poor and almost poor, in favor of the few favored by fortune. Salvador's resistance emerges as a determined effort to reassert inherited communal

values and a striving toward an older concept of justice, one that required those in authority to shelter the weak from the oppressions of
the strong. The 1837 revolt and the 1858 riot were both oriented toward restoring an earlier moral economy, not at upending the social
order. At root, the debate swirled around a definition of the good and
the proper, and the acute tension between individual freedom and the
general welfare.[39]

Liberal theory presupposed a society characterized by a more-or-
less equal distribution of wealth and power, but rank still seemed
natural in Brazil and remained generally unquestioned, even if some
objected to their particular place in the social pyramid. In a setting
of marked inequality, economically liberal measures allowed the few
to take over the market entirely for themselves. As the city council
understood it in 1858, "the existence of a monopoly in foodstuffs is
a fact, and it cannot be destroyed through commercial freedom, because this freedom is worthless where there is no free competition."[40]
Faced with an option, people preferred government paternalism, even
if it led to scarcity and a black market in foodstuffs, over a liberalism
that, through the seemingly inevitable processes of capitalism, led
to oligopolies and continued shortages and high prices. Everything
suggested to the people of Salvador that economic liberalism did not
work. It was useless theory.

CONCLUSION

IT'S EASY TO SAY SALVADOR'S was a society of orders, but what does that mean in terms of people's experience? What are the exceptions—in this case multitudinous—that stretch and bend the categories that are meant to contain them? Wealth and inherited status certainly played a large role in building an invisible tracery to keep people in place. Yet the vertical ordering of society was confounded by interpersonal contacts, status reversals, physical movement, and individual social mobility. This was true even metaphorically in regard to the city's physical arrangement. True, the upper city of government offices, baroque churches, and elegant stone houses seemed to distance itself from the lower one, with its narrow, grimy streets, its grains market, merchant houses, wharves, and warehouses. But street vendors plied their trade in both the upper and lower parts of the city, and the slaughterhouse, although originally outside the city, was on high ground. In every district could be found self-hired slaves, freed slaves, free-born blacks and mulattos, and whites—poor, rich, and middle class, Brazilian and Portuguese—all living and working in proximity. The African-born street vendor Ana de São José da Trindade, who eventually owned a three-story house with glass windows and gilt-framed English paintings, was noticeably wealthier than many Portuguese-born storekeepers. Enslaved boat captains exercised authority over free white sailors. Although neighborhoods seem to have contained more or less similar people in terms of their wealth, they lived cheek-by-jowl with those of differing color. Such mixed neighborhoods and daily business contacts tended to blur social distinctions and encourage shifting identities. At least one can say these markers were elastic, with overlapping categories ranged across a continuum of ranks. Multiple barriers were penetrable and subject to negotiation, so everyone had to be continually alert to shifting position.

The business and busy-ness of the food trade lay at the heart of city life. Those engaged in buying and selling foodstuffs worked energetically and constantly, constructing a vigorous and dynamic market system. Merchants bought cattle at interior fairs, and drovers brought them daily to the slaughterhouse, where muscular workers slaughtered, gutted, skinned, and bled with expertise, while others transported the quarters to butcher shops for sale to consumers. Boatmen took advantage of water transport to supply the city with its calories and much else. At the grains market women and men—some working on their own account and others as agents or clerks for others, some born in Portugal and others in Africa—bought corn, beans, rice and manioc meal from boat captains and sailors to resell to householders or to street vendors and grocers. They were assisted by those who did the heavy lifting and lugging: lightermen, stevedores, and porters, both slave and free. At the local grocer's the consumer found for sale manioc meal produced just across the bay, and spices imported from far-away India. The streets were filled with vendors hawking fruits and vegetables, eggs, manioc meal, salt, and cooked delicacies, both sweet and savory. Sailors and slaughtermen, stevedores and porters, Africans at the grains market and on the street—all confidently exercised precise skills. Differences emerged based on what people did, not always on who they were.

All these people were connected to one another. Not only were there the daily face-to-face contacts between suppliers and retailers, but there was the necessary advancing of credit down the ladder from large merchant houses to grocers and street vendors, and then steady repayments up again in reverse. Everyone sought to maintain or expand their network of patronage and clientage, building essential trust. Family, friends, and neighbors extended the network into the broader community.

This was a slave society. It seems at times that everyone who was not a slave owned one. Yet slaves were not merely chattel, and an urban setting made it impractical to treat them as such. They engaged in trade on their own account, keeping what they earned beyond a fixed amount and many times using their earnings to buy their freedom. Slavery also made possible the cruelty of stocks and shackles, thumb screws, cutting off a lip with the vicious swing of a fish knife. Contradictory realities confound simplistic conclusions.

Political events and changing notions on the role of government directly impacted the work of food traders. The year-long Independence War brought a sudden shift in reality and perceptions. The black militia cut off the supply of meat to the city, a crucial step in imposing a siege. Sailors and captains, mostly men of color and a large number enslaved, on the whole chose to take manioc meal to the insurgent army and not to the Portuguese ensconced in the city, despite the temptation to make a killing in profits. The war heightened differences between Brazilians and Portuguese, and linked white planters to non-white sailors and soldiers. At the same time war drew attention to the racial differences between the black and mulatto fighting men on the Brazilian side and the invariably white Portuguese soldiers. The tumult of war also weakened the slave system and stirred new fears among masters regarding all persons of color, so many of whom dealt in food.

This was never a harmonious society and became less so over the course of the years surveyed here. Mutinies of black soldiers were followed by a strike for higher wages among black slaughtermen. In 1835 a major uprising of Africans in the city, the "Malê" revolt, led to the discovery of a wide network of communication among them spanning not only the city, but reaching far into the interior. Two years later porters and stevedores, men of color, launched a strike as they refused to be regimented into work gangs captained by those chosen by whites. By November 1837 the rising cost of meat helped provoke a major revolt that opened space for the active participation of blacks and mulattos demanding greater attention to the plight of the poor during a time of rising prices.

These tensions are best understood within the context of a persistent cultural heritage that validated the notion of a ranked society as appropriate and just. The legitimacy of privilege, honor, and public esteem, awarded to some and denied to others, depended on the simultaneous conviction that those above would care for those below, especially when it came to the government's supervision of trading in food items of prime necessity. People believed that one of the most important roles of government consisted precisely in protecting the people in this way. It did so by enforcing price controls and regulating street vendors, grocers, boatmen, cattle dealers, butchers, and food traders. Regulations on the trade in manioc meal were long maintained, especially one requiring that no manioc meal could go to grocery stores or street vendors until it had first been placed for sale at the public grains market, where everyone could see the quantity, compare the quality, and make their household's purchases.

Political and intellectual leaders gradually accepted and applied diametrically contrary principles regarding the economy, principles derived from an individualistic liberal philosophy. The end of regulation drew support from grocers, cattle dealers, boatmen, and traders at the grains market, as well as from the Lisbon colonial secretary, a High Court judge, a local lawyer, and a warehouse owner who acted as spokesman for cattle dealers and boatmen. The city council at first objected, then grudgingly complied with directives based on the new notions of political economy.

The reformers, however, did not challenge the validity of social gradations and, in this way, exposed the new ideas to eventual rebuff. Such a switch in policy triggered a reaction from consumers—one that sometimes turned violent. The promised abundance and lowering of prices resulting from competition did not occur. When the city council allowed merchants to bypass the public grains market and buy directly from suppliers, stocking unlimited amounts, it laid the groundwork for accusations of hoarding. These accusations became especially strident at a time of scarcity in 1857–1858, resulting in riot. The real battle, however, was always an ideological one in which people debated competing views of the Good. The value of individual freedom versus general equity was in question. Some struggled for fairness, social dignity, and a just society in preference to that liberty.

Examining identifiable participants in the food trade makes possible a more nuanced understanding of Salvador's complex and variable society. The strength and creative inventiveness of the human spirit emerges as the driving force of that society—as is perhaps always true.

When the purchasing power of a currency varies significantly over time as it did in Brazil, an estate of several *contos* may be a sign of extraordinary wealth at one time and be relatively common among persons of a middling sort several decades later. One common technique used to solve this problem is simply to convert the currency at any one time to that of a more stable economy; for example, the pound sterling or the U.S. dollar.[1] One naturally asks, however, whether the foreign exchange rate is the best guide to local purchasing power, given that many of those at the lower end of the socioeconomic scale never, or rarely, bought imported goods nor depended directly on exports for their livelihood. For them, food is a more important criterion, and as a general rule, over time the price of all goods produced locally tends to move in tandem with the price of food. For this reason I have also included here the price of manioc meal and fresh meat. In addition, virtually every estate inventory in Salvador from 1780 to 1860 included slaves, even among those that listed very little else. It is well known that the prices of slaves increased dramatically during the period I am studying, albeit there were periods in which they declined,[2] so I determined to take their price into account also in calculating the real value of an estate. I chose the year 1824 as the base year for establishing an index, for several reasons. It lies roughly halfway through the period that I study here. By then the war for Brazilian independence had ended, but the political instability that ensued had not yet begun, so values continued to reflect colonial understandings of economic realities. The export economy of the region still prospered. And by this date I could include price data for all four items of my inquiry—that is, manioc meal, meat, slaves, and the pound sterling (or, rather, the pence sterling). I arbitrarily decided, following the example of others, to weigh these four factors equally.[3] The sources for the data are indicated in Table A.1.

Table A.1. Arriving at an Index of Prices and Exchange Rates for Salvador, 1790–1860, with a Conversion Multiplier

Year	Manioc meal price[a] (réis per liter)	5-yr avg.	Manioc meal index (1824 = 100)	Meat price[b] (réis per kg)	5-yr avg.	Meat index (1824 = 100)	FX-SSA[c] (d. per milréis)
1789	13.2			40.7			66
1790	10.6			40.7			66.4
1791	10	12.5	31	40.7	41.8	26	67.7
1792	13.4	13.4	33	40.7	44.5	28	70.9
1793	15.4	15.1	37	46.4	47.2	29	67.7
1794	17.6	17.2	43	54.2	50.4	31	63.9
1795	19.2	18.2	45	54.2	52.8	33	67.1
1796	20.4	19.5	48	56.3	61.0	38	
1797		23.0	57		68.0	42	
1798	20.7	24.2	60	79.3	74.9	47	
1799	31.62	24.0	59	82	82.9	52	
1800	24.26	22.7	56	82	83.6	52	
1801	19.27	23.2	57	88.4	84.8	53	
1802	17.49	20.1	50	86.5	84.6	53	
1803	23.34	17.6	44	84.9	84.9	53	63.4
1804	16.26	16.6	41	81	84.0	52	60.6
1805	11.58	17.2	42	83.8	85.6	53	60.8
1806	14.23	18.3	45	83.6	85.4	53	61.8
1807	20.38	17.3	43	94.7	84.2	52	64.2
1808	29.01	17.5	43	83.9	81.0	50	72
1809	11.3	18.9	47	75	81.7	51	73.6
1810	12.7	19.6	48	67.6	80.2	50	71.7
1811	21	17.5	43	87.2	80.5	50	73.6
1812	23.9	18.4	46	87.3	82.8	52	76.6
1813	18.4	19.9	49	85.4	86.1	54	76.6
1814	16	21.2	53	86.5	86.3	54	76.1
1815	20	25.5	63	84.1	87.8	55	64
1816	27.9	29.9	74	88	92.3	57	57
1817	45	30.6	76	95.1	103.0	64	72.3
1818	40.8	29.5	73	107.9	108.3	67	66.1

Year	FX-SSA (réis per d.)	5-yr. avg.	FX-SSA index (1824 = 100)	Avg. price of healthy, skilled male African slave (moço)[d] (in réis)	5-yr.avg.	Index of slave prices (1824 = 100)	Avg. index of manioc meal, meat, FX-SSA and slave price (1824 = 100)	Multiplier for any figure
1789	15	15	74					
1790	15	15	73					
1791	15	15	73				43	2.30
1792	14	15	74				45	2.23
1793	15	15	73				47	2.14
1794	16	15	74				49	2.03
1795	15	15	75				51	1.97
1796		15	76				54	1.85
1797		15	74				58	1.73
1798							53	1.88
1799							55	1.80
1800							54	1.85
1801							55	1.82
1802							51	1.95
1803	16	16	80				59	1.70
1804	17	16	80				58	1.73
1805	16	16	80				58	1.71
1806	16	16	78				59	1.70
1807	16	15	75				57	1.76
1808	14	15	72				55	1.80
1809	14	14	70				56	1.79
1810	14	14	67				55	1.81
1811	14	13	67	129,444	130,576	68	57	1.75
1812	13	13	66	118,000	129,182	68	58	1.73
1813	13	14	68	144,285	129,182	68	60	1.68
1814	13	14	72	125,000	131,821	69	62	1.62
1815	16	15	72		143,571	75	66	1.51
1816	18	15	75	140,000	146,250	77	71	1.41
1817	14	16	79	165,000	164,167	86	76	1.31
1818	15	17	82	155,000	172,280	90	78	1.28

(continued)

Table A.1. (*continued*)

Year	Manioc meal price[a] (réis per liter)	5-yr avg.	Manioc meal index (1824 = 100)	Meat price[b] (réis per kg)	5-yr avg.	Meat index (1824 = 100)	FX-SSA[c] (d. per milréis)
1819	19.4	27.9	69	139.8	114.4	71	57.8
1820	14.2	24.6	61	110.6	144.8	90	51.5
1821	19.9	35.2	87	118.7	160.9	100	50
1822	28.5	35.7	88	247.1	155.6	97	49
1823	94.2	37.3	92	188.3	166.8	104	50.7
1824	21.9	40.4	100	113.2	160.7	100	48.2
1825	22.2	40.4	100		131.8	82	51.8
1826	35.3	27.6	68	94	103.6	64	48.1
1827	28.6	36.4	90		119.4	74	35.2
1828	29.8	36.4	90		128.3	80	31.6
1829	65.9	33.8	84	144.8	152.9	95	24.6
1830	22.5	32.4	80	146.2	161.9	101	22.8
1831	22.2			167.7			25
1832	21.7			188.7			35.1
1833							37.8
1834							38.7
1835							39.2
1836							38.4
1837							29.5
1838							28.6
1839							31.6
1840							31
1841							30.3
1842							26.8
1843	19			173.6			25.8
1844	18.3			173.6			23.1
1845	37.4	36.7	91	217.1	200.14	125	25.4
1846	52.1	41.3	102	208	211	131	26.9
1847	56.7	46.3	115	228.4	223.78	139	28
1848	42.2	45.4	112	227.9	222.76	139	25
1849	43.2	43.1	107	237.5	224.24	140	25.8

Year	FX-SSA (réis per d.)	5-yr. avg.	FX-SSA index (1824 = 100)	Avg. price of healthy, skilled male African slave (moço)[d] (in réis)	5-yr.avg.	Index of slave prices (1824 = 100)	Avg. index of manioc meal, meat, FX-SSA and slave price (1824 = 100)	Multiplier for any figure
1819	17	17	85	196,666	178,280	94	80	1.26
1820	19	18	91	204,736	177,050	93	84	1.19
1821	20	19	96	170,000	176,550	93	94	1.06
1822	20	20	99	158,846	169,307	89	93	1.07
1823	20	20	99	152,500	174,421	91	97	1.03
1824	21	20	100	160,454	190,631	100	100	1.00
1825	19	22	108	230,303	210,771	111	100	1.00
1826	21	24	120	251,052	226,414	119	93	1.08
1827	28	28	139	259,545	260,323	137	110	0.91
1828	32	33	164	230,714	284,262	149	121	0.83
1829	41	37	183	330,000	305,265	160	130	0.77
1830	44	37	183	350,000	312,489	164	132	0.76
1831	40	36	178	356,065	333,872	175	176	0.57
1832	28	33	163	295,666	328,206	172	168	0.60
1833	26	29	145	337,631	326,933	172	158	0.63
1834	26	26	131	301,666	330,886	174	152	0.66
1835	26	28	136	343,635	349,753	183	160	0.63
1836	26	29	145	375,833	376,437	197	171	0.58
1837	34	30	151	390,000	406,656	213	182	0.55
1838	35	32	157	471,052	427,929	224	191	0.52
1839	32	33	164	452,758	446,845	234	199	0.50
1840	32	34	168	450,000	465,095	244	206	0.49
1841	33	35	171	470,416	478,551	251	211	0.47
1842	37	37	183	481,250	486,750	255	219	0.46
1843	39	38	190	538,333	486,416	255	223	0.45
1844	43	39	194	493,750	498,269	261	228	0.44
1845	39	39	192	448,333	510,176	268	169	0.59
1846	37	39	194	529,677	510,404	268	174	0.58
1847	36	38	189	540,789	505,233	265	177	0.56
1848	40	37	185	539,473	507,294	266	175	0.57
1849	39	37	182	467,894	520,807	273	175	0.57

(continued)

Table A.1. (*continued*)

Year	Manioc meal price[a] (réis per liter)	5-yr avg.	Manioc meal index (1824 = 100)	Meat price[b] (réis per kg)	5-yr avg.	Meat index (1824 = 100)	FX-SSA[c] (d. per milréis)
1850	32.6	39.0	96	212	221.88	138	28.7
1851	40.7	42.6	105	215.4	221.88	138	29.1
1852	36.1	44.1	109	216.6	218.68	136	27.4
1853	60.2	45.9	114	227.9	230.96	144	28.5
1854	50.7	50.4	125	221.5	251.66	157	27.6
1855	41.7	64.5	160	273.4	281.44	175	27.5
1856	63.5	72.9	180	318.9	327.74	204	27.5
1857	106.6	86.8	215	365.5	381.1	237	26.6
1858	101.9	99.7	247	459.4	427.7	266	25.5
1859	120.2	97.6	241	488.3	438.6	273	25.6
1860	106.2	85.8	212	506.4	430.14	268	25.8

Note: Exchange rates in Salvador are labeled FX-SSA.

[a]From Kátia M. de Queirós Mattoso, "Au nouveau monde: Une province d'un nouvel empire—Bahia au XIXe siècle" (Ph.D. diss., Université de Paris-Sorbonne, 1986), pp. 447–458. She has no data for 1833–1842.

[b]Ibid.

[c]FX-SSA refers to the foreign exchange rate in Salvador. From Kátia M. de Queirós Mattoso, *Bahia: A cidade de Salvador e seu mercado no século XIX*, Coleção Estudos Brasileiros, no. 12 (São Paulo and Salvador: HUCITEC and Secretaria Municipal de Educação e Cultura, 1978), p. 243n, with additional data on the Lisbon exchange rate for the period before 1808 compiled and calculated from http://gpih.ucdavis.edu/datafilelist.htm and from Nicolaas Wilhelmus Posthumus, *Inquiry into the History of Prices in Holland*, 2 vols. (Leiden: Brill, 1946–1964), 1: 607–616.

Year	FX-SSA (réis per d.)	5-yr. avg.	FX-SSA index (1824 = 100)	Avg. price of healthy, skilled male African slave (moço)[d] (in réis)	5-yr.avg.	Index of slave prices (1824 = 100)	Avg. index of manioc meal, meat, FX-SSA and slave price (1824 = 100)	Multiplier for any figure
1850	35	37	183	458,636	529,711	278	174	0.58
1851	34	36	178	597,241	557,623	293	178	0.56
1852	36	35	175	585,312	607,044	318	185	0.54
1853	35	36	177	679,032	698,174	366	200	0.50
1854	36	36	179	715,000	749,976	393	213	0.47
1855	36	36	180	914,285	853,851	448	241	0.42
1856	36	37	184	856,250	990,772	520	272	0.37
1857	38	38	187	1,104,687	1,047,772	550	297	0.34
1858	39	38	189	1,363,636	1,086,915	570	318	0.31
1859	39	39	192	1,000,000	1,144,581	600	327	0.31
1860	39	39	192	1,110,000	1,157,879	607	320	0.31

[d]From Maria José de Souza Andrade, A mão de obra escrava em Salvador, 1811–1860, Baianada 8 (São Paulo and Brasília: Corrupio and CNPq, 1988), pp. 207–208. Her study is based on 1,269 inventories from 1811 to 1860.

Appendix B. Volume of Foodstuff Handled at the Grains Market, 1785–1849 (in *alqueires*)

Year	Manioc Meal	%	Rice	%	Maize	%	Beans	%	Total	%
1785	83,949.75	88.88	6,003.75	6.36	2,522.50	2.67	1,973.50	2.09	94,449.50	100
1786	221,078.25	82.56	13,056.50	4.88	26,199.50	9.78	7,449.50	2.78	267,783.75	100
1787	230,060.50	82.03	18,169.50	6.48	24,539.00	8.75	7,675.25	2.74	280,444.25	100
1788	289,809.50	87.52	10,520.50	3.18	23,020.50	6.95	7,774.75	2.35	331,125.25	100
1789	269,992.75	86.55	7,247.00	2.32	28,840.25	9.25	5,856.00	1.88	311,936.00	100
1790	274,636.50	86.87	7,605.00	2.41	22,288.00	7.05	11,629.00	3.68	316,158.50	100
1791	289,648.50	91.05	11,157.00	3.51	10,581.50	3.33	6,745.75	2.12	318,132.75	100
1792	365,378.50	93.63	9,538.00	2.44	11,819.00	3.03	3,505.50	0.90	390,241.00	100
1793	257,502.50	90.12	10,087.00	3.53	12,621.00	4.42	5,513.00	1.93	285,723.50	100
1794	237,140.25	89.23	7,245.75	2.73	14,897.75	5.61	6,475.00	2.44	265,758.75	100
1795	282,444.00	89.03	7,416.75	2.34	21,418.50	6.75	5,967.00	1.88	317,246.25	100
1796	300,292.00	89.91	10,043.00	3.01	19,376.00	5.80	4,285.00	1.28	333,996.00	100
1797	289,089.00	89.61	7,077.00	2.19	18,497.00	5.73	7,954.00	2.47	322,617.00	100
1798	278,949.00	86.44	6,263.00	1.94	25,716.00	7.97	11,772.00	3.65	322,700.00	100
1799	288,611.00	87.66	10,243.00	3.11	24,006.00	7.29	6,375.00	1.94	329,235.00	100
1800	281,155.00	88.23	7,574.00	2.38	21,806.00	6.84	8,135.00	2.55	318,670.00	100
1801	279,908.00	89.17	5,610.00	1.79	23,091.00	7.36	5,299.00	1.69	313,908.00	100
1802	362,218.00	92.11	6,186.00	1.57	19,296.00	4.91	5,546.00	1.41	393,246.00	100
1803	302,031.00	87.81	9,641.00	2.80	25,797.00	7.50	6,472.00	1.88	343,941.00	100
1804	200,406.00	85.95	6,254.00	2.68	21,644.00	9.28	4,853.00	2.08	233,157.00	100
1805	287,181.00	86.73	17,407.00	5.26	21,216.00	6.41	5,316.00	1.61	331,120.00	100

(continued)

Year	Manioc Meal	%	Rice	%	Maize	%	Beans	%	Total	%
1806	347,083.00	84.76	29,721.00	7.26	27,244.00	6.65	5,434.00	1.33	409,482.00	100
1807	391,807.00	84.24	38,163.00	8.20	28,056.00	6.03	7,104.00	1.53	465,130.00	100
1808	297,751.00	81.25	32,202.00	8.79	30,150.00	8.23	6,370.00	1.74	366,473.00	100
1809	290,709.00	82.51	20,146.00	5.72	34,335.00	9.75	7,142.00	2.03	352,332.00	100
1810	311,376.00	84.53	17,435.00	4.73	33,898.00	9.20	5,656.00	1.54	368,365.00	100
1811	360,671.00	86.12	23,363.00	5.58	28,046.00	6.70	6,712.00	1.60	418,792.00	100
1812	327,691.00	79.51	45,799.00	11.11	29,860.00	7.25	8,773.00	2.13	412,123.00	100
1813	346,567.00	83.11	34,630.00	8.30	29,029.00	6.96	6,791.00	1.63	417,017.00	100
1814	325,259.00	76.16	64,707.00	15.15	32,529.00	7.62	4,590.00	1.07	427,085.00	100
1815	336,349.00	74.72	69,562.00	15.45	39,658.00	8.81	4,572.00	1.02	450,141.00	100
1816	368,837.00	80.05	55,654.00	12.08	32,439.00	7.04	3,831.00	0.83	460,761.00	100
1817	447,133.00	86.40	28,824.00	5.57	32,992.00	6.37	8,579.00	1.66	517,528.00	100
1818	335,368.00	82.60	20,774.00	5.12	38,043.00	9.37	11,832.00	2.91	406,017.00	100
1819	409,438.00	86.14	25,486.00	5.36	32,510.00	6.84	7,895.00	1.66	475,329.00	100
1820	431,345.00	89.58	21,174.00	4.40	22,712.00	4.72	6,264.00	1.30	481,495.00	100
1821	440,259.00	89.92	13,780.00	2.81	29,921.00	6.11	5,652.00	1.15	489,612.00	100
1822	348,934.00	89.54	11,849.00	3.04	23,983.00	6.15	4,921.00	1.26	389,687.00	100
1823	152,214.00	89.09	11,025.00	6.45	4,845.00	2.84	2,766.00	1.62	170,850.00	100
1824	336,234.00	92.69	16,698.00	4.60	7,898.00	2.18	1,921.00	0.53	362,751.00	100
1825	409,654.00	89.64	24,132.00	5.28	17,561.00	3.84	5,630.00	1.23	456,977.00	100
1826	399,369.00	90.29	19,893.00	4.50	17,347.00	3.92	5,732.00	1.30	442,341.00	100
1827	371,071.00	86.62	26,139.00	6.10	23,959.00	5.59	7,236.00	1.69	428,405.00	100

Year		%		%		%		%		%
1828	411,175.00	88.62	18,293.00	3.94	28,461.00	6.13	6,051.00	1.30	463,980.00	100
1829	433,011.00	83.47	39,811.00	7.67	37,126.00	7.16	8,844.00	1.70	518,792.00	100
1830	467,863.00	80.00	44,662.00	7.64	65,273.00	11.16	7,052.00	1.21	584,850.00	100
1831	401,377.00	83.52	25,587.00	5.32	48,412.00	10.07	5,173.00	1.08	480,549.00	100
1832	350,723.00	87.67	21,368.00	5.34	24,580.00	6.14	3,369.00	0.84	400,040.00	100
1833	341,343.00	91.20	14,520.00	3.88	15,171.00	4.05	3,262.00	0.87	374,296.00	100
1834	474,208.00	92.32	17,063.00	3.32	19,605.00	3.82	2,757.00	0.54	513,633.00	100
1835	478,931.00	87.27	25,118.00	4.58	37,173.00	6.77	7,590.00	1.38	548,812.00	100
1836	470,569.00	91.11	20,673.00	4.00	21,751.00	4.21	3,499.00	0.68	516,492.00	100
1837	462,023.00	91.72	12,705.00	2.52	27,403.00	5.44	1,588.00	0.32	503,719.00	100
1838	315,889.00	85.32	16,712.00	4.51	36,014.00	9.73	1,606.00	0.43	370,221.00	100
1839	380,110.00	90.12	17,929.00	4.25	22,802.00	5.41	930.00	0.22	421,771.00	100
1840	316,223.00	89.04	12,913.00	3.64	24,347.00	6.86	1,668.00	0.47	355,151.00	100
1841	368,350.00	92.69	12,475.00	3.14	15,223.00	3.83	1,337.00	0.34	397,385.00	100
1842	526,160.00	91.61	12,966.00	2.26	29,538.00	5.14	5,680.00	0.99	574,344.00	100
1843	381,006.00	88.01	20,295.00	4.69	30,127.00	6.96	1,473.00	0.34	432,901.00	100
1844	368,873.00	90.56	16,985.00	4.17	19,779.00	4.86	1,694.00	0.42	407,331.00	100
1845	375,888.00	90.76	26,106.00	6.30	11,342.00	2.74	837.00	0.20	414,173.00	100
1846	445,822.00	91.80	23,508.00	4.84	14,104.00	2.90	2,209.00	0.45	485,643.00	100
1847	441,426.00	93.92	15,938.00	3.39	10,013.00	2.13	2,621.00	0.56	469,998.00	100
1848	456,597.00	92.61	20,452.00	4.15	13,014.00	2.64	2,961.00	0.60	493,024.00	100
1849	261,931.00	92.21	10,442.50	3.68	9,145.00	3.22	2,535.00	0.89	284,053.50	100
Totals	22,386,098.00	87.44	1,292,022.25	5.05	1,576,610.50	6.16	346,710.25	1.35	25,601,441.00	100

Source: Mappa demonstrativo do numero de alqueires dos differentes generos que pagarão a contribuição e o rendimento, a despeza e o liquido, e teve principio em 9 de setembro de 1785 até 31 de maio de 1849, Arquivo Público do Estado da Bahia, M. 1611.

NOTES

ABBREVIATIONS

ABNRJ	*Anais da Biblioteca Nacional do Rio de Janeiro*
Admin.	Administrador
AHM	Arquivo Histórico Militar, Lisbon
AHU	Arquivo Histórico Ultramarino, Lisbon
AIHGB	Arquivo do Instituto Histórico e Geográfico Brasileiro, Rio de Janeiro
AMS	Arquivo Municipal de Salvador, Salvador
AN	Arquivo Nacional, Rio de Janeiro
ANTT	Arquivo Nacional da Torre do Tombo, Lisbon
APEB	Arquivo Público do Estado da Bahia, Salvador
ASCM	Arquivo da Santa Casa de Misericórdia, Salvador
BA	Bahia
BN/SM	Biblioteca Nacional, Seção de Manuscritos, Rio de Janeiro
CP	Colonial e Provincial
Cx.	Caixa
IT	Inventários e Testamentos
Inv.	Inventário
Jourdan, Breve noticia	Antonio Jourdan, Breve noticia sobre o provimento das carnes na Cidade da Bahia, 1818, AN, SPE, Cód. 807, Vol. 13
JP	Juiz de Paz
LB	*Colleção das Leis do Império do Brasil*
M.	Maço
MDU	Ministro e Secretário de Estado da Marinha e Domínios Ultramarinos, Portugal
MGuerra	Ministro de Guerra
MI	Ministro do Império
MJ	Ministro da Justiça
MM	Ministro da Marinha
MRE	Ministro (or Ministério) de Relações Exteriores
PP-BA	Presidente da Província, Bahia
PRO	Public Record Office, London
Ribeiro, Discurso	José da Silva Ribeiro, Discurso sobre o celleiro publico da Bahia, n.d. [1807], encl. in José da Silva Ribeiro, Memoria, n.d. [1808], BN/SM, II-33, 24, 40, Doc. 2
Ribeiro, Memória	José da Silva Ribeiro, Memoria, n.d. [1808], BN/SM, II-33, 24, 40, Doc. 1
Rio	Rio de Janeiro city
SH	Seção Histórica
SJ	Seção Judiciária
SL	Seção Legislativa

SPE   Seção do Poder Executivo
Test.   Testamento
uncat.   uncatalogued
VP   Vice Presidente

Note: Unless otherwise stated, all cited correspondence originated in Salvador. Many documents at the Arquivo Municipal de Salvador (AMS) that were uncatalogued when this research was carried out (and labeled here "uncat.") have since been catalogued. Some materials at the Arquivo Público do Estado da Bahia (APEB) have been recatalogued with new numbers after research was completed.

INTRODUCTION

1. For thinking about the history of the Atlantic World see David Eltis, "Atlantic History in Global Perspective," *Itinerario* 23, no. 2 (1999): 141–161; J. H. Elliott, "Atlantic History: A Circumnavigation," in *The British Atlantic World, 1500–1800*, ed. David Armitage and Michael J. Braddick (New York: Palgrave and Macmillan, 2002), 233–249; and Júnia Ferreira Furtado, ed., *Diálogos oceânicos: Minas Gerais e as novas abordagens para uma história do império ultramarino português* (Belo Horizonte: Editora UFMG, 2001).

2. On this variety and interconnectedness, see, for example, Laura de Mello e Souza, *Desclassificados do ouro: A pobreza mineira no século XVIII* (Rio de Janeiro: Graal, 1982); Vera Lúcia Ferlini, "Pobres do açucar: Estrutura produtiva e relações de poder no Nordeste colonial," in *História econômica do período colonial: Coletânea de textos apresentados no 1 Congresso Brasileiro de História Econômica (Campus da USP, setembro de 1993)*, ed. Tamás Szmrecsányi (São Paulo: HUCITEC, FAPESP, and Associação Brasileira de Pesquisadores em História Econômica, 1996), pp. 28–29, 31; and Luciano Figueiredo, *O avesso da memória: Cotidiano e trabalho da mulher em Minas Geraes no século XVIII* (Rio de Janeiro and Brasília: José Olympio and EDUNB, 1993). And on Spanish America, R. Douglas Cope, *The Limits of Racial Domination: Plebeian Society in Colonial Mexico City, 1660–1720* (Madison: University of Wisconsin Press, 1994).

3. On the worth of wills and testaments as historical documents, compare Sarah Cline, "Fray Alonso de Molina's Model Testament and Antecedents to Indigenous Wills in Spanish America," with Kevin Terraciano, "Native Expressions of Piety in Mextec Testaments," both in *Dead Giveaways: Indigenous Testaments of Colonial Mesoamerica and the Andes*, ed. Susan Kellogg and Matthew Restall (Salt Lake City: University of Utah Press, 1998), pp. 24–25 and 126–127. See also Kátia M. de Queirós Mattoso, *Testamentos de escravos libertos na Bahia no século XIX* (Salvador: Centro de Estudos Bahianos, Universidade Federal da Bahia, 1979), p. 21, and James Lockhart, *The Nahuas After the Conquest: A Social and Cultural History of the Indians of Central Mexico, Sixteenth Through Eighteenth Centuries* (Stanford, CA: Stanford University Press, 1992), pp. 251–252.

CHAPTER 1

1. Andrew Grant, *History of Brazil Comprising a Geographical Account of That Country, Together with a Narrative of the Most Remarkable Events Which*

Have Occurred There Since Its Discovery . . . (London: Henry Colburn, 1809), p. 205; Charles Darwin to Robert Waring Darwin (his father), [8 Feb.–1 Mar. 1832], in Charles Darwin, *The Life and Letters of Charles Darwin, Including an Autobiographical Chapter,* ed. Francis Darwin (New York: Appleton, 1898), p. 204. Many commented on the visual impact of the city: see Mrs. (Nathaniel) Kindersley, *Letters from the Island of Teneriffe, Brazil, the Cape of Good Hope, and the East Indies* (London: J. Nourse, 1776), p. 23. Johan Brelin, *De passagem pelo Brasil e Portugal em 1756* (Lisbon: Casa Portuguesa, 1955), p. 104, estimated that 1,200 to 1,400 ships could anchor in the bay at any one time.

2. Daniel P. Kidder, *Sketches of Residence and Travels in Brazil Embracing Historical and Geographical Notices of the Empire and Its Several Provinces,* 2 vols. [Philadelphia: Sorin and Ball, 1845], 2: 19, 63 [quoted]); James Prior, *Voyage Along the Eastern Coast of Africa to Mosambique, Johanna, and Quiloa; to St. Helena; to Rio de Janeiro, Bahia, and Pernambuco in Brazil, in the Nisus Frigate* (London: Richard Phillips, 1819), p. 100; Johann Baptist von Spix and Karl Friedrich Philipp von Martius, *Através da Bahia: Excerptos da obra "Reise in Brasilien,* 3rd ed., trans. Manuel Augusto Pirajá da Silva and Paulo Wolf, Brasiliana, Ser. 5, no. 118 (São Paulo: Editora Nacional, 1938), p. 89; Alcide d'Orbigny, *Viagem pitoresca através do Brasil,* Reconquista do Brasil, no. 29 (Belo Horizonte and São Paulo: Itatiaia and EDUSP, 1976), p. 103.

3. Ferdinand Denis, in Hippolyte Taunay and Ferdinand Denis, *Le Brésil, ou histoire, moeurs, usages et coutumes des habitans de ce royaume,* 6 vols. (Paris: Nepveu, 1822), 4: 59. On this lake called the Dique see also Maximilian [Emperor of Mexico (Ferdinand Joseph Maximilian of Austria)], *Recollections of My Life,* 3 vols. (London: Richard Bentley, 1868), 3: 135, and Robert Avé-Lallemant, *Viagens pelas províncias da Bahia, Pernambuco, Alagoas e Sergipe* (1859), trans. Eduardo de Lima Castro, Reconquista do Brasil, no. 19 (Belo Horizonte and São Paulo: Itatiaia and EDUSP, 1980), p. 28. On its history (it's partly man-made) see Braz Hermenegildo do Amaral, *História da Bahia do Império à República* (Salvador: Imp. Oficial do Estado, 1923), p. 184. On the date of Maps 1.2 and 1.3 see Bahia, Presidente da Província, *Falla,* 1846, p. 31 (I owe this reference to Cláudia Trindade).

4. José Maria dos Santos Lopes, Petition, Lisbon, n.d. [before 2 Mar. 1805], AHU, D. Cat. Bahia 28.366 (quoted); Fernando José de Portugal to Marquez Mordomo-Mor, 17 Sept. 1793, BN/SM, 1, 4, 11; Inv., José da Silva Maia, 1809, APEB, SJ, 04/1790/2260/01, fol. 4v; Taunay and Denis, *Le Brésil,* 4: 22, 71. A list of twelve wharf-side warehouses (*trapiches*) in 1829 appears in Domingos José Antonio Rebello, "Corographia, ou abreviada historia geographica do Imperio do Brasil," 2nd ed., *Revista do Instituto Geográfico e Histórico da Bahia* 55 (1929): 138. Also see Waldemar Mattos, *Panorama econômico da Bahia, 1808–1960: Edição comemorativa do sesquicentenário da Associação Comercial da Bahia* (Salvador: [Tip. Manu Editôra], 1961), pp. 13–14. A general notion of the social dimensions of the various sections of town can be found in Anna Amélia Vieira Nascimento, *Dez freguesias da cidade do Salvador: Aspectos sociais e urbanos do século XIX* (Salvador: Fundação Cultural do Estado da Bahia, 1986), pp. 33–34. The early borders and some physical features of each parish are presented in "Lista das informações e discripções [*sic*] das diversas freguezias do Arcebipado da Bahia, enviadas pela Frota de 1757 . . . ," in Eduardo de Castro e Almeida, ed., "Inventario dos docu-

mentos relativos ao Brasil existentes no Archivo de Marinha e Ultramar," *ABNRJ* 32 (1909): 177-184. On how the Brazilian slave trade was anchored in Brazil, see David Eltis, "The Volume and Structure of the Transatlantic Slave Trade: A Reassessment," *William and Mary Quarterly* Series 2, 58, no. 1 (January 2001): 30.

5. Kindersley, *Letters*, p. 33; Taunay and Denis, *Le Brésil*, 4: 26, 39-40; L. F. de Tollenare, *Notas dominicais tomadas durante uma viagem em Portugal e no Brasil em 1816, 1817, e 1818* (Salvador: Progresso, 1956), p. 307; Gustavo Beyer, "Ligeiras notas de viagem do Rio de Janeiro á capitania de S. Paulo, no Brasil, no verão de 1813, com algumas noticias sobre a cidade da Bahia e a ilha Tristão da Cunha, entre o Cabo e o Brasil e que ha pouco foi ocupada," trans. A. Löfgren, *Revista do Instituto Histórico e Geográfico de São Paulo* 11 (1907): 275-276. On the city council building and its jail see Rebello, "Corographia," p. 148.

6. Taunay and Denis, *Le Brésil*, 4: 34; d'Orbigny, *Viagem pitoresca*, p. 103; Queixoso: João Rolando, Queixado: João Batista de Figeiredo, 8 Mar. 1839, Auto crime, APEB, SJ, 04/128/12, fols. 2, 8v, 15v, 16.

7. Kidder, *Sketches of Residence*, p. 63 (quoted); Tollenare, *Notas dominicais*, p. 302; Maria Graham [Lady Maria Calcott], *Journal of a Voyage to Brazil and Residence There During Part of the Years 1821, 1822, 1823* (1824; reprint, New York: Praeger, 1969), p. 134; Robert Elwes, *A Sketcher's Tour Round the World* (London: Hurst and Blackett, 1854), p. 93; Avé-Lallemant, *Viagens . . . Bahia*, p. 26; José Francisco da Silva Lima, "A Bahia ha 66 anos," *Revista do Instituto Geográfico e Histórico da Bahia*, ano 15, no. 34 (1908): 115. On British citizens in Salvador, see Kidder, *Sketches of Residence*, 2: 25-26. On Portuguese merchants in the upper city, see Catherine Lugar, "The Merchant Community of Salvador, Bahia, 1780-1830" (Ph.D. diss., State University of New York at Stony Brook, 1980), p. 249, n. 23.

8. Inv., José da Silva Barros, 1823, APEB, SJ, 04/1826/2297/13, fols. 7, 8, 8v, 32; Câmara to Governador, 19 Nov. 1788, and enclosures, APEB, CP, M. 201-14, Doc. 5. Nascimento, *Dez freguesias*, p. 89; Patricia Ann Aufderheide, "Order and Violence: Social Deviance and Social Control in Brazil, 1780-1840" (Ph.D. diss., University of Minnesota, 1976), p. 97.

9. [Miguel Antonio de Mello], Informaçam da Bahia de Todos os Santos [1797], copy encl. in Rodrigo de Souza Coutinho to Fernando José de Portugal, Lisbon, 26 Sept. 1798, BN/SM, I-31, 21, 34, no. 2 (quoted); Mappa da enumeração da gente e povo desta capitania da Bahia, . . . 5 dec. 1780, in E. Almeida, "Inventario dos documentos," *ABNRJ* 32 (1910): 480; Governador [Conde da Ponte] to Visconde de Anadia, 16 June 1807, in *ABNRJ* 37 (1915): 460; Brazil, Directoria Geral de Estatística, *Recenseamento da população do Imperio do Brazil* [sic] *a que se procedeu no dia 1° de agosto de 1872* (Rio de Janeiro: Typ. Nacional, 1873-1876), Imperio, Bahia, Salvador. The censuses of the city before 1872 are discussed by Thales de Azevedo, *Povoamento da cidade do Salvador*, 3rd ed. (Salvador: Itapuã, 1969), pp. 181-200, 231-237; Kátia M. de Queirós Mattoso, *Bahia: A cidade de Salvador e seu mercado no século XIX*, Coleção Estudos Brasileiros, no. 12 (São Paulo and Salvador: HUCITEC and Secretaria Municipal de Educação e Cultura, 1978), pp. 127-133; Mattoso, *Bahia, século xix: Uma província no Império* (Rio de Janeiro: Nova Fronteira, 1992), pp. 83-87, 104-110; Nascimento, *Dez freguesias*, pp. 59-68; and, for the earlier censuses, Avelino de Jesus da Costa, "População

da cidade da Baía em 1775," in *Actas do V [Quinto] Colóquio Internacional de Estudos Luso-Brasileiros, Coimbra, 1963* (Coimbra: Gráfica de Coimbra, 1964), 1: 191–274. All of these figures are for the *município*, or county, which included some rural parishes.

10. Richard M. Morse, Michael L. Conniff, and John Wibel, eds., *The Urban Development of Latin America, 1750–1920* (Stanford, CA: Stanford University Center for Latin American Studies, 1971), pp. 23, 37, 54, 78, 95, 105; Nicolás Sánchez-Albornoz, *The Population of Latin America*, trans. W. A. R. Richardson (Berkeley: University of California Press, 1974), p. 128; Arnold J. Bauer, *Goods, Power, History: Latin America's Material Culture* (Cambridge, Eng.: Cambridge University Press, 2001), p. 91; Bailey W. Diffie, *A History of Colonial Brazil, 1500–1792* (Malbar, FL: Krieger, 1987), pp. 452–454; Campbell Gibson, "Population of the 100 Largest Cities and Other Urban Places in the United States, 1791–1990," in *U.S. Census Bureau, Population Division Working Paper*, No. 27 (n.d.), http://www.census.gov/population, Table 2.

11. PP-BA to MJ, 14 Feb. 1835, AN, SPE, Série Judiciária, IJ¹707, 1835; Avé-Lallemant, *Viagens . . . Bahia*, p. 22.

12. Stuart B. Schwartz, *Sugar Plantations in the Formation of Brazilian Society: Bahia, 1550–1835*, Cambridge Latin American Studies, no. 52 (Cambridge, Eng.: Cambridge Univ. Press, 1985), pp. 163–164; B. J. Barickman, *A Bahian Counterpoint: Sugar, Tobacco, Cassava, and Slavery in the Recôncavo, 1780–1860* (Stanford, CA: Stanford University Press, 1998), pp. 32–39.

13. For an account of the earlier slave trade see Luiz Felipe de Alencastro, *O trato dos viventes: A formação do Brasil no Atlântico Sul* (São Paulo: Companhia das Letras, 2000); for a summary of the later phase see Schwartz, *Sugar Plantations*, pp. 340–341.

14. Alexandre Vieira Ribeiro, "O comércio de escravos e a elite baiana no período colonial," in *Conquistadores e negociantes: Histórias de elites no Antigo Regime nos trópicos—América lusa, séculos XVI a XVIII*, ed. João Luís Ribeiro Fragoso, Carla Maria Carvalho de Almeida, and Antônio Carlos Jucá de Sampaio (Rio de Janeiro: Civilização Brasileira, 2007), pp. 314–324; Maria José de Souza Andrade, *A mão de obra escrava em Salvador, 1811–1860*, Baianada, no. 8 (São Paulo and Brasília: Corrupio and CNPq, 1988), pp. 188, 195, and 197 (in 1,269 inventories for the period 1811–1860, Andrade found 6,974 slaves, including 2,657 African men and 1,697 African women).

15. Andrade (*Mão de obra escrava*, p. 104) finds that 78.4 percent of the African slaves whose origin is indicated in postmortem estate inventories carried out from 1811 to 1888 were from areas bordering the Gulf of Benin, 19.3 percent were from Angola or the Congo, and 2.2 percent were from East Africa. Carlos Ott (*Formação e evolução étnica da cidade de Salvador: O folclore bahiano*, 2 vols., Evolução Histórica da Cidade do Salvador, no. 5 [Salvador: Manú Ed., 1955–1957], 1: 61, 68) counted the ethnic labels assigned to 57,500 slaves buried by a charitable institution and found that the proportion of West Africans to Central Africans dramatically increased after 1800. Two Quakers visiting Bahia in the 1850s reported that most of the city's slaves had been "brought from the coast of Benin near the province of Mina"; John Candler and William Burgess, *Narrative of a Recent Visit to Brazil to Present an Address on the Slave Trade and Slavery Is-*

sued by the Religious Society of Friends (London: Edward Marsh, 1853), pp. 11–12. See also Pierre Verger, *Trade Relations Between the Bight of Benin and Bahia from the 17th to 19th Century*, trans. Evelyn Crawford (Ibadan: Ibadan University Press, 1976), pp. 1–2; João José Reis and Beatriz Galloti Mamigonian, "Nagô and Mina: The Yoruba Diaspora in Brazil," in *The Yoruba Diaspora in the Atlantic World*, ed. Toyin Falola and Matt Childs (Bloomington: Indiana University Press, 2004), pp. 80–81; and David Eltis, "The Diaspora of Yoruba Speakers, 1650–1865: Dimensions and Implications," in the same volume, p. 31.

16. The erasure of particular ethnic identities in Brazil remains to be studied in depth; a start has been made by João José Reis, *Rebelião escrava no Brasil: A história do levante dos malês em 1835*, 2nd ed. (São Paulo: Companhia das Letras, 2003), pp. 307–319; also see Reis and Mamigonian, "Nagô and Mina," p. 84.

17. Corpo do Comércio e mais cidadãos to Prince-Regent João, n.d. [shortly after 28 Feb. 1814], in Ott, *Formação e evolução étnica*, 2: 107 (a translated version of this document appears in Robert Edgar Conrad, comp. and ed., *Children of God's Fire: A Documentary History of Black Slavery in Brazil* [Princeton, NJ: Princeton University Press, 1983], pp. 401–406); Candler and Burgess, *Narrative of a Recent Visit to Brazil*, p. 49.

18. On former slaves who owned slaves, see, besides evidence later in this book, the statement by Elwes, *Sketcher's Tour*, p. 97. Kátia M. de Queirós Mattoso (*Testamentos de escravos libertos na Bahia no século XIX* [Salvador: Centro de Estudos Bahianos, Universidade Federal da Bahia, 1979], p. 32) indicates that 50.8 percent of the wills left by freedmen in Salvador referred to the ownership of slaves, a proportion that rises to 75.5 percent in the case of freed women. Also see Iraci del Nero da Costa and Francisco Vidal Luna, "De escravo a senhor," *Revista do Arquivo Público Mineiro* 41 (July–Dec. 2005): 113, 115; and Sheila de Castro Faria, "Sinhás pretas, 'damas mercadoras': As pretas minas nas cidades do Rio de Janeiro e de São João del Rey (1700–1850)," unpublished MS tese de doutorado (Niterói: Universidade Federal Fluminense, 2004), pp. 160–161.

19. José da Silva Lisboa, "'Carta muito interessante do advogado da Bahia . . . para Domingos Vandelli, Bahia, 18 de outubro de 1781,' in Eduardo de Castro e Almeida, *Inventario dos documentos relativos ao Brasil existentes no Archivo de Marinha e Ultramar, Part II (Bahia, 1763–1786)*," *ABNRJ* 32 (1910): 505; Inv., José Pereira da Silva, 1846, APEB, SJ, 04/1973/2445/01, fol. 19. Also see Marcus J. M. de Carvalho, *Liberdade: Rotinas e rupturas do escravismo urbano, Recife, 1822–1850*, 2nd ed. (Recife: Editora da UFPE, 2002), p. 276.

20. On the age of freed females see Stuart B. Schwartz, "The Manumission of Slaves in Colonial Brazil: Bahia, 1684–1745," *Hispanic American Historical Review* 54, no. 4 (Nov. 1974): 615, 617. To my knowledge no systematic quantitative study has been made of gender among the owners who freed slaves in Salvador, but from my reading of numerous estate inventories, I expect such a study would reveal a situation similar to that in Mexico discussed by Frank "Trey" Proctor III, "Gender and the Manumission of Slaves in New Spain," *Hispanic American Historical Review* 86, no. 2 (May 2006): 309–336.

21. Mapa geral no qual se vem todas as moradas de cazas q. [h]a na cidade da Baia com a distinsam das q. tem cada uma das freguezias de que ela se compoem, seus fogos e numero dos clerigos q. tem e dos [h]omens brancos, pardos, e pretos,

cazados, viuvos, e solteiros, e igualm^{te} todas as mulheres cazadas, viuvas, e solteiras, com a distinsão de suas qualidades, e ultimam^{te} o numero dos escravos que tem esta cidade e o total de todas as almas, tudo com a maior clareza e distinsão possivel, Bahia, 20 de junho de 1775, Estampa 3, in Costa, "População da cidade," Appendix.

22. On water supply see Luís dos Santos Vilhena, *A Bahia no século XVIII*, 2nd ed., ed. Braz do Amaral, intro. by Edison Carneiro (Salvador: Itapuã, 1969), pp. 102–104; Taunay and Denis, *Le Brésil*, 4: 45; Tollenare, *Notas dominicais*, p. 299; Spix and Martius, *Através da Bahia*, pp. 139, 141; Conde de Suzannet, *O Brasil em 1845 (Semelhanças e diferenças após um século)*, trans. Márcia de Moura Castro, intro. by Austregésilo de Athayde (Rio de Janeiro: Casa do Estudante do Brasil, 1957), p. 184. Only at midcentury did the provincial government contract a private company to build a waterworks (Amaral, *História da Bahia*, p. 173); it relied on steam engines to pump water up the steep hills (Maximilian [Emperor of Mexico (Ferdinand Joseph Maximilian of Austria)], *Recollections*, 3: 177).

23. Quotations are from Lisboa, "'Carta muito interessante,'" p. 496; Kidder, *Sketches of Residence*, 2: 22; and French consul to Foreign Minister, 1844, quoted in Pierre Verger, *Notícias da Bahia—1850* (Salvador: Corrupío, 1981), p. 21. For other details see "Carta I" in João Rodrigues de Brito et al., *Cartas economico-politicas sobre a agricultura e commercio da Bahia* (Lisbon: Imp. Nacional, 1821), p. 27; and Oskar Canstatt, *Brasil: Terra e gente*, 2nd ed., trans. Eduardo de Lima Castro, intro. by Artur Cezar Ferreira Reis, Temas Brasileiros, no. 18 (Rio de Janeiro: Conquista, 1975), p. 190. To count streets and *ladeiras*, I used the list in Alexandre José de Mello Moraes [Pai], "Praças, largos, ruas, becos, travessas, templos, [e] edificios que contém as dez freguezias da cidade do Salvador, Bahia de Todos os Santos," in Moraes [Pai], ed., *Brasil historico* (Rio de Janeiro: Pinheiro, 1866), 2ª Serie, Tomo 1, p. 281.

24. Lima, "A Bahia ha 66 anos," p. 104; Alexander Majoribanks, *Travels in South and North America* (London and New York: Simpkin, Marshall and Appleton, 1853), p. 46. Also see Taunay and Denis, *Le Brésil*, 4: 85–86; Prinz von Maximilian Wied, *Viagem ao Brasil/Maximiliano, Principe de Wied-Neuwied*, trans. Edgar Sussekind de Mendonça and Flavio Poppe de Figueiredo, Brasiliana (Grande Formato), no. 1 (Belo Horizonte: Itatiaia and EDUSP, 1989), p. 469; and Canstatt, *Brasil: Terra e gente*, p. 194.

25. Taunay and Denis, *Le Brésil*, 4: 34, 85 (quoted); Kidder, *Sketches of Residence*, p. 21; Lima, "A Bahia ha 66 anos," 105n; João José Reis, "A greve negra de 1857 na Bahia," *Revista USP*, no. 18 (June–Aug. 1993): 13. On public space, I follow Maria Cecília Velasco e Cruz, "Puzzling Out Slave Origins in Rio de Janeiro Port Unionism: The 1906 Strike and the Sociedade de Resistência dos Trabalhadores em Trapiche e Café," *Hispanic American Historical Review* 86, no. 2 (May 2006): 217–218, 220–222.

26. Or at least that was so in Rio de Janeiro; see Thomas Ewbank, *Life in Brazil; or, A Journal of a Visit to the Land of the Cocoa and the Palm* . . . (1856; reprint, Detroit: Blaine Ethridge, 1971), p. 184.

27. Mattoso (*Bahia: A cidade de Salvador*, pp. 286–289) examines distinct categories of slave labor in more detail. For Rio see Leila Mezan Algranti, *O feitor*

ausente: Estudo sobre a escravidão urbana no Rio de Janeiro (Petrópolis: Vozes, 1988), esp. pp. 49 and 88; and Marilene Rosa Nogueira da Silva, *Negro na rua: A nova face da escravidão* (São Paulo: HUCITEC, 1988). Although self-hired slaves were also present in the British colonies, many of the subsequent North American states outlawed the practice; see Kenneth M. Stampp, *The Peculiar Institution: Slavery in the Ante-Bellum South* (New York: Vintage, 1956), p. 208; "Alabama Slave Code of 1852" [paragraph 1005], in Willie Lee Rose, ed., *A Documentary History of Slavery in North America* (New York: Oxford University Press, 1976), p. 181 (I owe these last two references to Sandra Lauderdale Graham).

28. Flávio Rabello Versiani, "Escravidão no Brasil: Uma análise econômica," *Revista Brasileira de Economia* 48, no. 4 (Dec. 1994): 463-478.

29. For example: Inv., Manoel Tavares, 1816, APEB, SJ, 04/1725/2195/09, fols. 132-133; Inv., José Gomes da Costa, 1824, APEB, SJ, 04/1783/2253/09, fol. 52; Inv., José Ferreira de Azevedo e sua mulher, 1838, APEB, SJ, 03/1063/1532/03, fols. 76, 79-81, 115; Inv. e Test., Joaquim Teixeira de Carvalho, 1846-1847, APEB, SJ, 04/1473/1942/05, fol. 14; Inv., Henrique José Teixeira Chaves, 1847, APEB, SJ, 04/1447/1916/05, fols. 83, 86; Inv. (2°), João Simões Coimbra, 1870 [1860], APEB, SJ, 03/1052/1521/02, fols. 35v, 231; Inv., Sabina da Cruz, 1872, APEB, SJ, 03/1100/1569/07, fols. 10v, 28. In Brazil the practice of allowing slaves to purchase their freedom depended entirely on custom until 1871, when it became enshrined in law (Lei n. 2040, 28 Sept. 1871, in Brazil, *Colleção das leis do Imperio do Brasil*, Art. 4, par. 2).

30. Test., 1 Mar. 1813, encl. in Inv., Ignacio José da Silva, 1817, and his inventário itself, APEB, SJ, 07/2873/04, fols. 4v, 9v, 11. On the prosperity of some former slaves and their ownership of slaves, see Faria, "Sinhás pretas," pp. 143-160, and Keila Grinberg, *O fiador dos brasileiros: Cidadania, escravidão e direito civil no tempo de Antônio Pereira Rebouças* (Rio de Janeiro: Civilização Brasileira, 2002), p. 184.

31. d'Orbigny, *Viagem pitoresca*, p. 106 (quoted); Avé-Lallemant, *Viagens . . . Bahia*, p. 24; Henry Martyn, *Memoir*, ed. John Sargent (London: J. Hatchard and Son, 1820), p. 141; Robert Walsh, *Notices of Brazil in 1828 and 1829*, 2 vols. (Boston: Richardson, Lord, and Holbrook & Carvill, 1831), 1: 204 and 2: 60. For priests see Júnia Ferreira Furtado, *Chica da Silva e o contratador dos diamantes: O outro lado do mito* (São Paulo: Companhia das Letras, 2003), p. 54; for militia officers see Hendrik Kraay, *Race, State, and Armed Forces in Independence-Era Brazil: Bahia, 1790s-1840s* (Stanford, CA: Stanford University Press, 2001), p. 98.

32. Nascimento, *Dez freguesias*, p. 95.

33. Corpo do Comércio e mais cidadãos to Prince-Regent João, n.d. [shortly after 28 Feb. 1814], in Ott, *Formação e evolução étnica*, 2: 107 (a translated version of this document appears in Conrad, *Children of God's Fire*, pp. 401-406). On the events of 1798 see Luís Henrique Dias Tavares, *História da sedição intentada na Bahia em 1798 ("A conspiração dos alfaiates")* (São Paulo: Livraria Pioneira, 1975); István Jancsó, *Na Bahia, contra o Império: História do ensaio de sedição de 1798*, Estudos Históricos, 24 (São Paulo and Salvador: HUCITEC and EDUFBA, 1995); and Arquivo Público do Estado da Bahia, *Autos da devassa da Conspiração dos Alfaiates* (Salvador: Secretaria da Cultura e Turismo, Arquivo Público do Estado, 1998).

34. Conde da Ponte to Visconde de Anadia, 16 July 1807, in Ignacio Accioli de Cerqueira e Silva, *Memórias históricas e políticas da província da Bahia*, 2nd ed., 6 vols., ed. Braz do Amaral (Salvador: Imprensa Official do Estado, 1919–1940), 3: 228–230; Conde dos Arcos to Marquês de Aguiar, 2 and 16 May, and 1 Sept. 1814, and enclosures, AN, SPE, IJJ⁹ 323, fols. 5–30, 42–47, 133–160. See also João José Reis, "Slave Resistance in Brazil: Bahia, 1807–1835," *Luso-Brazilian Review* 25, no. 1 (Summer 1988): 111–144; João José Reis, "'Nos achamos em campo a tratar da liberdade': A resistência negra no Brasil oitocentista," in *Viagem incompleta: A experiência brasileira (1500–2000), Vol. 1: Formação: Histórias*, ed. Carlos Guilherme Mota (São Paulo: SENAC, 2000), pp. 241–263.

35. João José Reis, *Slave Rebellion in Brazil: The Muslim Uprising of 1835 in Bahia*, trans. Arthur Brakel (Baltimore: Johns Hopkins University Press, 1993), passim; British consul Porter, Report, 1 Apr. 1847, FO 84/679, quoted in Verger, *Trade Relations*, p. 379.

36. Candido Mendes de Almeida, ed., *Codigo Philippino; ou Ordenações e leis do reino de Portugal recopiladas por mandado d'el rei D. Philippe I* . . . (Rio de Janeiro: Instituto Philomathico, 1870), Liv. 4, Tits. 46, 48, 96; Inv., Henrique José Teixeira Chaves, 1847, APEB, SJ, 04/1447/1916/05, fol. 91; Sandra Lauderdale Graham, "Making the Private Public: A Brazilian Perspective," *Journal of Women's History*, no. 1 (Spring 2003): 31–32; Alida C. Metcalf, *Family and Frontier in Colonial Brazil: Santana de Paranaíba, 1580–1822* (Berkeley: University of California Press, 1992), pp. 95–100.

37. For example, Inv. Bartolomeu Francisco Gomes, 1848, APEB, SJ, 04/1697/2167/06, fol. 4v.

38. John Turnbull, *A Voyage Round the World* . . . (London: Maxwell, 1813), p. 32; Pedro Moacir Maia, ed., *O Museu de Arte Sacra da Universidade Federal da Bahia* (São Paulo: Banco Safra, 1987); G. Oscar Oswaldo Campliglia, *Igrejas do Brasil: Fontes para a história da Igreja no Brasil* (São Paulo: Melhoramentos, n.d. [1957]), pp. 37–129, 345–357; Robert C. Smith, *Arquitetura colonial bahiana: Alguns aspectos de sua história*, Publicações do Museu do Estado, no. 14 (Salvador: Secretaria de Educação e Cultura, 1951); Jaime C. Diniz, *Mestres de capela da Misericórdia da Bahia, 1647–1810*, ed. Manuel Veiga (Salvador: Centro Editorial e Didático da UFBA, 1993), pp. 87–110; Diniz, *Organistas da Bahia, 1750–1850* (Rio de Janeiro and Salvador: Tempo Brasileiro and Fundação Cultural do Estado da Bahia, 1986), pp. 50–162.

39. Test. and Codicílio (1º), Innocencio José da Costa, 1805, APEB, SJ, 08/3465/02, fol. 3. For descriptions of some other oratórios, see Inv., José da Silva Barros, 1823, APEB, SJ, 04/1826/2297/13, fol. 8; Inv., José Gomes da Costa, 1824, APEB, SJ, 04/1783/2253/09, fol. 15; Inv., Joanna Maria da Conceição, 1816, APEB, SJ, 04/1715/2185/01, fol. 5; Inv., Manoel Tavares, 1816, APEB, SJ, APEB, SJ, 04/1725/2195/09, fol. 102v; Inv., Maria do Carmo, 1817, APEB, SJ, 01/02/02/03, fol. 8; Inv., Ignacio José da Silva, 1817, APEB, SJ, 07/2873/04, fol. 10; Inv., Antonio Moreira de Azevedo, 1834, APEB, SJ, 05/2019/2490/05, fol. 57.

40. Test., 11 July 1828, encl. in Inv., Joaquina Maria de Santana, 1829, APEB, SJ, 04/1845/2316/01, fol. 4v; Test., Francisco Joaquim de Brito (2º), 1855, APEB, SJ, 03/1354/1823/22, fol. 2 (on his occupation see Francisco Joaquim de Brito to PP-BA, n.d. [before 16 Apr. 1846], encl. in Câmara to PP-BA, 6 May 1846, APEB, CP, M.

1399, 1846, Doc. 14); Test. e Codicílio (1°), Innocencio José da Costa, 1805, APEB, SJ, 08/3465/02, fol. 1.

41. A. J. R. Russell-Wood, "Prestige, Power, and Piety in Colonial Brazil: The Third Orders of Salvador," *Hispanic American Historical Review* 69, no. 1 (February 1989): 61–89; Mattoso, *Bahia, século xix*, pp. 397–404.

42. Patricia Ann Mulvey, "The Black Lay Brotherhoods of Colonial Brazil" (Ph.D. diss., City University of New York, 1976); A. J. R. Russell-Wood, *The Black Man in Slavery and Freedom in Colonial Brazil* (New York: St. Martin's, 1982), pp. 128–160; Russell-Wood, "Black and Mulatto Brotherhoods in Colonial Brazil: A Study in Collective Behavior," *Hispanic American Historical Review* 54, no. 4 (November 1974): 567–602; Furtado, *Chica da Silva*, pp. 169–170, 174; Julita Scarano, "Black Brotherhoods: Integration or Contradiction?" *Luso-Brazilian Review* 16, no. 1 (Summer 1979): 1–17. On admission to the Santa Casa de Misericórdia see Russell-Wood, *Fidalgos and Philanthropists: The Santa Casa da Misericórdia of Bahia, 1550–1755* (Berkeley: University of California Press, 1968), pp. 124–125. For an example of a black brotherhood's charter see Kenneth Mills, William B. Taylor, and Sandra Lauderdale Graham, eds., *Colonial Latin America: A Documentary History* (Wilmington, DE: Scholarly Resources, 2002), pp. 280–296. On similar sodalities in Spanish America see Nicole von Germeten, *Black Blood Brothers: Confraternities and Social Mobility for Afro-Mexicans* (Gainesville: University Press of Florida, 2006) and sources referred to therein.

43. Martyn, *Memoir*, p. 153; Reis, *Slave Rebellion*, pp. 93–136.

44. William Scully, *Brazil: Its Provinces and Chief Cities . . .* (London: Trübner, 1868), p. 352; João José Reis, "Candomblé in Nineteenth Century Bahia: Priests, Followers, Clients," *Slavery and Abolition* 22, no. 1 (2001): 116–134; Rachel E. Harding, *A Refuge in Thunder: Candomblé and Alternative Spaces of Blackness* (Bloomington: Indiana University Press, 2000), esp. pp. 22, 23, 33–40, 57, 61–62; Edison (de Souza) Carneiro, *Candomblés da Bahia*, Publicações no. 8 (Salvador: Museu do Estado, 1948); Ruth Landes, *The City of Women* (1947; reprint, Albuquerque: University of New Mexico Press, 1994), esp. pp. 37, 226–227; Luís Nicolau Parés, "The 'Nagôization' Process in Bahian Candomblé," in *The Yoruba Diaspora in the Atlantic World*, ed. Toyin Falola and Matt Childs (Bloomington: Indiana University Press, 2004), pp. 185–208; Roger Bastide, *The African Religions of Brazil: Toward a Sociology of the Interpenetration of Civilizations*, trans. Helen Sebba (Baltimore: Johns Hopkins University Press, 1978); Eduardo França Paiva, *Escravidão e universo cultural na colônia: Minas Gerais, 1716–1789* (Belo Horizonte: Editora UFMG, 2001), p. 222. On African drumming elsewhere in the Atlantic World, see John Thornton, *Africa and Africans in the Making of the Atlantic World, 1400–1680* (Cambridge, Eng.: Cambridge University Press, 1992), pp. 226–228.

45. Taunay and Denis, *Le Brésil* 4: 65–66; Elwes, *Sketcher's Tour*, p. 98; Francisco Michelena y Rójas, *Exploración oficial por la primera vez desde el norte de la America del Sur siempre por rios . . . de 1855 hasta 1859* (Brussels: A. Locroix, Verboeckhoven, 1867), p. 658. On the prescientific mind-set reflected in ex-votos, see Guilherme Pereira das Neves, "O reverso do milagre: Ex-votos pintados e religiosidade em Angra dos Reis (RJ)," *Tempo* 7, no. 14 (Jan.–June 2003): 48. Even in the twentieth century the Brazilian police believed in the power of magic; see

Yvonne Maggie, *Medo do feitiço: Relações entre magia e poder no Brasil* (Rio de Janeiro: Arquivo Nacional, 1992).

46. James Wetherell, *Brazil: Stray Notes from Bahia, Being Extracts from Letters, Etc., During a Residence of Fifteen Years* (Liverpool: Webb and Hunt, 1860), p. 19. References to *bentinhos* are frequent in contemporary documents; see, for example, Inv., Joanna Maria de Assumpção, 1792, APEB, SJ, 07/3195/07, fol. 7v; Test., Rosa Maria da Conceição, 1805, APEB, SJ, 07/3243/39, fol. 1; Treslado de Test., 16 Jan. 1823, in Inv. e Test., Ana de São José da Trindade, 1823, APEB, SJ, 04/1840/2311/02, fol. (first set:) 6v; Inv., Ana Joaquina de Jesus, 1800, APEB, SJ, 04/1710/2180/02, fols. 4–4v.

47. Rolf Reichert, ed., trans., and comp., *Os documentos árabes do Arquivo do Estado da Bahia*, Publicações, no. 9 (Salvador: Centro de Estudos Áfro-Orientais, Universidade Federal da Bahia, 1970); Reis, *Slave Rebellion*, pp. 98–99. See illustrations in Carlos Julião, *Riscos illuminados de figurinhos de brancos e negros dos uzos do Rio de Janeiro e Serro do Frio*, intro. by Lygia da Fonseca Fernandes da Cunha (Rio de Janeiro: Biblioteca Nacional, 1960), plate 33; and Ewbank, *Life in Brazil*, p. 27. Also see Laura de Mello e Souza, *O diabo e a Terra de Santa Cruz: Feitiçaria e religiosidade popular no Brasil colonial* (São Paulo: Companhia das Letras, 1987), pp. 210–211, 214, 214n, 219–221; Eduardo França Paiva, "Celebrando a alforria: Amuletos e práticas culturais entre as mulheres negras e mestiças do Brasil," in *Festa: Cultura e sociabilidade na América portuguesa*, ed. Ístvan Jancsó and Íris Kantor (São Paulo: HUCITEC and EDUSP, 2001), p. 507n; and Márcio Sousa Soares, "Cirurgiões negros: Saberes africanos sobre o corpo e as doenças nas ruas do Rio de Janeiro durante a primeira metade do século XIX," *Locus: Revista de História* 8, no. 2 (2002): 44–50; Maximilian [Emperor of Mexico (Ferdinand Joseph Maximilian of Austria)], *Recollections*, 3: 114 (also see Tollenare, *Notas dominicais*, p. 298).

48. Peter Brown, "A More Glorious House," *New York Review of Books* 44, no. 9 (29 May 1997).

49. Charles R. Boxer, *Portuguese Society in the Tropics: The Municipal Councils of Goa, Macao, Bahia, and Luanda* (Madison: University of Wisconsin Press, 1965), pp. 6–7. In 1696 the king charged the High Court in Salvador with the task of deciding who would be eligible; see Affonso Ruy, *História da Câmara Municipal da cidade do Salvador*, 2nd ed. (Salvador: Câmara Municipal de Salvador, 1996), p. 46. The degree to which the governor could then influence or even determine the choice of councilmen is the subject of some controversy among historians: cf. Boxer, *Portuguese Society in the Tropics*, pp. 74–75, 75n, 177–179, with Eulália Maria Lahmeyer Lobo, *Processo Administrativo Ibero-Americano (Aspectos Sócio-Econômicos—Período Colonial)* (Rio de Janeiro: Biblioteca do Exército Editora, 1962), p. 397.

50. F. W. O. Morton, "The Conservative Revolution of Independence: Economy, Society and Politics in Bahia, 1790–1840" (Ph.D. diss., University of Oxford, 1974), pp. 65–66; Mattoso, *Bahia, século xix*, p. 256. On the broad electorate see Richard Graham, *Patronage and Politics in Nineteenth-Century Brazil* (Stanford, CA: Stanford University Press, 1990), pp. 103–109.

51. PP-BA to Câmara, 31 Jan. 1829, AMS, 111.7, fol. 116; Silva, *Memórias históricas*, 4: 249–250.

52. Câmara to Governador, 8 June 1807, AHU, Cat. 29.987; PP-BA to MI, 19 Jan. 1850, AN, SPE, IIJ⁹339, 1850.

CHAPTER 2

1. Licenças, 1807, AMS, 88.4, fol. 219; Treslado de Test., 16 Jan. 1823, in Inv., Ana de São José da Trindade, 1823, APEB, SJ, 04/1840/2311/02, fols. 4–9v.

2. Inv., Ana de São José da Trindade, 1823, APEB, SJ, 04/1840/2311/02, fols. 5v–8v and (second pagination) fols. 11, 25. Her estate totaled 2:711$475 after funeral expenses, or 2:792$819 after monetary correction to 1824 values (see Appendix A). Hereafter, monetary figures in parentheses or brackets refer to 1824 values. On rosaries in Brazil see Elizabeth W. Kiddy, *Blacks of the Rosary: Memory and History in Minas Gerais, Brazil* (University Park: Pennsylvania State University Press, 2005), pp. 16–19. For a different take on the mobility of blacks see Rachel E. Harding, *A Refuge in Thunder: Candomblé and Alternative Spaces of Blackness* (Bloomington: Indiana University Press, 2000), p. 15 and the works she cites. On women pawnbrokers in Spanish America see Jane E. Mangan, *Trading Roles: Gender, Ethnicity, and the Urban Economy in Colonial Potosí* (Durham, NC: Duke University Press, 2005), p. 108.

3. Test., copy encl. in Inv., and Inv. itself, Antônio José Pereira Arouca, 1825, APEB, SJ, 04/1717/2187/02, fols. 4, 15v–16; Licença, 23 Sept. 1815, AMS, 88.5, fol. 156 (listed as Antonio José Pereira Rouca).

4. Câmara to PP-BA, 30 Sept. 1851, APEB, CP, M. 1401; PP-BA (Francisco Gonçalves Martins), *Falla*, 1 Mar. 1852, pp. 18–19; Câmara to PP-BA, 22 Aug. 1854, APEB, CP, M. 1402; Commissão encarregada . . . Praça de S. João, [Relatorio], 21 Jan. 1857, copy encl. in Câmara to PP-BA, 22 Jan. 1857, APEB, CP, M. 1403; José Antonio de Araújo to PP-BA, 8 June 1878, and enclosures, APEB, CP, M. 4632.

5. Maximilian [Emperor of Mexico (Ferdinand Joseph Maximilian of Austria)], *Recollections of My Life*, 3 vols. (London: Richard Bentley, 1868), 3: 129; 1° Livro das Denunciações na Visitação do Santo Ofício, Bahia, ANTT, Manuscritos do Brasil, Liv. 16 (1591), quoted in Luiz Mott, "Subsídios à história do pequeno comércio no Brasil," *Revista de História*, no. 105 (1976): p. 87; A. C. de C. M. Saunders, *A Social History of Black Slaves and Freedmen in Portugal, 1441–1555* (Cambridge, Eng.: Cambridge University Press, 1982), pp. 77–78.

6. Richard Lander and John Lander, *Journal of an Expedition to Explore the Course and Termination of the Niger with a Narrative of a Voyage Down That River to Its Termination* (1832; reprint, New York: Harper, 1854), 2: 202–204; Joachim John Monteiro, *Angola and the River Congo* (London: Macmillan, 1875), 2: 25, 27–29. See also Robert A. Le Vine, "Sex Roles and Economic Change in Africa," in *Black Africa: Its People and Their Culture Today*, ed. John Middleton (London: Macmillan, 1970), pp. 177, 179; Niara Sudarkasa, *Where Women Work: A Study of Yoruba Women in the Marketplace and in the Home*, Anthropological Papers, no. 53 (Ann Arbor: Museum of Anthropology, University of Michigan, 1973), pp. 25–32; Toyin Falola, "Gender, Business, and Space Control: Yoruba Market Women and Power," in *African Market Women and Economic Power: The Role of Women in African Economic Development*, ed. Bessie House-Midamba and Felix K. Ekechi, Contributions in Afro-American and African Studies, no. 174

(Westport, CT: Greenwood, 1995), pp. 25–27; Selma Pantoja, "A dimensão atlântica das quitandeiras," in *Diálogos oceânicos: Minas Gerais e as novas abordagens para uma história do império ultramarino português*, ed. Júnia Ferreira Furtado, Humanitas, no. 67 (Belo Horizonte: Editora UFMG, 2001), pp. 45–67. There is an extensive literature on street vendors throughout the Atlantic World and beyond.

7. AMS, 88.1, fols. 198–201; AMS, 88.4, fols. 211–212v; AMS, 88.5, fols. 266–267v; AMS, 7.1, fols. 15–21. I thank Gail Sanders for assisting me in gathering this data.

8. Inv., José Pinto de Almeida, 1830, APEB, SJ, 04/1729/2199/03, fols. 118, 128, 328 (on Genoveva); Inv. (1º), José Caetano de Aquino, 1833, APEB, SJ, 05/2003/2474/03, fol. 47; Inv., Manoel José Dias, 1836, APEB, SJ, 05/1958/2430/08, fols. 11v–12. The archives are full of estate inventories that speak of owning vendors to be sent out on the street, but it is not always clear whether they worked for the owner directly or were rented to another; see, for example, these three: Inv. e Test., José Antonio Correia, 1838, APEB, SJ, 04/1602/2071/02, fol. 8; Inv., Manuel Gonçalves Ferreira, 1820, APEB, SJ, 04/1732/2201/03; Inv., José da Silva Barros, 1823, APEB, SJ, 04/1826/2297/13, fol. 7v. On the substantial wealth of some of these owners, see Licenças, 1789, AMS, 88.1, fol. 214v, and Inv., Rosa Maria de Jesus, 1808–1811, APEB, SJ, 01/269/514/02, fol. 18v; Inv., Maria do Carmo, 1817, APEB, SJ, 01/02/02/03; and Inv., Tomasia Maria do Sacramento, 1823, APEB, SJ, 04/1590/2059/02, fol. 4v. The practice of owning slaves to sell on the street was common in other Brazilian cities as well; see Mary C. Karasch, *Slave Life in Rio de Janeiro, 1808–1850* (Princeton, NJ: Princeton University Press, 1987), p. 206; Maria Odila Leite da Silva Dias, *Quotidiano e poder em São Paulo no século XIX: Ana Gertudes de Jesus* (São Paulo: Brasiliense, 1984), pp. 92–97.

9. Madre Maria Thereza Marianna, "Religiosa do Desterro," and Madre Julianna Tereza, "do Convento do Desterro," were listed among those who took out licenses for their slaves as vendors: Licenças, 1789, AMS, 88.1, fols. 210 and 213v. Also see Susan A. Soeiro, "The Social and Economic Role of the Convent: Women and Nuns in Colonial Bahia, 1677–1800," *Hispanic American Historical Review* 54, no. 2 (May 1974): 231; and Anna Amélia Vieira Nascimento, *Dez freguesias da cidade do Salvador: Aspectos sociais e urbanos do século XIX* (Salvador: Fundação Cultural do Estado da Bahia, 1986), p. 73.

10. Inv. (1º), José Caetano de Aquino, 1833, APEB, SJ, 05/2003/2474/03, fols. 46–46v.

11. João Rodrigues de Brito, "Carta I," in João Rodrigues de Brito et al., *Cartas economico-politicas sobre a agricultura e commercio da Bahia* (Lisbon: Imp. Nacional, 1821), p. 28; on Ludovica see Inv. (1º), José Caetano de Aquino, 1833, APEB, SJ, 05/2003/2474/03, fol. 46v.

12. José Francisco da Silva Lima, "A Bahia ha 66 anos," *Revista do Instituto Geográfico e Histórico da Bahia*, ano 15, no. 34 (1908): 94; Robert Dundas, *Sketches of Brazil Including New Views of Tropical and European Fever with Remarks on a Premature Decay of the System Incident to Europeans on Their Return from Hot Climates* (London: John Churchill, 1852), p. 202. See also Daniel P. Kidder, *Sketches of Residence and Travels in Brazil Embracing Historical and Geographical Notices of the Empire and Its Several Provinces*, 2 vols. (Philadelphia: Sorin and Ball, 1845), 2: 19; and James Prior, *Voyage Along the Eastern Coast*

of Africa to Mosambique, Johanna, and Quiloa; to St. Helena; to Rio de Janeiro, Bahia, and Pernambuco in Brazil, in the Nisus Frigate (London: Richard Phillips, 1819), p. 101.

13. Maximilian [Emperor of Mexico (Ferdinand Joseph Maximilian of Austria)], *Recollections* 3: 171–172, 284; Oskar Canstatt, *Brasil: Terra e gente*, 2nd ed., trans. Eduardo de Lima Castro, intro. by Artur Cezar Ferreira Reis, Temas Brasileiros, no. 18 (Rio de Janeiro: Conquista, 1975), p. 199; Inv. (1°), José Caetano de Aquino, 1833, APEB, SJ, 05/2003/2474/03, fol. 24, and Inv. (2°), José Caetano de Aquino, 1836, APEB, SJ, 05/1962/2434/04, fols. 14, 61.

14. Maximilian [Emperor of Mexico (Ferdinand Joseph Maximilian of Austria)], *Recollections*, 3: 172; Posturas approvadas pela Assembléia Legislativa, 18 May and 17 June, 1859, AMS, 115.9, fol. 111. For a similar measure adopted for the area around the churches of Bomfim and Monteserrat see Edital, 1 Oct. 1855, enclosed in Câmara to PP-BA, 20 May 1857, APEB, CP, M. 1403, and PP-BA to Câmara, 10 Oct. 1855, AMS, 111.12, fol. 262. Also see Maria Graham [Lady Maria Calcott], *Journal of a Voyage to Brazil and Residence There During Part of the Years 1821, 1822, 1823* (1824; reprint, New York: Praeger, 1969), p. 133.

15. Câmara to PP-BA, 20 Aug. 1831, AMS, 111.8, fol. 100; PP-BA to Câmara, 22 Aug. 1831, AMS, 111.7, fol. 244; letter from "Philopolito," in *O tolerante na Bahia,* 25 Apr. 1839, p. 1, col. 1, in Arquivo Histórico do Exército, Rio de Janeiro, D-26-709 (Hendrik Kraay kindly copied this document for me). On beggars at the council chambers see Walter Fraga Filho, *Mendigos, moleques e vadios na Bahia do século XIX* (São Paulo and Salvador: HUCITEC and EDUFBA, 1996), pp. 148–149.

16. Luís dos Santos Vilhena, *A Bahia no século XVIII*, 2nd ed., ed. Braz do Amaral, intro. by Edison Carneiro (Salvador: Itapuã, 1969), 1: 93. On other subsequent locations of *quitandas*, see Câmara, Edital, 25 May 1822, AMS, 116.6, fol. 63v; Câmara to PP-BA, 22 Feb. 1826, AMS, 111.6, fols. 201v–202; PP-BA to Câmara, 30 Jan. 1826, AMS, 111.7, fol. 18; AMS, 7.1, fols. 71–118; and *Jornal da Bahia,* 13 Jan. 1854, quoted in Pierre Verger, *Trade Relations Between the Bight of Benin and Bahia from the 17th to 19th Century*, trans. Evelyn Crawford (Ibadan: Ibadan University Press, 1976), p. 444.

17. Câmara to Governador, 18 July 1798, APEB, CP, M. 201-14, Doc. 64; Câmara to Fiscal Geral, 4 July 1835, AMS, 116.8, fol. 24. This was also the motivation in Minas Gerais; see Luciano Figueiredo, *O avesso da memória: Cotidiano e trabalho da mulher em Minas Geraes no século XVIII* (Rio de Janeiro and Brasília: José Olympio and EDUNB, 1993), p. 69. On the equivalent use of stalls in other countries see Fernando Iwasaki Cauti, "Ambulantes y comercio colonial: Iniciativas mercantiles en el virreinato peruano," *Jahrbuch für Geschichte von Staat, Wirtschaft und Gesellschaft Lateinamerikas* 24 (1987): 184, 200; Judith Marti, "Nineteenth-Century Views of Women's Participation in Mexico's Markets," in *Women Traders in Cross-Cultural Perspective: Mediating Identities, Marketing Wares*, ed. Linda J. Seligmann (Stanford, CA: Stanford University Press, 2001), pp. 26–29, 41–43; and Gracia Clark, *Onions Are My Husband: Survival and Accumulation by West African Market Women* (Chicago: University of Chicago Press, 1994), pp. 12–13. On the use of the word *quitanda* in Luanda, see Monteiro, *Angola and the River Congo*, 2: 25.

18. Antônio Calmon du Pin, Proposta [de lei] ao Conselho Geral da Província,

2 Dec. 1828, APEB, CP, M. 1070-4; Atas, Sessão 13 Jan. 1829 and Sessão 17 Jan. 1829, APEB, SL, 197, fols. 18v–19, 21–21v (also see fol. 41v); Chefe da Polícia to PP-BA, 27 Nov. 1835, quoted in João José Reis, *Slave Rebellion in Brazil: The Muslim Uprising of 1835 in Bahia*, trans. Arthur Brakel (Baltimore: Johns Hopkins University Press, 1993), p. 228; Câmara to PP-BA, 17 Oct. 1838, APEB, CP, M. 1397, Doc. 50; PP-BA to Câmara, 25 Oct. 1838, AMS, 111.10, fol. 71v; Lei 374, 12 Nov. 1849, in Bahia, *Colleção das leis e resoluções da Assemblea Legislativa e regulamentos do governo da provincia da Bahia*; Câmara to PP-BA, 26 Mar. 1857, and pencilled reply from the president, APEB, CP, M. 1403, as well as the related correspondence, Câmara to PP-BA, 20 Feb., 14 Mar., and 2 June, 1857, in ibid. Also see Manuela Carneiro da Cunha, *Negros, estrangeiros: Os escravos libertos e sua volta à África* (São Paulo: Brasiliense, 1985), p. 99. Similar to the 1820s exceptions for street vendors in Salvador were those prevalent in eighteenth-century Jamaica; see Sidney W. Mintz, *Caribbean Transformations* (1974; reprint, Baltimore: Johns Hopkins University Press, 1984), pp. 197–198, 205.

19. On non-food items sold by street vendors see Bando [no. 185], 12 Sept. 1788, BN/SM, II-33, 34, 1; Câmara to Governador, 29 Oct. 1800, AMS 111.4, fol. 176v; Maximilian [Emperor of Mexico (Ferdinand Joseph Maximilian of Austria)], *Recollections*, 3: 167, 172; Protest of Rita de Cássia de Jesus Ramalho, 1854, cited in Cecília Moreira Soares, "As ganhadeiras: Mulher e resistência em Salvador no século XIX," *Afro-Ásia*, no. 17 (1996): 69. On fresh meat, see Câmara to Almotacéis, 21 Mar. 1818, and Câmara, Edital, 23 July 1823, AMS, 116.6, fols. 7 and 81 (quoted); proposed ordinance encl. in Câmara to PP-BA, 18 Aug. 1847, APEB, CP, M. 1400; Postura encl. in Câmara to PP-BA, 18 Aug. 1847, AMS, 111.11, fol. 227; Posturas aprovadas pela Assembléia Geral, 18 May and 17 June 1859, AMS, 115.9, fol. 111.

20. Câmara, Edital, 21 Feb. 1824, AMS, 116.6, fols. 86v–87; and Câmara to PP-BA, 28 Feb. 1824, AMS, 111.6, fol. 181. This was still the rule in 1855; Câmara to PP-BA, 18 Sept. 1855, and enclosures, APEB, CP, M. 1402. I have found no reference to increased demand for fish during Lent. Although meat was generally proscribed by the Church during Lent, there were so many exceptions that it seems likely it made little difference in Salvador. For the exceptions see Sebastião Monteiro da Vide, *Constituições primeiras do arcebispado da Bahia, feitas e ordenadas pelo . . .* (São Paulo: Typographia "2 de Dezembro" de Antonio Louzada Antunes, 1853), Liv. 2, Tit. 16, paragraphs 394, 396, 397; Tit. 18, paragraphs 406, 408, 410; and Tit. 20, paragraph 412.

21. Maximilian [Emperor of Mexico (Ferdinand Joseph Maximilian of Austria)], *Recollections*, 3: 284.

22. Edital que o Conselho Geral [da Provincia] reputou Postura, 14 Aug. 1829, art. 15, AMS 119.5, fol. 9v; Vilhena, *Bahia no Século XVIII*, pp. 93, 129; Admin. do Curral to Câmara, 9 Nov. 1829, AMS, uncat., Correspondência recebida, Curral, 1829. For another instance of pilfered meat see Admin. do Curral to Câmara, 4 May 1816, AMS, 33.2, fols. 146v–147.

23. James Wetherell, *Brazil: Stray Notes from Bahia, Being Extracts from Letters, Etc., During a Residence of Fifteen Years* (Liverpool: Webb and Hunt, 1860), p. 21; Vilhena, *Bahia no século XVIII*, pp. 93, 130. On whale meat also see Hippolyte Taunay and Ferdinand Denis, *Le Brésil, ou histoire, moeurs, usages et coutumes des habitans de ce royaume*, 6 vols. (Paris: Nepveu, 1822), 4: 53; L. F. de Tol-

lenare, *Notas dominicais tomadas durante uma viagem em Portugal e no Brasil em 1816, 1817, e 1818* (Salvador: Progresso, 1956), pp. 293, 340; Kidder, *Sketches of Residence,* 2: 24–25; Daniel Parish Kidder and James Cooley Fletcher, *Brazil and the Brazilians Portrayed in Historical and Descriptive Sketches* (Philadelphia: Childs and Peterson, 1857), p. 485; and Myriam Ellis, *A baleia no Brasil colonial* (São Paulo: Melhoramentos and EDUSP, 1969), pp. 41–42.

24. Manuel Querino, "Dos alimentos puramente africanos," in Edison (de Souza) Carneiro, comp., *Antologia do negro brasileiro* (Rio de Janeiro: Edições de Ouro, 1967), pp. 449–453; Robert W. Slenes, *Na senzala uma flor: Esperanças e recordações na formação da família escrava—Brasil sudeste, século XIX* (Rio de Janeiro: Nova Fronteira, 1999), pp. 190–194. On spices see Carlos Ott, *Formação e evolução étnica da cidade de Salvador: O folclore bahiano,* 2 vols., Evolução Histórica da Cidade do Salvador, no. 5 (Salvador: Manú Ed., 1955–1957), 1: 145. Also see Ruth Landes, *The City of Women* (1947; reprint, Albuquerque: University of New Mexico Press, 1994), p. 119. Religious taboos today regarding food, even when prepared for public sale, are mentioned in *Correio da Bahia,* 26 Nov. 2001, p. 2. On cooking in the street itself, see Prinz von Maximilian Wied, *Viagem ao Brasil/Maximiliano, Principe de Wied-Neuwied,* trans. Edgar Sussekind de Mendonça and Flavio Poppe de Figueiredo, Brasiliana (Grande Formato), no. 1 (Belo Horizonte: Itatiaia and EDUSP, 1989), p. 469.

25. Ellena, quoted by Reis, *Slave Rebellion,* p. 167. The work of several authors have been helpful in writing this paragraph: João José Reis, "A greve negra de 1857 na Bahia," *Revista USP,* no. 18 (June–August 1993): 11–12; Marco Aurélio A. de Filgueiras Gomes, "Escravismo e cidade: Notas sobre a ocupação da periferia de Salvador no século XIX," *Rua: Revista de Arquitetura e Urbanismo* 3, no. 4–5 (June–Dec. 1990): 10; Sidney W. Mintz, "The Role of the Middleman in the Internal Distribution System of a Caribbean Peasant Economy," *Human Organization* 15, no. 2 (Summer 1956): 21; Mintz, *Caribbean Transformations,* p. 213; Clifford Geertz, *Peddlers and Princes* (Chicago: University of Chicago Press, 1963), pp. 32–33; Clifford Geertz et al., *Meaning and Order in Moroccan Society: Three Essays in Cultural Analysis* (Cambridge, Eng.: Cambridge University Press, 1979), pp. 222, 225, 227; Craig Muldrew, *The Economy of Obligation: The Culture of Credit and Social Relations in Early Modern England* (London and New York: Macmillan and St. Martin's, 1998), p. 43; and Clark, *Onions Are My Husband,* pp. 128–140. I also draw on my own experience on bargaining in interior Brazil.

26. Advertisements for three runaway slaves appear in *Jornal da Bahia,* 10 Feb. 1854, 4 Mar. 1857, 18 May 1854, quoted in Verger, *Trade Relations,* p. 444; Johann Moritz Rugendas, *Malerische Reise in Brasilien* (1835; facsim. ed., Stuttgart: Daco-Verlag, 1986), 2ᵉ Div., plate 8; Robert Elwes, *A Sketcher's Tour Round the World* (London: Hurst and Blackett, 1854), p. 94; Maximilian [Emperor of Mexico (Ferdinand Joseph Maximilian of Austria)], *Recollections,* 3: 144; Canstatt, *Brasil: Terra e gente,* p. 192; Alexander Majoribanks, *Travels in South and North America* (London and New York: Simpkin, Marshall and Appleton, 1853), p. 46.

27. Robert Avé-Lallemant, *Viagens pelas províncias da Bahia, Pernambuco, Alagoas e Sergipe (1859),* trans. Eduardo de Lima Castro, Reconquista do Brasil, no. 19 (Belo Horizonte and São Paulo: Itatiaia and EDUSP, 1980), p. 24 (quoted); Inv., Ana de São José da Trindade, 1823, APEB, SJ, 04/1840/2311/02, fol. (second

set) 20; Test., Rosa Maria da Conceição, 1805, APEB, SJ, 07/3243/39; Silvia Hunold Lara, "Signs of Color: Women's Dress and Racial Relations in Salvador and Rio de Janeiro, ca. 1750-1815," *Colonial Latin American Review* 6, no. 2 (1997): 213. On slaves always being barefoot, see (among many sources) Andrew Grant, *History of Brazil* . . . (London: Henry Colburn, 1809), p. 236, and Majoribanks, *Travels*, p. 42.

28. Rugendas, *Malerische Reise*, 2ᵉ Div., plate 8; Johan Brelin, *De passagem pelo Brasil e Portugal em 1756* (Lisbon: Casa Portuguesa, 1955), p. 104; Tollenare, *Notas dominicais*, p. 298; John Candler and William Burgess, *Narrative of a Recent Visit to Brazil to Present an Address on the Slave Trade and Slavery Issued by the Religious Society of Friends* (London: Edward Marsh, 1853), p. 53. For examples of their jewelry see the magnificent illustrations in Edward J. Sullivan, ed., *Brazil: Body and Soul* (New York: Guggenheim Museum, 2001), pp. 272-281.

29. Ana de Lourdes Ribeiro da Costa, "Moradia de escravos em Salvador no século XIX," *Clio: Revista de Pesquisa Histórica* [Série História do Nordeste], no. 11 (1988): 99. According to this same author's thesis (as cited in Fraga Filho, *Mendigos, moleques*, p. 26), 30 percent of those who lived in these basement rooms in a central parish were self-hired slaves who lived on their own, and 79 percent were blacks or mulattos. An African renter of such a room is mentioned in Inv., José Pedro de Torres, 1829, APEB, SJ, 04/1710/2180/06, fols. 42, 44. See also Reis, *Slave Rebellion*, p. 75.

30. Inv., Ana de São José da Trindade, 1823, APEB, SJ, 04/1840/2311/02, fols. (second set) 10-11, 19v.

31. Licenças, 1819, AMS, 88.5, fol. 176v; Test., Rosa Maria da Conceição, 1838, APEB, SJ, Registro de Testamentos, Liv. 27, fols. 148v-150; records on Maria da Cruz in Irmão Mordomo dos presos pobres to Provedor and Mesarios, 28 Nov. 1852, ASCM, Despesa desencadernada, 1852/53, M. 339; Test., Maria da Cruz, [signed 1849] 1853, APEB, SJ, 05/2105/2575A/41, fol. 2.

32. Maria Inês Côrtes de Oliveira, *O liberto: O seu mundo e os outros (Salvador, 1790-1890)*, Baianada, 7 (São Paulo and Brasília: Corrupio and CNPq, 1988), p. 36; Sheila de Castro Faria, "Mulheres forras: Riqueza e estigma social," *Tempo*, no. 9 (July 2000): 65-92; Faria, "Sinhás pretas, 'damas mercadoras': As pretas minas nas cidades do Rio de Janeiro e de São João del Rey (1700-1850)," unpublished MS tese de doutorado (Niterói: Universidade Federal Fluminense, 2004); Júnia Ferreira Furtado, *Chica da Silva e o contratador dos diamantes: O outro lado do mito* (São Paulo: Companhia das Letras, 2003), pp. 105-111, 129-131, 135, 139-141, 144, 151-152. Also see Kátia M. de Queiroz Mattoso, *Testamentos de escravos libertos na Bahia no século XIX* (Salvador: Centro de Estudos Bahianos, Universidade Federal da Bahia, 1979), pp. 11-12. On the wealth of a freed African male in Rio de Janeiro see Zephyr Frank, *Dutra's World: Wealth and Family in Nineteenth-Century Rio de Janeiro* (Albuquerque: University of New Mexico Press, 2004), pp. 131-140.

33. Subdelegado do Curato da Sé to Chefe da Polícia, 11 Dec. 1871, APEB, CP, M. 6241, 1871, caderno 4 (I owe this reference to Sandra Lauderdale Graham); Inv., Benedita Maria Carneiro, 1798, APEB, SJ, 04/1604/2073/03, fols. 1-15v (she took out a license as a street vendor herself in 1789; Licenças, 1789, AMS, 88.1, fol. 212v); Fraga Filho, *Mendigos, moleques*, p. 69.

34. Inv., surgeon's bill in José Pinto de Almeida, 1830, APEB, SJ, 04/1729/2199/03,

242 NOTES TO PAGES 46–48

fol. 231; advertisements for runaways in *Jornal da Bahia,* 10 Feb. 1854, and 4 Mar. 1857, quoted in Verger, *Trade Relations,* p. 444; Inv., José Botelho de Siqueira, 1821, APEB, SJ, 03/1093/1562/01, fol. 3. See also illnesses described in postmortem estate inventories cited by Maria José de Souza Andrade, *A mão de obra escrava em Salvador, 1811–1860,* Baianada, 8 (São Paulo and Brasília: Corrupio and CNPq, 1988), p. 154. On abandonment of ill slaves see A. J. R. Russell-Wood, *The Black Man in Slavery and Freedom in Colonial Brazil* (New York: St. Martin's, 1982), p. 46.

35. "No esquife denominado Bangué," Escrivão da Santa Casa de Misericórdia, Atestado, 4 Feb. 1835, in Inv., José Pinto de Almeida, 1830, APEB, SJ, 04/1729/2199/03, fol. 240v; João José Reis, *A morte é uma festa: Ritos fúnebres e revolta popular no Brasil do século XIX* (São Paulo: Companhia das Letras, 1991), pp. 146–147, 193–200.

36. Juiz de Paz (Vitória) to PP-BA, [?] Sept. 1832, and enclosures, especially Delegado (Districto do Rio Vermelho) to Juiz de Paz, 24 May 1832; idem., Deposition, 4 June 1832; interrogation of Maria Joaquina de Santa Anna, 22 June 1832, at chambers of the Juiz de Paz; A Justiça contra Maria Joaquina de Santa Anna (a court record); and Maria Joaquina de Santa Anna, petition to be released on bail, all in APEB, SJ, Juizes de Paz, 1ª Vara, Cx. 1048, M. 2682 [pasta 4]. Also see Brazil, *Código criminal do Império,* Arts. 202 and 280, for the legal basis for the charges against Maria Joaquina.

37. See Sandra Lauderdale Graham, "Slavery's Impasse: Slave Prostitutes, Small-Time Mistresses, and the Brazilian Law of 1871," *Comparative Studies in Society and History* 33, no. 4 (Oct. 1991): 686–689; Alexandra Kelly Brown, "'On the Vanguard of Civilization': Slavery, the Police, and Conflicts Between Public and Private Power in Salvador da Bahia, Brazil, 1835–1888" (Ph.D. diss., University of Texas at Austin, 1998), pp. 224–237.

38. Câmara, Edital, 14 May 1823, AMS, 116.6, fols. 69v–70.

39. Inv., Manoel Ferreira Dias, 1807, APEB, SJ, 04/1771/2241/10, fol. 11; Inv., José Pinto de Almeida, 1830, APEB, SJ, 04/1729/2199/03, fols. 21–21v; Inv. e Test., Antonio José Ferreira Sampaio, 1834, APEB, SJ, 05/1999/2470/05, fols. 2, 8; *Correio Mercantil* (Salvador), 26 Oct. 1835, enclosed in APEB, SJ, Auto crimes, 09/313, M. 3181, Doc. 1, p. 4, col. 2; Inv. e Test., Antonio José Pinto (2º), 1855 [1854], APEB, SJ, 05/2152/2621/03, fol. 1. Cf. the French use of the word *chez* or the English "merchant house." Although stores were licensed, I have found no evidence (except for butcher shops) that the city specified where they could be located, unlike the practice in Potosí, Bolivia (Mangan, *Trading Roles,* pp. 48–57).

40. For the interchangeability of *venda* and *armazém* for stores selling only foodstuffs and drink, see Inv., José Pinto de Almeida, 1830, APEB, SJ, 04/1729/2199/03, fols. 15, 21, 25, 43; and Commodidades que o marechal de campo graduado Luiz Paulino de Oliveira Pinto da França offerece para o estabelecimento de uma feira, in "Decreto," 9 Aug. 1819, LB, 1819. On the interchangeability of *venda* and *tenda* see Inv., Ana Joaquina de Jesus, 1800, APEB, SJ, 04/1710/2180/02, fols. 7–7v. On the dictionary definition of *tenda* see Rafael Bluteau, *Diccionario da lingua portugueza,* rev. Antonio de Moraes Silva (Lisbon: Simão Thaddeo Ferreira, 1789). On the use of *venda* and *taverna* for the same establishment see Inv., Antonio Lopes da Silva, 1827, APEB, SJ, 04/1702/2172/05, fols. 7 and 22; and Inv., Bartolomeu Francisco Gomes, 1848, APEB, CP, 04/1697/2167/06. Even *armazem*

and *taberna* are conflated in Câmara to PP-BA, 23 Mar. 1830, AMS, 111.8, fol. 9. Sometimes the word *loja* was used (e.g., Inv., Henrique José Teixeira Chaves, 1847, APEB, SJ, 04/1447/1916/05, fol. 14), but only rarely for a store selling foodstuffs, in contrast to the situation in Minas Gerais, as described by Júnia Ferreira Furtado, *Homens de negócio: A interiorização da metrópole e do comércio nas Minas setecentistas* (São Paulo: HUCITEC, 1999), pp. 241–243 (cf. Figueiredo, *Avesso da memória*, p. 41).

41. Inv., José Pinto de Almeida, 1830, APEB, SJ, 04/1729/2199/03, fol. 19v (quoted); Inv., Antonio Lopes da Silva, 1827, APEB, SJ, 04/1702/2172/05, fol. 22; Inv., José Pereira de Carvalho, 1846, APEB, SJ, 03/1063/1532/05, fol. 11; Inv., Manoel Ferreira Dias, 1807, APEB, SJ, 04/1771/2241/10 (I was led to this last reference by Hendrik Kraay).

42. Testimony of Antonio Pedro de Alcântara, 1822, in "Documentos relativos ao governo da Bahia, 1822," in APEB, *Anais*, 27 (1941), p. 134. On the perishable nature of the goods in general stores see Inv., Bartolomeu Francisco Gomes, 1848, APEB, SJ, 04/1697/2167/06, fol. 5, and Inv. José Pinto de Almeida, 1830, APEB, SJ, 04/1729/2199/03, fol. 21. Mappa de importação . . . a Bahia . . . anno de 1809, AN, SPE, IJJ⁹319, fol. 15, shows that 17.5 percent of all imports to Salvador from Portugal between 1796 and 1811 consisted of foodstuffs. See also José Jobson de A. Arruda, *O Brasil no comércio colonial* (São Paulo: Ática, 1980), Table 20B, p. 200.

43. Inv., Balthazar de Andrade Bastos, 1865, APEB, SJ, 05/1965/2437/06, fol. 5.

44. Lima, "A Bahia ha 66 anos," p. 96; Grant, *History of Brazil*, p. 233. Also see Alcide d'Orbigny, *Viagem pitoresca através do Brasil*, Reconquista do Brasil, no. 29 (Belo Horizonte and São Paulo: Itatiaia and EDUSP, 1976), p. 105.

45. Inv., José Pinto de Almeida, 1830, APEB, SJ, 04/1729/2199/03, fols. 8v–9v.

46. AMS, 88.1, fols. 198–201; AMS, 88.4, fols. 211–212v; AMS, 88.5, fols. 266–267v. I again thank Gail Sanders for assisting me in gathering this data. On women and *vendas* in Minas Gerais during the eighteenth century, cf. Furtado, *Homens de negócio*, p. 256, with Figueiredo, *Avesso da memória*, pp. 55–56.

47. Inv. Ana Rosa de Jesus, 1796, APEB, SJ, 04/1586/2055/07, fol. 5v; *Cidade d'Ouro*, 1815 (no. 72), 1816 (no. 76), 1819 (nos. 34, 46), and 1823 (no. 12), all quoted in Maria Beatriz Nizza da Silva, "Mulheres e patrimônio familiar no Brasil no fim do período colonial," *Acervo* 9, no. 1–2 (Dec. 1996): 97 (the same information is found in Maria Beatriz Nizza da Silva, "Mulheres brancas no fim do período colonial," *Cadernos Pagu: Fazendo história das mulheres*, no. 4 [1995]: 80); Correição feita no sitio da Fonte de S. Pedro, 26 Jun. 1780, AMS, 45.2, fol. 198v; and Soares, "As ganhadeiras," p. 68.

48. Inv., Ana Joaquina de Jesus, 1800, APEB, SJ, 04/1710/2180/02; Inv., Florinda de Aragão, 1805, APEB, SJ, 04/1766/2336/07.

49. On a Brazilian owner of a store see Inv., Bartolomeu Francisco Gomes, 1848, APEB, SJ, 04/1697/2167/06, fols. 6, 7; on the slave store owner see João José Reis, "Domingos Pereira Sodré: Um sacerdote africano na Bahia oitocentista," *Afro-Ásia*, no. 34 (2006): 266; on the "Commercial Body," see Ignacio Madeira de Mello (army commander) to El-Rey, 2 Apr. 1822, AHM, 2ª Div., 1ª Sec., Cx. 39, No. 1.

50. Francisco de Sierra y Mariscal, "Idéas geraes sobre a revolução do Brazil [sic] e suas consequencias," *ABNRJ* 43–44 (1920–1921): 55–56; Henry Koster, *Travels in Brazil in the Years from 1809 to 1815* (London: Longman Hurst, Reese, Orme and

Brown, 1816), p. 170. See also Stuart B. Schwartz, "The Formation of a Colonial Identity in Brazil," in *Colonial Identity in the Atlantic World, 1500–1800*, ed. Nicholas Canny and Anthony Pagden (Princeton, NJ: Princeton University Press, 1987), pp. 19, 24.

51. Test. e Codicílio, Inocencio José da Costa, 1805, APEB, SJ, 08/3465/02, fol. 1; Test., Joaquim José de Oliveira, 25 June 1831, APEB, SJ, Registro de Testamentos, Liv. 20, fols. 102–102v; Test., 24 Sept. 1856, encl. in Inv., Antonio Pinto Rodrigues da Costa, 1860/62, APEB, SJ, 06/2873/07, fols. 1 and 6v. On the mob action see F. W. O. Morton, "The Conservative Revolution of Independence: Economy, Society and Politics in Bahia, 1790–1840" (Ph.D. diss., University of Oxford, 1974), pp. 299–307, 321; João José Reis, "A elite baiana face os movimentos sociais, Bahia: 1824–1840," *Revista de História* 54, no. 108 (Dec. 1976): 347–351, 363–367. On the comparable situation in Pernambuco see Jeffrey C. Mosher, *Political Struggle, Ideology, and State Building: Pernambuco and the Construction of Brazil, 1817–1850* (Lincoln: University of Nebraska Press, 2008), pp. 197–201.

52. Inv., Luiz Antonio Soares, 1808, APEB, SJ, 05/2033/2504/10, fol. 13; Inv., Manoel Tavares, 1816, APEB, SJ, 04/1725/2195/09, fols. 43v, 59; Lima, "A Bahia ha 66 anos," p. 96.

53. Inv., Bartolomeu Francisco Gomes, 1848, APEB, SJ, 04/1697/2167/06, fols. 3, 4; Test., Joaquim José de Oliveira, 25 June 1831, APEB, SJ, Registro de Testamentos, Liv. 20, fol. 100; and Inv. (2º), Joaquim José de Oliveira, 1831 and 1832, APEB, SJ, 02/875/1344/03, fol. 8. I found only one reference to a black woman clerking (Termo de exame, enclosed in Almotacel to Governador, 19 Nov. 1801, APEB, CP, M. 209-1), in contrast to the situation in Minas Gerais; see Mafalda P. Zemella, *O abastecimento da capitania das Minas Gerais no século XVIII*, 2nd ed. (São Paulo: HUCITEC and EDUSP, 1990), p. 164; Furtado, *Homens de negócio*, pp. 255–256.

54. Reis, *Slave Rebellion*, p. 171.

55. Copy of petition enclosed in Rodrigo de Souza Coutinho to Fernando José de Portugal, Palacio Queluz [Lisbon], 6 Nov. 1798, APEB, CP, M. 86, fols. 276–276v. On petitions to the Crown see A. J. R. Russell-Wood, "'Acts of Grace': Portuguese Monarchs and Their Subjects of African Descent in Eighteenth-Century Brazil," *Journal of Latin American Studies* 32, no. 2 (May 2000): 307–332.

56. Autuação da petição de Joaquim de Almeida, 1834, Auto crime, APEB, SJ, 04/128/3 (M. 3175, no. 3), fols. 7v, 10, 35v–36v, and Acareação e inquirição ad perpetuam, enclosed in ibid., but separately paged, fols. 4–4v, 6v.

57. "[Discussion]," London, 14 Aug. 1804, Chatham Papers, PRO, 30/8/345, pt. 2, fol. 233, as cited in Kenneth Maxwell, *Conflicts and Conspiracies: Brazil and Portugal, 1750–1808*, Cambridge Latin American Studies no. 16 (Cambridge, Eng.: Cambridge University Press, 1973), p. 215; Vilhena, *Bahia no século XVIII*, p. 244.

CHAPTER 3

1. Kátia M. de Queirós Mattoso, *Bahia, século XIX: Uma província no Império* (Rio de Janeiro: Nova Fronteira, 1992), p. 151; Conde de Suzannet, *O Brasil em 1845 (Semelhanças e diferenças após um século)*, trans. Márcia de Moura Castro, intro. by Austregésilo de Athayde (Rio de Janeiro: Casa do Estudante do

Brasil, 1957), p. 47 (quoted). See also Donald Ramos, "Marriage and the Family in Colonial Vila Rica," *Hispanic American Historical Review* 55, no. 2 (May 1975): 207–209, 218; Emílio Willems, *Latin American Culture: An Anthropological Synthesis* (New York: Harper and Row, 1975), p. 53; Júnia Ferreira Furtado, *Chica da Silva e o contratador dos diamantes: O outro lado do mito* (São Paulo: Companhia das Letras, 2003), pp. 69, 266–267; Maria Beatriz Nizza da Silva, *Sistema de casamento no Brasil colonial*, Coleção Coroa Vermelha, Estudos Brasileiros, no. 6 (São Paulo: T. A. Queiroz and EDUSP, 1984), pp. 50, 53–56. On Church requirements, see Sheila de Castro Faria, *A colônia em movimento: Fortuna e família no cotidiano colonial* (Rio de Janeiro: Nova Fronteira, 1998), pp. 58–61. In smallholding rural areas of the province of Rio de Janeiro, formal marriage may have been more prevalent; ibid., p. 148.

 2. E.g., Inv., José Pinto de Almeida, 1830, APEB, SJ, 04/1729/2199/03, fol. 104v. The quoted phrase dates back at least to the Philippine Code of 1603; Candido Mendes de Almeida, ed., *Codigo Philippino; ou, Ordenações e leis do reino de Portugal recopiladas por mandado d'el rei D. Philippe I . . .* (Rio de Janeiro: Instituto Philomathico, 1870), Liv. 4, Tit. 46, paragraph 2, col. 1, n. 1. As explained in col. 2, n. 1, and specifically referenced in Tit. 92, par. 1, concubinage did not lead to joint property, as between man and wife, but only to their children's right to inherit. For an alternative view on the meaning of "concubine," based on records from the Inquisition, see Ronaldo Vainfas, "Moralidades brasílicas: Deleites sexuais e linguagem erótica na sociedade escravista," in *História da vida privada no Brasil, 1: Cotidano e vida privada na América portuguesa*, ed. Laura de Mello e Souza; Fernando A. Novais, gen. ed. (São Paulo: Companhia das Letras, 1997), pp. 236–238; but cf. Silva, *Sistema de casamento*, p. 44. The practice in the Portuguese world contrasts sharply with the principles laid out in Spanish law: *Las siete partidas del sabio rey D. Alonso el IX con las variantes de más interés, y con la glosa del lic. Gregorio Lopez* (Barcelona: Antonio Bergens, 1844), Partida 4, Title 14, Law 3, pp. 1055–1056.

 3. Muriel Nazzari, "Concubinage in Colonial Brazil: The Inequalities of Race, Class, and Gender," *Journal of Family History* 21, no. 2 (April 1996): 107–118; Test., Antonio José Pinto (2º), 1855 [1854], APEB, SJ, 05/2152/2621/03, fol. 1; Inv. e Test., Antonio José Ferreira Sampaio, 1834, APEB, SJ, 05/1999/2470/05, fol. 4v. An example, however, of the equality of an unmarried couple in Salvador is that of Faustina dos Passos, who had a small fortune of her own to add to that of her conjugal partner; Henrique José Teixeira Chaves to José Thomas dos Santos, 17 Jan. 1846, encl. in Inv., Henrique José Teixeira Chaves, 1847, APEB, SJ, 04/1447/1916/05, fol. 147, and this inventário itself, fol. 177v. Also see Anna Amélia Vieira Nascimento, *Dez freguesias da cidade do Salvador: Aspectos sociais e urbanos do século XIX* (Salvador: Fundação Cultural do Estado da Bahia, 1986), p. 125; and Furtado, *Chica da Silva*, p. 55.

 4. Test. 16 Nov. 1848, encl. in Inv., Bartolomeu Francisco Gomes, 1848, APEB, SJ, 04/1697/2167/06, fol. 6; Inv., José Pinto de Almeida, 1830, APEB, SJ, 04/1729/2199/03, fols. 1, 73, 89, 99, 299v; Test. 4 Feb. 1822, encl. in Inv., José Gomes da Costa, 1824, APEB, SJ, 04/1783/2253/09, fol. 4v.

 5. See, for example, Inv., José da Silva Barros, 1823, APEB, SJ, 04/1826/2297/13, fols. 53–53v, 55v. A testator needed specifically to deny paternity if he wanted a

court subsequently to reject claims to inheritance rights made by children of a woman with whom he had lived; Test., 24 Sept. 1856, encl. in Inv., Antonio Pinto Rodrigues da Costa, 1860/62, APEB, SJ, 06/2873/07, fols. 4, 5, 6v, 7v. Alida Metcalf (*Family and Frontier in Colonial Brazil: Santana de Parnaíba, 1580–1822* [Berkeley: University of California Press, 1992], pp. 101–102) reports that disinheriting natural children was a common practice in the town she studied, but I did not find that to be the case in Salvador.

6. Test. 18 June 1807, and Inv., João Nunes, 1808, APEB, SJ, 05/2048/2519/17, fols. 1–6; Licenças, 1789, AMS, 88, fol. 211.

7. Inv., José da Silva Barros, 1823, APEB, SJ, 04/1826/2297/13, fols. 53–55v, 61, 66.

8. Luzia Pedreira de Sales Lobo e Maia, Declaration, in Inv., Antonio Pedreiras Jiquitibá Rebouças, 1829, APEB, SJ, 08/3440/27, fol. 1; Test., 1 Feb. 1806, encl. in Inv., Felix Ferreira de Santana, 1806, APEB, SJ, 04/1770/2240/04, fol. 6v.

9. Furtado, *Chica da Silva*, p. 46.

10. Test., 25 Aug. 1827, copy in Treslado de Test., Francisco Ferreira da Gama, 1836, APEB, SJ, 03/1276/1745/24, fols. [2–5].

11. Slave prostitution was not uncommon. See Mary C. Karasch, *Slave Life in Rio de Janeiro, 1808–1850* (Princeton, NJ: Princeton University Press, 1987), p. 346; A. J. R. Russell-Wood, *The Black Man in Slavery and Freedom in Colonial Brazil* (New York: St. Martin's, 1982), p. 37; Sandra Lauderdale Graham, "Slavery's Impasse: Slave Prostitutes, Small-Time Mistresses, and the Brazilian Law of 1871," *Comparative Studies in Society and History* 33, no. 4 (Oct. 1991): 669–694. Prostitution was not illegal in Brazil, so records are not numerous. Historians have often been too eager to ignore the possibility of sex for a woman's pleasure, freely chosen.

12. Felix Justiniano de Albuquerque (Alferes), Report, 7 June 1859, copy encl. in Francisco Felix da Fonseca Pereira e Pinto (Comandante das Armas) to Antonio Ladislau de Figueiredo Rocha (Chefe de Polícia), 9 June 1859, APEB, CP, M. 6461 (I was led to this document by Hendrik Kraay); L. F. de Tollenare, *Notas dominicais tomadas durante uma viagem em Portugal e no Brasil em 1816, 1817, e 1818* (Salvador: Progresso, 1956), p. 299.

13. Ana de Lourdes Ribeiro da Costa, "Moradia de escravos em Salvador no século XIX," *Clio: Revista de Pesquisa Histórica* [Série História do Nordeste], no. 11 (1988): 99, 102; Kátia M. de Queiroz Mattoso, *Testamentos de escravos libertos na Bahia no século XIX* (Salvador: Centro de Estudos Bahianos, Universidade Federal da Bahia, 1979), p. 39; Isabel Cristina Ferreira dos Reis, *Histórias de vida familiar e afetiva de escravos na Bahia do século XIX* (Salvador: Centro de Estudos Baianos, 2001), pp. 104–105, 115–116, 162–164.

14. Oskar Canstatt, *Brasil: Terra e gente*, 2nd ed., trans. Eduardo de Lima Castro, intro. by Artur Cezar Ferreira Reis, Temas Brasileiros, no. 18 (Rio de Janeiro: Conquista, 1975), p. 192; Test., 16 Jan. 1823, encl. in Inv., Ana de São José da Trindade, 1823, APEB, SJ, 04/1840/2311/02, fol. 6; on Benedita see Inv. e Test., Manuel José da Cunha, 1821, APEB, SJ, 04/1740/2210/01, fol. 10.

15. See Florence E. Babb, *Between Field and Cooking Pot: The Political Economy of Marketwomen in Peru*, 2nd ed. (Austin: University of Texas Press, 1998), p. 53; Linda J. Seligman, ed., *Women Traders in Cross-Cultural Perspective: Me-*

diating Identities, Marketing Wares (Stanford, CA: Stanford University Press, 2001), p. 4.

16. Reis, *Histórias de vida familiar*, pp. 31–32; José Roberto de Góes and Manolo Florentino, "Crianças escravas, crianças dos escravos," in *História das crianças no Brasil*, ed. Mary del Priore (São Paulo: Editora Contexto, 2000), pp. 182–183.

17. Sandra Lauderdale Graham, *Caetana Says No: Women's Stories from a Brazilian Slave Society* (Cambridge, Eng.: Cambridge University Press, 2002), pp. 44–49; Stuart B. Schwartz, *Slaves, Peasants, and Rebels: Reconsidering Brazilian Slavery* (Urbana: University of Illinois Press, 1992), pp. 137–160.

18. Test., 21 Mar. 1864, Manoel José dos Reis, 1873, APEB, SJ, 05/2190/2663/15, fol. 2; Test., 1868, encl. in Inv., Sabina da Cruz, 1872, APEB, SJ, 03/1100/1569/07, fols. 1 and 2v (I owe this last reference to Sandra Lauderdale Graham).

19. Acareação e inquirição ad perpetuam, encl. in Autuação da petição de Joaquim de Almeida, 1834, APEB, SJ, Auto crime, 04/128/3, fols. 4v–6v; Queixoso: José Callisto de Oliveira; Queixado: Luiz Baptista Correia, Salvador, 25 Aug. 1834, Auto crime, APEB, SJ, 04/128/4 (M. 3175, no. 4), fols. 12, 24–33.

20. Commandante de Armas to Chefe de Polícia, 8 Apr. 1870, APEB, CP, M. 6464 (I owe this reference to Hendrik Kraay); Canstatt, *Brasil: Terra e gente*, pp. 192, 199; Maximilian [Emperor of Mexico (Ferdinand Joseph Maximilian of Austria)], *Recollections of My Life*, 3 vols. (London: Richard Bentley, 1868), 3: 108.

21. Acusação de Bento Alvares de Carvalho e Manoel Rodrigues Branco, 1832, Auto crime, APEB, SJ, 04/127/2 (M. 3175, no. 2), 2ª parte.

22. Test. e Inv. (1º), Manuel José da Cunha, 1821, APEB, SJ, 04/1740/2210/01, fol. 10; Quadro da População do 21º quarteirão do Curato da Sé, [1855], APEB, CP, M. 1602, fols 3, 7. See also Costa, "Moradia de escravos," p. 100.

23. Edital, 2 Sept. 1853, encl. in Câmara to PP-BA, 20 May 1857, APEB, CP, M. 1403; Postura no. 65, 25 Feb. 1831, AMS, 119.5, fol. 37.

24. In contrast see Cheryl English Martin, *Governance and Society in Colonial Mexico: Chihuahua in the Eighteenth Century* (Stanford, CA: Stanford University Press, 1996), pp. 135–139; and Jane E. Mangan, *Trading Roles: Gender, Ethnicity, and the Urban Economy in Colonial Potosí* (Durham, NC: Duke University Press, 2005), p. 215, n. 64.

25. Ellena quoted in João José Reis, *Slave Rebellion in Brazil: The Muslim Uprising of 1835 in Bahia*, trans. Arthur Brakel (Baltimore: Johns Hopkins University Press, 1993), p. 167; Postura no. 35, in Posturas do Senado da Câmara [1716] . . . fielmente copiadas . . . 1785, ANRJ, SH, Cód. 90, fol 7.

26. Hendrik Kraay, *Race, State, and Armed Forces in Independence-Era Brazil: Bahia, 1790s–1840s* (Stanford, CA: Stanford University Press, 2001), pp. 199, 202; Alexandra Kelly Brown, "'On the Vanguard of Civilization': Slavery, the Police, and Conflicts Between Public and Private Power in Salvador da Bahia, Brazil, 1835–1888" (Ph.D. diss., University of Texas at Austin, 1998), pp. 87–89.

27. Câmara to Governador, 24 Oct. 1801, APEB, CP, M. 209-1 (also in AMS, 111.4, fol. 184v) (quoted); Tenente Coronel Joaquim José Velloso to Commandante das Armas, 9 Oct. 1832, APEB, CP, M. 3394; Câmara to PP-BA, 26 Feb. 1834, AMS, 111.8, fol. 236v; Letter from "Philopolito" in *O tolerante na Bahia*, 25 Apr. 1839,

p. 1, col. 1, Arquivo Histórico do Exército, Rio de Janeiro, D-26-709; PP-BA to Commandante das Armas Interino, 24 Mar. 1824 in *O Independente Constitucional*, 5 Apr. 1824, p. 2, col. 1, in AN, IG[1] 249/432 (I owe these last two references to Hendrik Kraay). On the copper currency see F. W. O. Morton, "The Conservative Revolution of Independence: Economy, Society and Politics in Bahia, 1790–1840" (Ph.D. diss., University of Oxford, 1974), pp. 326–327; and João José Reis, "A elite baiana face os movimentos sociais, Bahia: 1824–1840," *Revista de História* 54, no. 108 (Dec. 1976): 354–357.

28. Traslado dos Autos de Summaria [a] que se procederão no Juizo de Paz da Freguezia da Conceição da Praia pela sublevação dos prezos da Justiça na Fortaleza do Mar, 1833, APEB, CP, M. 2853, fol. 46.

29. Reis, *Slave Rebellion*, pp. 73–75, 167, 184–185. Also see Keila Grinberg, *O fiador dos brasileiros: Cidadania, escravidão e direito civil no tempo de Antônio Pereira Rebouças* (Rio de Janeiro: Civilização Brasileira, 2002), p. 142.

30. Licenças, 1807, AMS, 88.4, fols. 218 and 219v; Queixosa: Thereza Maria de Jesus; Queixado: Gonçalo José dos Santos Paz (or Pereira), Juizado de Paz de Santo Antonio Além do Carmo, 29 Oct. 1838, Auto crime, APEB, SJ, 09/313/11, no. 6.

31. Waldemar Mattos, *Panorama econômico da Bahia, 1808–1960: Edição comemorativa do sesquicentenário da Associação Comercial da Bahia* (Salvador: [Tip. Manu Editôra], 1961), pp. 66–67; José Antônio Caldas, *Noticia geral de toda esta capitania da Bahia desde o seu descobrimento até o presente anno de 1759*, facsim. ed. (Salvador: Câmara de Vereadores, 1951), fols. 525–533. More on the rankings of merchant houses can be found in Mesa de Inspeção to Rainha, 23 Feb. 1789, ANTT, Junta do Commercio, M. 10, no. 20. Most grocers would not have been mentioned in any of these sources. Also see Catherine Lugar, "The Merchant Community of Salvador, Bahia, 1780–1830" (Ph.D. diss., State University of New York at Stony Brook, 1980), pp. 32–34, 53–56.

32. Inv. José da Silva Maia,1809, APEB, SJ, 04/1790/2260/01, passim, and Inv., José Pinto de Almeida, 1830, APEB, SJ, 04/1729/2199/03, fols. 15–19, 25, 143 (on Silva Maia's rank within the merchant community see Lugar, "Merchant Community," p. 169); Account presented by Joaquim Carneiro de Campos for Sept. 1821 ordered paid on 14 Oct. 1821, ASCM, Pacote 224; Ignacio Madeira de Mello to MGuerra, 1 Apr. 1822, AHM, 2ª Div. 1ª Sec., Cx. 39, no. 1; Abaixo Assignado, n.d. [before 28 June 1851], APEB, CP, M. 3784; Inv., Manoel Tavares, 1816, APEB, SJ, 04/1725/2195/09, fols. 22, 26–28v, 30, 99v, 101, 104. Tavares's estate was valued at 5:256$469 (7:411$621).

33. Some store owners were specifically reported to lack the necessary funds to be registered at the Board of Trade; Juiz de Fora dos Orfãos to El-Rey, 6 Sept. 1822, copy encl. in idem to El-Rey, 16 May 1823, AHU, Bahia, Avulsos, Cx. 265, Doc. 68; Luís dos Santos Vilhena, *A Bahia no século XVIII*, 2nd ed., ed. Braz do Amaral, intro. by Edison Carneiro (Salvador: Itapuã, 1969), 1: 57, 131. On their military service see, for example, Inv., Manoel Ferreira Dias, 1807, APEB, SJ, 04/1771/2241/10, fol. 1, and Queixoso: Luiz Baptista Correia; Queixado: José Callisto de Oliveira, 25 Aug. 1834, Auto crime, APEB, SJ, 04/128/4 (M. 3175, no. 4), fol. 24. Also see Lugar, "Merchant Community," p. 220.

34. *Relatorio apresentado á Mesa e Junta da Casa da Santa Misericordia da Capital da Bahia pelo provedor Conde de Pereira Marinho por occasião da posse em 2 de julho de 1885* (Salvador: Tourinho, 1885); Eul-Soo Pang, *In Pursuit of*

Honor and Power: Noblemen of the Southern Cross in Nineteenth-Century Brazil (Tuscaloosa: University of Alabama Press, 1988), pp. 120, 250; Pierre Verger, *Trade Relations Between the Bight of Benin and Bahia from the 17th to 19th Century*, trans. Evelyn Crawford (Ibadan: Ibadan University Press, 1976), pp. 398–399, and p. 324, n. 30; B. J. Barickman, *A Bahian Counterpoint: Sugar, Tobacco, Cassava, and Slavery in the Recôncavo, 1780–1860* (Stanford, CA: Stanford University Press, 1998), p. 136; Eul-Soo Pang, *O Engenho Central do Bom Jardim na economia baiana: Alguns aspectos de sua história, 1875–1891* (Rio de Janeiro: Arquivo Nacional and Instituto Histórico e Geográfico Brasileiro, 1979), p. 42n; Mattoso, *Bahia, século XIX*, p. 497.

35. Livro de Notas de Francisco Ribeiro Neves, 1840–1842, APEB, SJ, 15, 27, fol. 79; Inv., Luiz Manoel da Rocha, 1853, APEB, SJ, 04/1689/2159/03, fols. 3, 19, 119, 380.

36. Test., Luiz Manoel da Rocha, 1853, APEB, SJ, 05/2105/275A/35, fol. 1; Inv., Luiz Manoel da Rocha, 1853, APEB, SJ, 04/1689/2159/03, fols. 11v–13, 14–18, 19–26v, 29–37, 38, 54, 56. Debts reduced his estate's value to 4:117$705 (2:058$853); fols. 620–621.

37. Test., copy encl. in Inv., and Inv. itself, Bartolomeu Francisco Gomes, 1848, APEB, SJ, 04/1697/2167/06, fols. 1–4, 6–7, 19–23v, 37–37v, 39, 54, 168, 169, 171 (the estate was worth 1:269$460 [723$592], fol. 175); Marchantes chamados ao curral em 1839 pelo presidente da Câmara, encl. in Câmara to PP-BA, 14 Jan 1839, APEB, CP, M. 1397, and covering letter. On his landlord's dry goods business see Test. (1°), 24 Oct. 1844, encl. in Test. (2°), Estevão Vaz de Carvalho, 1867, APEB, SJ, 05/2186/2655/52, unnumbered fol.

38. Inv., Luiz Manoel da Rocha, 1853, APEB, SJ, 04/1689/2159/03, fol. 12; Inv., Balthazar de Andrade Bastos, 1865, APEB, SJ, 05/1965/2437/06, fols. 38v–40; Inv., Paulo José Fernandes, 1820–1824, APEB, SJ, 07/3267/15, fol. 36. On Africa see Gareth Austin, "Indigenous Credit Institutions in West Africa, c. 1750–c. 1960," in *Local Suppliers of Credit in the Third World, 1750–1960*, ed. Gareth Austin and Kaoru Sugihara (New York: St. Martin's, 1993), p. 101.

39. Inv., Ana de São José da Trindade, 1823, APEB, SJ, 04/1840/2311/02, fol. 8; Joaquina leant Manoel 1:200$000 (1:284$000), Test., Manoel José Machado, 19 July 1821 (deceased 16 Apr. 1824), APEB, SJ, Registro de testamentos, Liv. 10, fol. 158; Câmara to PP-BA, 12 Jan. 1846, AMS, 111.11, fol. 163v. On similar practices elsewhere, see S[arah] L. Cline, *Colonial Culhuacan, 1580–1600: A Social History of an Aztec Town* (Albuquerque: University of New Mexico Press, 1986), pp. 90–97; Mangan, *Trading Roles*, p. 116; and Afonso de Alencastro Graça Filho, *A princesa do oeste e o mito da decadência de Minas Gerais: São João del Rei, 1831–1888* (São Paulo: Annablume, 2002), p. 72. Still today, throughout Brazil, it is common to see signs in small grocery shops announcing that they do not sell on credit, which means many customers expect to buy on credit.

40. Inv. Antônio José Pereira Arouca, 1825, APEB, SJ, 04/1717/2187/02, fol. 6; José Francisco da Silva Lima, "A Bahia ha 66 anos," *Revista do Instituto Geográfico e Histórico da Bahia*, ano 15, no. 34 (1908): 95. On the transatlantic flow of credit during the first half of the eighteenth century, see Luís Lisanti [Filho], ed., *Negócios coloniais (Uma correspondência comercial do século XVIII)* (Brasília and São Paulo: Ministério da Fazenda and Visão Editorial, 1973), 4: 563, 606.

41. On banks see Inv., Antonio da Cunha Bastos, 1856, SJ, 4/1671/2141/11,

fols. 42–49, 90, 95; Lima, "A Bahia ha 66 anos," 95; Thales de Azevedo and Edilberto Quintela Vieira Lins, *História do Banco da Bahia, 1858–1958*, Documentos Brasileiros, no. 132 (Rio de Janeiro: J. Olympio, 1969), pp. 48–89, esp. pp. 56–67. On institutional lending to planters see Stuart B. Schwartz, *Sugar Plantations in the Formation of Brazilian Society: Bahia, 1550–1835*, Cambridge Latin American Studies, no. 52 (Cambridge, Eng.: Cambridge University Press, 1985), pp. 204–212; A. J. R. Russell-Wood, *Fidalgos and Philanthropists: The Santa Casa da Misericórdia of Bahia, 1550–1755* (Berkeley: University of California Press, 1968), pp. 106, 197; Susan A. Soeiro, "A Baroque Nunnery: The Economic and Social Role of a Colonial Convent—Santa Clara do Destêrro, Salvador, Bahia, 1677–1800" (Ph.D. diss., New York University, 1974), pp. 115–154. There was, it is true, a savings bank (Caixa Econômica) founded in 1834 (Francisco Marques de Góes Calmon, *Vida econômico-financeira da Bahia (elementos para a história) de 1808–1899* [Salvador: Imp. Official do Estado, 1925], p. 54), but I found no references to it until much later; Test., 21 Mar. 1864, Manoel José dos Reis, 1873, APEB, SJ, 05/2190/2663/15, fol. 2. On how the similar coffee-dominated economy of Rio was financed in the second quarter of the nineteenth century, see Joseph E. Sweigart, *Coffee Factorage and the Emergence of a Brazilian Capital Market, 1850–1888* (New York: Garland, 1987), pp. 109–116.

42. "Discurso preliminar, historico, introductivo com natureza de descripção economica da comarca, e cidade da Bahia . . . [1789–1808?]," *ABNRJ* 27 (1905): 348; Inv. e Test. [2°], Antonio José Pinto, 1855 [1854], APEB, SJ, 05/2152/2621/03, fol. 1v. For an example of a money lender, see Inv., Antonio da Cruz Velloso, 1811, APEB, SJ, 04/1709/2179/02.

43. Inv., José Pinto de Almeida, 1830, APEB, SJ, 04/1729/2199/03, fols. 4, 6v, 7v, 19, 19v, 22, 24, 461v (his estate totaled 14:648$916 [11:133$176]); Inv. e Test., Antonio José Ferreira Sampaio, 1834, APEB, SJ, 05/1999/2470/05, fols. 6v–7.

44. José da Silva Lisboa, "'Carta muito interessante do advogado da Bahia . . . para Domingos Vandelli, Bahia, 18 de outubro de 1781,' in Eduardo de Castro e Almeida, "Inventario dos documentos relativos ao Brasil existentes no Archivo de Marinha e Ultramar, Part II (Bahia, 1763–1786)," *ABNRJ* 32 (1910): 504; Governador to Martinho de Mello e Castro, 15 Sept. 1795, BN/SM, 1, 4, 11, fol. 217. The government, however, presumably because a loan to it was judged more secure, was able to borrow money at only 5 percent; see Test., Inocencio José da Costa, 1805, APEB, SJ, 08/3465/02.

45. Balthazar de Andrade Bastos to Domingos de Almeida Carmo, 12 Aug. 1865, encl. in Inv., Balthazar de Andrade Bastos, 1865, APEB, SJ, 05/1965/2437/06, fol. 43 (quoted), and see fols. 42, 91; Inv., José Teixeira de Sousa, 1814, APEB, SJ, 05/2213/2713/29, fols. 91–91v. On patron-client ties see Richard Graham, *Patronage and Politics in Nineteenth-Century Brazil* (Stanford, CA: Stanford University Press, 1990), pp. 242, 247, 249. Jay Kinsbruner (*The Colonial Spanish-American City: Urban Life in the Age of Atlantic Capitalism* [Austin: University of Texas Press, 2005], p. 148, n. 19), in denying the presence of patron-client relations in credit transactions, misunderstands the generally ambiguous and ambivalent nature of all such relations.

46. Inv., Henrique José Teixeira Chaves, 1847, APEB, SJ, 04/1447/1916/05, fol. 15 (he stated that he kept each item with a note on who had pawned it, when, and for

how much); Inv., Ana de São José da Trindade, 1823, APEB, SJ, 04/1840/2311/02, fol. 8. I am not aware of city regulations on pawning such as those in Mexico City; Marie Eileen Francois, *A Culture of Everyday Credit: Housekeeping, Pawnbroking, and Governance in Mexico City, 1750–1920* (Lincoln: University of Nebraska Press, 2006), pp. 49–52, 56–58.

47. John Turnbull, *A Voyage Round the World, in the Years 1800, 1801, 1802, 1803, and 1804* . . . (London: Maxwell, 1813), p. 47; Andrew Grant, *History of Brazil Comprising a Geographical Account of That Country, Together with a Narrative of the Most Remarkable Events Which Have Occurred There Since Its Discovery* . . . (London: Henry Colburn, 1809), p. 229.; Tollenare, *Notas dominicais*, p. 352. On foreclosure see, for example, Exequente: Bernardino José de Almeida, Executado: Jeronimo Ribeiro de Queiroz, APEB, SJ, Cachoeira, 1860, M. 1662, no. 8. Few were the creditors who could, for instance, attach a lighter when a payment was not received; Inv., José Pereira de Carvalho, 1846, APEB, SJ, 03/1063/1532/05, fol. 50.

48. Inv., José Pinto de Almeida, 1830, APEB, SJ, 04/1729/2199/03, fol. 43. The very same words are reported for an auction of a food store and some slaves a quarter of a century later; Inv., Antonio da Cunha Bastos, 1856, APEB, SJ, 4/1671/2141/11, fol. 10v.

49. The drawback of merely oral agreements is demonstrated by the case of a freed African woman who traded in textiles, was illiterate, and kept no written records; at her death, creditors presented their bills to the executor, but he had no way of finding those who owed her money; Inv., Sabina da Cruz, 1872, APEB, SJ, 03/1100/1569/07, fol. 39 (I owe this reference to Sandra Lauderdale Graham). On orality see Mattoso, *Testamentos de escravos*, p. 42, and, for eighteenth-century France, Steven L. Kaplan, *Provisioning Paris: Merchants and Millers in the Grain and Flour Trade During the Eighteenth Century* (Ithaca, NY: Cornell University Press, 1984), p. 354.

CHAPTER 4

1. *Livro que dá razão do Estado do Brasil* (1612; facsim. ed., Rio de Janeiro: Instituto Nacional do Livro and Ministério da Educação e Cultura, 1968), p. 39; Mapa geral de toda qualidade de embarcasoens que [h]a na Capitania da Bahia e navegão para a Costa da el'Mina, Angola, e outros portos de Africa e de todas as que navegão de porto a porto para o Rio de Janeiro, Pernambuco, Pará, e outros portos desta costa do Brazil, como tão bem dos barcos, lanxas e outras pequenas embarcações que navegão pelos rios e ribeiras desta Capitania na condusão dos viv[e]res e pescado para a sua manutensão . . . Baia, 27 de maio de 1775, facsim. in Avelino de Jesus da Costa, "População da cidade da Baía em 1775," in *Actas do V [Quinto] Colóquio Internacional de Estudos Luso-Brasileiros, Coimbra, 1963* (Coimbra: Gráfica de Coimbra, 1964); Estampa 5 (a copy of this document, with a slightly different title, can be found enclosed in Manuel da Cunha Menezes to Martinho de Mello e Castro, 3 July 1775, AIHGB, Arq. 1-1-19, fol. 229); Governador to El-Rey, 28 Feb. 1798, APEB, CP, M. 158, fol. 282; Capitania dos Portos da Bahia, Mapa demonstrativo das embarcações nacionaes da navegação de longo curso e cabotagem bem como do trafico dos portos . . . e dos individuous que n'ellas

ر

trabalhão ou se empregão, 31 Dec. 1856, encl. in Diogo Ignacio Tavares (chefe da capitania do porto) to MM, 20 Feb. 1857, AN, SPE, XM-183. I have found nothing to suggest even remotely that 800 to 1,000 vessels docked every *day*, as alleged by Kátia M. de Queirós Mattoso, *Bahia: A cidade de Salvador e seu mercado no século XIX*, Coleção Estudos Brasileiros, no. 12 (São Paulo and Salvador: HUCITEC and Secretaria Municipal de Educação e Cultura, 1978), p. 143.

2. Denis, in Hippolyte Taunay and Ferdinand Denis, *Le Brésil, ou histoire, moeurs, usages et coutumes des habitans de ce royaume*, 6 vols. (Paris: Nepveu, 1822), 4: 27, 40; Andrew Grant, *History of Brazil Comprising a Geographical Account of That Country . . .* (London: Henry Colburn, 1809), p. 239; Daniel P. Kidder, *Sketches of Residence and Travels in Brazil Embracing Historical and Geographical Notices of the Empire and Its Several Provinces*, 2 vols. (Philadelphia: Sorin and Ball, 1845), 2: 19.

3. Manuel da Cunha Menezes to Martinho de Mello e Castro, 3 Mar. 1775, in Costa, "População da cidade," p. 273. This was still an issue in 1857; Diogo Ignacio Tavares (Chefe da Capitania do Porto) to José da Silva Paranhos (MM), 20 Feb. 1857 and enclosures.

4. On part ownership by captains, see Relação das farinhas exportadas para o celleiro público da Bahia desde 1 de 8bro até 31 do mesmo de 1826, [Jaguaripe], ABEB, CP, M. 1609—see, for example, the entry for Silvestre Francisco Canedo; on this dispute between owner and captain, see Carlos Antonio de Cerqueira, Auto, 26 Apr. 1793, APEB, CP, M. 201-31, Doc. 2.

5. [Illegible] to José Nunes Freire, Vila Viçosa, 25 Sept. 1822, APEB, CP, M. 4631.

6. Inspector de farinha to Governador, Nazaré, 14 Apr. 1794, APEB, CP, M. 201-31, Doc. 5; Relação da Bahia, Accordão, 22 Sept. 1821, copy encl. in Ouvidor do Crime to [Governador], 6 Oct. 1821, APEB, CP, M. 245; and Traslado do officio do secretario da Commissão Militar desta Villa [de Valença] e inventario que se procedeu . . . , 14 Dec. 1822, BN/SM, I-31, 6, 1, Doc. 53.

7. João Damaceno Palmeira to Conselho Interino, Maragogipe, n.d. [shortly before 2 Apr. 1823], and enclosures, APEB, CP, M. 4631; *Correio Mercantil* (Salvador), 2 May 1843, p. 4, quoted in Isabel Cristina Ferreira dos Reis, *Histórias de vida familiar e afetiva de escravos na Bahia do século XIX* (Salvador: Centro de Estudos Baianos, 2001), p. 55; Lista das embarcações que tem saido do porto da Vila de Maragogipe . . . desde o primeiro de agosto de 1786, n.d. [ca. 5 Sept. 1786], BN/SM, II-33, 21, 88; Relação das farinhas exportadas deste porto para o celleiro público da Bahia em o presente mez de julho 1826, Jaguaripe, APEB, CP, M. 1609, s.v. "barco Santa Rita."

8. I draw here on William Jeffrey Bolster, "African-American Seamen: Race, Seafaring Work, and Atlantic Maritime Culture, 1750–1860" (Ph.D. diss., Johns Hopkins University, 1991), pp. 426–438.

9. Câmara to Governador, 25 Nov. 1809, APEB, CP, M. 127; Chefe de Policia de Ilhéus, 6 Dec. 1837, in Arquivo do Estado da Bahia, *Publicações* (1941),4: 415; *Gazeta Commercial da Bahia*, no. 11, 24 May 1833 (I owe this reference to João José Reis); Inv., Manoel Tavares, 1816, APEB, SJ, 04/1725/2195/09, fols. 101, 101v, 104; João José Reis, *Rebelião escrava no Brasil: A história do levante dos malês, 1835* (São Paulo: Brasiliense, 1986), p. 264.

10. Inv., Rosa Maria de Jesus, 1808–1811, APEB, SJ, 01/269/514/02, fols. 4–5v, 10–11, 14–15 (the appraised value of the entire estate was 18:360$540 [37:639$107]); Licenças, 1789, AMS, 88.1, fol. 214v; Abaixo assinado 9 May 1823, AHM, 2ª Div., 1ª Sec., Cx. 41, No. 5, s.v. Manuel José dos Santos. On other wealthy ship owners who transported foodstuffs, see Test., copy encl. in Inv., and Inv. itself, Antônio José Pereira Arouca, 1825, APEB, SJ, 04/1717/2187/02, fols. 4, 15v–16; Licença, 23 Sept. 1815, AMS, 88.5, fol. 156 (listed as Antonio José Pereira Rouca); Junta Provisória to Campos, 18 June 1823, AHM, 2ª Div., 1ª Sec, Cx. 40, No. 1-1; Inv., Luiz José Pereira Rocha, 1843, APEB, SJ, 04/1751/2221/03, fols. 4–5, 15–17.

11. Capitania dos Portos da Bahia, Mapa demonstrativo das embarcações nacionaes . . . , 31 Dec. 1856, AN, SPE, XM-183; Mapa geral de toda qualidade de embarcasoens. . . . Baia, 27 de maio de 1775, facsim. in Costa, "População da cidade," Estampa 5; Manoel da Cunha Menezes to Martinho de Melo e Castro, 3 Mar. 1775, in ibid., pp. 272–273. On oarsmen, see Inv. e Test., Manuel José da Cunha, 1821, APEB, SJ, 04/1740/2210/01, fol. 10; Inv., Antonio Moreira de Azevedo, 1834, APEB, SJ, 05/2019/2490/05, fol. 23v; Inv., Antonio José de Andrade, 1820, APEB, SJ, 04/1747/2217/06, fol. 4. On lighterage service, see Inv., José Ferreira de Azevedo e Maria Francisca da Conceição Azevedo, 1838, APEB, SJ, 03/1063/1532/03, fols. 8–10v. On training young men as sailors, see Inv., Rosa Maria de Jesus, 1808-1811, APEB, SJ, 01/269/514/02, fol. 4.

12. Manoel da Cunha Menezes to Martinho de Melo e Castro, 3 Mar. 1775, in Costa, "População da cidade," p. 273; Inv. e Test., José Antonio Correia, 1838, APEB, SJ, 04/1602/2071/02, fols. 5, 5v, 8; Réo: Hygino Pires Gomes e seus escravos marinheiros, 1851, Auto crime, APEB, SJ, 08/260/6497.

13. Inv. e Test., Antonio Pinto Rodrigues da Costa, 1860/62, APEB, SJ, 06/2873/07, fol. 6; Relação geral de todos os moradores do 6° quarteirão da Freguezia da Rua do Passo [1855], APEB, CP, M. 1602, fol. [7], entry for Rufino, aged twenty-five. From postmortem inventories it is often difficult to know whether self-hired slaves lived with the master or on their own.

14. Inv., Florinda de Aragão, 1805, APEB, SJ, 04/1766/2336/07, fols. 4–5, 6; John Thornton, *Africa and Africans in the Making of the Atlantic World, 1400–1680* (Cambridge, Eng.: Cambridge University Press, 1992), pp. 19–20, 37; Robert Smith, "The Canoe in West African History," *Journal of African History* 11, no. 4 (1970): 517–519, 522; W[illiam] Jeffrey Bolster, *Black Jacks: African American Seamen in the Age of Sail* (Cambridge, MA: Harvard University Press, 1997), pp. 45, 49, 51, 55.

15. Inv., Florinda de Aragão, 1805, APEB, SJ, 04/1766/2336/07, fols. 4–5. On the dangers of tar see U.S. Department of Labor, Occupational and Health Administration, *Regulations* (www.osha.gov). I was led to think about this aspect by Luiz Geraldo Silva, *A faina, a festa e o rito: Uma etnografia histórica sobre as gentes do mar, sécs. XVII ao XIX* (Campinas: Papirus, 2001), p. 189.

16. [J. M.] Marcus Carvalho ("Os caminhos do rio: Negros canoeiros no Recife da primeira metade do século XIX," *Afro-Ásia* 19/20 [1997]: 92), makes a similar point, as does Bolster ("African-American Seamen," p. 430).

17. Capitania dos Portos da Bahia, Mapa demonstrativo das embarcações nacionaes . . . , 31 Dec. 1856, AN, SPE, XM-183; Inv., Pedro do Espírito Santo, 1850, APEB, SJ, 04/1624/2093/05, fol. 59; Inv. José Ferreira de Azevedo e Maria Francisca

da Conceição Azevedo, 1838, APEB, SJ, 03/1063/1532/03, fols. 76, 79–80v; Inv. e Test., Joaquim Teixeira de Carvalho, 1846–1847, APEB, SJ, 04/1473/1942/05, fols. 10v, 14; João Pereira dos Santos to Madeira and enclosures, 30 May 1823, BN/SM, II-33, 36, 17.

18. Mapa geral de toda qualidade de embarcasoens. . . . Baia, 27 de maio de 1775, facsim. in Costa, "População da cidade," Estampa 5; Capitania dos Portos da Bahia, Mapa demonstrativo das embarcações nacionaes . . . , 31 Dec. 1856, AN, SPE, XM-183; Antônio Alves Câmara, *Ensaio sobre as construções navais indígenas do Brasil*, 2nd ed., Brasiliana, 92 (São Paulo: Editora Nacional, 1976), pp. 56–63; Inv., João Ferreira de Oliveira Silva, 1856–1874, APEB, SJ, 04/1658/2127/05, fol. 23v. On their sails, see James Wetherell, *Brazil: Stray Notes from Bahia, Being Extracts from Letters, Etc., During a Residence of Fifteen Years* (Liverpool: Webb and Hunt, 1860), p. 26 (quoted). For their value, see Inv., Joanna Maria da Conceição, 1816, APEB, SJ, 04/1715/2185/01, fol. 17. Other descriptions can be found in George Gardner, *Travels in the Interior of Brazil, Principally Through the Northern Provinces and the Gold and Diamond Districts During the Years 1836–1841* (1846; reprint, Boston: Milford House, 1973), p. 118; Robert Avé-Lallemant, *Viagens pelas províncias da Bahia, Pernambuco, Alagoas e Sergipe (1859)*, trans. Eduardo de Lima Castro, Reconquista do Brasil, no. 19 (Belo Horizonte and São Paulo: Itatiaia and EDUSP, 1980), pp. 81, 98, and 272; and Maximilian [Emperor of Mexico (Ferdinand Joseph Maximilian of Austria)], *Recollections of My Life*, 3 vols. (London: Richard Bentley, 1868), 3: 254.

19. Câmara, *Ensaio sobre as construções navais*, pp. 145–191; Pedro Agostinho [Silva], *Embarcações do Recôncavo: Estudo de origens*, A Bahia e o Recôncavo, no. 3 (Salvador: Museu do Recôncavo Wanderley Pinho, 1973); Theodor Selling Júnior, *A Bahia e seus veleiros: Uma tradição que desapareceu* (Rio de Janeiro: Serviço de Documentação Geral da Marinha, 1976), pp. 47–48. One estate inventory referred to a boat that was just under 29'4" in length and 10'3" wide; Inv. e Test., Manoel de Araújo Cortez, 1846, APEB, SJ, 04/1438/1907/04, fol. 28v. Another one listed two, one 39 feet long and the other 34 feet; Inv. (traslado), Antonio Pedroso de Albuquerque, Itaparica, 1878, APEB, SJ, 07/3213/17 (I owe this reference to Sandra Lauderdale Graham).

20. Avé-Lallemant, *Viagens . . . Bahia*, p. 32.

21. On the interchangeability of names for boat types, see Selling Júnior, *A Bahia e seus veleiros*, p. 37. Câmara (*Ensaio sobre as construções navais*, pp. 191, 196) admits as much, but insists on the classification. An example, out of many, in which the word *saveiro* is used interchangeably with *lancha* is Inv., José Ferreira de Azevedo, 1838, APEB, SJ, 03/1063/1532/03, fols. 20, 23, 27v; *lancha* and *barco* are equated in Inv., José da Silva Maia, APEB, SJ, 04/1790/2260/01, fols. 8–9; *alvarengas* were equated to *lanchas* in Joaquim José Corrêa (Intendente da Marinha) to João Felix de Campos, Salvador, 17 Jun. 1823, AHU, Bahia, Avulsos, Cx. 266, Doc. 43. The use of the word *saveiro* for a lighter has to be deduced from context, as in Inv., Bartolomeu Francisco Gomes, 1848, APEB, SJ, 04/1697/2167/06, fol. 37v, although occasionally the phrase was *saveiro de desembarque;* Inv. e Test., Antonio de Oliveira, 1855, APEB, SJ, 03/1354/1823/39, fol. 1v. See also the usage in Kidder, *Sketches of Residence* 2: 87. Finding an adequate English translation for this general type of boat is difficult since *barco* is reminiscent of "bark," a very

different kind of vessel, and "launch," despite its etymological origin in *lancha*, today implies the use of oars primarily.

22. Cecília Maria Westphalen, *Porto de Paranaguá, um sedutor* (Curitiba: Secretaria de Estado da Cultura, 1998), pp. 67–68, 87–88. On ship building in Salvador see José Antonio Saraiva (MM) to Felipe José Ferreira (Intendente da Marinha da Bahia), Rio, 6 Aug. 1858, AN, SPE, IX-M 84; Grant, *History of Brazil*, p. 215; Avé-Lallemant, *Viagens . . . Bahia*, p. 145; José Roberto do Amaral Lapa, *A Bahia e a carreira da Índia* (São Paulo: Editôra Nacional and EDUSP, 1968), pp. 51–81; Shawn William Miller, *Fruitless Trees: Portuguese Conservation and Brazil's Colonial Timber* (Stanford, CA: Stanford University Press, 2000), p. 207.

23. Relação da Bahia, Accordão, 22 Sept. 1821, copy encl. in Ouvidor do Crime to [Governador], 6 Oct. 1821, APEB, CP, M. 245.

24. José da Silva Lisboa, "'Carta muito interessante do advogado da Bahia . . . para Domingos Vandelli, Bahia, 18 de outubro de 1781,' in Eduardo de Castro e Almeida, Inventario dos documentos relativos ao Brasil existentes no Archivo de Marinha e Ultramar, Part II (Bahia, 1763–1786)," *ABNRJ* 32 (1910): 504; Governador to El-Rey, 28 Feb. 1798, APEB, CP, M. 158, fol. 282. On canoes' more perishable cargoes see Wetherell, *Brazil: Stray Notes from Bahia*, p. 27.

25. William O. Jones, *Manioc in Africa* (Stanford, CA: Stanford University Press, 1959), pp. 3–5, 11, 15–17, 21–23, 25, 118; James H. Cock, "Cassava: A Basic Energy Source in the Tropics," *Science* 218 (19 Nov. 1982): 755–762; and B. J. Barickman, *A Bahian Counterpoint: Sugar, Tobacco, Cassava, and Slavery in the Recôncavo, 1780–1860* (Stanford, CA: Stanford University Press, 1998), pp. 44–96, 163–68.

26. Robert Elwes, *A Sketcher's Tour Round the World* (London: Hurst and Blackett, 1854), p. 89. The technique is still widely used in the backlands of Brazil, as I have observed many times. An illustration can be found in Charles Ribeyrolles, *Brasil pitoresco: História, descrições, viagens, colonização, intituitções, acompanhado de um álbum de vistas, panoramas, paisagens, costumes, etc. por Victor Frond*, 2nd ed., 2 vols., trans. Gastão Penalva, intro. by Afonso d'E. Taunay (São Paulo and Brasília: Martins and Instituto Nacional do Livro, 1976), Plate 56, between pp. 96 and 97. Estate inventories that mention this equipment include Inv., Manoel Carlos Gomes, 1803, APEB, SJ, 05/2023/2494/09, fol. 15v; Inv., Raimunda Maria dos Anjos and Pedro José de Brito, 1806, APEB, SJ, 04/1823/2294/03, fol. 16v; Inv., Manuel Lopes dos Santos, 1817, APEB, SJ, 01/03/03/04, fols. 13v, 14v; Inv., Antonio José Pereira de Arouca, 1825, APEB, SJ, 04/1717/2187/02, fol. 42v–43; Inv., Pedro Felix de Andrade, 1836, APEB, SJ, 04/1822/2293/02, fol. 12v; Inv., Francisco José de Andrada, 1838, APEB, SJ, 04/1824/2295/02, unnum. fol.; Inv., João Simões Coimbra, 1860, APEB, SJ, 03/1242/1711/07, fols. 18, 20, 66; Inv., Manoel José de Souza, 1861, APEB, SJ, 04/1516/1985/04, fol. 6.

27. Hernani da Silva Pereira, *Considerações sobre a alimentação no Brazil: These para o doutoramento em medicina apresentada à Faculdade da Bahia* (Salvador: Imp. Popular, 1887), p. 74; Maria Graham [Lady Maria Calcott], *Journal of a Voyage to Brazil and Residence There During Part of the Years 1821, 1822, 1823* (1824; reprint, New York: Praeger, 1969), p. 148; Robert Walsh, *Notices of Brazil in 1828 and 1829*, 2 vols. (Boston: Richardson, Lord, and Holbrook & Carvill, 1831), 1: 284 and 2: 15; Wetherell, *Brazil: Stray Notes from Bahia*, p. 124; C[hristopher]

C[olumbus] Andrews, *Brazil: Its Condition and Prospects* . . . *with an Account of the Downfall of the Empire, the Establishment of the Republic and the Reciprocity Treaty,* 3rd ed. (New York: Appleton, 1891), p. 253. On the diet in Rio see Jean Baptiste Debret, *Viagem pitoresca e histórica ao Brasil,* 2nd ed., 2 vols., trans. Sérgio Milliet, intro. by Rubens Borba de Moraes (São Paulo: Martins and EDUSP, 1972), 1: 138–139.

28. Luís dos Santos Vilhena, *A Bahia no século XVIII,* 2nd ed., ed. Braz do Amaral, intro. by Edison Carneiro (Salvador: Itapuã, 1969), p. 159; Inv., Luiz José Pereira Rocha, 1843, APEB, SJ, 04/1751/2221/03, fol. 17; Walsh, *Notices of Brazil,* 1: 281.

29. An *alqueire* (or bushel), as known in Bahia, was equivalent to 36.27 liters, so ¹⁄₄₀ of an *alqueire* would be 0.907 liter. On its weight, see Barickman, *Bahian Counterpoint,* p. 214, n. 5. The invariability of the daily ration over space and time is striking; e.g., Lisboa, "Carta muito interessante, [*ABNRJ*]," p. 503; ANTT, Junta do Commercio, [n.d.], Liv. 302, fols. 42, 65; Vilhena, *Bahia no século XVIII,* 1: 186; Salvador Pereira da Costa to Conselho Interino, Quartel de Nazareth, 16 Nov. 1822, BN/SM, I-31, 6, 3, Doc. 52; Decisão, no. 151 (Marinha), 25 Aug. 1829, and no. 45 (Marinha), 20 May 1846, in Brazil, *Collecção das decisões do governo do Imperio do Brasil;* Inv. (1⁰), José Caetano de Aquino, 1833, APEB, SJ, 05/2003/2474/03, fols. 3, 60v; Despesas, Feb. 1844, ASCM, G, 1ª, 1071, fols. 1–51v; Contrato celebrado pelo Dr. Chefe da Policia com a Santa Casa de Misericórdia, 31 Jan. 1860, APEB, CP, M. 6418.

30. Carla Rahn Phillips, *Six Galleons for the King of Spain* (Baltimore: Johns Hopkins University Press, 1986), p. 167; Antonio Fernández García, *El abastecimiento de Madrid en el reinado de Isabel II,* intro. by Vicente Palacio Atard, Biblioteca de Estudios Madrileños no. 14 (Madrid: Instituto de Estudios Madrileños, 1971), p. xi; Philip D. Curtin, *Death by Migration: Europe's Encounter with the Tropical World in the Nineteenth Century* (Cambridge, Eng.: Cambridge University Press, 1989), p. 126; Michel Morineau, "Rations militaires et rations moyennes en Holland au XVII siécles," *Annales: Economies, Sociétés, Civilisations* 18, no. 3 (May–June 1963): 521–531; Emmanuel Le Roy Ladurie, *The Peasants of Languedoc,* trans. John Day (Urbana: University of Illinois Press, 1974), p. 102.

31. Josué de Castro, *O problema da alimentação no Brasil (Seu estudo fisiológico),* Brasiliana, Ser. 5, no. 29 (São Paulo: Editora Nacional, 1938), p. 157; Caribbean Food and Nutrition Institute, *Food Composition Tables for Use in the English-Speaking Caribbean* (Kingston, Jamaica: Caribbean Food and Nutrition Institute, 1974), Table 1, pp. 13, 15; Anna Curtenius Roosevelt, *Parmana: Prehistoric Maize and Manioc Cultivation Along the Amazon and Orinoco* (New York: Academic Press, 1980), pp. 119–137; and Luís Lisanti, "Sur la nourriture des 'paulistas' entre le XVIIIᵉ et XIXᵉ siècles," *Annales: Economies, Sociétés, Civilisations* 18, no. 3 (May–June 1963): 531–540. On the daily caloric requirement, see Jones, *Manioc in Africa,* p. 8; and Phillips, *Six Galleons,* p. 241. On the challenge of calculating food values in past time, see John C. Super, *Food, Conquest, and Colonization in Sixteenth-Century Spanish America* (Albuquerque: University of New Mexico Press, 1988), pp. 5–6.

32. Tabella do arbitramento dos preços para se pagarem as etapes e forragens á tropa, encl. in PP-BA to MI, 25 Jan. 1834, AN-SPE, Interior, IJJ⁹337 (1833–1838), Doc. 1834/6. Similar calculations appear in Junta da Fazenda Real to Câmara, 24 Nov.

1807, AMS, 33.2; João Felix Pereira de Campos to José Antonio Rodrigues Vianna e Cia, 23 Feb. 1823, encl. in Campos to Ignácio da Costa Quintella (Minister of the Navy in Portugal), 24 Mar. 1823, AHU, Bahia, Avulsos, Cx. 265, Doc. 50.

33. Antonio Pedro Gurgalho to PP-BA, 28 Sept. 1826, BN/SM, II-34, 1, 6, Doc. 6; João Rodriges de Brito, "Carta I," in João Rodrigues de Brito et al., *Cartas economico-politicas sobre a agricultura e commercio da Bahia* (Lisbon: Imp. Nacional, 1821), pp. 38–39. On the dangers of relying on official statements regarding rations for soldiers, seamen, or slaves, see Fernand Braudel, *The Mediterranean and the Mediterranean World in the Age of Philip II*, 2 vols., trans. Siân Reynolds (New York: Harper and Row, 1972), 1: 459–460.

34. Mappa demonstrativo do numero d'alqueires dos differentes generos que pagarão a contribuição e o rendimento, a despeza, e o liquido, e teve principio em 9 de setembro de 1785 até 31 de maio de 1849, APEB, CP, M. 1611. Slightly different data are presented in the magnificent circular chart Escrivão do celeiro [público], Diagrama da produção agricola da capitania da Bahia, 1785–1812, AN, Cód. 623. The problems with these data are outlined by Barickman (*Bahian Counterpoint*, pp. 71–85) and were known at the time; Câmara to PP-BA, 17 May 1826, AMS, 111.6. On the growth of the population see Mattoso, *Bahia: A cidade de Salvador*, pp. 129, 138. No reliable source gives credence to the claim made by Lisboa ("'Carta muito interessante,'" p. 503) that the city consumed over a million bushels per year.

35. Lisboa, "'Carta muito interessante,'" p. 503; Breve compendio de reflexões sobre a Vila de Jaguaripe e o estado atual da mandioca . . . , n.d., AHU, Bahia, Cx. [*sic*] 19,754, cited in Francisco Carlos Teixeira da Silva, "A morfologia da escassez: Crises de subsistência e política econômica no Brasil colônia (Salvador e Rio de Janeiro, 1680–1790)" (Ph.D. diss., Universidade Federal Fluminense, 1990), p. 140; Barickman, *Bahian Counterpoint*, pp. 13–14, 163–168.

36. Relação das farinhas exportadas deste porto para o celleiro publico da Bahia em o presente mez de julho 1826, Jaguaripe, and Relação das farinhas exportadas para o celleiro publico da Bahia desde 1 de 8bro até 31 do mesmo de 1826, [Jaguaripe], both in APEB, CP, M. 1609. For other data on the size of *barcos* and *lanchas* see José Gomes da Cruz to Governador, Barra da Villa de N. S. da Abadia, 7 May 1793, APEB, CP, M. 201-40, Doc. 2; Abaixo assinado to Prince-Regent, 1808, BNRJ/SM, II-34, 8, 20, Doc. 1, fol. 2v; Passaporte de Ignacio Antonio Alexandrino, Caravellas, 22 Oct. 1822, APEB, CP, M. 4631; Francico Manuel de Castro (deputado commissário) to Miguel Calmon du Pin e Almeida, Nazaré, 19 May 1823, BN/SM, II-34, 10, 33. For smacks, *iates*, and brigantines see Escrivão e tesoureiro do Celeiro Público to Admin., 30 July 1839, encl. in Adminstrador do Celeiro to PP-BA, 30 July 1839; Admin. do Celeiro to PP-BA, 22 Apr. 1842; and Admin. do Celeiro to PP-BA, 16 Sept. 1842, all in APEB, CP, M. 1610, as well as PP-BA to MI, 1 Aug. 1834, AN, SPE, IJJ⁹337, 1834.

37. Thomaz Tamayo de Vargas, "A restauração da cidade do Salvador, Bahia de Todos os Santos, na provincia do Brasil pelas armas de D. Felippe IV, rei catholico das hespanhas e indias, publicada em 1628," trans. and ed. Ignacio Accioli de Cerqueira e Silva, *Revista do Instituto Geográfico e Histórico da Bahia*, no. 56 (1930): 139; Lisboa, "Carta muito interessante,'" p. 498; Antonio de Sousa Lima to PP-BA, Quartel do Comando Militar de Itaparica, 9 Dec. 1837, BN/SM, II-33, 18, 16.

38. Lisboa, "Carta muito interessante,'" p. 496 (quoted); Conselho Interino to

Caixa Militar de Caravellas, 20 June 1823, APEB, CP, M. 1617; Admin. do Celeiro to PP-BA, 20 June 1842 (also see 22 Apr.), APEB, CP, M. 1610. Because at a lowering tide a wide expanse of the bay fed into this narrow channel, it was often called Funil (funnel); Ignacio Accioli de Cerqueira e Silva, *Memórias históricas e políticas da província da Bahia*, 2nd ed., 6 vols., ed. Braz do Amaral (Salvador: Imprensa Official do Estado, 1919–1940), 3: 371n.

39. Câmara, *Ensaio sobre as construções navais*, pp. 61, 148; Luiz José da Cunha Grã Ataíde e Mello, Conde de Povolide, to Martinho de Mello e Castro, 3 July 1771, AIHGB, Arq. 1-1-19, fol. 224v (quoted). On the canal see Affonso Ruy, *História da Câmara Municipal da cidade do Salvador*, 2nd ed. (Salvador: Câmara Municipal de Salvador, 1996), p. 298. On sandbars see Lapa, *A Bahia e a carreira da Índia*, pp. 142–144.

40. Johann Baptist von Spix and Karl Friedrich Philipp von Martius, *Através da Bahia: Excerptos da obra "Reise in Brasilien"*, 3rd ed., trans. Manuel Augusto Pirajá da Silva and Paulo Wolf, Brasiliana, Ser. 5, no. 118 (São Paulo: Editora Nacional, 1938), p. 222; Kidder, *Sketches of Residence*, p. 17.

41. Pierre Verger, *Trade Relations Between the Bight of Benin and Bahia from the 17th to 19th Century*, trans. Evelyn Crawford (Ibadan: Ibadan University Press, 1976), p. 286; Abaixo assinado, São Francisco do Conde, 24 Feb. 1816, encl. in Alexandre Gomes Ferrão to Marquês de Aguiar, 14 Mar. 1816, BN/SM, C. 9.5 (quoted); Luís Henrique Dias Tavares, *História da sedição intentada na Bahia em 1798 ("A conspiração dos alfaiates")* (São Paulo: Livraria Pioneira, 1975), pp. 79–91; Kátia M. de Queirós Mattoso, *Presença francesa no movimento democrático baiano de 1798* (Salvador: Itapuã, 1969). See also Julius Sherrard Scott III, "The Common Wind: Currents of Afro-American Communication in the Era of the Haitian Revolution" (Ph.D. diss., Duke University, 1986), esp. pp. 64–67; and Peter Linebaugh and Marcus Rediker, "The Many-Headed Hydra: Sailors, Slaves, and the Atlantic Working Class in the Eighteenth Century," *Journal of Historical Sociology* 3, no. 3 (Sept. 1990): 234.

42. PP-BA to MJ, 14 Feb. 1835, AN, SPE, Justiça, IJ¹707; João José Reis, *Slave Rebellion in Brazil: The Muslim Uprising of 1835 in Bahia*, trans. Arthur Brakel (Baltimore: Johns Hopkins University Press, 1993), pp. 109, 212–214; Chief of Police, Rio, 5 Dec. 1849, quoted by Carlos Eugênio Líbano Soares, *A capoeira escrava e outras tradições rebeldes no Rio de Janeiro (1808–1850)* (Campinas: Ed. Unicamp, 2001), pp. 387–388; John Candler and William Burgess, *Narrative of a Recent Visit to Brazil to Present an Address on the Slave Trade and Slavery Issued by the Religious Society of Friends* (London: Edward Marsh, 1853), pp. 38–39.

CHAPTER 5

1. Luís dos Santos Vilhena, *A Bahia no século XVIII*, 2nd ed., ed. Braz do Amaral, intro. by Edison Carneiro (Salvador: Itapuã, 1969), p. 124 (quoted); Ribeiro, Discurso, fol. 65; El-Rey to Câmara, 13 Jan. 1751, AMS, 126.4 , fols. 81–81v; Câmara to Governador, 24 (quoted) and 31 Jan. 1781, AMS, 126.4, fols. 66v–67.

2. Vilhena, *Bahia no século XVIII*, p. 419; Governador to Câmara, 7 Sept. 1785, copy encl. in Câmara to PP-BA, 14 Apr. 1845, APEB, CP, M. 1399, 1845, Doc. 19; Rodrigo José de Meneses to Martinho de Melo e Castro, 10 Oct. 1785, in

Copias extrahidas do Archivo do Conselho Ultramarino, AIHGB, Arq., 1, 1, 20 (a printed version appears in Eduardo de Castro e Almeida, ed., "Inventario dos documentos relativos ao Brasil existentes no Archivo de Marinha e Ultramar," *ABNRJ* 32 [1910]: 586).

3. Joel Serrão, *Dicionário de história de Portugal* (Porto: Iniciativas Editoriais, 1979), 6: 165, s.v. Terreiro do Trigo; Edital da Câmara, Lisbon, 4 Feb. 1774, in Antonio Delgado da Silva, *Collecção da legislação portuguesa desde a ultima compilação das ordenações . . .* , 2nd ed. (Lisbon: Typ. L.C. da Cunha and Typ. Maigrense, 1833-1858), 2: 753, which refers to the relevant Postura of 1532. Such grains markets were common in Europe; Fernand Braudel, *The Mediterranean and the Mediterranean World in the Age of Philip II*, 2 vols., trans. Siân Reynolds (New York: Harper and Row, 1972), 1: 329.

4. Prologue, Regimento do Celeiro Publico, copy encl. in Câmara to PP-BA, 14 Apr. 1845, APEB, CP, M. 1399, 1845, Doc. 19 (another copy was encl. in MRE to MI, Rio, 22 Jan. 1845, BN/SM, II-33, 24, 40, and a printed version can be found in Ignacio Accioli de Cerqueira e Silva, *Memórias históricas e políticas da província da Bahia*, 2nd ed., 6 vols., ed. Braz do Amaral [Salvador: Imprensa Official do Estado, 1919-1940], 3: 173n); B. J. Barickman, *A Bahian Counterpoint: Sugar, Tobacco, Cassava, and Slavery in the Recôncavo, 1780-1860* (Stanford, CA: Stanford University Press, 1998), pp. 73-74. The continuing effect of Governor Menezes's work can be seen by comparing these regulations with the very similar ones issued in 1851: "Regulamento de 15 de maio de 1851," in Bahia, *Colleção das leis e resoluções da Assemblea Legislativa e regulamentos do governo da província da Bahia*, 1851, pp. 391-398. The rationale of transparency also operated in France; Steven L. Kaplan, *Provisioning Paris: Merchants and Millers in the Grain and Flour Trade During the Eighteenth Century* (Ithaca, NY: Cornell University Press, 1984), p. 374.

5. José de Souza Azevedo Pizarro e Araújo, *Memórias históricas do Rio de Janeiro [1820-1822]*, 2nd ed., ed. Rubens Borba de Moraes, Biblioteca Popular Brasileira nos. 4-12 (Rio de Janeiro: Instituto Nacional do Livro, 1945-1948), Vol. 8, Tomo 2: 35-48 (also see Tomo 1: 44); Kenneth Maxwell, *Conflicts and Conspiracies: Brazil and Portugal, 1750-1808*, Cambridge Latin American Studies no. 16 (Cambridge, Eng.: Cambridge University Press, 1973), pp. 90, 98; M[anuel] F[erreira] da C[âmara], "Carta II," in João Rodrigues de Brito et al., *Cartas economico-politicas sobre a agricultura e commercio da Bahia* (Lisbon: Imp. Nacional, 1821), p. 85 (quoted); Representação do Senado da Câmara da Cidade da Bahia . . . , 4 June 1785, in Almeida, "Inventario dos documentos," *ABNRJ* 32 (1910), pp. 575-576.

6. On the building's earlier uses, location, and description, see Intendente do Arsenal da Marinha to Governador, 27 Oct. 1797, copy encl. in idem to [?], 28 Apr. 1798, in Codex, Prospectos e plantas do R¹ Arsenal da Marinha, BN/SM, I-2, 4, 27, fol. 3v, and Planta 1; Fernando José de Portugal to Rodrigo de Souza Coutinho, 29 Mar. 1799, BN/SM, 1, 4, 13; Ribeiro, Discurso, fol. 65; Vilhena, *Bahia no século XVIII*, p. 94; Braz do Amaral, "Notas," in ibid., p. 113; Intendente da Marinha to Governador, 21 Aug. 1817, APEB, CP, M. 234; PP-BA to Câmara, 22 July 1853, AMS, 111.12, fol. 210; and Domingos José Antonio Rebello, "Corographia, ou abreviada historia geographica do Imperio do Brasil [2nd ed.]," *Revista*

do Instituto Geográfico e Histórico da Bahia 55 (1929): 140. The building is also referred to by Maximilian [Emperor of Mexico (Ferdinand Joseph Maximilian of Austria)], *Recollections of My Life*, 3 vols. (London: Richard Bentley, 1868), 3: 99; and Oskar Canstatt, *Brasil: Terra e gente*, 2nd ed., trans. Eduardo de Lima Castro, intro. by Artur Cezar Ferreira Reis, Temas Brasileiros, no. 18 (Rio de Janeiro: Conquista, 1975), p. 190. An old photograph labeled "Arsenal da Marinha" is printed in Paulo Ormindo de Azevedo, *A alfândega e o mercado: Memória e restauração* (Salvador: Secretaria de Planejamento, Ciência, e Tecnologia do Estado da Bahia, 1985), p. 19.

7. On size and construction of bins see Ribeiro, Discurso, fols. 70, 70v; Ignacio de Andrada Soutomayor Rendon to Viceroy, Marapicuru (Rio de Janeiro), 7 Dec. 1788, enclosure, AN, Cx. 484, Pac. 2; and Fernando José de Portugal to Martinho de Melo e Castro, 5 Feb. 1789, BN/SM, 1, 4, 10, fol. 72v. On the number of bins and chests, see Rendimento do celeiro publico, encl. in Câmara to PP-BA, 20 May 1857, APEB, CP, M. 1403. On the upper floor and its misuse, see Vilhena, *Bahia no século XVIII*, pp. 71, 104; and Câmara to PP-BA, 29 July 1857, APEB, CP, M. 1403.

8. Vilhena, *Bahia no século XVIII*, p. 419; Ribeiro, Discurso, fol. 66; Governador to Câmara, 15 Sept. 1785, copy encl. in Câmara to PP-BA, 14 Apr. 1845, APEB, CP, M. 1399, 1845, Doc. 19; Câmara, Portaria, n.d. [1785], AMS, 116.4, fol. 206; Mappa demonstractivo do numero d'alqueires dos differentes generos que pagarão a contribuição e o rendimento e a despesa e o liquido, e teve principio em 9 de setembro de 1785 até 31 de maio de 1849, APEB, CP, M. 1611 (these data are also printed in Silva, *Memórias históricas*, 3: insert between pp. 14 and 15).

9. Regimento [1785], copy encl. in Câmara to PP-BA, 14 Apr. 1845, APEB, CP, M. 1399, 1845, Doc. 19 (hereafter, Regimento [1785]), Chaps. 1, 9, 10 (also encl. in MRE to MI, Rio, 22 Jan. 1845, BN/SM, II-33, 24, 40). A printed version is available in Silva, *Memórias históricas*, 3: 73n–77n. The tax was still being charged at the same rate in 1849; Lei no. 374, 12 Nov. 1849, Bahia, *Colleção das leis*, Art. 2, paragraph 36.

10. Regimento [1785], Chap. 3; João Rodrigues de Brito, "Carta I," in Brito et al., *Cartas economico-politicas*, p. 22.

11. Governador to Câmara, 7 Sept. 1785, copy encl. in Câmara to PP-BA, 14 Apr. 1845, APEB, CP, M. 1399, 1845, Doc. 19; Test. e Codicílio, Inocencio José da Costa, 1805, APEB, SJ, 08/3465/02; Hendrik Kraay, *Race, State, and Armed Forces in Independence-Era Brazil: Bahia, 1790s–1840s* (Stanford, CA: Stanford University Press, 2001), pp. 93, 95.

12. Ribeiro, Memoria, fol. 62; Procurador da Câmara to Governador, n.d. [9 Feb. 1797], APEB, CP, M. 201-14, Doc. 52; Inv., Adriano de Araujo Braga, 1816, APEB, SJ, 03/1341/1810/02, fols. [5–6, 7v–8v], 27v–31, 37, 38v–39v, 59, 128ff., 146, 870ff.

13. Inv., José da Silva Maia, 1809, APEB, SJ, 04/1790/2260/01, fols. 3–3v, 4v, 8–9, 12–56; Ribeiro, Memoria, fol. 63. On his being a sugar factor, see Claudio José Pereira da Costa to Ouvidor Geral do Crime, 22 Jan. 1806, in Stuart B. Schwartz, "Resistance and Accommodation in Eighteenth-Century Brazil: The Slaves' View of Slavery," *Hispanic American Historical Review* 57, no. 1 (Feb. 1977): 79.

14. Governador (Conde da Ponte) to Visconde de Anadia, 18 Sept. 1807, AN,

SPE, Cód. 9, fols. 55, 59ff.; Ribeiro, Discurso, fols. 61, 73; Catherine Lugar, "The Merchant Community of Salvador, Bahia, 1780–1830" (Ph.D. diss., State University of New York at Stony Brook, 1980), pp. 169–170. For complaints against Coelho, see Governo Interino to Câmara, 17 July 1809, AMS, III.5, fol. 57v (the original of this letter is in AMS, [Oficios/Câmara, 1797–1813], uncat.).

15. Regimento [1785], Chaps. 4–7; Admin. do Celeiro to PP-BA, 17 Apr. 1846, APEB, CP, M. 1611; Ribeiro, Discurso, fols. 65, 65v; Francisco José de Portugal to Souza Coutinho, 9 Apr. 1799, BN/SM, 1, 4, 13, no. 501.

16. Anonymous protest encl. in Câmara to Governador, 24 Apr. 1793, APEB, CP, M. 201-14, Doc. 30; Câmara to PP-BA, 13 May 1826, AMS, III.6, fol. 209; Inspector das farinhas to Governador, Nazaré, 17 Mar. 1794, APEB, CP, M. 201-31, Doc. 3; president's marginal note in Admin. do Celeiro to PP-BA, 31 Jan. 1834, APEB, CP, M. 1609.

17. Ribeiro, Memoria, fols. 61, 62, 63–63v; Procurador da Câmara to Governador, n.d. [9 Feb. 1797], APEB, CP, M. 201-14, Doc. 52. For more on Francisco Dias Coelho, see Governo Interino to Câmara, 17 July 1809, AMS, III.5, fol. 57v (the original of this letter is in AMS, [Ofícios/Câmara, 1797–1813], uncat.).

18. Correspondence in BN/SM, II-33, 24, 40, Docs. 5, 6, 8, 13, 15–20, 22–25; and Admin. do Celeiro to PP-BA, 16 Apr. 1842, APEB, CP, M. 1610. On França's Brazilian birth, see Test. João Pereira de Araujo França, 1848, APEB, SJ, 08/3489/11, fols. 1–2. On the prevalent xenophobia, see, among others, Jeffrey C. Mosher, *Political Struggle, Ideology, and State Building: Pernambuco and the Construction of Brazil, 1817–1850* (Lincoln: University of Nebraska Press, 2008), pp. 197–201. On the subsequent presence of Portuguese traders at the grains market, see Requerimentos, 1857, AMS, quoted in João José Reis and Márcia Gabriela D. de Aguiar, "'Carne sem osso e farinha sem caroço': O motim de 1858 contra a carestia na Bahia," *Revista de História*, no. 135 (2° semestre 1996): 154.

19. Test., Antonio de Oliveira, 1855, APEB, SJ, 03/1354/1823/39, fols. 1–3v; Inv., Antonio de Oliveira, 1855–1865, APEB, SJ, 04/1671/2141/04.

20. Governador to Câmara, 15 Sept. 1785, copy encl. in Câmara to PP-BA, 14 Apr. 1845, APEB, CP, M. 1399, 1845, Doc. 19 (the governor's words were parroted in Câmara, Portaria, n.d. [1785], AMS, 116.4, fol. 206); Admin. do Celeiro to [PP-BA], 6 Sept. 1836, APEB, CP, M. 1609.

21. Comerciantes da vila de Nazaré, Abaixo assinado, 1858, APEB, SL, M. 984, quoted by João José Reis, "A greve negra de 1857 na Bahia," *Revista USP*, no. 18 (June–August 1993): 16; and João José Reis and Beatriz Galloti Mamigonian, "Nagô and Mina: The Yoruba Diaspora in Brazil," in *The Yoruba Diaspora in the Atlantic World*, ed. Toyin Falola and Matt Childs (Bloomington: Indiana University Press, 2004), p. 87. On the deep division between Africans and Brazilian-born blacks, see João José Reis, *Slave Rebellion in Brazil: The Muslim Uprising of 1835 in Bahia*, trans. Arthur Brakel (Baltimore: Johns Hopkins University Press, 1993), p. 142. On the African background, see Niara Sudarkasa, *Where Women Work: A Study of Yoruba Women in the Marketplace and in the Home*, Museum of Anthropology Anthropological Papers, no. 53 (Ann Arbor: Museum of Anthropology, University of Michigan, 1973), p. 30.

22. Admin. do Celeiro to PP-BA, 22 Feb. 1842 and 7 Dec. 1844, both in APEB,

CP, M. 1610; Rendimento do celeiro publico, encl. in Câmara to PP-BA, 20 May 1857, APEB, CP, M. 1403.

23. Admin. do Celeiro to PP-BA, 31 Aug. and 7 Dec. 1844, APEB, CP, M. 1610.

24. Abaixo assinado to V.A.R. [Prince-Regent], 1808, BN/SM, II-34, 8, 20, Doc. 1, fols. 1, 5; Requerimentos, 1857, AMS, quoted in Reis and Aguiar, "'Carne sem osso,'" p. 154.

25. Admin. do Celeiro to PP-BA, 23 and 25 Apr. 1834, APEB, CP, M. 1609; Admin. do Celeiro to PP-BA, 22 Feb. 1842, APEB, CP, M. 1610.

26. Abaixo assinado to V.A.R. [Prince-Regent], 1808, BN/SM, II-34, 8, 20, Doc. 1, fol. 3; Ribeiro, Discurso, fols. 68, 68v, 70v, 71v.

27. Reis, "Greve negra," p. 13; Maximilian [Emperor of Mexico (Ferdinand Joseph Maximilian of Austria)], Recollections, 3: 163, 165.

28. Lei 14, 2 July 1835, and Regulamento para a formação de capatasias, 14 Apr. 1836 (arts. 2 and 13 quoted), Bahia, Colleção das leis. See also PP-BA to Juizes de Paz, 28 May 1836, copy encl. in Secretary of PP-BA to Assemblea Legislativa, 8 Mar. 1837, APEB, SL, M. 1148.

29. Juiz de Paz de Conceição da Praia and Juiz de Paz de Pilar to PP-BA, 7 and 8 Mar. 1837, copies encl. in Secretary of PP-BA to Assembléia Legislativa, 8 Mar. 1837 (and see this covering letter itself), APEB, SL, M. 1148. In other parishes the enforcement had begun earlier, and the reaction was less abrupt but effective nevertheless; Reis, "Greve negra," pp. 19–20.

30. Reis, "Greve negra," pp. 14–15, 26–27. On pp. 17–20, Reis provides further details on the events I narrate here. Also see Reis, Slave Rebellion, pp. 227–228.

31. Câmara to PP-BA, 21 Feb. 1850, AMS, 111.11, fol. 320v; PP-BA (Francisco Gonçalves Martins), Acto, 5 Oct. 1850, quoted in Braz Hermenegildo do Amaral, História da independência na Bahia, 2nd ed., Marajoara, no. 19 (Salvador: Livraria Progresso, 1957), p. 179; Bahia, Presidente da Província, Falla, 1 Mar. 1851, pp. 33–35; British Consul quoted by Pierre Verger, Trade Relations Between the Bight of Benin and Bahia from the 17th to 19th Century, trans. Evelyn Crawford (Ibadan: Ibadan University Press, 1976), p. 473; Antônio Alves Câmara, Ensaio sobre as construções navais indígenas do Brasil, 2nd ed. (1st ed., 1888), Brasiliana, no. 92 (São Paulo: Editora Nacional, 1976), p. 193; João Lins Vieira Cansansão de Sinimbu, penciled marginal comment on Câmara to PP-BA, 26 Mar. 1857, APEB, CP, M. 1403; Secretário da Polícia to PP-BA, 3 Nov. 1853, APEB, CP, M. 3118 (I owe this reference to Sandra Lauderdale Graham); Agentes dos remadores de saveiros to PP-BA, 20 Oct. 1857, and Comissão encarregada to PP-BA, 9 Oct. 1879, both in APEB, CP, M. 1570. The story is repeated by Amaral (História da Independência, p. 173), and the entire incident is described by Manuela Carneiro da Cunha (Negros, estrangeiros: Os escravos libertos e sua volta a África [São Paulo: Brasiliense, 1985], pp. 96–97).

32. Licenças, 31 Jan. 1789, AMS, 88.1, fol. 213v; Inv., Manuel Carlos Gomes, 1803, APEB, SJ, 05/2023/2494/09, fols. 4v, 15v, 16, 21v, 24, and Appenso no. 2, fol. 3.

33. Abaixo assinado, 9 May 1823, AHM, 2ª Div., 1ª Sec., Cx. 41, n. 5; Inv., Joanna Maria da Conceição, 1816, APEB, SJ, 04/1715/2185/01, fols. 5v, 15, 17, 37, 38; Licenças, 7 Feb. 1789, AMS, 88.1, fol. 215. I judge Joana to be a woman of color because she belonged to the Irmandade do Rosário de Itapagipe.

CHAPTER 6

1. Câmara to Governador, 7 Sept. 1799, APEB, CP, M. 201-14, Doc. 71; Admin. do Curral to Câmara, 15 Feb. 1830 and 18 Jan. 1834, AMS, Câmara, Correspondência recebida, Curral, [1830]–1834, uncat.; Thales de Azevedo, *Povoamento da cidade do Salvador*, 3d ed. (Salvador: Itapuã, 1969), p. 331n.

2. The basic law, addressed to Portugal but extended to the colonies, was incorporated into a legal code issued in 1603; Candido Mendes de Almeida, ed., *Codigo Philippino; ou, Ordenações e leis do reino de Portugal recopiladas por mandado d'el rei D. Philippe I* . . . (Rio de Janeiro: Instituto Philomathico, 1870), Liv. I, Tit. 66, par. 8.

3. Summary accounts of this cattle trade include Rollie Poppino, "The Cattle Industry in Colonial Brazil," *Mid-America* 31, no. 4 (October 1949): 219–247; and Francisco Carlos Teixeira da Silva, "Elevage et marché interne dans le Brésil de l'époque coloniale," in *Pour l'histoire du Brésil: Hommage à Kátia de Queirós Mattoso*, ed. François Crouzet, Philippe Bonnichon, and Denis Rolland (Paris: L'Harmattan, 2000), pp. 321–330.

4. Document dated 1732 quoted by Luiz Mott, "Subsídios à história do pequeno comércio no Brasil," *Revista de História*, no. 105 (1976): 88; Câmara, Regência da Feira de Capoame, 18 Apr. 1801, copy currently attached to Câmara to Governador, 28 Jan. 1801, APEB, CP, M. 209-1, Arts. 1–2; Câmara to Admin. do Curral, 1 July 1809, AMS, 116.5, fol. 27v; Câmara to Registrador do Cajueiro, 8 Nov. 1806, AMS, 33.2, fols. 17 and 17v. For a description of the facilities, see Câmara to Governador, 14 Aug. 1784 (second one of this date), AMS, 111.4, fol. 99; and Jourdan, Breve noticia, fol. 42. On the Estrada das Boiadas in later years see PP-BA to Câmara, 22 Sept. 1834, AMS, 98.1, fol. 121; Câmara to PP-BA, 29 Mar. 1843 and 6 May 1846, AMS, 111.11, fols. 79 and 178; and Câmara to PP-BA, 29 July 1857, APEB, CP, M. 1403.

5. Ordem Régia, April 1706, ANTT, MSS do Brasil, Liv. 26, cited by Mott, "Subsídios à história do pequeno comércio," pp. 96–97; Provisão Real, 4 Mar. 1763, AMS, 126.5, fols. 19v–20; Câmara to Governador, 25 Dec. 1782, AMS, 111.4, fol. 78.

6. Câmara to Governador, 12 May 1781 and 26 May 1783, AMS, 111.4, fols. 68 and 79; Procurador da Câmara, Memoria sobre o contrato das carnicerias, n.d., encl. in Câmara to Governador, 15 Mar. 1809, APEB, CP, M. 127.

7. Câmara, Portaria, n.d. [March 1783], AMS, 116.4, fol. 159; Registro de uma informação que dá o Senado aos Senhores Governadores com os pareceres de cada um dos vereadores por escripto sobre a [re]presentação que aos mesmos Sn^res fez o administrador dos talhos das rendas do Senado, 4 Oct. 1783, AMS, 111.4, fols. 86v–91; Câmara to Governador, 27 Sept. 1783, AMS, 111.4, fol. 85v. For later accounts see Governador to Câmara, 10 Dec. 1806 and 10 Mar. 1807, AMS, 111.5, fols. 13 and 18; and Jourdan, Breve noticia, fol. 41.

8. Plano estabelecido para a administração das marchantarias, 28 Mar. 1784, copy encl. in Procurador da Câmara to Governador, [9 Feb. 1797], APEB, CP, M. 201-14, Doc. 52. Most of its provisions were repeated with additional details in 1801; Câmara, Edital, 11 Mar. 1801; Câmara, Regência da Feira do Capoame, 18 Apr. 1801; and Câmara, Regência dos Currais, 4 Nov. 1801, all currently at-

tached to Câmara to Governador, 28 Jan. 1801, APEB, CP, M. 209-1. On slaughter-men, see Procurador da Câmara, Memoria sobre o contrato das carnecerias, n.d., encl. in Câmara to Governador, 15 Mar. 1809, APEB, CP, M. 127, and Câmara, Editaes, 23 Aug. 1826, 15 Feb. 1830, 21 Oct. 1830, AMS, 116.6, fols. 156, 242v, 271. On conflicts of interest, see Governador to Câmara, 10 Mar. 1807, AMS, 111.5, fol. 19v. On butchers, see Procurador da Câmara to Câmara, n.d., encl. in Câmara to Governador, 8 Feb. 1797, APEB, CP, M. 201-14, Doc. 51; Termos de entrega e rece-bimento de talhos e balanças, 1790, AMS, 176.1 (quoted); and Admin. do Curral, Mappa das Rezes, 11 Apr. 1807, AMS, 148.3, fol. 52v.

9. On manifests see Câmara to Governador, 20 Mar. 1790, APEB, CP, M. 201-14, Doc. 8; and Câmara to Francisco da Costa Passos, 29 May 1813, AMS, 33.2, fol. 100v. The continued reliance on and reapproval of the 1784 system can be traced in the following correspondence from Governador to Câmara, all in AMS, 111.5: 5 Mar. 1811, fol. 108; 12 Mar. 1814, fol. 171; 4 Feb. 1815, fol. 179; 15 Mar. 1816, fol. 187; 17 Mar. 1817, fol. 194; 6 Mar. 1818, fol. 202; 7 Mar. 1820, fol. 218.

10. Quotations are from Plano estabelecido para a administração das marchan-tarias, 28 Mar. 1784, copy encl. in Procurador da Câmara to Governador, n.d. [9 Feb. 1797], APEB, CP, M. 201-14, Doc. 52; Governador to Câmara, 8 Mar. 1809, AMS, 111.5, fol. 42v; and João Rodrigues de Brito, "Carta I," in João Rodrigues de Brito et al., Cartas economico-politicas sobre a agricultura e commercio da Bahia (Lisbon: Imp. Nacional, 1821), p. 22. On the inadequacy of one nominee, see Francisco José de Portugal to Souza Coutinho, 15 Apr. 1799, BN/SM, 1, 4, 13, no. 509.

11. Câmara, Edital, 8 Aug. 1818, AMS, 116.6, fol. 14v; petition referred to in "Decreto," 9 Aug. 1819, LB (also in António d'Oliveira Pinto da França, ed., Cartas baianas, 1821–1824: Subsídios para o estudo dos problemas da opção na in-dependência brasileira, Brasiliana no. 372 [São Paulo: Editora Nacional, 1980], p. 162); José Joaquim de Almeida e Arnizau, "Memoria topographica, historica, commercial e politica da villa de Cachoeira da provincia da Bahia [1825]," Revista do Instituto Historico e Geographico Brasileiro 25 (1862): 134 [written in 1824]; Câmara to PP-BA, 3 Sept. 1855, AMS, 111.13, fol. 118. See also Brazil, Ministério da Agricultura, Imperial Instituto Bahiano de Agricultura, Relatório (1871), p. 10; Rollie Poppino, Feira de Santana, trans. Arquimedes Pereira Guimarães (Salva-dor: Itapuã, 1968), p. 57; Stuart B. Schwartz, Sugar Plantations in the Formation of Brazilian Society: Bahia, 1550–1835, Cambridge Latin American Studies, no. 52 (Cambridge, Eng.: Cambridge University Press, 1985), p. 90; and Azevedo, Povoa-mento da cidade, p. 322.

12. Luís dos Santos Vilhena, A Bahia no século XVIII, 2nd ed., ed. Braz do Amaral, intro. by Edison Carneiro (Salvador: Itapuã, 1969), p. 160; Jourdan, Breve noticia, fol. 41v; João Rodrigues de Brito, "Carta I," in Brito et al., Cartas economico-politicas, pp. 4–5.

13. Câmara to Admin. do Curral, 19 Dec. 1821, 16 Jan. 1822, and 28 Feb. 1824, and Câmara, Edital, 11 Nov. 1826, AMS, 116.6, fols. 59, 60, 88, and 158v; Commis-são . . . carnes verdes, "Parecer," among the separately paged "Documentos An-nexos" in Bahia, Presidente da Provincia, Relatorio (1866), p. 3. On the pasture's location see Câmara to PP-BA, 2 Apr. 1830, AMS, 111.8, fol. 13v; PP-BA to Câmara, 26 July 1845, AMS, 111.10, fol. 262; and Câmara to PP-BA, 1 Aug. 1845, APEB, CP, M. 1399, 1845, Doc. 36 (a copy of this letter is also in AMS, 111.11, fol. 156).

14. Câmara, Instruções . . . ao Admin. dos pastos da Campina, 15 Nov. 1826, AMS, 116.6, fols. 159v–160v; Admin. do Curral to Câmara, 27 Nov. 1829, AMS, Câmara, Correspondência recebida, Curral, 1829, uncat.; PP-BA to Câmara, 30 Oct. 1839, AMS, 111.10, fol. 93.

15. Governador to Câmara, 25 Aug. 1807, AMS, 111.5, fols. 28–28v; Administrator do Curral to Câmara, 13 Jan. 1830, AMS, Câmara, Correspondência recebida, Curral, 1830, uncat.; Admin. do Curral to Câmara, 9, 12, 18 Feb. and 24 May 1833, AMS, Câmara, Cartas recebidas, Curral, 1833, uncat.; Câmara to Fiscal da Freguezia de Pilar, 7 Feb. 1833, AMS, 116.7, fols. 91–92; Fiscal da Freguezia da Penha to Câmara, 4 Mar. 1839, encl. in Câmara to PP-BA, 4 Mar. 1839, APEB, CP, M. 1397, 1839, Doc. 6.

16. Chefe de Polícia to Câmara, 23 Dec. 1844 and 11 Jan. 1845, and Câmara to Chefe de Polícia, 10 Jan. 1845, all encl. in PP-BA to Minister of Empire, 16 Jan. 1845, AN, SPE, IJJ⁹338, 1845; Câmara to PP-BA, 18 Jan. 1845, APEB, CP, M. 1399, 1845, Doc. 6, a copy of which is in AMS, 111.11, fol. 134. For the description of the scene, I draw on my childhood memories of the state of Goiás, where cattle were driven along the unpaved main street of a small town. On the fact they were longhorns, see George Gardner, *Travels in the Interior of Brazil, Principally Through the Northern Provinces and the Gold and Diamond Districts During the Years 1836–1841* (1846; reprint, Boston: Milford House, 1973), p. 278.

17. Administração dos Currais [Report], n.d. [after 1789], BN/SM, 3, 1, 5 (quoted); Câmara to Governador, 14 Aug. 1784, AMS, 111.4, fol. 98v (quoted). On the location of the earlier, privately held slaughterhouses, see Governador to Juiz de Fora, 3 Apr. 1723, in Biblioteca Nacional do Rio de Janeiro, *Documentos Históricos* (Rio de Janeiro: Biblioteca Nacional, 1928–1960), 87: 182; Lista das informações e discripções [sic] das diversas freguezias do Arcebispado da Bahia . . . 1757, in Eduardo de Castro e Almeida, ed., "Inventario dos documentos relativos ao Brasil existentes no Archivo de Marinha e Ultramar," *ABNRJ* 31 (1909): 183; Alexandre José Mello Moraes [Pai], "Praças, largos, ruas, becos, travessas, templos, [e] edificios que contém as dez frequezias da cidade do Salvador, Bahia de Todos os Santos," in Moraes [Pai], ed., *Brasil historico* (Rio de Janeiro: Pinheiro, 1866), 2ª Serie, Tomo I, p. 270; Azevedo, *Povoamento da cidade*, p. 334. For the location of the new slaughterhouse, see Admin. do Curral to Câmara, 11 Apr. 1835, AMS, Câmara, Correspondência recebida, Curral, 1835, uncat.; Amaral, "Notas" in Vilhena, *Bahia no século XVIII*, p. 86.

18. Vilhena, *Bahia no século XVIII*, pp. 69–70; Jourdan, Breve noticia, fols. 41–43. On sleeping quarters, see Câmara to PP-BA, 30 July 1845, AMS, 111.11, fol. 155. On other facilities, see Admin. do Curral to Câmara, 19 June 1830, AMS, Câmara, Correspondência recebida, Curral, 1830, uncat.; Câmara to Inspector das Obras, 31 July 1834, AMS, 116.7, fol. 196, and Commissão do Matadouro Público to Câmara, 13 Sept. 1843, encl. in Câmara to PP-BA, 13 Sept. 1843, APEB, CP, M. 1399, 1843, Doc. 48.

19. Vilhena, *Bahia no século XVIII*, p. 70; Admin. do Curral to Câmara, 9 May and 4 July 1829, AMS, Câmara, Correspondência recebida, 1829, uncat.; Câmara to PP-BA, 26 Jan. and 13 Mar. 1849, AMS, 111.11, fols. 285 and 289.

20. Jourdan, Breve noticia, fol. 42v; Câmara to Admin. do Curral, 1 July 1822, AMS, 116.6, fols. 65v–66; PP-BA to Câmara, 10 Dec. 1825, AMS, 111.7, fol. 14; Admin. do Curral to Câmara, 18 Mar. 1830, AMS, Câmara, Correspondên-

cia recebida, Curral, 1830, uncat.; Admin. do Curral to Vereador Encarregado do Matadouro, 6 Sept. 1843, AMS, Câmara, Correspondência recebida, Curral, 1843, uncat.; and Câmara to PP-BA, 22 Oct. 1845, APEB, CP, M. 1399, 1845, Doc. 40. On vultures see James Wetherell, *Brazil: Stray Notes from Bahia, Being Extracts from Letters, Etc., During a Residence of Fifteen Years* (Liverpool: Webb and Hunt, 1860), p. 87. On miasmas see João José Reis, *A morte é uma festa: Ritos fúnebres e revolta popular no Brasil do século XIX* (São Paulo: Companhia das Letras, 1991), pp. 252-262.

21. *Grito da Razão*, 12 Mar. 1824, p. 2 (I owe this reference to Hendrik Kraay); Câmara, Edital, 13 Mar. 1824; and Câmara to Admin. do Curral, 3 Apr. 1824, 22 Sept. and 6 Oct. 1827, all in AMS, 116.6, fols. 91, 94v, 175v, and 177; Câmara to PP-BA, 2 Apr. 1830, AMS, 111.8, fol. 13v; Admin. do Curral to Câmara, 11 Sept. 1830, AMS, Câmara, Correspondência recebida, Curral, 1830, uncat.

22. Câmara, Regência dos Currais, 4 Nov. 1801, copy currently attached to Câmara to Governador, 28 Jan. 1801, APEB, CP, M. 209-1, Art. 13; Admin. do Curral to Câmara, 4 May 1816, encl. in Antonio Jourdan to Luiz Antonio Barbosa de Oliveira, 25 May 1816, AMS, 33.2, fol. 147; Jourdan, Breve noticia, fol. 43; Admin. do Curral to Câmara, 9 May 1829, AMS, Câmara, Correspondência recebida, Curral, 1829, uncat. On the cemetery's location see marginal note on Admin. do Curral to Câmara, 24 Nov. 1829, AMS, Câmara, Correspondência recebida, Curral, 1829, uncat.

23. Admin. do Curral to Câmara, 9 May 1829, AMS, Câmara, Correspondência recebida, Curral, 1829, uncat.; Câmara to Admin. do Curral, 8 Apr. and 17 May 1837, AMS, 111.8, fols. 198 and 206; Admin. do Curral to Vereador Encarregado do Matadouro, 6 Sept. 1843, AMS, Câmara, Correspondência recebida, Curral, 1843, uncat.; Commissão do Matadouro Público to Câmara, 13 Sept. 1843, encl. in Câmara to PP-BA, 13 Sept. 1843, APEB, CP, M. 1399, 1843, Doc. 48.

24. Câmara to Admin. do Curral, 9 June 1819, AMS, 116.6, fol. 23; Instruções para o Admin., encl. in Administração dos Currais, n.d. [after 1789], BN/SM, 3, 1, 5; *O Mercantil*, 26 June 1848, p. 3. The rules for the slaughterhouse were often repeated, most notably in the city ordinances dated 17 June 1844, AMS, 119.5, fols. 75v-77.

25. Governador to El-Rey, 14 Apr. 1798, APEB, CP, M. 138, fols. 274-274v; Rodrigo de Souza Coutinho to Fernando José de Portugal, Queluz Palace (Portugal), 4 Oct. 1798, APEB, CP, M. 86, fol. 188; Governador to Câmara, 19 June 1802 and 13 Dec. 1806, AMS, Ofícios/Câmara, 1798-1813, uncat.

26. *Almanach para a Cidade da Bahia: Anno 1812* [facsim. ed.] (Salvador: Conselho Estadual de Cultura, 1973), p. 181; Portarias 15 Jan. and 22 Apr. 1829, AMS, 116.6, fols. 208 and 212; Câmara to PP-BA, 17 June 1829, AMS, 111.6, fol. 281v; PP-BA to Câmara, 23 Apr. 1855, AMS, 111.12, fol. 247v.

27. Instruções para o Admin., encl. in Administração dos Currais, n.d. [after 1789], BN/SM, 3, 1, 5.

28. Câmara, Regência dos Currais, 4 Nov. 1801, copy currently attached to Câmara to Governador, 28 Jan. 1801, APEB, CP, M. 209-1, Art. 7; Regulamento da Capatazia do Matadouro, 3 Feb. 1857, encl. in Câmara to PP-BA, 6 Mar. (and again on 13 May) 1857, APEB, CP, M. 1403. On their number and organization, see Representação dos marchantes to Câmara, n.d., encl. in Câmara to Governa-

dor, 13 Sept. 1797, APEB, CP, M. 201-14, Doc. 59; Câmara, Editaes, 23 Aug. 1826, 15 Feb. 1830, 21 Oct. 1830, AMS, 116.6, fols. 156, 242v, 271; and Admin. do Curral quoted in Câmara to PP-BA, 21 Oct. 1835, APEB, CP, M. 1395. The claim of eighty or a hundred slaughtermen is in Vilhena, *Bahia no século XVIII*, p. 130.

29. Jourdan, Breve noticia, fol. 42v. On Brazilian-born blacks as slaughtermen, see Admin. do Curral to Presidente da Câmara, 19 Apr. 1834, AMS, Câmara, Correspondência recebida, Curral, 1834, uncat.; and *Correio Mercantil* (Salvador), 26 Oct. 1835, p. 4, col. 2, encl. in Auto crime, APEB, SJ, 09/313/3181/01, fols. 5–6. On African slaughtermen, see Câmara to PP-BA, 6 Oct. 1843, AMS, 111.11, fol. 105; *O Mercantil*, 26 June 1848, p. 3; and, on their exclusion, Regulamento da Capatazia do Matadouro, encl. in Câmara to PP-BA, 13 May 1857, APEB, CP, M. 1403. On damaged hides see Procurador da Câmara to Câmara, encl. in Câmara to Governador, 8 Feb. 1797, APEB, M. 201-14, Doc. 51. On curing the meat see John Turnbull, *A Voyage Round the World* . . . (London: Maxwell, 1813), p. 48.

30. Admin. do Curral to Câmara, 12 Feb. 1830, AMS, Câmara, Correspondência recebida, Curral, 1830, uncat.; Câmara to Admin. do Curral, 27 July 1831, AMS, 116.7, fols. 8–8v; *O Mercantil*, 26 June 1848, p. 3.

31. Admin. do Curral to Câmara, 4 May 1816, AMS, 33.2, fols. 146v–147; Admin. do Curral to Câmara, 9 Nov. 1829, AMS, Câmara, Correspondência recebida, Curral, 1829, uncat. Also see idem to idem, 15 Feb. 1830, AMS, Câmara, Correspondência recebida, Curral, 1830, uncat.

32. Jourdan, Breve notícia, fol. 42v; Posturas 110–112 in Posturas do Senado da Câmara [1716] . . . fielmente copiadas . . . 1785, AN, SH, Cód. 90, fol. 17; Câmara, Edital, 9 Dec. 1830, AMS, 119.5, fol. 91v. On how they were suspected of misconduct, see Câmara to Admin. do Curral, 8 Dec. 1817, AMS, 33.2, fol. 180. On how they were perceived as dangerous, see Admin. do Curral quoted in Câmara to PP-BA, 21 Oct. 1835, APEB, CP, M. 1395, 1835-a, Doc. 21 (also in AMS, 111.9, fol. 42v).

33. Câmara to Governador, 20 Mar. 1790, APEB, CP, M. 201-14, Doc. 8; Câmara to Admin. do Curral, 22 Aug. 1827, AMS, 116.6, fol. 172; Postura no. 10, revised 1843, AMS, 119.5, fol. 68 (also see fol. 11v).

34. Jourdan, Breve noticia, fol. 43; Instruções para o Admin. encl. in Administração dos Currais, n.d. [after 1789], BN/SM, 3, 1, 5; Inv. João Simões Coimbra, 1870 [1860], APEB, SJ, 03/1052/1521/02, fol. 155.

35. Câmara, Edital, 11 Mar. 1801, currently attached to Câmara to Governador, 28 Jan. 1801, APEB, CP, M209-1, Regulation no. 5; Governador to Câmara, 17 Sept. 1806, AMS, Oficios/Câmara, 1798–1813, uncat.; Câmara to Governador, 18 Feb. 1809, APEB, CP, M. 127; Jourdan, Breve noticia, fol. 42v.

36. On the rationale for grouping shops, see, for example, Câmara, Edital, 7 May 1839, AMS, 116.9, fol. 25; and Câmara to PP-BA, 17 June 1839, APEB, CP, M. 1397, Doc. 20. On the location of butcher shops, see Vilhena, *Bahia no século XVIII*, p. 69; Governador to Câmara, 10 Mar. 1807, AMS, 111.5, fols. 20–20v; Descrição da Bahia [1813?], AIHGB, L.399, Doc. 2, fols. 288–289; Junta Provisória to Câmara, 2 Nov. 1821, AMS, 111.5, fol. 234; and Joaquim José da Silva Maia (Procurador da Câmara) to Câmara. n.d. [1820 or 1821], BN/SM, I-31, 14, 3.

37. Procurador da Câmara, Memoria sobre o contrato das carnecerias, n.d., encl. in Câmara to Governador, 15 Mar. 1809, APEB, M. 127; Jourdan, Breve noti-

cia, fol. 43v; Instruções para o Admin., in Administração dos Currais, n.d. [after 1789], MS, BN/SM, 3, 1, 5; Câmara to Admin. do Curral, 21 July 1817, AMS, 33.2, fol. 169. Because they brought in the tax, they were sometimes called *cobradores*—that is, collectors. On bids for butcher shops offered in 1805, see AMS, 18.1, fols. 44v–76, and for a list of shops in 1810, AMS, 148.3, fols. 241–242.

38. Câmara to Procurador da Câmara, 31 July 1833, AMS, 116.7, fol. 128; Câmara to PP-BA, 18 June 1839, APEB, CP, M. 1397, Doc. 20; PP-BA to Câmara, 29 July 1836, AMS 98.1, fols. 265–266.

CHAPTER 7

1. Câmara to Governador, 20 Nov. 1802, APEB, CP, M. 209-1, Doc. 99 (also in AMS, 111.4, fol. 193v); Admin. do Curral to Câmara, 10 Mar. 1830, AMS, Câmara, Correspondência recebida, Curral, 1830, uncat.; Câmara quoted in Governador to Câmara, 21 Mar. 1809, and Governador to Câmara, 27 Sept. 1815, AMS, 111.5, fols. 43v and 184v.

2. Câmara to Governador, 21 June 1809 and enclosures, APEB, CP, M. 127; Câmara to PP-BA, 14 Jan. 1839 and enclosures, APEB, CP, M. 1397; Inv. Bartolomeu Francisco Gomes, 1848, APEB, SJ, 04/1697/2167/06, fols. 3, 4, 6–6v, 19–23v, 37v, 54, 62, 168.

3. Câmara, Edital, 11 Mar. 1801, currently filed with Câmara to Governador, 28 Jan. 1801, APEB, CP, M. 209-1, para. 3; Governador to Câmara, 18 Mar. 1807, AMS, 111.5, fol. 21. In 1807 the required real property had to be worth at least 50,000 cruzados(i.e., 20:000$000 [42:$000$000 in 1824 values]).

4. Procurador da Câmara, Memoria sobre o contrato da carneceria, n.d., encl. in Câmara to Governador, 15 Mar. 1809, APEB, CP, M. 127; Governador to Câmara, 21 Mar. 1809, AMS, 111.5, fol. 43v (quoted). On exports see José Jobson de A. Arruda, *O Brasil no comércio colonial* (São Paulo: Ática, 1980), Table 22, p. 204, and Table 23, p. 206.

5. Câmara to Governador, 10 Mar. 1802, APEB, CP, M. 209-1 (quoted); Governador to Câmara, 21 Jan. 1807, AMS, 111.5, fols. 14v–15; record of bids for butcher shops, AMS, 18.1, fols. 44v–69. The term *plebe* was an eighteenth-century neologism; Stuart B. Schwartz, "'Gente da terra braziliense da nasção,' Pensando o Brasil: A construção de um povo," in *Viagem incompleta: A experiência brasileira (1500–2000)—Formação, histórias*, ed. Carlos Guilherme Mota (São Paulo: SENAC, 2000), pp. 119–120.

6. Câmara to Governador, 6 May and 29 Aug. 1789, APEB, CP, M. 485-1, Docs. 4 and 8; Câmara to PP-BA, 21 July 1830, AMS, 111.8, fol. 43v.

7. AMS, 18.1, fol. 54v; Inv. Jacinto Vieira Rios, 1818, APEB, SJ, 04/1738/2208/03, fols. 5v–6, 7v, 11v–12v, 138v. His estate was worth 2:024$220 (2:651$728).

8. AMS, 18.1, fols. 49v, 59v, 64v, 65v; Inv. Alexandre Gomes de Brito, 1826, APEB, SJ, 08/3470/01, fols. 1, 2v, 4, 5, 27, 31, 60v, 67. In 1809 Brito was a lieutenant in the *pardo* militia; personal communication from Hendrik Kraay, 21 Jan. 2008. At Brito's death, he was referred to as "captain." On his son-in-law, Gualter Martins da Silva Bahia, see Câmara to Admin. do Curral, 9 Nov. 1825 and 23 Oct. 1826, AMS, 116.6, fols. 120 and 154v.

9. Test. 18 June 1860, copy in Inv. e Test., João Simões Coimbra, 1860, APEB,

SJ, 03/1242/1711/07, fols. 30–31, 35–35v, 37; Inv. João Simões Coimbra, 1870 [1860], APEB, SJ, 03/1052/1521/02, fols. 16v–18v, 19v–20v, 26, 27–27v, 63v, 65–65v, 67v–68, 93, 94, 139, 145, 155; Procurador da Câmara, Memoria sobre o contrato das carnecerias, n.d., encl. in Câmara to Governador, 5 Mar. 1809, APEB, CP, M. 127; Inv. Alexandre Gomes de Brito, 1826, APEB, SJ, 08/3470/01, fols. 32v, 33; Câmara to PP-BA, 14 Jan. 1839 and enclosures, APEB, CP, M. 1397; José Luiz Teixeira, Informação dos officiaes do 4° regimento de milicias desta Cid^e e Capitania da Bahia, 31 Dec. 1809, APEB, CP, M. 247-6 (I owe this reference to Hendrik Kraay); Coimbra's estate was worth 142:987$520 (44:326$131).

10. Inv. Alexandre Gomes de Brito, 1826, APEB, SJ, 08/3470/01, fols. 32–33, 35.

11. Câmara to Governador, 23 Aug. 1780, AMS, 111.4, fol. 61; Câmara to Assembléia Provincial, 27 Feb. 1836, encl. in Câmara to PP-BA, 4 Aug. 1836, APEB, CP, M. 1396 (also in AMS, 111.9, fol. 77–82v); Ouvidor to Governador, 4 Sept. 1785, encl. in Governador to Martinho de Mello e Castro, 4 Feb. 1786, in Eduardo de Castro e Almeida, ed., "Inventario dos documentos relativos ao Brasil existentes no Archivo de Marinha e Ultramar," *ABNRJ* 34 (1912): 9.

12. Câmara, Regência da Feira do Capoame, 18 Apr. 1801, copy currently attached to Câmara to Governador, 28 Jan. 1801, APEB, M. 209-1, Arts. 1, 19, and 22; José Joaquim de Almeida e Arnizau, "Memoria topographica, historica, commercial e politica da villa de Cachoeira da provincia da Bahia [1825]," *Revista do Instituto Historico e Geographico Brasileiro* 25 (1862): 127.

13. Câmara to PP-BA, 1 Oct. 1829, AMS, 111.6, fol. 223; Diretor da Campina, quoted in Câmara to PP-BA, 8 Aug. 1831, AMS, 111.8, fol. 98; Câmara to PP-BA, 1 Sept. 1858, APEB, CP, M. 1404 (also in AMS, 111.13, fol. 255).

14. Câmara to Governador, 14 Sept. 1782, AMS, 111.4, fol. 75v; Governador to Câmara, 10 Mar. 1807, AMS, 111.5, fol. 18v; Câmara to Superintendente da Feira, 10 Mar. 1810, AMS, 33.2, fol. 37.

15. Câmara to Governador, 12 Mar. 1806 and enclosures, APEB, CP, M. 209-1, 1806, Doc. 108.

16. Procurador da Câmara, Memoria sobre o contrato das carnicerias, n.d., encl. in Câmara to Governador, 15 Mar. 1809, APEB, CP, M. 127; Inv., Alexandre Gomes de Brito, 1826, APEB, SJ, 08/3470/01, fol. 35; Governador (Conde da Ponte) to Câmara, 12 Nov. 1806, AMS, Ofícios/Câmara, 1797–1813, uncat.; Governador to Câmara, 14 Nov. 1806, and 22 Nov. 1806, AMS, 111.5, fols. 10 and 11; entry for 12 Nov. 1806 in "Descrição da Bahia [1813?]," MS, AIHGB, Lata 399, Doc. 2, fol. 211.

17. Procurador da Câmara to Câmara, encl. in Câmara to Governador, 8 Feb. 1797, APEB, M. 201-14, Doc. 51; Governador to El-Rey, 14 Apr. 1798, APEB, CP, M. 138, fol. 274–274v.

18. Procurador da Câmara to Câmara encl. in Câmara to Governador, 8 Feb. 1797, APEB, CP, M. 201-14, Doc. 51; Câmara to PP-BA, 14 Jan. 1839 and enclosures, APEB, CP, M. 1397; Procurador da Câmara, Memoria sobre o contrato das carnicerias, n.d., encl. in Câmara to Governador, 15 Mar. 1809, APEB, CP, M. 127.

19. Câmara to PP-BA, 4 Aug. 1836, AMS, 111.6, fol. 107; copy of proposed contract, encl. in Câmara to PP-BA, 15 Dec. 1836, APEB, CP, M. 1396 (also in AMS, 111.9, fols. 129v–130v); PP-BA to Câmara, 20 Dec. 1836, AMS, 98.1, fol. 291; Câmara to Admin. do Curral, 22 Dec. 1836, AMS, 116.8, fol. 167v (see also 181v).

20. Test., Manoel José dos Reis, 1864/1873, APEB, SJ, 05/2194/2263/15, fols. 1–2; Inv., João Antonio Maria Pereira, APEB, SJ, 03/1001/1470/12, fol. 12 (Hendrik Kraay shared with me his notes on this case). On the Bank of Brazil branch see Francisco Marques de Góes Calmon, *Vida econômico-financeira da Bahia (elementos para a história) de 1808–1899* (Salvador: Imp. Official do Estado, 1925), p. 19; and Thales de Azevedo and Edilberto Quintela Vieira Lins, *História do Banco da Bahia, 1858–1958,* Documentos Brasileiros, no. 132 (Rio de Janeiro: J. Olympio, 1969), p. 55.

21. Test., Antonio Pedrozo de Albuquerque [Pai], 1878, APEB, SJ, 01/88-A/125/02, fols. 1, 37v, 200–203, 306, 351–357v (I owe this reference to Sandra Lauderdale Graham); Pierre Verger, *Trade Relations Between the Bight of Benin and Bahia from the 17th to 19th Century,* trans. Evelyn Crawford (Ibadan: Ibadan University Press, 1976), pp. 363, 367, 372, 398, 404; Stanley J. Stein, *The Brazilian Cotton Manufacture: Textile Enterprise in an Underdeveloped Area, 1850–1950* (Cambridge, MA: Harvard University Press, 1957), pp. 21, 54. On his wife's property, see Francisco Antonio Dória and Jorge Ricardo de Almeida Fonseca, "Marechal José Inácio Acciaiuoli: Um potentado baiano no início do século XIX," *Revista do Instituto Geográfico e Histórico da Bahia,* no. 90 (1992): 138. Their son, Antonio Pedroso de Albuquerque [Filho], married Teodora Ignez Peçanha Martins, daughter of Francisco Gonçalves Martins, Visconde de São Lourenço; on Martins's, political career see José Wanderley Pinho [de Araújo], *Cotegipe e seu tempo: Primeira phase, 1815–1867,* Brasiliana no. 85 (São Paulo: Editora Nacional, 1937), pp. 494–498.

22. Câmara to PP-BA, 17 Jan. 1837, AMS, 111.9, fol. 144; Câmara to PP-BA, 3 Feb. 1837 and enclosures, PP-BA quoted in Câmara to PP-BA, 17 Feb. 1837, Câmara to PP-BA, 22 July 1837, all in APEB, CP, M. 1396.

23. João Pereira da Motta (for the company) to Câmara, 31 Jan. 1837, copy encl. in Câmara to PP-BA, 3 Feb. 1837; Câmara to PP-BA, 22 July 1837; Companhia de Fornecimento de Carnes Verdes to Câmara, n.d., encl. in Câmara to PP-BA, 16 Mar. 1837, all in APEB, CP, M. 1396; Câmara to Admin. do Curral, 19 July 1837, AMS, 116.8, fol. 221v.

24. Companhia de Fornecimento de Carnes Verdes to Câmara, n.d., encl. in Câmara to PP-BA, 16 Mar. 1837, and Câmara to PP-BA, 22 July, 14 Aug., and 19 Sept. 1837, all in APEB, CP, M. 1396. This last letter, but bearing the date of 16 Sept., is also in AMS, 111.9, fols. 181v–186.

25. See, for example, Sidney Chalhoub, "Dependents Play Chess: Political Dialogues in Machado de Assis," in *Machado de Assis: Reflections on a Brazilian Master Writer,* ed. Richard Graham (Austin: University of Texas Press, 1995), pp. 51–84.

26. Procurador da Câmara to Câmara, encl. in Câmara to Governador, 8 Feb. 1797, APEB, M. 201-14, Doc. 51.

27. Câmara, Edital, 11 Mar. 1801, currently filed with Câmara to Governador, 28 Jan. 1801, APEB, CP, M. 209-1; Instruções para o Admin., encl. in Administração dos Currais [Report], n.d. [after 1789], BN/SM, 3, 1, 5; João Rodrigues de Brito, "Carta I," in João Rodrigues de Brito et al., *Cartas economico-politicas sobre a agricultura e commercio da Bahia* (Lisbon: Imp. Nacional, 1821), p. 14.

28. The 1826 experience was recalled by Admin. do Curral, quoted in Câmara to PP-BA, 28 Feb. 1829, AMS, 111.6, fol. 273.

29. Admin. do Curral to Câmara, 19 Aug. 1829; 15 and 18 Feb.; 25 Sept.; 7, 16, and 19 Oct.; and 5 Nov. 1830 (two letters of this last date and the marginal draft of a reply), all in AMS, Câmara, Correspondência recebida, Curral, 1830, uncat. Also see his letters of 3 and 19 June 1830 in ibid.

30. Admin. do Curral to Câmara, 6 Nov., 22 Dec. 1830, AMS, Câmara, Correspondência recebida, Curral, 1830, uncat.; Câmara, Anuncio, 12 and 18 Nov. 1830, AMS, 116.6, fols. 274 and 275.

31. Câmara to PP-BA, 30 July 1845, APEB, CP, M. 1399, 1845, Doc. 35 (also in AMS, 111.11, fols. 154v–155); O Mercantil, 26 June 1848, p. 3. On the other hand, it seems that by 1857 they were paid 240 réis per head, a three-fold increase in twelve years; Regulamento da Capatazia do Matadouro, 3 Feb. 1857 (a printed flyer), encl. in Câmara to PP-BA, 26 Mar. 1857, APEB, CP, M. 1403.

32. Admin. do Curral, n.d. [after 1789], BN/SM, 3, 1, 5; Câmara to Admin. do Curral, 29 July 1818, AMS, 33.2, fol. 186v; Jourdan, Breve notícia, fol. 43; Luís dos Santos Vilhena, A Bahia no século XVIII, 2d ed., ed. Braz do Amaral, intro. by Edison Carneiro (Salvador: Itapuã, 1969), p. 130.

33. João José Reis, Slave Rebellion in Brazil: The Muslim Uprising of 1835 in Bahia, trans. Arthur Brakel (Baltimore: Johns Hopkins University Press, 1993), pp. 166–67, 170 (the men may have worked for butchers and not at the slaughterhouse; the same word applies to both); Admin. do Curral, quoted in Câmara to PP-BA, 21 Oct. 1835, and marginal draft of reply, APEB, CP, M. 1395, 1835-a, Doc. 21 (copies of this request and reply [dated 23 Oct.] are in AMS, 111.9, fol. 42v, and AMS, 98.1, fol. 218); Admin. do Curral, quoted in Câmara to PP-BA, 9 Oct. 1838, APEB, CP, M. 1397, Doc. 47.

CHAPTER 8

1. Except where otherwise noted, the next paragraphs on events in Portugal and Rio de Janeiro are primarily based on Francisco Adolfo de Varnhagen, História da independência do Brasil até ao reconhecimento pela antiga metrópole, compreendendo, separadamente, a dos sucessos ocorridos em algumas províncias até essa data, 3rd ed., ed. Baron of Rio Branco and Hélio Vianna (São Paulo: Melhoramentos, 1957); and Tobias Monteiro, História do Império: A elaboração da Independência, 2nd ed., Reconquista do Brasil, n.s., No. 39–40 (Belo Horizonte and São Paulo: Itatiaia and EDUSP, 1981). Additional information was drawn from Manuel de Oliveira Lima, O movimento da independência: O Império brasileiro (1821–1889), 2nd ed. (São Paulo: Melhoramentos, 1957), pp. 11–324. I have also profited from Roderick J. Barman, Brazil: The Forging of a Nation, 1798–1852 (Stanford, CA: Stanford University Press, 1988), pp. 65–107; José Honório Rodrigues, Independência: Revolução e contra-revolução, 5 vols. (Rio de Janeiro: Francisco Alves, 1975–1976), 1: 169–300; Carlos Guilherme Mota, ed., 1822: Dimensões (São Paulo: Perspectiva, 1972); and Neill Macaulay, Dom Pedro: The Struggle for Liberty in Brazil and Portugal, 1798–1834 (Durham, NC: Duke University Press, 1986). See also the perceptive historiographical essay on Brazilian independence as seen

from both sides of the Atlantic in Márcia Regina Berbel, *A nação como artefato: Deputados do Brasil nas Cortes portuguesas (1821-1822)* (São Paulo: HUCITEC, 1999), pp. 20-29.

2. The conflict of interests was well summarized by L. F. de Tollenare, *Notas dominicais tomadas durante uma viagem em Portugal e no Brasil em 1816, 1817, e 1818* (Salvador: Progresso, 1956), p. 127.

3. On attitudes in Portugal see Luís Henrique Dias Tavares, *A independência do Brasil na Bahia*, 3rd ed. (Salvador: EDUFBA, 2005), p. 66; Lima, *Movimento da independencia*, p. 223; Lúcia Maria Bastos P[ereira das] Neves, *Corcundas, constitucionais e pés-de-chumbo: A cultura política da Independência, 1820-1822* (Rio de Janeiro, 2002), p. 279; and José Hermano Saraiva, *História de Portugal* (Lisbon: Publicações Europa-América, 1993), pp. 328, 355. On resentments in Brazil of Rio's predominance see James Prior, *Voyage Along the Eastern Coast of Africa . . .* (London: Richard Phillips, 1819), p. 105; and Marcus J. M. de Carvalho, "Cavalcantis e cavalgados: A formação das alianças políticas em Pernambuco, 1817-1824," *Revista Brasileira de História* 18, no. 36 (1998): 333-334. On the actions of the Cortes see Berbel, *Nação como artefato*, pp. 96-97, 109, 117, 127ff.; Berbel, "A retórica da recolonização," in *Independência: História e historiografia*, ed. István Jancsó (São Paulo: HUCITEC and FAPESP, 2005), pp. 791-808; and Andréa Slemian and João Paulo G. Pimenta, *O "nascimento político" do Brasil: As origens do estado e da nação (1808-1825)* (Rio de Janeiro: DP&A, 2003), pp. 75, 77.

4. Not all historians agree on these points, especially on the number of combatants. I have followed Varnhagen, *História da independência do Brasil*, with special regard for the notes by the baron of Rio Branco, pp. 100, 110n, 271n; and Lima, *Movimento da independencia*, p. 143. But c.f. Tavares, *Independência na Bahia*, p. 71; and Macaulay, *Dom Pedro*, p. 116.

5. The events in Bahia are described by Braz Hermenegildo do Amaral, *História da independência na Bahia*, 2nd ed., Marajoara, no. 19 (Salvador: Livraria Progresso, 1957); and Ignacio Accioli de Cerqueira e Silva, *Memórias históricas e políticas da província da Bahia*, 2nd ed., 6 vols., ed. Braz do Amaral (Salvador: Imprensa Official do Estado, 1919-1940), 3: 293-561 and 4: 1-81. A useful summary is Varnhagen, *História da independência do Brasil*, pp. 260-286, and I have drawn additional information from Tavares, *Independência na Bahia*. Also see Luiz Alberto Moniz Bandeira, *O feudo—A Casa da Torre de Garcia d'Avila: Da conquista dos sertões à independência do Brasil* (Rio de Janeiro: Civilização Brasileira, 2000), pp. 389-462.

6. José Couto de Paiva Pereira to El-Rey, aboard the *Glória*, port of Lisbon, 6 Oct. 1821, AHU, Bahia, Avulsos, Cx. 254, Doc. 32.

7. Comandante da Força Marítima to Secretário dos Negócios da Marinha, 24 Aug. 1821, AHU, Bahia, Avulsos, Cx. 254, Doc. 39.

8. Luís dos Santos Vilhena, *A Bahia no século XVIII*, 2nd ed., ed. Braz do Amaral, intro. by Edison Carneiro (Salvador: Itapuã, 1969), pp. 245, 249-252; Maria Graham [Lady Maria Calcott], *Journal of a Voyage to Brazil and Residence There During Part of the Years 1821, 1822, 1823* (1824; reprint, New York: Praeger, 1969), pp. 141-142; F. W. O. Morton, "The Military and Society in Bahia, 1800-1821," *Journal of Latin American Studies* 7, no. 2 (Nov. 1975): 250, 254, 263; Hen-

drik Kraay, *Race, State, and Armed Forces in Independence-Era Brazil: Bahia, 1790s–1840s* (Stanford, CA: Stanford University Press, 2001), p. 87.

9. Câmara to Governador, 20 Nov. 1802, APEB, CP, M. 209-1, Doc. 99 (also in AMS, 111.4, fol. 193v); José Luiz Teixeira, Informação dos officiaes do 4° regimento de milicias desta Cid^e e Capitania da Bahia, 31 Feb. 1809, APEB, CP, M. 247-6; Queixosa: Thereza Maria de Jesus, Queixado: Gonçalo José dos Santos Paz [or Pereira], Juizado de Paz de Santo Antonio além do Carmo, 29 Oct. 1838, Auto crime, APEB, SJ, 09/313/11, No. 6 (crime de responsabilidade); João José Reis, *Slave Rebellion in Brazil: The Muslim Uprising of 1835 in Bahia*, trans. Arthur Brakel (Baltimore: Johns Hopkins University Press, 1993), pp. 225–226; Stuart B. Schwartz, "The Formation of a Colonial Identity in Brazil," in *Colonial Identity in the Atlantic World, 1500–1800*, ed. Nicholas Canny and Anthony Pagden (Princeton, NJ: Princeton University Press, 1987), p. 48; Inv., Ana de São José da Trindade, 1823, APEB, SJ, 04/1840/2311/02, fol. 20 of second set.

10. On the events of 18–20 Feb. 1822, see Conselho de Investigação mandado fazer . . . para se conhecer os factos acontecidos . . . , 13 May 1822; and Bernardino Alvares de Araújo (commander of Forte de São Pedro) to Madeira, 16 Apr. 1822, both in Amaral, *História da Independência*, pp. 85–113, as well as the documents in Silva, *Memórias históricas*, 3: 293–329, 454–480, and 488–519. On the emigration of the Brazilian contingent of the army, including officers, see Madeira to El-Rey, 20 [not 26] Aug. 1822, BN/SM, 5, 3, 45, Doc. 130; and Luís Paulino d'Oliveira Pinto da França Garcês to his father, 3 July 1822, in António d'Oliveira Pinto da França, ed., *Cartas baianas, 1821–1824: Subsídios para o estudo dos problemas da opção na independência brasileira*, Brasiliana no. 372 (São Paulo: Editora Nacional, 1980), p. 75.

11. Albert Roussin (commander of French naval station) to French Navy Minister, on board the *Amazone*, 21 June 1822, in Kátia M. de Queirós Mattoso, ed., "Albert Roussin: Testemunha das lutas pela independência da Bahia (1822)," *Anais do Arquivo [Público] do Estado da Bahia* 41 (1973): 129. On the Portuguese who sided with the Brazilians, see Alexandre José Mello Moraes [Pai], *A independencia e o Imperio do Brazil [sic]* . . . (Rio de Janeiro: Typ. do Globo, 1877), pp. 137 and 137n.

12. Felisberto Caldeira Brant Pontes to Joaquim Pereira d'Almeida, 31 Oct. 1820, in Felisberto Caldeira Brant Pontes (Marquês de Barbacena), *Economia açucareira do Brasil no séc. XIX*, comp. Carmen Vargas, Coleção Canavieira, no. 21 (Rio de Janeiro: Instituto do Açucar e do Álcool, 1976), p. 174.

13. Madeira to El-Rey, 7 July and 20 Aug. 1822, with enclosures, BN/SM, 5, 3, 45, Docs. 100 and 130; Ata de Vereação da Vila de São Francisco do Conde, 29 June 1822, in Silva, *Memórias históricas*, 3: 350 (quoted).

14. Antonio José de Melo to [Junta Provisória], Camamu, 16 Aug. 1822, encl. in Madeira to El-Rey, 20 Aug. 1822, BN/SM, 5, 3, 45, Doc. 173; Junta Governativa to Conselho Interino, Porto Seguro, 26 Nov. 1822, BN/SM, I-31, 6, 3, Doc. 79; Bispo Capellão de Porto Seguro to Prince-Regent Pedro, Porto Seguro, n. d., AN, SPE, IJJ⁹329; F. W. O. Morton, "The Conservative Revolution of Independence: Economy, Society and Politics in Bahia, 1790–1840" (Ph.D. diss., University of Oxford, 1974), p. 281.

15. Antonio de Meneses Vasconcellos de Drummond, "Anotações a sua bio-graphia publicada em 1836 na *Biographie universelle et portative des contempo-rains,*" *ABNRJ* 13, pt. 3 (1885–1886): 32.

16. Quotations are from Conselho Interino to Ouvidor desta Comarca, 13 Nov. 1822; idem to Inspector do Comissariado, 23 Nov. 1822, both dated from Cacho-eira, BN/SM, 9, 2, 30, Doc. 96, fol. 31, and Doc. 172, fol. 57; and from Mauricio Mendes da Silva (captain of *lancha*) to Joaquim Pires de Carvalho e Albuquerque, Paripe, 27 Nov. 1822, in Amaral, *História da Independência,* p. 249. On the need for cash, see Conselho Interino to Tesoureiro Geral, Cachoeira, 19 Dec. 1822, BN/SM, 9, 2, 30, Doc. 601, fols. 154v–155. On the force sent to Nazaré, see Madeira to El-Rey, 20 Aug. 1822, BN/SM, 5, 3, 45, Doc. 130. On the food supply agency, see Miguel Calmon du Pin e Almeida (Marquês de Abrantes), *Relatorio dos trabalhos do Conselho Interino do governo da Provincia da Bahia, 1823,* 2nd ed. (Rio de Janeiro: Typ. do "Jornal do Commercio," 1923), p. 28.

17. Commissão [Militar] to Conselho Interino, Nazaré, 16 Oct. 1822, BN/SM, I-31, 6, 1, Doc. 55 (quoted); Conselho Interino to Labatut, Cachoeira, 21 Nov. 1822, in Arquivo Público do Estado da Bahia, *Anais,* 41 (1973), p. 31; Conselho Interino, Portaria, Cachoeira, 29 Nov. 1822, BN/SM, 9, 2, 30, Doc. 158, fols. 52–53; José Fer-reira da Rocha to [Joaquim Pires de Carvalho e Albuquerque], Itapoã, 24 Sept. 1822, and Joaquim Pires de Carvalho e Albuquerque to [?], Santo Amaro, 3 Dec. 1822, both in Amaral, *História da Independência,* pp. 248 and 258; Conselho In-terino, Portaria, 15 May 1823, APEB, CP, Cx. 320; Conselho Interino to Inspec-tor do Commissariado das Munições de Boca, to Monges Beneditinos, and to Capitão-Mor da Trindade, all three dated from Cachoeira, 29 Dec. 1822, BN/SM, 9, 2, 30, Docs. 256, 257, and 259, fols. 82v–83; loose sheet headed "Lagarto," n.p., n.d. [1822?], APEB, CP, Cx. 320.

18. Francisco Rodrigues Gomes de Sousa to Secretario do Conselho Interino, Forte de Paraguassú, 6, 8, and 12 Nov. 1822, BN/SM, I-31, 6, 3, Docs. 12, 17, and 59; Antonio de Souza Lima to Secretario do Conselho Interino, Quartel de Itaparica, 14 Dec. 1822, quoted in Alexandre José Mello Moraes[Pai], *Historia do Brasil-Reino e do Brasil-Imperio,* 2 vols. (Rio de Janeiro: Typ. Pinheiro, 1871–1873), 2: 40. On morale, see, for example, Michael Seidman, *Republic of Egos: A Social History of the Spanish Civil War* (Madison: University of Wisconsin Press, 2002), pp. 219–220.

19. Felisberto Gomes Caldeira to Euzebio Vanerio, Quartel de Itapoã, 9 Nov. 1822, APEB, CP, Cx. 315. On supplying the army, see Conselho Interino to Inspec-tor do Commissariado das Munições de Boca, Cachoeira, 31 Dec. 1822; and to Co-mandante do Destacamento de Acupe, Cachoeira, 4 Dec. 1822, both at BN/SM, 9, 2, 30, Doc. 263, fol. 85, and Doc. 207, fol. 69; Bento de Araújo Lopes Villasboas to Miguel Calmon du Pin e Almeida, São Francisco do Conde, 2 Nov. 1822, BN/SM, I-31, 6, 2, Doc. 77.

20. Miguel Calmon du Pin e Almeida and Francisco Elesbão Paes de Carvalho e Albuquerque to Labatut, Cachoeira, 11 Dec. 1822, BN/SM, I-31, 6, 2, Doc. 47; Con-selho Interino to Antonio Francisco Dias, Cachoeira, 18 Dec. 1822, and to Victor da Silva Torres, Cachoeira, 28 Dec. 1822, BN/SM, 9, 2, 30, Doc. 239, fols. 78–79, and Doc. 251, fol. 81v; Manoel Diogo de Sá Barreto e Aragão to Conselho Interino, São Francisco do Conde, 13 June 1823, BN/SM, II-33, 36, 19.

21. Câmara, Edital, 20 July 1822, AMS, 116.6, fol. 66. The Henriques were later placed under the command of a wealthy sugar planter, who then received most of the credit for their action; cf. Amaral, *História da Independência*, pp. 184–185, with Morton, "Conservative Revolution," p. 260.

22. Conselho Interino to Commissão da Caixa Militar de Nazaré, Cachoeira, 10 Feb. 1823, BN/SM, I-7, 2, 26, Doc. [267], fols. 79v–81; Albert Roussin to French Navy Minister, Salvador, 17 July 1822, in Mattoso, "Albert Roussin," pp. 139–140.

23. Junta Provisória to Felipe Ferreira de Araujo e Castro, 8 Oct. 1822, AHU, Bahia, Avulsos, Cx. 262, Doc. 36; Commissão da Caixa Militar to Conselho Interino, Valença, 17 Oct. 1822, quoted in Moraes [Pai], *Historia do Brasil-Reino*, 2: 8; Joaquim José Correia (Intendente da Marinha) to Minister of the Navy, 24 Nov. 1822, AHU, Bahia, Avulsos, Cx. 263, Doc. 32 (a copy of this document is in Cx. 264, Doc. 35).

24. On the importance of this point see Anthony Oberschall and Michael Seidman, "Food Coercion in Revolution and Civil War: Who Wins and How They Do It," *Comparative Studies in History and Society* 47, no. 2 (July 2005): 398.

25. Catherine Lugar, "The Merchant Community of Salvador, Bahia, 1780–1830" (Ph.D. diss., State University of New York at Stony Brook, 1980), p. 86 (see also p. 69).

26. Madeira to El-Rey, 2 Apr. 1822, AHM, 2ª Div., 1ª Sec., Cx. 39, No. 1; Maria Bárbara Garcês Pinto de Madureira to Luís Paulino d'Oliveira Pinto de França, 28 June and postscript dated 30 June 1822, in França, *Cartas baianas*, p. 70.

27. Capitão-Mor de Maragogipe to Governador, Engenho de Capanema, 17 July 1819, APEB, CP, M. 415. On the July attempt, see the officer quoted by Drummond, "Anotações," p. 31; Antonio de Souza Lima to Miguel Calmon du Pin e Almeida, [Quartel de São Lourenço, Itaparica], 13 Sept. 1822, in Moraes[Pai], *Historia do Brasil-Reino*, 2: 5; and Graham [Lady Maria Calcott], *Journal*, p. 215. On the January attempt, see Bento José Cardoso to Joaquim José da Cunha, aboard the *Constituição*, 9 Jan. 1823, enclosed in Cunha to Campos, aboard the *Audaz*, 10 Jan. 1823, AHU, Bahia, Avulsos, Cx. 265, Doc. 8; Conselho Interino to José Bonifácio de Andrada e Silva, Cachoeira, 13 Jan. 1823, in Raul Lima, ed., *A Junta Governativa da Bahia e a Independência* (Rio de Janeiro: Arquivo Nacional, 1973), pp. 269–270; and Campos to Minister of the Navy, 2 Feb. 1823, AHU, Bahia, Avulsos, Cx. 265, Doc. 20.

28. Junta Provisória to Felipe Ferreira de Araujo e Castro, 8 Oct. 1822, AHU, Bahia, Avulsos, Cx. 262, Doc. 36.

29. João Felix Pereira de Campos to Minister of the Navy, 7 Nov. 1822, AHU, Bahia, Avulsos, Cx. 263, No. 11; Anonymous to Felisberto Gomes Caldeira, 7 Dec. 1822, quoted in Moraes [Pai], *Historia do Brasil-Reino*, 2: 38. On the difficulty of pursuing shallow-draft vessels at later times, see PP-BA to Antonio Pereira Rebouças, n.p., n.d. [after 2 Dec. 1837], in "A Sabinada nas cartas de Barreto Pedroso a Rebouças," *ABNRJ* 88 (1968): 216; and Marcus J. M. de Carvalho, *Liberdade: Rotinas e rupturas do escravismo urbano, Recife, 1822–1850*, 2nd ed. (Recife: Editora da UFPE, 2002), pp. 132–133.

30. Abaixo assinado, 4 Nov. 1822, and Campos to Madeira, 14 Nov. 1822, both in AHU, Bahia, Avulsos, Cx. 263, Doc. 34; *Idade d'Ouro do Brasil*, no. 93 (1822), in Maria Beatriz Nizza da Silva, *A primeira gazeta da Bahia: "Idade d'Ouro do*

Brasil" (São Paulo and Brasília: Cultrix and Instituto Nacional do Livro, 1978), p. 195.

31. Campos to Minister of the Navy, 2 Feb. 1823; Junta Provisória to Felipe Ferreira de Araujo e Castro, 21 Feb. 1823; Madeira to El-Rey, 13 Feb. 1823, AHU, Bahia, Avulsos, Cx. 265, Docs. 20, 37, and 33 (another copy of Madeira's letter, misdated 13 Dec. 1822, is in AHM, 2ª Div., 1ª Sec., Cx.39, No. 1; this misdated version has been printed in Amaral, *História da Independência*, pp. 295–297); and Bento da França Pinto d'Oliveira to his father, Luís Paulino d'Oliveira Pinto da França, n.d. [Feb. 1823], in França, *Cartas baianas*, p. 95.

32. Conselho Interino to José Bonifácio de Andrade e Silva, Cachoeira, 16 Apr. 1823, AN, SPE, IJJ⁹329 (quoted). On the numbers of Portuguese combatants in the city, see Campos to Minister of the Navy, 7 Nov. 1822 and 2 Feb. 1823, both at AHU, Bahia, Avulsos, Cx. 263, No. 11, and Cx. 265, Doc. 20; Mappa de todos os corpos da Primeira Linha da Guarnição em Bahia, 14 Feb. 1823, AHM, 2ª Div., 1ª Sec., Cx. 40, No. 6; Ignacio Rufino da Costa Lima (for the Junta da Fazenda) to Secretary of Junta Provisória, 23 Apr. 1823, in Amaral, *História da Independência*, p. 331. These numbers have been the subject of some confusion among historians; Varnhagen (*História da independência do Brasil*, p. 272n) calculated the number of Portuguese men under arms in November 1822 as 8,621, perhaps because he included militiamen who would have been there anyway. Probably relying on this figure, Macaulay (*Dom Pedro*, p. 143) and Barman (*Brazil: Forging a Nation*, p. 104) round the number up to 9,000, and Barman (p. 105) incorrectly puts just the reinforcements at "nearly 4,000." But the number of Portuguese soldiers, not sailors, reported in November 1822 was 3,507; Mappa da força militar portugueza ao presente destacada na Bahia, Lisbon, 11 Nov. 1822, AHU, Bahia, Avulsos, Cx. 263, No. 20.

33. Junta Provisória to Juiz de Fora do Civil interino, 22 Aug. 1822, AMS, 111.5, fol. 253; Madeira to El-Rey, 13 Feb. 1823, AHU, Bahia, Avulsos, Cx. 265, Doc. 33; Inv., Ana de São José Trindade, 1823, APEB, SJ, 04/1840/2311/02; Inv., Tomasia Maria do Sacramento, 1823, APEB, SJ, 04/1590/2059/02, fol. 54.

34. Conselho Interino to José Bonifácio de Andrade e Silva, Cachoeira, 16 Apr. 1823, AN, SPE, IJJ⁹329.

35. Conselho Interino, Circular, 28 Apr. 1823, encl. in Francisco Elesbão Pires de Carvalho e Albuquerque to José Bonifácio de Andrade e Silva, [Cachoeira], 28 May 1823, AN, SPE, IJJ⁹329; Almeida, *Relatorio*, p. 43. For more on this naval effort see Brian Vale, *Independence or Death! British Sailors and Brazilian Independence, 1822–1825* (London: British Academic Press/I. B. Taurus Publishers, 1996), pp. 45–61; and Max Justo Guedes, "Guerra de Independência: As forças do mar," in *História da Independência: Edição comemorativea*, ed. Josué Montello (Rio de Janeiro, 1972), 2: 167–211.

36. Campos to Madeira, sailing off Salvador, 6 May 1823, copy encl. in Campos to El-Rey, 26 May 1823, AHU, Bahia, Avulsos, Cx. 265, Doc. 71; Madeira to Campos, 19 May 1823 (also in Amaral, *História da Independência*, p. 363), and Madeira to El-Rey, 31 May 1823, both in AHM, 2ª Div., 1ª Sec., Cx. 40, No. 1, and Cx. 39, No. 1-1; Junta Provisória to Campos, 18 June 1824, AHM, 2ª Div., 1ª Sec., Cx.40, No. 1-1 (also in Amaral, *História da Independência*, pp. 428–430).

37. Junta Provisória to El-Rey, 10 June 1823, AHM, 2ª Div., 1ª Sec., Cx. 41,

No. 4; Joaquim José Correia to Campos, 17 June 1823, AHU, Bahia, Avulsos, Cx. 266, Doc. 43.

38. Mappa dos generos que se tem recebido abordo da corveta Quatro de Julho para entregar na Bahia, Lisbon, 7 Apr. 1823; Campos to Minister of the Navy, 9 June 1823; and Madeira to Junta Provisória, 23 June, 1823, all in AHU, Bahia, Avulsos, Cx. 265, Doc. 58, and Cx. 266, Docs. 11 and 74; Madeira to El-Rey, 31 May 1823, AHM, 2ª Div., 1ª Sec., Cx. 39, No. 1.1.

39. Madeira to Joaquim José Correia (Intendente da Marinha), 28 May 1823, in Amaral, História da Independência, p. 472; Câmara to Almotacé, 4 June 1823, AMS, 116.6, fol. 71v; Licença, guia, e relação de tripulantes da sumaca Patrocinio, [1822–]1823, BN/SM, II-33, 36, 17; Junta Provisória to El-Rey, 10 June 1823, AHM, 2ª Div., 1ª Sec., Cx. 41, No. 4 (also in AHU, Bahia, Avulsos, Cx. 266, Doc. 57); Graham [Lady Maria Calcott], Journal, p. 255; Almeida, Relatorio, p. 42. Also see Campos to Madeira, 9 June 1823, AHU, Bahia, Avulsos, Cx. 266, Doc. 11.

40. Madeira [Bando], 9 May 1823, in Amaral, História da Independência, pp. 355–356; entry for 10 May 1823 in [Francisco da Silva Barros], Chronica dos acontecimentos da Bahia, 1809–1828, BN/SM, II-33, 25, 53, No. 1, fol. 32v (for the name of the author cf. fol. 35 with Inv. José da Silva Barros, 1823, APEB, SJ, 04/1826/2297/13, fol. 1; for a printed version see [Francisco da Silva Barros], "Chronica dos acontecimentos da Bahia, 1809–1828," Anais do Arquivo Público do Estado da Bahia 26 [1938]: 79); Affonso Ruy, História da Câmara Municipal da cidade do Salvador, 2nd ed. (Salvador: Câmara Municipal de Salvador, 1996), pp. 243–244.

41. Madeira to Campos, 19 May 1823, in Amaral, História da Independência, p. 363; Abaixo assinado, 23 May 1823, AHM, 2ª Div., 1ª Sec., Cx. 41, No. 5 (also in Amaral, História da Independência, pp. 386–388). Madeira to Campos, 23 May 1823; Campos to Madeira, 23 May 1823; Manoel de Vasconcellos Pereira de Melo to Madeira, 24 May 1823; Madeira to Campos, 24 May 1823; and Campos to Madeira, 24 May 1823, all in Amaral, História da Independência, pp. 383–384, 388–390. Note that Madeira was also roundly criticized, even by his own officers; Drummond, "Anotações," p. 38.

42. Câmara to Junta Provisória, 14 June 1823, quoted in Ruy, História da Câmara, p. 248.

43. This paragraph is based on the following documents: Joaquim José Correia (Intendente da Marinha) to Madeira, 15 May 1823; Madeira to Campos, 17 May 1823; Madeira to El-Rey, 31 May 1823; Campos to Junta Provisória, 12 and 17 June 1823; Junta Provisória to Campos, 18 June 1823; and Madeira to El-Rey, aboard the Constituição, 21 July 1823, all of which are in AHM, 2ª Div., 1ª Sec., Cx. 39, No. 1-1, Cx. 40, Nos. 1 and 1-1, and Cx. 41, No. 4, and Campos to Madeira, 29 June 1823, AHU, Bahia, Avulsos, Cx. 266, Doc. 80. Printed versions of most of them are available in Amaral, História da Independência, pp. 361–362, 415–422, 426–430, and 472–473.

44. Relação dos navios de guerra e transportes em que se devem embarcar as tropas da Divisão, familias, e officiaes avulsos, 26 June 1823, AHU, Bahia, Avulsos, Cx. 266, Doc. 80; Copia do termo feito abordo do navio Conde de Palma, 6 July 1823, and Campos to Conde de Subserra, 10 Sept. 1823, AHU, Bahia, Avulsos, Cx. 266, Doc. 85, and Doc. 118; Relação dos officiais do [2º Batalhão do Regimento de

Infantaria No. 12] e familias para serem pagos das comedorias que vencerão como embarcados da Bahia à cidade de Lisboa, 19 Nov. 1823, AHM, 2ª Div., 1ª Sec., Cx. 36, No. 9.

45. Staff summary of correspondence, Portuguese Minister of Foreign Affairs to Minister of War, Lisbon, 14 Nov. 1823, in Amaral, *História da Independência*, pp. 469-470; Campos to Conde Subserra, 10 Sept. 1823, AHU, Bahia, Avulsos, Cx. 266, Doc. 118; Cochrane quoted by Graham [Lady Maria Calcott], *Journal*, p. 259.

46. Almeida, *Relatorio*, p. 28. On the number of troops entering the city, see Silva, *Memórias históricas*, 4: 59n. On the total number of troops on the Brazilian side in early April 1823, see ibid., 4: 41n, but I assume those stationed at other points of the Recôncavo did not enter the city.

47. Mappa demonstrativo do numero de alqueires dos differentes generos que pagarão a contribuição e o rendimento, a despeza, e o liquido, e teve principio em 9 de setembro de 1785 até 31 de maio de 1849, APEB, M. 1611; Câmara, Edital, 23 July 1823, AMS, 116.6, fols. 77v-78v.

CHAPTER 9

1. On members of the advisory committee see Abaixo assinado, 9 May 1823, AHM, 2ª Div., 1ª Sec., Cx. 41, No. 5 (a printed version with several omitted or truncated names is in Braz Hermenegildo do Amaral, *História da independência na Bahia*, 2nd ed., Marajoara, no. 19 [Salvador: Livraria Progresso, 1957], p. 354); Catherine Lugar, "The Merchant Community of Salvador, Bahia, 1780-1830" (Ph.D. diss., State University of New York at Stony Brook, 1980), pp. 169, 179, 190; Junta Provisória to Campos, 18 June 1823, AHM, 2ª Div., 1ª Sec., Cx. 40, No. 1-1; entry for Antonio Bernardo Pereira de Carvalho in Joaqum José de Carvalho, Conta da despesa que fiz na dispensa no mez de agosto de 1821, 16 Dec. 1821, ASCM, Pacote 224; Inv., Rosa Maria de Jesus (wife of Manoel José dos Santos), 1808-1811, APEB, SJ, 01/269/514/02, fols. 4-5v, 10-11, 14-15v; Câmara to Governador, 25 Nov. 1809, APEB, CP, M. 127; Inv., Joanna Maria da Conceição, 1816, APEB, SJ, 04/1715/2185/01, fol. 37. The attitude of the Portuguese business community was well captured by Francisco de Sierra y Mariscal, "Idéas geraes sobre a revolução do Brazil [*sic*] e suas consequencias," *ABNRJ* 43-44 (1920-1921): 56-57.

2. Madeira to El-Rey, aboard the *Constituição*, 21 July 1823, AHM, 2ª Div., 1ª Sec., Cx. 39, No. 1-1 (also in Braz Hermenegildo do Amaral, *História da Bahia do Império à República* [Salvador: Imp. Oficial do Estado, 1923], p. xvi); *Idade d'Ouro do Brasil*, no. 94 (1822), in Maria Beatriz Nizza da Silva, *A primeira gazeta da Bahia: "Idade d'Ouro do Brasil"* (São Paulo and Brasília: Cultrix and Instituto Nacional do Livro, 1978), pp. 195-96; Joaquim José Correia (Intendente da Marinha) to Minister of the Navy, 19 Dec. 1822, AHU, Bahia, Avulsos, Cx. 264, Doc. 35.

3. Licenças, 27 Jan. 1819, AMS, 88.4, fol. 212; Test., Joaquim José de Oliveira, 25 June 1831, APEB, SJ, Registro de Testamentos (Capital), Liv. 20, fols. 97v-99v, 101, 102; Inv. (2⁰), Joaquim José de Oliveira, 1831-1832, APEB, SJ, 02/875/1344/03, fol. 8; Inv. (1⁰), Joaquim José de Oliveira, 1831, APEB, SJ, 02/748/1213/02, fol. 634.

4. Campos to Governo Provisório, 30 Jan. 1823, AHU, Bahia, Avulsos, Cx. 265, Doc. 19.

5. Câmara, Editaes, 14 and 21 May 1823, AMS, 116.6, fols. 69v–70v; Madeira to Junta Provisória, 23 June 1823, AHU, Bahia, Avulsos, Cx. 266, Doc. 74.

6. Entry for 16 May 1823 in [Francisco da Silva Barros], Chronica dos Acontecimentos da Bahia, 1809–1828, BN/SM, II-33, 25, 53, Doc. 1, fol. 33 (for a printed version see [Francisco da Silva Barros], "Chronica dos acontecimentos da Bahia, 1809–1828," *Anais do Arquivo Público do Estado da Bahia* 26 [1938]: 79–80); Junta Provisória to Madeira, 12 June 1823, AHU, Bahia, Avulsos, Cx. 266, Doc. 17.

7. Junta Provisória to Câmara, 9 Oct. 1822, AMS, 111.5, fol. 254.

8. On Portuguese deserters, see Madeira to El-Rey, 28 Nov. 1822, AHU, Bahia, Avulsos, Cx. 263, Doc. 73; Madeira to El-Rey, aboard the *Constituição*, 21 July 1823, AHM, 2ª Div., 1ª Sec., Cx. 39, No. 1-1 (also in Amaral, *História da Bahia*, p. xvi); Campos to Madeira, 29 June 1823, and Campos to Conde de Subserra, n.p. [Lisbon?], 10 Sept. 1823, both at AHU, Bahia, Avulsos, Cx. 266, Docs. 80 and 118.

9. Manoel da Cunha Menezes to MI, 21 Oct. 1826, quoted by João José Reis and Eduardo Silva, *Negociação e conflito: A resistência negra no Brasil escravista* (São Paulo: Companhia das Letras, 1989), p. 97; Maria Graham [Lady Maria Calcott], *Journal of a Voyage to Brazil and Residence There During Part of the Years 1821, 1822, 1823* (1824; reprint, New York: Praeger, 1969), pp. 246–247.

10. João José Reis, *Slave Rebellion in Brazil: The Muslim Uprising of 1835 in Bahia*, trans. Arthur Brakel (Baltimore: Johns Hopkins University Press, 1993), p. 41; João José Reis, "Domingos Pereira Sodré: Um sacerdote africano na Bahia oitocentista," *Afro-Ásia*, no. 34 (2006): esp. p. 284; Marco Aurélio A. de Filgueiras Gomes, "Escravismo e cidade: Notas sobre a ocupação da periferia de Salvador no século XIX," *Rua: Revista de Arquitetura e Urbanismo* 3, no. 4–5 (June–Dec. 1990): 16–17.

11. Labatut to Conselho Interino, GHQ at Engenho Novo, 22 Nov. 1822, in Alexandre José Mello Moraes[Pai], *Historia do Brasil-Reino e do Brasil-Imperio*, 2 vols. (Rio de Janeiro: Typ. Pinheiro, 1871–1873), 2: 27; Labatut to MGuerra, 11 Dec. 1822, in Ignacio Accioli de Cerqueira e Silva, *Memórias históricas e políticas da província da Bahia*, 2nd ed., 6 vols., ed. Braz do Amaral (Salvador: Imprensa Oficial do Estado, 1919–1940), 4: 13–14, n. 7; Madeira, Proclamação, 29 Mar. 1822, APEB, M. 2860, cited in João José Reis, "'Nos achamos em campo a tratar da liberdade': A resistência negra no Brasil oitocentista," in *Viagem incompleta: A experiência brasileira (1500–2000)*, [Vol. 1:] *Formação: Histórias*, ed. Carlos Guilherme Mota (São Paulo: SENAC, 2000), p. 251; Madeira to El-Rey, 7 July 1822, BN/SM, 5, 3, 45, Doc. 100; Conselho Interino to Francisco Gomes Brandão Montezuma and Simão Gomes Ferreira Velloso (its delegates to the Rio government), Cachoeira, 16 Dec. 1822, in Moraes [Pai], *Historia do Brasil-Reino*, 2: 42. These events are recounted in Amaral, *História da Independência*, pp. 284–285, although he dates them to December, not November, and counts the women as eighteen, not twenty.

12. Luiz Mott, ed. and trans., "Um documento inédito para a história da Independência," in *1822: Dimensões*, ed. Carlos Guilherme Mota (São Paulo: Perspectiva, 1972), pp. 478–479.

13. Madeira to Junta Provisória, 9 May 1823, in Amaral, *História da Independência*, pp. 358–359; Câmara to El-Rey, 4 June 1823, in Affonso Ruy, *História*

da Câmara Municipal da cidade do Salvador, 2nd ed. (Salvador: Câmara Municipal de Salvador, 1996), p. 247; Madeira to El-Rey, 31 May 1823, and aboard the *Constituição,* 21 July 1823, AHM, 2ª Div., 1ª Sec., Cx. 39, No. 1-1 (also in Amaral, *História da independência,* pp. 415–422); Amaral, *História da Bahia,* p. xvi; and Tobias Monteiro, *História do Império: A elaboração da Independência,* 2nd ed., Reconquista do Brasil, n.s., no. 39–40 [Belo Horizonte and São Paulo: Itatiaia and EDUSP, 1981], p. 582).

14. Marcus J. M. Carvalho, "Os negros armados pelos brancos e suas independências no Nordeste (1817–1848)," in *Independência: História e historiografia,* ed. Istvan Jancsó (São Paulo: HUCITEC and FAPESP, 2005), pp. 897–98, 912–13. On postwar unrest see Moraes [Pai], *Historia do Brasil-Reino,* vol. 2, passim; and João José Reis and Hendrik Kraay, "'The Tyrant Is Dead!' The Revolt of the Periquitos in Bahia, 1824," *Hispanic American Historical Review* 89, no. 3 (Aug. 2009): 399–434.

15. Manuel Ferreira Gomes, Petition [to Conselho Interino], n.p., n.d., APEB, CP, Cx. 322; Inv., José Gomes da Costa, 1824, APEB, SJ, 04/1783/2253/09, fol. 23; Decisão, 30 July 1823, in Brazil, *Collecção das decisões do governo do Imperio do Brasil,* 1823, no. 113 Império; MI, Portaria, 10 Jan. 1824, in Amaral, *História da Independência,* p. 292. On the practice generally, see Hendrik Kraay, "'The Shelter of the Uniform': The Brazilian Army and Runaway Slaves, 1800–1888," *Journal of Social History* 29, no. 3 (March 1996): 637–657.

16. Governo Provisório, Bando, 6 Aug. 1823, in Amaral, *História da Independência,* pp. 293–294; newspaper quoted by Isabel Cristina Ferreira dos Reis, *Histórias de vida familiar e afetiva de escravos na Bahia do século XIX* (Salvador: Centro de Estudos Baianos, 2001), p. 92. On fear of slaves among whites, see Albert Roussin to French Navy Minister, 17 July 1822, in Kátia M. de Queirós Mattoso, ed., "Albert Roussin: Testemunha das lutas pela independência da Bahia (1822)," *Anais do Arquivo [Público] do Estado da Bahia* 41 (1973): 140. Also see Hendrik Kraay, "'Em outra coisa não falavam os pardos, cabras, e crioulos': O 'recrutamento' de escravos na guerra da Independência na Bahia," *Revista Brasileira de História* 22, no. 43 (2002): 109–126. On the situation in Spanish America, see Richard Graham, *Independence in Latin America: A Comparative Approach* (New York: McGraw-Hill, 1994), pp. 148–149.

17. Coronel Commandante to Miguel Calmon du Pin e Almeida, São Francisco do Conde, 15 Nov. 1822, and Commandante to Secretario do Conselho Interino, Santo Amaro, 18 Nov. 1822, both at BN/SM, I-31, 6, 3, Docs. 45 and 60; Antonio Maria da Silva Torres to Conselho Interino, Quartel de Saubara, 4 Dec. 1822, quoted in Moraes [Pai], *Historia do Brasil-Reino,* 2: 36 (also see p. 42); Miguel Calmon du Pin e Almeida (Marquês de Abrantes), *Relatorio dos trabalhos do Conselho Interino do governo da Provincia da Bahia, 1823,* 2nd ed. (Rio de Janeiro: Typ. do "Jornal do Commercio," 1923), p. 32.

18. Madeira to Joaquim José Correia (Intendente da Marinha), 28 May 1823, in Amaral, *História da Independência,* p. 472; Câmara to Almotacé, 4 June 1823, AMS, 116.6, fol. 71v.

19. Conselho Interino da Bahia, Portaria, Cachoeira, 10 Mar. 1823; Conselho Interino, À todas as autoridades, Cachoeira, 14 Mar. 1823; Conselho Interino, Portaria, Cachoeira, 24 Mar. 1823; and Conselho Interino, Portaria, Cachoeira,

22 Apr. 1823, all at BN/SM, I-7, 2, 26, Docs. 420, 449, 529, and 650, fols. 127v, 137v–138, 163v–165, and 212v. Copies of most of this correspondence were enclosed in Conselho Interino to José Bonifácio, Cachoeira, 16 Apr. 1823, AN, SPE, IJJ⁹329, and many of the documents sent to Bonifácio (cited here and hereafter) are printed in Raul Lima, ed., *A Junta Governativa da Bahia e a Independência* (Rio de Janeiro: Arquivo Nacional, 1973).

20. Capitão Comandante das Ordenanças, Passaporte, Quartel de São Gonçalo [São Francisco do Conde], 4 Mar. 1823, and Declaration, 8 Apr. 1823, both enclosed in José Ferreira de Carvalho to Conselho Interino, n.p. [Nazaré], n.d. [Apr. 1823], APEB, CP, Cx. 322. A similar passport permitted another vessel to leave Ilhéus to go to Rio de Janeiro; Passaporte do Hiate Lanuta, Cachoeira, 26 Feb. 1824 [1823], BN/SM, I-7, 2, 26, Doc. 361, fol. 105.

21. Ignacio de Faria Andrade to Conselho Interino, São José da Barra do Rio das Contas [Itacaré], 17 Oct. 1822, APEB, CP, Cx. 315, unnum. cód., Doc. 8. On the common practice among *juizes ordinários* of taking turns, see Patricia Ann Aufderheide, "Order and Violence: Social Deviance and Social Control in Brazil, 1780–1840" (Ph.D. diss., University of Minnesota, 1976), p. 266.

22. Francisco Xavier de Figueiredo and others to Secretario do Conselho Interino, Valença, 8 Oct. 1822, BN/SM, I-31, 6, 1, Doc. 12; Junta Provisória to Câmara de S. Mateus, 26 Nov. 1822, AN, SPE, IJJ⁹329 (for a printed version see Lima, *Junta Governativa*, p. 267).

23. Junta Provisória to Câmara de S. Mateus, Salvador, 26 Nov. 1822, AN, SPE, IJJ⁹329; Madeira to El-Rey, 23 Dec. 1822, and Junta Provisória to Felipe Ferreira de Araujo e Castro, 8 Oct. 1822, both at AHU, Bahia, Avulsos, Cx. 264, Doc. 35, and Cx. 262, Doc. 36.

24. Conselho Interino to Antonio Francisco Dias, Cachoeira, 18 Dec. 1822, BN/SM, 9, 2, 30, Doc. 239, fols. 78–79.

25. On Labatut's effort to free slaves for the war, see Labatut to Conselho Interino, GHQ at Engenho Novo, 30 Dec. 1822, in Moraes [Pai], *Historia do Brasil-Reino*, 2: 48; Labatut, Declaration, Cangurungú, 3 Apr. 1823, and Conselho Interino to Câmara of Maragogipe, Cachoeira, 8 Apr. 1823, both in Amaral, *História da Independência*, pp. 291–292; Kraay, *Race, State, and Armed Forces*, p. 128; Kraay, "'Em outra coisa não falavam'," passim. See also "O batalhão dos libertos," in Edison (de Souza) Carneiro, comp., *Antologia do negro brasileiro* (Rio de Janeiro: Edições de Ouro, 1967), pp. 163–164.

26. Manoel Diogo de Sá Barreto e Aragão to Conselho Interino, São Francisco do Conde, 13 June 1823, BN/SM, II-33, 36, 19; Reis and Silva, *Negociação e conflito*, pp. 92–98; Kraay, "'Em outra coisa não falavam'," p. 110.

27. Antonio Joaquim Pires de Carvalho e Albuquerque to Labatut, n.p. [Santo Amaro], n.d. [just before 17 Nov. 1822], BN/SM, I-31, 6, 3, Doc. 53 (also found in Moraes [Pai], *Historia do Brasil-Reino*, 2: 27); Commissão da Caixa Militar to [Conselho Interino], Nazaré, 6 Jan. 1823, BN/SM, II-31, 35, 1, Doc. 5. A similar charge was made by Conselho Interino to Francisco Gomes Brandão Montezuma and Simão Gomes Ferreira Velloso (emissaries in Rio), Cachoeira, 16 Dec. 1822, in Moraes [Pai], *Historia do Brasil-Reino*, 2: 42.

28. Jacques Guinebeau (French consul) to [?], 22 May 1822, quoted by Reis and Silva, *Negociação e conflito*, p. 93.

CHAPTER 10

1. Carta Régia de 7 de março de 1810, in José Luís Cardoso, ed., *A economia política e os dilemas do império luso-brasileiro (1790–1822)* (Lisbon: Comissão Nacional para as Comemorações dos Descobrimentos Portugueses, 2001), p. 204, italics added.

2. Candido Mendes de Almeida, ed., *Codigo Philippino; ou, Ordenações e leis do reino de Portugal recopiladas por mandado d'el rei D. Philippe I . . .* (Rio de Janeiro: Instituto Philomathico, 1870), Liv. I, Tit. 66, Preamble; Governador to Câmara, 7 Sept. 1785, copy encl. in Câmara to PP-BA, 14 Apr. 1845, APEB, CP, M. 1399, 1845, Doc. 19. On Spanish American city councils see Jay Kinsbruner, *The Colonial Spanish-American City: Urban Life in the Age of Atlantic Capitalism* (Austin: University of Texas Press, 2005), p. 40.

3. Raymond de Roover, "The Concept of the Just Price: Theory and Economic Policy," *Journal of Economic History* 18, no. 4 (Dec. 1958): 426–429; de Roover, "Scholastic Economics: Survival and Lasting Influence from the Sixteenth Century to Adam Smith," *Quarterly Journal of Economics* 69, no. 2 (May 1955): 179, 184, 186; Henri Pirenne, *Medieval Cities: Their Origin and the Revival of Trade*, trans. Frank D. Halsey (Garden City, NY: Doubleday, 1925), p. 148; Steven L. Kaplan, *Provisioning Paris: Merchants and Millers in the Grain and Flour Trade During the Eighteenth Century* (Ithaca, NY: Cornell University Press, 1984), pp. 25–26, 594; E. P. Thompson, "The Moral Economy of the English Crowd in the Eighteenth Century," *Past & Present*, no. 50 (Feb. 1971): 83–88, 94–107. See also Adam Smith, *An Inquiry Into the Nature and Causes of the Wealth of Nations*, 6th[?] ed., ed. Edwin Cannan (Chicago: University of Chicago Press, 1976), 2: 35 and 40 [Bk. 4, Chap. 5].

4. Three examples of prevailing notions about "monopolists" are: Governador to Câmara, 7 Sept. 1785, copy encl. in Câmara to PP-BA, 14 Apr. 1845, APEB, CP, M. 1399, 1845, Doc. 19; Capitão Mor de Sergipe to Governador da Bahia, Estância, 9 Mar. 1808, APEB, Cartas do Governo à várias autoridades, vol. 210, fol. 23v, quoted by Kátia M. de Queirós Mattoso, "Conjoncture et société au Brésil a la fin du XVIIIᵉ siècle: Prix et salaires à la veille de la Révolution des Alfaiates, Bahia, 1798," *Cahiers des Ameriques Latines* 5 (1970): 40, n. 29; and PP-BA to Presidente da Província de Pernambuco, 13 May 1834, encl. in PP-BA to MI, 1 Aug. 1834, AN, SPE, IJJ⁹337. These understandings were widespread in premodern societies; Steven L. Kaplan, *Bread, Politics and Political Economy in the Reign of Louis XV*, 2 vols. continuously paged (The Hague: Martinus Nijhoff, 1976), 2: 516; F. J. Fisher, "The Development of the London Food Market, 1540–1640," *Economic History Review* 5, no. 2 (Apr. 1935): 63; John Bohstedt, *Riots and Community Politics in England and Wales, 1790–1810* (Cambridge, MA: Harvard University Press, 1983), p. 238, n. 72; Peter T. Bauer, *West African Trade: A Study of Competition, Oligopoly, and Monopoly in a Changing Economy* (Cambridge, Eng.: Cambridge University Press, 1954), p. 9; Enrique Florescano, "El abasto y la legislación de granos en el siglo XVI," *Historia Mexicana* 14, no. 4 (Apr.–June 1965): 610.

5. Here too Brazil was far from unique; see, for example, Kaplan, *Provisioning Paris*, p. 205; Rebecca Horn, "Testaments and Trade: Interethnic Ties Among Petty Traders in Central Mexico (Coyoacan, 1550–1620)," in *Dead Giveaways:*

Indigenous Testaments of Colonial Mesoamerica and the Andes, ed. Susan Kellogg and Matthew Restall (Salt Lake City: University of Utah Press, 1998), p. 73; Fernando Iwasaki Cauti, "Ambulantes y comercio colonial: Iniciativas mercantiles en el virreinato peruano," *Jahrbuch für Geschichte von Staat, Wirtschaft und Gesellschaft Lateinamerikas* 24 (1987): 185. This hostility appears even today in many places; on Spanish America see R. J. Bromley and Richard Symanski, "Marketplace Trade in Latin America," *Latin American Research Review* 9, no. 3 (Fall 1974): 9. Some U.S. historians seem to share this hostility; for example, Kinsbruner, *Colonial Spanish-American City,* p. 76.

6. Almeida, *Codigo Philippino,* Liv. V, Tit. 76, prologue and Arts. 4–5; law dated 2 Oct. 1704 in ANTT, Manuscritos do Brasil, Liv. 26, cited by Luiz Mott, "Subsídios à história do pequeno comércio no Brasil," *Revista de História,* no. 105 (1976): 96 (also referred to by Luís dos Santos Vilhena, *A Bahia no século XVIII,* 2nd ed., ed. Braz do Amaral, intro. by Edison Carneiro [Salvador: Itapuã, 1969], p. 159); Governador to Câmara, 6 July 1723, and Governador to Juiz de Fora, 28 July 1724, in Biblioteca Nacional do Rio de Janeiro, *Documentos Históricos* (Rio de Janeiro: Biblioteca Nacional, 1928–1960), 87: 186, 200.

7. Governador to Câmara, 15 Sept. 1785, copy encl. in Câmara to PP-BA, 14 Apr. 1845, APEB, CP, M. 1399, 1845, Doc. 19. Hoarding and the creation of monopolies or oligopolies were often alleged and condemned as well in other places and at other times; see, for example, John C. Super, *Food, Conquest, and Colonization in Sixteenth-Century Spanish America* (Albuquerque: University of New Mexico Press, 1988), pp. 30, 45; Eric Van Young, *Hacienda and Market in Eighteenth-Century Mexico: The Rural Economy of the Guadalajara Region, 1675–1820* (Berkeley: University of California Press, 1981), p. 93; Karen J. Friedmann, "Victualling Colonial Boston," *Agricultural History* 47, no. 3 (July 1973): 192; Mario Augusto da Silva Santos, "Sobrevivência e tensões sociais: Salvador (1890–1930)" (Ph.D. diss., Universidade de São Paulo, 1982), pp. 270–274.

8. De Roover, "Concept of the Just Price," pp. 425, 427–428; de Roover, "Scholastic Economics," p. 186; Craig Muldrew, *The Economy of Obligation: The Culture of Credit and Social Relations in Early Modern England* (London and New York: Macmillan and St. Martin's, 1998), pp. 47–48; Sidney Webb and Beatrice Webb, "The Assize of Bread," *Economic Journal* 14 (June 1904): 196n, 199–201, 217–218; Thompson, "Moral Economy," pp. 107–115; Friedmann, "Victualling Colonial Boston," p. 193. On Spain and Spanish America see Antonio Fernández García, *El abastecimiento de Madrid en el reinado de Isabel II,* intro. by Vicente Palacio Atard, Biblioteca de Estudios Madrileños, no. 14 (Madrid: Instituto de Estudios Madrileños, 1971), pp. 35–36; Raymond L. Lee, "Grain Legislation in Colonial Mexico, 1575–1585," *Hispanic American Historical Review* 27, no. 4 (Nov. 1947): 651–653 (but cf. Irene Vasquez de Warman, "El pósito y la ahóndiga en la Nueva España," *Historia Mexicana* 17, no. 3 [Jan.–Mar. 1968]: 412); Ward Barrett, "The Meat Supply of Colonial Cuernavaca," *Annals of the Association of American Geographers* 64, no. 4 (Dec. 1974): 539–540; Van Young, *Hacienda and Market,* p. 43; Iwasaki Cauti, "Ambulantes y comercio colonial," p. 191; and Kinsbruner, *Colonial Spanish-American City,* pp. 40, 74, 77.

9. Regimento do Governador Geral do Brasil, Tomé de Sousa, 17 Dec. 1548, AHU, Cód. 112, fol. 4v, and [royal order] 5 Apr. 1706, ANTT, Manuscritos do Bra-

sil, Liv. 26, both quoted in Mott, "Subsídios à história do pequeno comércio," pp. 93 and 96–97; Almeida, *Codigo Philippino*, Liv. I, Tit. 66, par. 32, 34, and 34, nn. 1 and 3; Governador to Câmara, [?] Jan. 1701, in Biblioteca Nacional do Rio de Janeiro, *Documentos Históricos*, 87: 36.

10. Câmara to Governador, 17 June 1780, AMS, 111.4, fol. 56; Governador to Câmara, 10 Mar. 1807, AMS, 111.5, fol. 18v; Câmara, Edital, 23 July 1823 [?], AMS, 116.6, fol. 81. References to *forminas* or *fulminas* (also spelt *furmina* and even *formiga*) pepper the documents, but this word does not appear in dictionaries of the epoch or since. The word *fulmina* was referred to as a "phrase of this region" in "Commodidades que o marechal de campo graduado Luiz Paulino de Oliveira Pinto da França offerece para o estabelecimento de uma feira," quoted in full in "Decreto," 9 Aug. 1819, LB, 1819, par. 9 (another version of this decree, presumably printed at that time, uses *formiga*: António d'Oliveira Pinto da França, ed., *Cartas baianas, 1821–1824: Subsídios para o estudo dos problemas da opção na independência brasileira*, Brasiliana no. 372 [São Paulo: Editora Nacional, 1980], p. 165). There is possibly a connection to the verb *fulminar*, which, besides meaning to fulminate, also came to mean "to scheme . . . to work astutely to do harm [machinar, ... obrar astutamente para fazer mal]" (Antonio de Moraes Silva, *Diccionario da lingua portugueza*, 8th ed. [Rio de Janeiro: Empreza Litteraria Fluminense de A. A. da Silva Lobo, 1889]); also see Rafael Bluteau, *Diccionario da lingua portugueza*, rev. Antonio de Moraes Silva (Lisbon: Simão Thaddeo Ferreira, 1789), s.v. *fulminar*. Alternatively, the word may derive from the French *fornir*, to supply, to fatten, to make corpulent—that is, to engross. The fact that it was occasionally spelt *formiga*—that is, "ant"—suggests a possible connection to a seventeenth-century belief in Spain that ants are the reincarnation of greedy hoarders; Sebastián de Covarrubias Orozco, *Tesoro de la lengua castellana o española* [1611], 2nd rev. ed., ed. Felipe C. R. Maldonado (Madrid: Editorial Castalia, 1995) (I owe this information to Richard Flint). In eighteenth-century Portugal an antlike thief (*ladrão formigueiro*) was a petty thief who stole small things.

11. Câmara to Governador, 21 June 1809 and enclosures, APEB, CP, M. 127; Câmara to Admin. do Curral, n.d. [Aug. 1805], AMS, 116.5, fol. 2; Câmara to Governador, 18 Feb. 1809, APEB, CP, M. 127. On selling by the piece, see Câmara to Governador, 7 Nov. 1792, and 22 Dec. 1792, APEB, CP, M. 201-14, Docs. 25 and 27. In 1488 a city ordinance in Madrid also made a distinction between selling meat by the piece and selling it by weight, with only the latter being subject to price controls; Antonio Matilla Tascón, *Abastecimiento de carne a Madrid (1477–1678)*, Colección Biblioteca de Estudios Madrileños, no. 26 (Madrid: Instituto de Estudios Madrileños, 1994), p. 51.

12. Governador (Interino) to Câmara, 10 Apr. 1810; Governador to Câmara, 9 Mar. 1821; and Junta Provisória to Câmara, 2 Nov. 1821, AMS, 111.5, fols. 82, 227, 234; Jourdan, Breve noticia, fol. 42v; Joaquim José da Silva Maia (Procurador da Câmara) to Câmara, n.d. [1820 or 1821], BN/SM, I-31, 14, 3; and Câmara, Edital, 31 Mar. 1821, AMS, 116.6, fol. 53v.

13. Câmara to Governador, 29 Oct. 1800, AMS, 111.4, fol. 176v; Posturas nos. 25 and 26, approved 25 Feb. 1831, AMS, 119.5, fol. 18.

14. Almeida, *Codigo Philippino*, Liv. I, Tit. 18, par. 28, 41ff.; Atas do Conselho Geral, 1 Apr. 1830, APEB, SL, 197, fol. 83; Câmara to Governador, 6 June 1787 and

29 Oct. 1800, AMS, III.4, fols. 118 and 175; Câmara to Governador, 29 Oct. 1800, AMS, III.4, fol. 175v.

15. Postura no. 11, Posturas do Senado da Câmara [1716] . . . fielmente copiadas . . . 1785, AN, SH, Cód. 90, fol. 4v.; Câmara to Governador, 25 Oct. 1800, AMS, III.4, fol. 176; Correição feita no sitio do Forte de S. Pedro, 26 June 1780, AMS, 45.2, fol. 198v.

16. Câmara, Postura, 15 Nov. 1785, AMS, 119.1, fol. 123; Posturas 19, 24, 113, 115, and two unnumbered ones in Posturas do Senado da Câmara [1716] . . . fielmente copiadas . . . 1785, AN, SH, Cód. 90, fols. 5–6, 17, 28v, and 31; Correição feita no sítio do Forte de S. Pedro, 26 June 1780, AMS, 45.2, fol. 198v; Câmara to Governador, 29 Oct. 1800, AMS, III.4, fol. 176v; Almeida, *Codigo Philippino*, Liv. I, Tit. 18, par. 28, 36, 38, 43, and 50; Vilhena, *Bahia no século XVIII*, 1: 73, 132.

17. Requerimento dos lanxeiros da Villa de Camamu, encl. in Governador to Câmara, 5 Oct. 1801, AMS, Correspondência do Governo, uncat. (a similar complaint was lodged five years later in Francisco de Faria to Governador, n.d. [after 12 Nov. 1806], presumably sent to the Câmara but now separated from the covering letter; AMS, Correspondência do Governo, uncat.); Antonio Xavier da Silveira (almotacel) to Câmara, 30 May 1807, quoted in João José Reis and Márcia Gabriela D. de Aguiar, "'Carne sem osso e farinha sem caroço': O motim de 1858 contra a carestia na Bahia," *Revista de História*, no. 135 (2° semestre 1996): 152.

18. Francisco Carlos Teixeira da Silva, "A morfologia da escassez: Crises de subsistência e política econômica no Brasil colônia (Salvador e Rio de Janeiro, 1680–1790)" (Ph.D. diss., Universidade Federal Fluminense, 1990), p. 315. This was also the understanding elsewhere; Kaplan, *Provisioning Paris*, p. 36, and Super, *Food, Conquest*, pp. 39–40. Also see de Roover, "Scholastic Economics," pp. 162–163.

19. Alvará, 21 Feb. 1765, in Antonio Delgado da Silva, *Collecção da legislação portuguesa desde a ultima compilação das ordenações . . .* , 2nd ed. (Lisbon: Typ. L. C. da Cunha and Typ. Maigrense, 1833–1858), 2: 151 (the first edition had, through a printer's error, misdated this Alvará to 20 Feb. 1765; see index to second edition). In the 1780s the High Court in Salvador specifically noted that this decree did not apply there; Representação a S.M.R. dos vivandeiros e conductores de mantimentos, 25 Jan. 1798, BN/SM, II-33, 25, 52, fol. 131v.

20. Kaplan, *Bread, Politics*, 1: xxvii–xxviii, 97–163 (esp. 90–95, 101–106, 126–144, and 113–116), 405–407, 552, and 2: 660–664, 670; Kaplan, *Provisioning Paris*, pp. 170–171, 595–598. Similar measures were adopted in Spain in 1765; John Lynch, "The Origins of Spanish American Independence," in *The Cambridge History of Latin America*, ed. Leslie Bethell (Cambridge, Eng.: Cambridge University Press, 1985), 3: 4. Also see Fernández García, *Abastecimiento de Madrid*, esp. pp. ix–x, 35–36.

21. Edwin Cannan, "Introduction," in Smith, *Wealth of Nations*, 1: xxiv–liii, esp. xxxv–xxxvii. Smith acknowledges the work of the French physiocrats while arguing with them; 2: 182–183, 193, 195ff., 199–200, and 207–208. On combinations among employers, see 1: 74–76.

22. Rodrigo de Souza Coutinho to João Paulo Bezerra [Lisbon, 1778], in Andrée Mansuy-Diniz Silva, *Portrait d'un homme d'etat: D. Rodrigo de Souza Coutinho, Comte de Linhares, 1755–1812*, 2 vols. (Lisbon and Paris: Fundação Calouste

Gulbenkian and Centre Culturel Calouste Gulbenkian, 2003–2006), 1: 651 (also see pp. 118 and 243). Besides relying on this work, this paragraph is based on Cardoso, "Nas malhas do império"; Kenneth Maxwell, *Conflicts and Conspiracies: Brazil and Portugal, 1750–1808*, Cambridge Latin American Studies, no. 16 (Cambridge, Eng.: Cambridge University Press, 1973), pp. 179, 206–207, 230–235; and Lúcia Maria Bastos P[ereira das] Neves, "Intelectuais brasileiros no oitocentos: A constituição de uma 'família' sob a proteção do poder imperial (1821–1838)," in *O estado como vocação: Idéias e práticas políticas no Brasil oitocentista*, ed. Maria Emília Prado (Rio de Janeiro: Access, 1999), pp. 9–32.

23. Quotations are from original sources quoted in Cardoso, "Nas malhas do império," pp. 79–83, 94, 98, 99, 103; and in Cardoso, ed., *A economia política e os dilemas do império luso-brasileiro (1790–1822)* (Lisbon: Comissão Nacional para as Comemorações dos Descobrimentos Portugueses, 2001), 204–207. I have also drawn on Antonio Penalves Rocha, "A economia política na desagregação do império português," in ibid., p. 154. On Adam Smith's influence upon Souza Coutinho, see António Almodovar and José Luís Cardoso, *A History of Portuguese Economic Thought* (London and New York: Routledge, 1998), pp. 49–50.

24. José da Silva Lisboa, "'Carta muito interessante do advogado da Bahia . . . para Domingos Vandelli, Bahia, 18 de outubro de 1781,' in Eduardo de Castro e Almeida, Inventario dos documentos relativos ao Brasil existentes no Archivo de Marinha e Ultramar, Part II (Bahia, 1763–1786)," *ABNRJ* 32 (1910): 494–506.

25. Decreto, 23 Feb. 1808, copy in José da Silva Lisboa, Petition, Rio, 28 Mar. 1808 (a printed version is in Cardoso, *Economia política*, p. 203); José da Silva Lisboa to [?], [Rio], 24 Aug. 1808; and José da Silva Lisboa, Petition, n.d., [Rio], all at AN, AP 1 (Fundo Visc. de Cairu), Cx. 1, Pasta 1, Docs. 3, 1, and 5. On his life see Antonio Paim, *Cairu e o liberalismo económico* (Rio de Janeiro: Tempo Brasileiro, 1968), pp. 23–38; António Almodovar, "Processos de difusão e institucionalização da economia política no Brasil," in *A economia política e os dilemas do império Luso-Brasileiro (1790–1822)*, ed. José Luís Cardoso (Lisbon: Comissão Nacional para as Comemorações dos Descobrimentos Portugueses, 2001), pp. 122–123, 132–134, 137–142; and the introduction by Fernando Antônio Novais and José Jobson de Andrade Arruda to José da Silva Lisboa [Visconde de Cairu], *Observações sobre a franqueza da indústria, e estabelecimento de fábricas no Brasil* (Brasília: Senado Federal, 1999), pp. 9–29. On the importance of Silva Lisboa's *Princípios de economia política* see Rocha, "Economia política," p. 153. On his opposition to the physiocrats also see Cardoso, *O pensamento económico em Portugal nos finais do século XVIII, 1780–1808* (Lisbon: Editorial Estampa, 1989), pp. 289–290. On the ethical or moral thought that restrained his full adoption of a Smithian outlook, see Guilherme Pereira das Neves, "As Máximas do Marquês: Moral e política na trajetória de Mariano José da Fonseca," in *Retratos do Império: Trajetórias individuais no mundo português nos séculos XVI a XIX*, ed. Ronaldo Vainfas, Georgina Silva dos Santos, and Guilherme Pereira das Neves (Niterói: Editora da Universidade Federal Fluminense, 2006), pp. 300–303. Also see Maria Eugénia Mata, "Economic Ideas and Policies in Nineteenth-Century Portugal," *Luso-Brazilian Review* 39, no. 1 (Summer 2002): 31.

26. In 1809 an English visitor to Salvador noted that "many of the more opulent inhabitants" had in their "scanty libraries" works by European writers, in-

cluding Adam Smith; Andrew Grant, *History of Brazil Comprising a Geographical Account of That Country* . . . (London: Henry Colburn, 1809), p. 230. Also see J. F. Normano, *Brazil: A Study of Economic Types* (Chapel Hill: University of North Carolina Press, 1935), pp. 85–89; Kenneth Maxwell, "The Generation of the 1790s and the Idea of Luso-Brazilian Empire," in *Colonial Roots of Modern Brazil: Papers of the Newberry Library Conference*, ed. Dauril Alden (Berkeley and Los Angeles: University of California Press, 1973), p. 122; and E. Bradford Burns, "The Enlightenment in Two Colonial Brazilian Libraries," *Journal of the History of Ideas* 25, no. 3 (July–Sept. 1964): 435–436.

27. Ribeiro, Discurso, fols. 69, 72. On his background, see Ribeiro, Memoria, fols. 62–62v, and Câmara to Governador, 29 Oct. 1800, AMS, III.4, fol. 177.

28. Ribeiro, Memoria, fol. 61v–62; idem, Discurso, fol. 66; Rodrigo de Souza Coutinho to Fernando José de Portugal, Palácio de Queluz, 4 Oct. 1798, APEB, CP, M. 86, fol. 188v.

29. Abaixo assinado ou requerimento, presented to the Câmara, 8 Feb. 1797, encl. in Câmara to Governador, 4 Mar. 1797, APEB, CP, M. 201-14, Doc. 53. Cf. Smith, *Wealth of Nations*, 2: 41–42 [Bk. 4, Chap. 5].

30. Câmara to Governador, 4 Mar. 1797, APEB, M. 201-14, Doc. 53.

31. Câmara to Governador, 7 Sept. 1799, which quotes Governador to Câmara, 15 Sept. 1797, APEB, CP, M. 201-14, Doc. 65.

32. Representação a S.M.R. dos vivandeiros e conductores de mantimentos, 25 Jan. 1798, BN/SM, II-33, 25, 52, fols. 129–132v (Silva ["Morfologia da escassez," p. 12n] indicates that this representação is also at BN/SM, I-8, 4, 8). As to the document's authorship, see Rodrigo de Souza Coutinho to Fernando José de Portugal, Palacio de Queluz [Lisbon], 24 Sept. 1798, APEB, CP, M. 86, fol. 125, which refers to an enclosed complaint of Ribeiro and the *lancha* owners of Cairu, Boipeba, Camamu, Rio de Contas, and Ilhéus; the enclosed petition is missing, as well as the next four folios, but these missing folios, without Ribeiro's name, are the representação cited above.

33. Governador to Câmara, 16 Nov. 1799, quoted in Câmara, Edital, 11 Jan. 1800, copy encl. in Câmara to Governador, 19 Jan. 1800, APEB, CP, M. 209-1. The date of the order from Souza Coutinho to the governor is given as 11 July 1798 in Câmara, Edital, 11 Mar. 1801, currently filed with Câmara to Governador, 28 Jan. 1801, APEB, CP, M. 209-1; if this date is correct, the governor took more than a year to pass it on to the city council.

34. Câmara to Governador, Salvador, 29 Oct. 1800, AMS, III.4, fols. 173v, 177v, and 176 (a nearly verbatim copy of this letter, but oddly bearing the date 18 Nov. 1808, is in BN/SM, II-33, 24, 40; perhaps it was copied in response to a later complaint of Ribeiro addressed to the prince-regent in Brazil); Câmara, Edital, 11 Mar. 1801, now filed with Câmara to Governador, 28 Jan. 1801, APEB, CP, M. 209-1.

35. Brito, "Carta I," in João Rodrigues de Brito et al., *Cartas economico-politicas sobre a agricultura e commercio da Bahia* (Lisbon: Imp. Nacional, 1821), pp. 2, 74.

36. Ibid., p. 19.

37. Ibid., p. 9.

38. Ibid., pp. 20–21.

39. Ibid., pp. 11–14.

40. Conde da Ponte to Visconde de Anadia, 27 Aug. 1807, AHU, Bahia, Cat. 29.985.

41. On the role of Silva Lisboa in opening the ports of Brazil and the background and effects of this measure, see José Wanderley Pinho [de Araújo], "A abertura dos portos—Cairu," *Revista do Instituto Histórico e Geográfico Brasileiro* 243 (Apr.–June 1959): 94–147, and the many texts he quotes verbatim in his notes. This article is ably summarized by Alan K. Manchester, "The Transfer of the Portuguese Court to Rio de Janeiro," in *Conflict and Continuity in Brazilian Society,* ed. Henry H. Keith and S. F. Edwards (Columbia: University of South Carolina Press, 1969), pp. 164–167. A useful but confusingly written summary of the historiography on this act and its instigators appears in José Honório Rodrigues, *História da história do Brasil,* vol. 2, tomo 1: *A historiografia conservadora,* Brasiliana, Grande Formato, no. 23 (São Paulo and Brasília: Editora Nacional and Instituto Nacional do Livro, 1988), pp. 146–154.

42. Alvará, 21 Feb. 1765, in Silva, *Collecção da legislação portuguesa desde a ultima compilação das ordenações . . . ,* 2: 151; Governador to Câmara, 2 Oct. 1801, quoted in Câmara to Governador, 10 Mar. 1804, APEB, M. 209-1 (a copy is in AMS, 111.4, fol. 195v); Requerimento dos moradores desta Cidade, n.d., encl. in Governador (interino) to Câmara, 20 Oct. 1809, AMS, 111.5, fol. 70.

43. Governador to Câmara, 23 Nov. 1810, 27 Feb. 1812, 27 Sept. 1815, 15 Oct. 1816, and 19 Sept. 1817, AMS, 111.5, fols. 103, 139, 184v, 192v, and 196v; Câmara, Edital, 11 Mar. 1820, AMS, 116.6, fols. 32v–33.

44. *Idade d'Ouro do Brazil,* 23 July 1813, pp. 1–2 (I owe this reference to Hendrik Kraay).

CHAPTER 11

1. Brazil, *Constituição política do Império do Brasil,* Art. 179, par. 22 and 24.

2. Joaquim José da Silva Maia to Junta Provisória, n.d. [between 10 Feb. and 20 Mar. 1821], BN/SM, I-31, 14, 3; the 1824 provision is described in Câmara to PP-BA, 13 July 1825, AMS, 111.6, fols. 193v–194, 196; Edital, 1 July 1826, APEB, M. 1395; Câmara to Admin. do Curral, 27 Sept. 1828, AMS, 116.6, fols. 202v–203; Edital que o Conselho Geral [da Provincia] reputou Postura, 14 Aug. 1829, Art. 8, AMS, 119.5, fol. 6v; Edital, 11 June 1833, AMS, 116.7, fol. 118v; Câmara to PP-BA, 18 June 1839, APEB, CP, M. 1397, 1839, Doc. 20.

3. Edital, 11 June 1833, AMS, 116.7, fol. 118v.

4. Edital, 1 July 1826, APEB, M. 1395 (also found in AMS, 116.6, fols. 142v–143v); Câmara to PP-BA, 13 Sept. 1826, AMS, 111.6, fol. 219v; Proposta de postura de Santo Amaro, quoted in debate of 1 Apr. 1830, Bahia, Conselho Geral, Atas, APEB, SL, M. 197, fol. 74v; and José Joaquim de Almeida e Arnizau, "Memoria topographica, historica, commercial e politica da villa de Cachoeira da provincia da Bahia [1825]," *Revista do Instituto Historico e Geographico Brasileiro* 25 (1862): 130, 134.

5. Inv., Pedro do Espírito Santo, 13 Aug. 1850, APEB, SJ, 04/1624/2093/05, fols. 5–34v, 43, 130–131 (the estate was valued at 239:106$575 [129:117$551]); Admin. do Curral to Câmara, 19 July 1828, Câmara to Admin. do Curral, 19 July

1828, and Câmara to PP-BA, 26 July 1828, all in AMS, 116.6, fols. 189v and 253; Admin. da Campina to Câmara, 18 Feb. 1839, encl. in Câmara to PP-BA, 4 Mar. 1839, APEB, CP, M. 1397, Doc. 6; Câmara to PP-BA, 9 June 1855, AMS, 111.13, fol. 107.

6. Câmara, Sessão ordinaria, 1 Apr. 1841, AMS, 9.44, fol. 37 (I owe this reference to Hendrik Kraay); José Pereira Monteiro to PP-BA, n.d. [before 5 Oct. 1841], APEB, CP, M. 4631.

7. A characteristic also noted in prerevolutionary France; Steven L. Kaplan, *Provisioning Paris: Merchants and Millers in the Grain and Flour Trade During the Eighteenth Century* (Ithaca, NY: Cornell University Press, 1984), p. 215.

8. Lei, 11 July 1821, in *LB* (sometimes this law is referred to as dated 5 July 1821, the date on which it was approved by the Cortes; it was cosigned by the king six days later and published in the *Diario do Governo* on 24 July 1821). For its application in Rio, see Fabricantes de pão, Petition, Rio de Janeiro, 6 Oct. 1821, BN/SM, II-34, 27, 21; "Resolução" of 16 Aug. 1823, repeated in the Provisão da Mesa do Desembargo do Paço, 20 Nov. 1823, in Brazil, *Collecção das decisões do governo do Imperio do Brasil*, 1823, Decisão no. 162; and Maria de Fátima Silva Gouvêa, "Poder, autoridade e o Senado da Câmara do Rio de Janeiro, ca. 1780–1820," *Tempo* 7, no. 13 (July 2002): 147–148. The Rio provisions did not become specifically applicable in all Brazilian cities until 1827; Decreto s. n. [do poder legislativo], 15 Oct. 1827, Brazil, *Collecção das decisões*, 1827.

9. Lei, 20 Oct. 1823, and Lei, 1 Oct. 1828, Art. 66, par. 8–10, in *LB*. Also see the debate in Brazil, Assemblea Geral Constituinte e Legislativa do Imperio do Brasil, *Diario . . . 1823*, facsim. ed. (Brasília: Senado Federal, 1973), 1: 24, 267, 270, 415–416, 483–484, 664–665, 681, 756–761, and 2: 74–79, 99–105, 128–130, and 265.

10. In colonial times the number of butcher shops had varied from 34 in 1797 to 42 by 1807, 48 by 1810, and back to 42 in 1820; Representação dos marchantes, encl. in Câmara to Governador, 13 Sept. 1797, APEB, CP, M. 201-14, Doc. 59; Governador to Câmara, 10 Mar. 1807, AMS, 111.5, fol. 19; Registro dos currais, 1806–1811, AMS, 148.3, fol. 241–242; Joaquim José da Silva Maia (Procurador da Câmara) to Câmara, n.d. [1820 or 1821], BN/SM, I-31, 14, 3. On subsequent numbers see Admin. do Curral to Câmara, 31 July 1830, AMS, Câmara, Correspondência recebida, Curral, 1830, uncat.; and Câmara to PP-BA, 4 Aug. 1836, APEB, M. 1396 (also in AMS, 111.9, fols. 106v–110v). By extrapolating from known censuses, one historian estimates that the city's population increased 30 to 40 percent from 1810 to 1830/1836; Kátia M. de Queirós Mattoso, *Bahia: A cidade de Salvador e seu mercado no século XIX*, Coleção Estudos Brasileiros, no. 12 (São Paulo and Salvador: HUCITEC and Secretaria Municipal de Educação e Cultura, 1978), p. 138.

11. Câmara, Edital, 9 Mar. 1822, AMS, 116.6, fols. 60–60v.

12. Câmara to PP-BA, Salvador, 14 June 1832, AMS, 111.8, fol. 145 (the same phrases are used in Edital, 11 June 1833, AMS, 116.7, fol. 118v); Câmara to PP-BA, 4 Aug. 1836, and Câmara to Assembléia Provincial, 27 Feb. 1836, encl. in ibid., CP, M. 1396 (also in AMS, 111.9, fols. 77–82v, 106v–110v); PP-BA to Câmara, Salvador, 19 Feb. 1834, AMS, 98.1, fol. 97v, referring to a representação (not enclosed) from José Alvares de Sousa.

13. PP-BA to Câmara, 24 [or 23?] Jan. 1833, AMS, 98.1, fol. 35; PP-BA to MI, 8 Nov. 1833, APEB, M. 681, fol. 35.

14. Câmara to Admin. da Campina, 6 Apr. (two letters of this date) and 18 Apr. 1831, AMS, 116.6, fols. 286, 286v, 288; prices reported in Inv. (1⁰), José Caetano de Aquino, 1833, APEB, SJ, 05/2003/2474/03, fol. 48. A succinct account of these political upheavals and their social matrix is presented by João José Reis, *Slave Rebellion in Brazil: The Muslim Uprising of 1835 in Bahia*, trans. Arthur Brakel (Baltimore: Johns Hopkins University Press, 1993), pp. 13–39.

15. Plano de governo pelo systema federativo, MS copy, 27 Apr. 1833, Arts. 11 and 18, AN, SPE, Justiça, IJ¹707 (a printed version can be found in Braz Hermenegildo do Amaral, *História da Bahia do Império à República* [Salvador: Imp. Oficial do Estado, 1923], p. 104); PP-BA to MI, 25 Jan. 1834, AN, SPE, IJJ⁹337; Visconde de Pirajá, Manifesto (printed), addressed to PP-BA and presumably forwarded to MJ, 14 Nov. 1836, AN, SPE, IJ¹708.

16. Câmara to PP-BA, 4 Aug. 1836, APEB, M. 1396 (also in AMS, 111.9, fols. 106v–110v); Câmara to PP-BA, 16 Mar. 1837, AMS, 111.9, fols. 150–150v.

17. Câmara to PP-BA, 19 Sept., 28 Sept., and 13 Oct. 1837, APEB, CP, M. 1396 (copies of these letters with slightly different dates are in AMS, 111.9, fols. 182–183, 187–190v, and 191–192); PP-BA to Câmara, 23 Sept. and 4 Oct. 1837, AMS, 111.10, fols. 28, and 30.

18. PP-BA to Câmara, 16 Oct. 1837, AMS, 111.10, fol. 32v; Câmara, Annuncio, 25 Oct. 1837, AMS, 116.8, fols. 239v–240; Câmara to PP-BA, 16 May 1838, AMS, 111.9, fol. 207v. On the threat of a food riot, see Felix da Graça P. Lisboa to Chefe de Polícia, 3 Sept. 1837, APEB, M. 3139-9, quoted in João José Reis and Márcia Gabriela D. de Aguiar, "'Carne sem osso e farinha sem caroço': O motim de 1858 contra a carestia na Bahia," *Revista de História*, no. 135 (2⁰ semestre 1996): 154.

19. Acta (printed), 7 Nov. 1837, AN, SPE, IJ¹708; Manifesto (MS), 7 Nov. 1837, encl. in Albino José Barbosa de Oliveira (Juiz de Direito) to MJ, Caravellas, 2 Jan. 1838, AN, SPE, IJ¹708. The reference is to the resignation of Diogo Antônio Feijó and his substitution by Pedro de Araújo Lima as Brazil's regent.

20. Manifesto, 7 Nov. 1837, encl. in Albino José Barbosa de Oliveira (Juiz de Direito) to MJ, Caravellas, 2 Jan. 1838, AN, SPE, IJ¹708. For the traditional interpretation see, for example, José Wanderley Pinho [de Araújo], "A Bahia, 1808–1856," in *História geral da civilização brasileira*, ed. Sérgio Buarque de Holanda (São Paulo: Difusão Européia do Livro, 1964), pp. 282–284; and Roderick J. Barman, *Brazil: The Forging of a Nation, 1798–1852* (Stanford, CA: Stanford University Press, 1988), pp. 195–197. For the newer interpretation consult Paulo César Souza, *A Sabinada: A revolta separatista da Bahia* (São Paulo: Brasiliense, 1987), passim; and Hendrik Kraay, "'As Terrifying as Unexpected': The Bahian Sabinada, 1837–1838," *Hispanic American Historical Review* 72, no. 4 (Nov. 1992): 501–527. On the racial makeup of the revolutionaries, also see João Francisco Cabassu to José Martiniano de Alencar, [Salvador?], 11 Apr. 1838, in "Correspondência passiva do Senador José Martiniano de Alencar," *ABNRJ* 86 (1966): 331; Robert Dundas, *Sketches of Brazil Including New Views of Tropical and European Fever* . . . (London: John Churchill, 1852), p. 395; George Gardner, *Travels in the Interior of Brazil* . . . (1846; reprint, Boston: Milford House, 1973), p. 78; Robert Avé-Lallemant, *Viagens pelas províncias da Bahia, Pernambuco, Alagoas e Sergipe [1859]*, trans. Eduardo de Lima Castro, Reconquista do Brasil, no. 19 (Belo Horizonte and São Paulo: Itatiaia and EDUSP, 1980), p. 51; and Keila Grinberg, *O fiador dos brasileiros: Cidadania,*

escravidão e direito civil no tempo de Antônio Pereira Rebouças (Rio de Janeiro: Civilização Brasileira, 2002), p. 151.

21. PP-BA to Câmara, Salvador, 8 May 1838, AMS, 111.10, fol. 50; Câmara to PP-BA, Salvador, 16 May 1838, AMS, 111.9, fol. 207v; Bahia, Assembléia Provincial, [Aprovação de Posturas], 31 July 1838, AMS [119.6, Posturas das Câmaras Municipaes, 1837–1847], fol. 71; Câmara to PP-BA, 8 Mar. 1839, AMS, 111.9, fol. 246v; Câmara to PP-BA, 27 Dec. 1847, AMS, 111.11, fol. 245v; Câmara to PP-BA, 16 Oct. 1845, APEB, CP, M. 1399, 1845, Doc. 38 (italics added).

22. Câmara, Edital, 17 May 1826, AMS, 116.6, fol. 134.

23. Câmara, Edital, 17 May 1826, AMS, 116.6, fols. 133v–134v; Câmara, Edital, 30 Jan. 1833, and Câmara to fiscal, 8 Feb. 1833, both in AMS, 116.7, fols. 90 and 93; Câmara to PP-BA, 4 and 10 May 1842, AMS, 111.11, fols. 55–56 (also in APEB, CP, M. 1398, 1842, Doc. 14).

24. Câmara to PP-BA, 10 May 1842, AMS, 111.11, fol. 56v (also in APEB, CP, M. 1398, Doc. 14); PP-BA to Câmara, 18 May 1842, 20 Aug. and 25 Nov. 1845, all in AMS, 111.10, fols. 156, 263, 275.

25. Câmara to PP-BA, 12 Jan. 1846, AMS, 111.11, fols. 162v–164.

26. Joaquim Torquato Carneiro de Campos, Luiz Antonio de Sampaio Vianna, and Victor d'Oliveira to PP-BA, 27 Apr. 1847, APEB, CP, M. 1611.

27. Admin. do Celeiro to PP-BA, 26 Apr. 1849, APEB, CP, M. 1611; Câmara to PP-BA, 18 July 1849, APEB, CP, M. 1400. Their wording followed the language of a report from a council committee; Comissão de Justiça to Câmara, 30 June 1849, AMS, 9.47, fols. 7v–9.

28. Contemporary narrative accounts of the events I summarize here are, from a point of view friendly to that of the city council, British Consul John Morgan Junior to British Minister Plenipotentiary Peter Campbell, 3 Mar. 1858, and idem to Foreign Minister the Earl of Clarendon, 16 Mar. 1858, both at PRO, London, F.O. 13, No. 365, fols. 52–67 (microfilm), and from an opposing point of view, Bahia, Presidente da Província, *Relatorio*, 13 May 1858, pp. 2–4, and Chefe de Polícia to PP-BA, n.d., enclosed in ibid., separately paged. The best historical account is the brilliant article by Reis and Aguiar, "'Carne sem osso.'" When not otherwise indicated, these sources form the basis of this and the following paragraphs. Other brief accounts that do not indicate sources are Braz Hermenegildo do Amaral, "Motim de carne sem osso e farinha sem caroço," *Revista do Instituto Geográfico e Histórico da Bahia*, no. 43 (1917): 110–114; João Craveiro Costa, *O visconde de Sinimbu: Sua vida e sua atuação na política nacional (1840–1889)*, Biblioteca Pedagógica Brasileira, série 5, vol. 79 (São Paulo: Editora Nacional, 1937), pp. 150–155; Manoel Pinto de Aguiar, *Abastecimento: Crises, motins e intervenção*, Redescobrimento do Brasil, no. 4 (Rio de Janeiro: Philobiblion, 1985), pp. 61–71; and Affonso Ruy, *História da Câmara Municipal da cidade do Salvador*, 2nd ed. (Salvador: Câmara Municipal de Salvador, 1996), pp. 218–221.

29. Proposed postura, encl. in Câmara to PP-BA, 12 Jan. 1857, APEB, CP, 1403; *Jornal da Bahia*, 19 Jan., 11 Mar., and 4 Apr. 1857, quoted in Ellen Melo dos Santos Ribeiro, "Abastecimento de farinha da cidade do Salvador, 1850–1870: Aspectos históricos," unpublished master's thesis (Universidade Federal da Bahia, 1982), pp. 49, 94–95. Also, on rising prices, see *Jornal da Bahia*, 16 Feb. 1857, encl. in Câmara to PP-BA, 16 July 1857, APEB, CP, M. 1403; and the graph presented by B. J.

Barickman, *A Bahian Counterpoint: Sugar, Tobacco, Cassava, and Slavery in the Recôncavo, 1780–1860* (Stanford, CA: Stanford University Press, 1998), p. 80. One historian has calculated that the percentage of a stonemason's income spent on three essential foodstuffs (manioc meal, fresh meat, and beans) for a family of five rose by more than 10 percent between 1854 and 1858; Mattoso, *Bahia: A cidade de Salvador*, pp. 369–370.

30. Câmara to PP-BA, 23 Apr. 1857, AMS, 111.13, fols. 196v–197; *Jornal da Bahia*, 27 Apr. 1857, quoted in Ribeiro, "Abastecimento de farinha," p. 98; Câmara to PP-BA, 14 Nov. 1857, APEB, CP, M. 1403; Costa, *Visconde de Sinimbu*, pp. 46–49. William Scully, *Brazil: Its Provinces and Chief Cities . . .* (London: Trübner, 1868), p. 351; Scully identifies Sinimbu's wife as being "of English origin."

31. Câmara to PP-BA, 25 Jan. 1858, APEB, CP, M. 1404; British Consul to British Foreign Minister, 16 Mar. 1858, PRO, F.O. 13, No. 365, fol. 65.

32. PP-BA to Câmara, 1 and 24 Feb. 1858, AMS, 111.14, fols. 31v–34v.

33. Câmara to PP-BA, 25 Feb. 1858, in Aguiar, *Abastecimento*, pp. 63–66; PP-BA to Dr. Francisco Antonio Pereira Rocha, 28 Feb. 1858, AMS, 111.14, fol. 35; Manoel Geronimo Ferreira to PP-BA, 1 Mar. 1858, APEB, M. 1404, quoted in Reis and Aguiar, "'Carne sem osso,'" pp. 141–142; British Consul to British Minister Plenipotentiary, 3 Mar. 1858, PRO, F.O. 13, No. 365, fols. 56 and 59. Sinimbu was referring to Brazil, *Codigo criminal do Imperio do Brasil*, Art. 154 (Aguiar, *Abastecimento*, p. 70, mistakenly cites Art. 164). The British Consul alleged that several leading authorities agreed with the city council's legal position; British Consul to British Foreign Minister, 16 Mar. 1858, PRO, F.O. 13, No. 365, fol. 66. The council members were indicted by a judge, but Sinimbu's decision was overturned by a higher court; Bahia, Presidente da Provincia, *Relatório*, 24 Nov. 1858; Livro de Correspondência da Câmara à Assembléia Provincial, no. 2, fol. 94v, in Ruy, *História da Câmara*, p. 305. Also see Ribeiro, "Abastecimento de farinha," pp. 103–104.

34. British Consul to Foreign Minister, 16 Mar. 1858, PRO, F.O. 13, No. 365, fol. 56v; Chefe de Polícia to PP-BA, n.d., enclosed in Bahia, Presidente da Província, *Relatorio*, 11 May 1858 (separately paged), p. 5; illustration in Reis and Aguiar, "'Carne sem osso,'" p. 143. For an account that labels the rioters as "scum [canalha]" and Sinimbu as "noble," see Avé-Lallemant, *Viagens . . . Bahia*, pp. 52–54. On remodeling the governor's palace, see Scully, *Brazil: Its Provinces and Chief Cities*, p. 351.

35. Bahia, Presidente da Província, *Relatorio*, 13 May 1858, p. 3. A slightly different chronology of events is found in José Alvares do Amaral, "Resumo chronologico e noticioso da Provincia da Bahia desde seu descobrimento em 1500" [1881], ed. J. Teixeira Bastos, *Revista do Instituto Geográfico e Histórico da Bahia*, no. 47 (1921–1922): 149, 176–77. On the symbolic meanings of these actions, I draw on points made by John Bohstedt, *Riots and Community Politics in England and Wales, 1790–1810* (Cambridge, MA: Harvard University Press, 1983), p. 3.

36. Câmara to PP-BA, 1 Mar. 1858, APEB, CP, M. 1404; Sinimbu quoted in Reis and Aguiar, "'Carne sem osso,'" pp. 141, 144; Associação Commercial to PP-BA, 3 Mar. 1858, APEB, CP, M. 1404; British Consul to British Foreign Minister, 16 Mar. 1858, PRO, F.O. 13, fol. 59. On the Commercial Association's makeup, see Eugene Ridings, *Business Interest Groups in Nineteenth-Century Brazil* (Cambridge, Eng.: Cambridge University Press, 1994), p. 32.

37. Câmara to Assembléia Legislativa, [?] Sept. 1858, as quoted in Thales de Azevedo and Edilberto Quintela Vieira Lins, *História do Banco da Bahia, 1858–1958*, Documentos Brasileiros, no. 132 (Rio de Janeiro: J. Olympio, 1969), p. 12; Câmara to Assembléia Legislativa, 24 Nov. 1858, in Ruy, *História da Câmara*, p. 305; *Jornal da Bahia*, 4 and 6 Apr. 1859, Parecer da Commissão Especial Sobre as Causas da Carestia da Farinha, 18 May 1859, in Ribeiro, "Abastecimento de farinha," pp. 131–132; Postura No. 143, approved 1 June 1859, AMS, 119.5, fol. 109v.

38. Ribeiro, "Abastecimento de farinha", pp. 52, 61–62, 65, 107, 112, 121; Bahia, Presidente da Província, *Relatorio*, 1866, pp. 20, 25; José Antonio de Araujo to PP-BA, 8 June 1878, and enclosures, APEB, CP, M. 4632. Cf. Kátia M. de Queirós Mattoso, "Conjoncture et société au Brésil a la fin du XVIIIᵉ siècle: Prix et salaires à la veille de la Révolution des Alfaiates, Bahia, 1798," *Cahiers des Ameriques Latines* 5 (1970): 40 (Mattoso dates the end of the grains market to 1834). For the building's later fate see Braz do Amaral, "Notas," in Luís dos Santos Vilhena, *A Bahia no século XVIII*, 2nd ed., ed. Braz do Amaral, intro. by Edison Carneiro (Salvador: Itapuã, 1969), p. 113.

39. The *locus classicus* on the moral economy is E. P. Thompson, "The Moral Economy of the English Crowd in the Eighteenth Century," *Past & Present*, no. 50 (Feb. 1971): 76–136. A critic who often misses his mark is John Bohstedt, "The Moral Economy and the Discipline of Historical Context," *Journal of Social History* 26, no. 2 (1992): 265–284. See also Francisco Carlos Teixeira da Silva, "A morfologia da escassez: Crises de subsistência e política econômica no Brasil colônia (Salvador e Rio de Janeiro, 1680–1790)" (Ph.D. diss., Universidade Federal Fluminense, 1990), pp. 270–275.

40. Câmara to PP-BA, 17 Feb. 1858, and "Parecer da Commissão Especial sobre as causas da carestia da farinha," *Jornal da Bahia*, 18 May 1859, both quoted in Aguiar, *Abastecimento*, pp. 62, 132. Silva ("Morfologia da escassez," pp. 356ff.) makes the same point about social inequality.

APPENDIX A

1. For a discussion of the various approaches to the study of purchasing power over time, with special reference to Brazil, see Nathaniel H. Leff, *Underdevelopment and Development in Brazil*, Vol. I: *Economic Structure and Change, 1822–1947* (London: Allen and Unwin, 1982), pp. 97–130. An alternative approach can be found in Afonso de Alencastro Graça Filho, *A princesa do oeste e o mito da decadência de Minas Gerais: São João del Rei, 1831–1888* (São Paulo: Annablume, 2002), pp. 154–155, 180–181.

2. Kátia M. de Queirós Mattoso, Herbert S. Klein, and Stanley L. Engerman, "Trends and Patterns in the Prices of Manumitted Slaves: Bahia, 1819–1888," *Slavery and Abolition* 7, no. 1 (May 1986): 59–67.

3. A fuller discussion of my method and its justifications appears in Richard Graham, "Purchasing Power: A Tentative Approach and an Appeal," *Boletim de História Demográfica*, ano 12, no. 36 (Apr. 2005) (http://www.brnuede.com, link at p. 2).

SOURCES

ARCHIVES

Arquivo da Santa Casa de Misericórdia, Salvador (ASCM)
Arquivo do Instituto Histórico e Geográfico Brasileiro, Rio de Janeiro (AIHGB)
Arquivo Histórico Militar, Lisbon (AHM)
Arquivo Histórico Ultramarino, Lisbon (AHU)
Arquivo Municipal de Salvador, Salvador (AMS)
Arquivo Nacional, Rio de Janeiro (AN)
    Seção do Poder Executivo (SPE)
    Seção Histórica (SH)
Arquivo Nacional da Torre do Tombo, Lisbon (ANTT)
Arquivo Público do Estado da Bahia, Salvador (APEB)
    Colonial e Provincial (CP)
    Inventários e Testamentos (IT)
    Seção Judiciária (SJ)
    Seção Legislativa (SL)
Biblioteca Nacional, Seção de Manuscritos, Rio de Janeiro (BN/SM)
Public Record Office, London (microfilm) (PRO)

PRINTED MATERIALS, THESES, AND DISSERTATIONS

Agostinho [Silva], Pedro. *Embarcações do Recôncavo: Estudo de origens.* A Bahia e o Recôncavo, no. 3. Salvador: Museu do Recôncavo Wanderley Pinho, 1973.

Aguiar, Manoel Pinto de. *Abastecimento: Crises, motins e intervenção.* Rio de Janeiro: Philobiblion, 1985.

Alencastro, Luiz Felipe de. *O trato dos viventes: A formação do Brasil no Atlântico Sul.* São Paulo: Companhia das Letras, 2000.

Algranti, Leila Mezan. *O feitor ausente: Estudo sobre a escravidão urbana no Rio de Janeiro.* Petrópolis: Vozes, 1988.

Almanach para a Cidade da Bahia: Anno 1812. Facsim. ed. Salvador: Conselho Estadual de Cultura, 1973.

Almeida, Candido Mendes de, ed. *Codigo Philippino; ou, Ordenações e leis do reino de Portugal recopiladas por mandado d'el rei D. Philippe I . . .* Rio de Janeiro: Instituto Philomathico, 1870.

Almeida, Eduardo de Castro e, ed. "Inventario dos documentos relativos ao Brasil existentes no Archivo de Marinha e Ultramar." *ABNRJ* 31 (1909), 32 (1910), 34 (1912), 36 (1914), 37 (1915), 71 (1947).

Almeida, Miguel Calmon du Pin e (Marquês de Abrantes). *Relatorio dos trabalhos do Conselho Interino do governo da Provincia da Bahia, 1823.* 2nd ed. Rio de Janeiro: Typ. do "Jornal do Commercio," 1923.

Almodovar, António. "Processos de difusão e institucionalização da economia política no Brasil." In *A economia política e os dilemas do império Luso-*

Brasileiro (1790–1822), edited by José Luís Cardoso, 111–145. Lisbon: Comissão Nacional para as Comemorações dos Descobrimentos Portugueses, 2001.

Almodovar, António, and José Luís Cardoso. *A History of Portuguese Economic Thought*. London and New York: Routledge, 1998.

Amaral, Braz Hermenegildo do. *História da Bahia do Império à República*. Salvador: Imp. Oficial do Estado, 1923.

———. *História da independência na Bahia*. 2nd ed. Marajoara, no. 19. Salvador: Livraria Progresso, 1957.

———. "Motim de carne sem osso e farinha sem caroço." *Revista do Instituto Geográfico e Histórico da Bahia*, no. 43 (1917): 110–114.

Amaral, José Alvares do. "Resumo chronologico e noticioso da Provincia da Bahia desde seu descobrimento em 1500 [1881]." Edited by J. Teixeira Bastos. *Revista do Instituto Geográfico e Histórico da Bahia*, no. 47 (1921–1922): 71–559.

Andrade, Maria José de Souza. *A mão de obra escrava em Salvador, 1811–1860*. Baianada 8. São Paulo and Brasília: Corrupio and CNPq, 1988.

Andrews, C[hristopher] C[olumbus]. *Brazil: Its Condition and Prospects . . . with an Account of the Downfall of the Empire, the Establishment of the Republic and the Reciprocity Treaty*. 3rd ed. New York: Appleton, 1891.

Arnizau, José Joaquim de Almeida e. "Memoria topographica, historica, commercial e politica da villa de Cachoeira da provincia da Bahia [1825]." *Revista do Instituto Historico e Geographico Brasileiro* 25 (1862): 127–142.

Arquivo do Estado da Bahia. *Publicações*. 1937–1948.

Arquivo Público do Estado da Bahia. *Anais*.

———. *Autos da devassa da Conspiração dos Alfaiates*. Salvador: Secretaria da Cultura e Turismo, Arquivo Público do Estado, 1998.

Arruda, José Jobson de A. *O Brasil no comércio colonial*. São Paulo: Ática, 1980.

Aufderheide, Patricia Ann. "Order and Violence: Social Deviance and Social Control in Brazil, 1780–1840." Ph.D. diss., University of Minnesota, 1976.

Austin, Gareth. "Indigenous Credit Institutions in West Africa, c. 1750–c. 1960." In *Local Suppliers of Credit in the Third World, 1750–1960*, edited by Gareth Austin and Kaoru Sugihara, 93–159. New York: St. Martin's, 1993.

Avé-Lallemant, Robert. *Viagens pelas províncias da Bahia, Pernambuco, Alagoas e Sergipe, 1859*. Translated by Eduardo de Lima Castro. Reconquista do Brasil, no. 19. Belo Horizonte and São Paulo: Itatiaia and EDUSP, 1980.

Azevedo, Paulo Ormindo de. *A alfândega e o mercado: Memória e restauração*. Salvador: Secretaria de Planejamento, Ciência, e Tecnologia do Estado da Bahia, 1985.

Azevedo, Rubens de, comp. *Atlas geográfico Melhoramentos*. 28th ed. São Paulo: Companhia Melhoramentos, 1968.

Azevedo, Thales de. *Povoamento da cidade do Salvador*. 3rd ed. Salvador: Itapuã, 1969.

Azevedo, Thales de, and Edilberto Quintela Vieira Lins. *História do Banco da Bahia, 1858–1958*. Documentos Brasileiros, no. 132. Rio de Janeiro: J. Olympio, 1969.

Babb, Florence E. *Between Field and Cooking Pot: The Political Economy of Marketwomen in Peru*. 2nd ed. Austin: University of Texas Press, 1998.

Bahia. *Colleção das leis e resoluções da Assemblea Legislativa e regulamentos do governo da provincia da Bahia.*

Bahia, Presidente da Província. *Falla.* 1846.

——. *Relatorio.* 1866.

Bahia, Secretaria dos Transportes e Comunicações. *Mapa do sistema de transportes.* Salvador: [Bahia, Secretaria dos Transportes e Comunições], 1981.

Bandeira, Luiz Alberto Moniz. *O feudo—A Casa da Torre de Garcia d'Avila: Da conquista dos sertões à independência do Brasil.* Rio de Janeiro: Civilização Brasileira, 2000.

Barickman, B. J. *A Bahian Counterpoint: Sugar, Tobacco, Cassava, and Slavery in the Recôncavo, 1780–1860.* Stanford, CA: Stanford University Press, 1998.

Barman, Roderick J. *Brazil: The Forging of a Nation, 1798–1852.* Stanford, CA: Stanford University Press, 1988.

Barrett, Ward. "The Meat Supply of Colonial Cuernavaca." *Annals of the Association of American Geographers* 64, no. 4 (December 1974): 525–540.

[Barros, Francisco da Silva]. "Chronica dos acontecimentos da Bahia, 1809-1828." *Anais do Arquivo Público do Estado da Bahia* 26 (1938): 46–95.

Bastide, Roger. *The African Religions of Brazil: Toward a Sociology of the Interpenetration of Civilizations.* Translated by Helen Sebba. Baltimore: Johns Hopkins University Press, 1978.

Bauer, Arnold J. *Goods, Power, History: Latin America's Material Culture.* Cambridge, Eng.: Cambridge University Press, 2001.

Bauer, Peter T. *West African Trade: A Study of Competition, Oligopoly, and Monopoly in a Changing Economy.* Cambridge, Eng.: Cambridge University Press, 1954.

Berbel, Márcia Regina. "A retórica da recolonização." In *Independência: História e historiografia,* edited by István Jancsó, 791–808. São Paulo: HUCITEC and FAPESP, 2005.

——. *A nação como artefato: Deputados do Brasil nas Cortes portuguesas (1821–1822).* São Paulo: HUCITEC, 1999.

Beyer, Gustavo. "Ligeiras notas de viagem do Rio de Janeiro á capitania de S. Paulo, no Brasil, no verão de 1813, com algumas noticias sobre a cidade da Bahia e a ilha Tristão da Cunha, entre o Cabo e o Brasil e que ha pouco foi ocupada." Translated by A. Löfgren. *Revista do Instituto Histórico e Geográfico de São Paulo* 11 (1907): 275–311.

Biblioteca Nacional do Rio de Janeiro. *Anais* (*ABNRJ*).

——. *Documentos Históricos.* Rio de Janeiro: Biblioteca Nacional, 1928–1960.

Bluteau, Rafael. *Diccionario da lingua portugueza.* Revised by Antonio de Moraes Silva. Lisbon: Simão Thaddeo Ferreira, 1789.

Bohstedt, John. "The Moral Economy and the Discipline of Historical Context." *Journal of Social History* 26, no. 2 (1992): 265–284.

——. *Riots and Community Politics in England and Wales, 1790-1810.* Cambridge, MA: Harvard University Press, 1983.

Bolster, William Jeffrey. "African-American Seamen: Race, Seafaring Work, and Atlantic Maritime Culture, 1750–1860." Ph.D. diss., Johns Hopkins University, 1991.

————. *Black Jacks: African American Seamen in the Age of Sail.* Cambridge, MA: Harvard University Press, 1997.

Boxer, Charles R. *Portuguese Society in the Tropics: The Municipal Councils of Goa, Macao, Bahia, and Luanda.* Madison: University of Wisconsin Press, 1965.

Brant Pontes (Marquês de Barbacena), Felisberto Caldeira. *Economia açucareira do Brasil no séc. XIX: Cartas.* Compiled by Carmen Vargas. Coleção Canavieira, no. 21. Rio de Janeiro: Instituto do Açucar e do Álcool, 1976.

Braudel, Fernand. *The Mediterranean and the Mediterranean World in the Age of Philip II.* 2 vols. Translated by Siân Reynolds. New York: Harper and Row, 1972.

Brazil. *Código criminal do Império.*

————. *Collecção das decisões do governo do Imperio do Brasil.*

————. *Colleção das leis do Imperio do Brasil.*

————. *Constituição política do Império do Brasil.*

Brazil, Assemblea Geral Constituinte e Legislativa do Imperio do Brasil. *Diario ... 1823.* Facsim. ed. Brasília: Senado Federal, 1973.

Brazil, Directoria Geral de Estatística. *Recenseamento da população do Imperio do Brazil [sic] a que se procedeu no dia 1º de agosto de 1872.* Rio de Janeiro: Typ. Nacional, 1873–1876.

Brazil, Ministério da Agricultura. Imperial Instituto Bahiano de Agricultura. *Relatório,* 1871.

Brelin, Johan. *De passagem pelo Brasil e Portugal em 1756.* Lisbon: Casa Portuguesa, 1955.

Brito, João Rodrigues de, et al. *Cartas economico-politicas sobre a agricultura e commercio da Bahia.* Lisbon: Imp. Nacional, 1821.

Bromley, R. J., and Richard Symanski. "Marketplace Trade in Latin America." *Latin American Research Review* 9, no. 3 (Fall 1974): 3–38.

Brown, Alexandra Kelly. "'On the Vanguard of Civilization': Slavery, the Police, and Conflicts Between Public and Private Power in Salvador da Bahia, Brazil, 1835–1888." Ph.D. diss., University of Texas at Austin, 1998.

Brown, Peter. "A More Glorious House." *New York Review of Books* 44, no. 9 (29 May 1997).

Burns, E. Bradford. "The Enlightenment in Two Colonial Brazilian Libraries." *Journal of the History of Ideas* 25, no. 3 (July–September 1964): 430–438.

Caldas, José Antônio. *Noticia geral de toda esta capitania da Bahia desde o seu descobrimento até o presente anno de 1759.* Facsim. ed. Salvador: Câmara de Vereadores, 1951.

Calmon, Francisco Marques de Góes. *Vida econômico-financeira da Bahia (elementos para a história) de 1808–1899.* Salvador: Imp. Official do Estado, 1925.

Câmara, Antônio Alves. *Ensaio sobre as construções navais indígenas do Brasil.* 2nd ed. São Paulo: Editora Nacional, 1976.

Campliglia, G. Oscar Oswaldo. *Igrejas do Brasil: Fontes para a história da Igreja no Brasil.* São Paulo: Melhoramentos, n.d. [1957].

Candler, John, and William Burgess. *Narrative of a Recent Visit to Brazil to Present an Address on the Slave Trade and Slavery Issued by the Religious Society of Friends.* London: Edward Marsh, 1853.

Cannan, Edwin. "Introduction." In Adam Smith, *An Inquiry Into the Nature and Causes of the Wealth of Nations*. 6th[?] ed. Edited by Edwin Cannan. Chicago: University of Chicago Press, 1976.

Canstatt, Oskar. *Brasil: Terra e gente*. 2nd ed. Translated by Eduardo de Lima Castro, with an introduction by Artur Cezar Ferreira Reis. Temas Brasileiros, no. 18. Rio de Janeiro: Conquista, 1975.

Cardoso, José Luís, "Nas malhas do império: A economia política e a política colonial de D. Rodrigo de Souza Coutinho." In *A economia política e os dilemas do império luso-brasileiro (1790–1822)*, edited by José Luís Cardoso, 63–109. Lisbon: Comissão Nacional para as Comemorações dos Descobrimentos Portugueses, 2001.

———. *O pensamento económico em Portugal nos finais do século XVIII, 1780–1808*. Lisbon: Editorial Estampa, 1989.

———, ed. *A economia política e os dilemas do império luso-brasileiro (1790–1822)*. Lisbon: Comissão Nacional para as Comemorações dos Descobrimentos Portugueses, 2001.

Caribbean Food and Nutrition Institute. *Food Composition Tables for Use in the English-Speaking Caribbean*. Kingston, Jamaica: Caribbean Food and Nutrition Institute, 1974.

Carneiro, Edison [de Souza]. *Candomblés da Bahia*. Publicações no. 8. Salvador: Museu do Estado, 1948.

———, comp. *Antologia do negro brasileiro*. Rio de Janeiro: Edições de Ouro, 1967.

Carvalho, Marcus J. M. de. "Os caminhos do rio: Negros canoeiros no Recife da primeira metade do século XIX." *Afro-Ásia* 19/20 (1997): 75–93.

———. "Cavalcantis e cavalgados: A formação das alianças políticas em Pernambuco, 1817–1824." *Revista Brasileira de História* 18, no. 36 (1998): 331–365.

———. *Liberdade: Rotinas e rupturas do escravismo urbano, Recife, 1822–1850*. 2nd ed. Recife: Editora da UFPE, 2002.

———. "Os negros armados pelos brancos e suas independências no Nordeste (1817–1848)." In *Independência: História e historiografia*, edited by Istvan Jancsó, 881–914. São Paulo: HUCITEC and FAPESP, 2005.

Castro, Josué de. *O problema da alimentação no Brasil (Seu estudo fisiológico)*. Brasiliana, ser. 5, no. 29. São Paulo: Editora Nacional, 1938.

Chalhoub, Sidney. "Dependents Play Chess: Political Dialogues in Machado de Assis." In *Machado de Assis: Reflections on a Brazilian Master Writer*, edited by Richard Graham, 51–84. Austin: University of Texas Press, 1995.

Clark, Gracia. *Onions Are My Husband: Survival and Accumulation by West African Market Women*. Chicago: University of Chicago Press, 1994.

Cline, Sarah L. *Colonial Culhuacan, 1580–1600: A Social History of an Aztec Town*. Albuquerque: University of New Mexico Press, 1986.

———. "Fray Alonso de Molina's Model Testament and Antecedents to Indigenous Wills in Spanish America." In *Dead Giveaways: Indigenous Testaments of Colonial Mesoamerica and the Andes*, edited by Susan Kellogg and Matthew Restall, 13–33. Salt Lake City: University of Utah Press, 1998.

Cock, James H. "Cassava: A Basic Energy Source in the Tropics." *Science* 218 (19 November 1982): 755–762.

Conrad, Robert Edgar, comp. and ed. *Children of God's Fire: A Documentary History of Black Slavery in Brazil*. Princeton, NJ: Princeton University Press, 1983.

Cope, R. Douglas. *The Limits of Racial Domination: Plebeian Society in Colonial Mexico City, 1660–1720*. Madison: University of Wisconsin Press, 1994.

Costa, Ana de Lourdes Ribeiro da. "Moradia de escravos em Salvador no século XIX." *Clio: Revista de Pesquisa Histórica* [Série História do Nordeste], no. 11 (1988): 95–104.

Costa, Avelino de Jesus da. "População da cidade da Baía em 1775." In *Actas do V [Quinto] Colóquio Internacional de Estudos Luso-Brasileiros, Coimbra, 1963*, 1: 191–274. Coimbra: Gráfica de Coimbra, 1964.

Costa, Iraci del Nero da, and Francisco Vidal Luna. "De escravo a senhor." *Revista do Arquivo Público Mineiro* 41 (July–December 2005): 106–115.

Costa, João Craveiro. *O visconde de Sinimbu: Sua vida e sua atuação na política nacional (1840–1889)*. São Paulo: Editora Nacional, 1937.

Covarrubias Orozco, Sebastián de. *Tesoro de la lengua castellana o española*. 1611. 2nd rev. ed. Edited by Felipe C. R. Maldonado. Madrid: Editorial Castalia, 1995.

Cruz, Maria Cecília Velasco e. "Puzzling Out Slave Origins in Rio de Janeiro Port Unionism: The 1906 Strike and the Sociedade de Resistência dos Trabalhadores em Trapiche e Café." *Hispanic American Historical Review* 86, no. 2 (May 2006): 205–245.

Cunha, Manuela Carneiro da. *Negros, estrangeiros: Os escravos libertos e sua volta à África*. São Paulo: Brasiliense, 1985.

Curtin, Philip D. *Death by Migration: Europe's Encounter with the Tropical World in the Nineteenth Century*. Cambridge, Eng.: Cambridge University Press, 1989.

Darwin, Charles. *The Life and Letters of Charles Darwin, Including an Autobiographical Chapter*. Edited by Francis Darwin. New York: Appleton, 1898.

Debret, Jean Baptiste. *Viagem pitoresca e histórica ao Brasil*. 2 vols. 2nd ed. Translated by Sérgio Milliet, with an introduction by Rubens Borba de Moraes. São Paulo: Martins and EDUSP, 1972.

de Roover, Raymond. "The Concept of the Just Price: Theory and Economic Policy." *Journal of Economic History* 18, no. 4 (December 1958): 418–434.

———. "Scholastic Economics: Survival and Lasting Influence from the Sixteenth Century to Adam Smith." *Quarterly Journal of Economics* 69, no. 2 (May 1955): 161–190.

"Descrição da Bahia." [1813?]. MS, AIHGB, Lata 399, Doc. 2.

Dias, Maria Odila Leite da Silva. *Quotidiano e poder em São Paulo no século XIX: Ana Gertudes de Jesus*. São Paulo: Brasiliense, 1984.

Diffie, Bailey W. *A History of Colonial Brazil, 1500–1792*. Malbar, FL: Krieger, 1987.

Diniz, Jaime C. *Mestres de capela da Misericórdia da Bahia, 1647–1810*. Edited by Manuel Veiga. Salvador: Centro Editorial e Didático da UFBA, 1993.

———. *Organistas da Bahia, 1750-1850*. Rio de Janeiro and Salvador: Tempo Brasileiro and Fundação Cultural do Estado da Bahia, 1986.

"Discurso preliminar, historico, introductivo com natureza de descripção economica da comarca, e cidade da Bahia. . . ." [1789–1808?]. *ABNRJ* 27 (1905): 283–348.

d'Orbigny, Alcide. *Viagem pitoresca através do Brasil.* Belo Horizonte and São Paulo: Itatiaia and EDUSP, 1976.

Dória, Francisco Antonio, and Jorge Ricardo de Almeida Fonseca. "Marechal José Inácio Acciaiuoli: Um potentado baiano no início do século XIX." *Revista do Instituto Geográfico e Histórico da Bahia,* no. 90 (1992): 133–142.

Drummond, Antonio de Meneses Vasconcellos de. "Anotações a sua biographia publicada em 1836 na *Biographie universelle et portative des contemporains.*" *ABNRJ* 13, pt. 3 (1885–1886): 1–149.

Dundas, Robert. *Sketches of Brazil Including New Views of Tropical and European Fever with Remarks on a Premature Decay of the System Incident to Europeans on Their Return from Hot Climates.* London: John Churchill, 1852.

Elliott, J. H. "Atlantic History: A Circumnavigation." In *The British Atlantic World, 1500–1800,* edited by David Armitage and Michael J. Braddick, 233–249. Houndmills, Basingstoke, Hampshire, and New York: Palgrave and Macmillan, 2002.

Ellis, Myriam. *A baleia no Brasil colonial.* São Paulo: Melhoramentos and EDUSP, 1969.

Eltis, David. "Atlantic History in Global Perspective." *Itinerario* 23, no. 2 (1999): 141–161.

———. "The Diaspora of Yoruba Speakers, 1650–1865: Dimensions and Implications." In *The Yoruba Diaspora in the Atlantic World,* edited by Toyin Falola and Matt D. Childs, 17–39. Bloomington: Indiana University Press, 2004.

———. *Economic Growth and the Ending of the Transatlantic Slave Trade.* New York: Oxford, 1987.

———. "The Volume and Structure of the Transatlantic Slave Trade: A Reassessment." *William and Mary Quarterly* Series 2, 58, no. 1 (January 2001): 17–46.

Eltis, David, Stephen D. Behrendt, David Richardson, and Herbert S. Klein. *The Transatlantic Slave Trade: A Database on CD-ROM.* Cambridge, Eng.: Cambridge University Press, 1999.

Elwes, Robert. *A Sketcher's Tour Round the World.* London: Hurst and Blackett, 1854.

Ewbank, Thomas. *Life in Brazil; or, A Journal of a Visit to the Land of the Cocoa and the Palm, with an Appendix Containing Illustrations of Ancient South American Arts in Recently Discovered Implements and Products of Domestic Industry and Works in Stone, Pottery, Gold, Silver, Bronze, &C.* 1856. Reprint, Detroit: Blaine Ethridge, 1971.

Falola, Toyin. "Gender, Business, and Space Control: Yoruba Market Women and Power." In *African Market Women and Economic Power: The Role of Women in African Economic Development,* edited by Bessie House-Midamba and Felix K. Ekechi, 23–40. Contributions in Afro-American and African Studies, no. 174. Westport, CT: Greenwood, 1995.

Faria, Sheila de Castro. *A colônia em movimento: Fortuna e família no cotidiano colonial.* Rio de Janeiro: Nova Fronteira, 1998.

———. "Mulheres forras: Riqueza e estigma social." *Tempo*, no. 9 (July 2000): 65–92.

———. "Sinhás pretas, 'damas mercadoras': As pretas minas nas cidades do Rio de Janeiro e de São João del Rey (1700–1850)." Unpublished MS tese de doutorado. Niterói: Universidade Federal Fluminense, 2004.

Ferlini, Vera Lúcia. "Pobres do açucar: Estrutura produtiva e relações de poder no Nordeste colonial." In *História econômica do período colonial: Coletânea de textos apresentados no 1 Congresso Brasileiro de História Econômica (Campus da USP, setembro de 1993)*, edited by Tamás Szmrecsányi, 21–34. São Paulo: HUCITEC, FAPESP, and Associação Brasileira de Pesquisadores em História Econômica, 1996.

Fernández García, Antonio. *El abastecimiento de Madrid en el reinado de Isabel II*. With an introduction by Vicente Palacio Atard. Biblioteca de Estudios Madrileños, no. 14. Madrid: Instituto de Estudios Madrileños, 1971.

Figueiredo, Luciano. *O avesso da memória: Cotidiano e trabalho da mulher em Minas Geraes no século XVIII*. Rio de Janeiro and Brasília: José Olympio and EDUNB, 1993.

Fisher, F. J. "The Development of the London Food Market, 1540–1640." *Economic History Review* 5, no. 2 (April 1935): 46–64.

Florescano, Enrique. "El abasto y la legislación de granos en el siglo XVI." *Historia Mexicana* 14, no. 4 (April–June 1965): 567–630.

Fraga Filho, Walter. *Mendigos, moleques e vadios na Bahia do século XIX*. São Paulo and Salvador: HUCITEC and EDUFBA, 1996.

França, António d'Oliveira Pinto da, ed. *Cartas baianas, 1821–1824: Subsídios para o estudo dos problemas da opção na independência brasileira*. São Paulo: Editora Nacional, 1980.

Francois, Marie Eileen. *A Culture of Everyday Credit: Housekeeping, Pawnbroking, and Governance in Mexico City, 1750–1920*. Lincoln: University of Nebraska Press, 2006.

Frank, Zephyr. *Dutra's World: Wealth and Family in Nineteenth-Century Rio de Janeiro*. Albuquerque: University of New Mexico Press, 2004.

Friedmann, Karen J. "Victualling Colonial Boston." *Agricultural History* 47, no. 3 (July 1973): 189–205.

Furtado, Júnia Ferreira, *Chica da Silva e o contratador dos diamantes: O outro lado do mito*. São Paulo: Companhia das Letras, 2003.

———. *Homens de negócio: A interiorização da metrópole e do comércio nas Minas setecentistas*. São Paulo: HUCITEC, 1999.

———, ed. *Diálogos oceânicos: Minas Gerais e as novas abordagens para uma história do império ultramarino português*. Humanitas, no. 67. Belo Horizonte: Editora UFMG, 2001.

Gardner, George. *Travels in the Interior of Brazil, Principally Through the Northern Provinces and the Gold and Diamond Districts During the Years 1836–1841*. 1846; reprint, Boston: Milford House, 1973.

Geertz, Clifford. *Peddlers and Princes*. Chicago: University of Chicago Press, 1963.

Geertz, Clifford, Hildred Geertz, Lawrence Rosen, and Paul Hyman. *Meaning and Order in Moroccan Society: Three Essays in Cultural Analysis*. Cambridge, Eng.: Cambridge University Press, 1979.

Germeten, Nicole von. *Black Blood Brothers: Confraternities and Social Mobility for Afro-Mexicans*. Gainesville, FL: University Press of Florida, 2006.

Gibson, Campbell. "Population of the 100 Largest Cities and Other Urban Places in the United States, 1791–1990." In *U.S. Census Bureau, Population Division Working Paper*, No. 27, n.d.

Góes, José Roberto de, and Manolo Florentino. "Crianças escravas, crianças dos escravos." In *História das crianças no Brasil*, edited by Mary del Priore, 177–191. São Paulo: Editora Contexto, 2000.

Gomes, Marco Aurélio A. de Filgueiras. "Escravismo e cidade: Notas sobre a ocupação da periferia de Salvador no século XIX." *Rua: Revista de Arquiteura e Urbanismo* 3, no. 4–5 (June–December 1990): 9–19.

Gouvêa, Maria de Fátima Silva. "Poder, autoridade e o Senado da Câmara do Rio de Janeiro, ca. 1780–1820." *Tempo* 7, no. 13 (July 2002): 111–155.

Graça Filho, Afonso de Alencastro. *A princesa do oeste e o mito da decadência de Minas Gerais: São João del Rei, 1831–1888*. São Paulo: Annablume, 2002.

Graham, Maria [Lady Maria Calcott]. *Journal of a Voyage to Brazil and Residence There During Part of the Years 1821, 1822, 1823. 1824*. Reprint, New York: Praeger, 1969.

Graham, Richard. *Independence in Latin America: A Comparative Approach*. New York: McGraw-Hill, 1994.

———. *Patronage and Politics in Nineteenth-Century Brazil*. Stanford, CA: Stanford University Press, 1990.

Grant, Andrew. *History of Brazil Comprising a Geographical Account of That Country, Together with a Narrative of the Most Remarkable Events Which Have Occurred There Since Its Discovery; a Description of the Manners, Customs, Religion, Etc. of the Natives and Colonists; Interspersed with Remarks on the Nature of Its Soil, Climate, Production, and Foreign and Internal Commerce, to Which Are Subjoined Cautions to New Settlers for the Preservation of Health*. London: Henry Colburn, 1809.

Grinberg, Keila. *O fiador dos brasileiros: Cidadania, escravidão e direito civil no tempo de Antônio Pereira Rebouças*. Rio de Janeiro: Civilização Brasileira, 2002.

Guedes, Max Justo. "Guerra de Independência: As forças do mar." In *História da Independência: Edição comemorativea*, edited by Josué Montello, vol. 2, 167–211. Rio de Janeiro, 1972.

Harding, Rachel E. *A Refuge in Thunder: Candomblé and Alternative Spaces of Blackness*. Bloomington: Indiana University Press, 2000.

Horn, Rebecca. "Testaments and Trade: Interethnic Ties Among Petty Traders in Central Mexico (Coyoacan, 1550–1620)." In *Dead Giveaways: Indigenous Testaments of Colonial Mesoamerica and the Andes*, edited by Susan Kellogg and Matthew Restall, 59–83. Salt Lake City: University of Utah Press, 1998.

Iwasaki Cauti, Fernando. "Ambulantes y comercio colonial: Iniciativas mercantiles en el virreinato peruano." *Jahrbuch für Geschichte von Staat, Wirtschaft und Gesellschaft Lateinamerikas* 24 (1987): 179–211.

Jancsó, István. *Na Bahia, contra o Império: História do ensaio de sedição de 1798.* Estudos Históricos, 24. São Paulo and Salvador: HUCITEC and EDUFBA, 1995.

Jones, William O. *Manioc in Africa.* Stanford, CA: Stanford University Press, 1959.

Julião, Carlos. *Riscos illuminados de figurinhos de brancos e negros dos uzos do Rio de Janeiro e Serro do Frio.* With an introduction by Lygia da Fonseca Fernandes da Cunha. Rio de Janeiro: Biblioteca Nacional, 1960.

Kaplan, Steven L. *Bread, Politics and Political Economy in the Reign of Louis XV.* 2 vols., continuously paged. The Hague: Martinus Nijhoff, 1976.

———. *Provisioning Paris: Merchants and Millers in the Grain and Flour Trade During the Eighteenth Century.* Ithaca, NY: Cornell University Press, 1984.

Karasch, Mary C. *Slave Life in Rio de Janeiro, 1808–1850.* Princeton, NJ: Princeton University Press, 1987.

Kidder, Daniel P. *Sketches of Residence and Travels in Brazil Embracing Historical and Geographical Notices of the Empire and Its Several Provinces.* 2 vols. [Philadelphia: Sorin and Ball, 1845].

Kidder, Daniel Parish, and James Cooley Fletcher. *Brazil and the Brazilians Portrayed in Historical and Descriptive Sketches.* Philadelphia: Childs and Peterson, 1857.

Kiddy, Elizabeth W. *Blacks of the Rosary: Memory and History in Minas Gerais, Brazil.* University Park: Pennsylvania State University Press, 2005.

Kindersley, Mrs [Nathaniel]. *Letters from the Island of Teneriffe, Brazil, the Cape of Good Hope, and the East Indies.* London: J. Nourse, 1776.

Kinsbruner, Jay. *The Colonial Spanish-American City: Urban Life in the Age of Atlantic Capitalism.* Austin: University of Texas Press, 2005.

Koster, Henry. *Travels in Brazil in the Years from 1809 to 1815.* London: Longman Hurst, Reese, Orme and Brown, 1816.

Kraay, Hendrik. "'As Terrifying as Unexpected': The Bahian Sabinada, 1837–1838." *Hispanic American Historical Review* 72, no. 4 (November 1992): 501–527.

———. "'Em outra coisa não falavam os pardos, cabras, e crioulos': O 'recrutamento' de escravos na guerra da Independência na Bahia." *Revista Brasileira de História* 22, no. 43 (2002): 109–126.

———. *Race, State, and Armed Forces in Independence-Era Brazil: Bahia, 1790s–1840s.* Stanford, CA: Stanford University Press, 2001.

———. "'The Shelter of the Uniform': The Brazilian Army and Runaway Slaves, 1800–1888." *Journal of Social History* 29, no. 3 (March 1996): 637–657.

Lander, Richard, and John Lander. *Journal of an Expedition to Explore the Course and Termination of the Niger with a Narrative of a Voyage Down That River to Its Termination.* 1832. Reprint, New York: Harper, 1854.

Landes, Ruth. *The City of Women.* 1947. Reprint, Albuquerque: University of New Mexico Press, 1994.

Lapa, José Roberto do Amaral. *A Bahia e a carreira da Índia.* São Paulo: Editôra Nacional and EDUSP, 1968.

Lara, Silvia Hunold. "Signs of Color: Women's Dress and Racial Relations in Salvador and Rio de Janeiro, ca. 1750–1815." *Colonial Latin American Review* 6, no. 2 (1997): 205–224.

Lauderdale Graham, Sandra. *Caetana Says No: Women's Stories from a Brazilian Slave Society.* Cambridge, Eng.: Cambridge University Press, 2002.

———. "Making the Private Public: A Brazilian Perspective." *Journal of Women's History* 15, no. 1 (Spring 2003): 28–42.

———. "Slavery's Impasse: Slave Prostitutes, Small-Time Mistresses, and the Brazilian Law of 1871." *Comparative Studies in Society and History* 33, no. 4 (October 1991): 669–694.

Lee, Raymond L. "Grain Legislation in Colonial Mexico, 1575–1585." *Hispanic American Historical Review* 27, no. 4 (November 1947): 647–660.

Le Roy Ladurie, Emmanuel. *The Peasants of Languedoc.* Translated by John Day. Urbana: University of Illinois Press, 1974.

Le Vine, Robert A. "Sex Roles and Economic Change in Africa." In *Black Africa: Its People and Their Culture Today,* edited by John Middleton, 174–180. London: Macmillan, 1970.

Lima, José Francisco da Silva. "A Bahia ha 66 anos." *Revista do Instituto Geográfico e Histórico da Bahia,* ano 15, no. 34 (1908): 93–117.

Lima, Manuel de Oliveira. *O movimento da independência: O Império brasileiro (1821–1889).* 2nd ed. São Paulo: Melhoramentos, 1957.

Lima, Raul, ed. *A Junta Governativa da Bahia e a Independência.* Rio de Janeiro: Arquivo Nacional, 1973.

Linebaugh, Peter, and Marcus Rediker. "The Many-Headed Hydra: Sailors, Slaves, and the Atlantic Working Class in the Eighteenth Century." *Journal of Historical Sociology* 3, no. 3 (September 1990): 225–252.

Lisanti, Luís. "Sur la nourriture des 'paulistas' entre le XVIIIᵉ et XIXᵉ siècles." *Annales: Economies, Sociétés, Civilisations* 18, no. 3 (May–June 1963): 531–540.

Lisanti [Filho], Luís, ed. *Negócios coloniais (Uma correspondência comercial do século XVIII).* Brasília and São Paulo: Ministério da Fazenda and Visão Editorial, 1973.

Lisboa, José da Silva. "'Carta muito interessante do advogado da Bahia . . . para Domingos Vandelli, Bahia, 18 de outubro de 1781,' in Eduardo de Castro e Almeida, *Inventario dos documentos relativos ao Brasil existentes no Archivo de Marinha e Ultramar,* Part II (Bahia, 1763–1786)." *ABNRJ* 32 (1910): 494–506.

———. *Observações sobre a franqueza da indústria, e estabelecimento de fábricas no Brasil.* With an introduction by Fernando Antônio Novais and José Jobson de Andrade Arruda. Brasília: Senado Federal, 1999.

Livro que dá razão do Estado do Brasil. 1612. Facsim. ed., Rio de Janeiro: Instituto Nacional do Livro and Ministério da Educação e Cultura, 1968.

Lobo, Eulália Maria Lahmeyer. *Processo Administrativo Ibero-Americano (Aspectos Sócio-Econômicos—Período Colonial).* Rio de Janeiro: Biblioteca do Exército Editora, 1962.

Lockhart, James. *The Nahuas After the Conquest: A Social and Cultural History of the Indians of Central Mexico, Sixteenth Through Eighteenth Centuries.* Stanford, CA: Stanford University Press, 1992.

Lugar, Catherine. "The Merchant Community of Salvador, Bahia, 1780–1830." Ph.D. diss., State University of New York at Stony Brook, 1980.

Lynch, John. "The Origins of Spanish American Independence." In *The Cam-*

bridge History of Latin America, edited by Leslie Bethell, 3: 3–50. Cambridge, Eng.: Cambridge University Press, 1985.

Macaulay, Neill. Dom Pedro: The Struggle for Liberty in Brazil and Portugal, 1798–1834. Durham, NC: Duke University Press, 1986.

Maggie, Yvonne. Medo do feitiço: Relações entre magia e poder no Brasil. Rio de Janeiro: Arquivo Nacional, 1992.

Maia, Pedro Moacir, ed. O Museu de Arte Sacra da Universidade Federal da Bahia. São Paulo: Banco Safra, 1987.

Majoribanks, Alexander. Travels in South and North America. London and New York: Simpkin, Marshall and Appleton, 1853.

Manchester, Alan K. "The Transfer of the Portuguese Court to Rio de Janeiro." In Conflict and Continuity in Brazilian Society, edited by Henry H. Keith and S. F. Edwards, 148–183. Columbia: University of South Carolina Press, 1969.

Mangan, Jane E. Trading Roles: Gender, Ethnicity, and the Urban Economy in Colonial Potosí. Durham, NC: Duke University Press, 2005.

Marti, Judith. "Nineteenth-Century Views of Women's Participation in Mexico's Markets." In Women Traders in Cross-Cultural Perspective: Mediating Identities, Marketing Wares, edited by Linda J. Seligmann, 27–44. Stanford, CA: Stanford University Press, 2001.

Martin, Cheryl English. Governance and Society in Colonial Mexico: Chihuahua in the Eighteenth Century. Stanford, CA: Stanford University Press, 1996.

Martyn, Henry. Memoir. Edited by John Sargent. London: J. Hatchard and Son, 1820.

Mata, Maria Eugénia. "Economic Ideas and Policies in Nineteenth-Century Portugal." Luso-Brazilian Review 39, no. 1 (Summer 2002): 29–42.

Matilla Tascón, Antonio. Abastecimiento de carne a Madrid (1477–1678). Colección Biblioteca de Estudios Madrileños, no. 26. Madrid: Instituto de Estudios Madrileños, 1994.

Mattos, Waldemar. Panorama econômico da Bahia, 1808–1960: Edição comemorativa do sesquicentenário da Associação Comercial da Bahia. Salvador: [Tip. Manu Editôra], 1961.

Mattoso, Kátia M. de Queirós. "Au nouveau monde: Une province d'un nouvel empire—Bahia au XIXe siècle." Ph.D. diss., Université de Paris–Sorbonne, 1986.

———. Bahia: A cidade de Salvador e seu mercado no século XIX. Coleção Estudos Brasileiros, no. 12. São Paulo and Salvador: HUCITEC and Secretaria Municipal de Educação e Cultura, 1978.

———. Bahia, século XIX: Uma província no Império. Rio de Janeiro: Nova Fronteira, 1992.

———. "Conjoncture et société au Brésil a la fin du XVIIIᵉ siècle: Prix et salaires à la veille de la Révolution des Alfaiates, Bahia, 1798." Cahiers des Ameriques Latines 5 (1970): 33–53.

———. Presença francesa no movimento democrático baiano de 1798. Salvador: Itapuã, 1969.

———. Testamentos de escravos libertos na Bahia no século XIX. Salvador: Centro de Estudos Bahianos, Universidade Federal da Bahia, 1979.

———, ed. "Albert Roussin: Testemunha das lutas pela independência da Bahia." 1822. Anais do Arquivo [Público] do Estado da Bahia 41 (1973): 116–168.

Maximilian [Emperor of Mexico (Ferdinand Joseph Maximilian of Austria)]. *Recollections of My Life*. 3 vols. London: Richard Bentley, 1868.

Maximilian Wied, Prinz von. *Viagem ao Brasil/Maximiliano, Principe de Wied-Neuwied*. Translated by Edgar Sussekind de Mendonça and Flavio Poppe de Figueiredo. Brasiliana (Grande Formato), no. 1. Belo Horizonte: Itatiaia and EDUSP, 1989.

Maxwell, Kenneth. *Conflicts and Conspiracies: Brazil and Portugal, 1750–1808*. Cambridge Latin American Studies, no. 16. Cambridge, Eng.: Cambridge University Press, 1973.

————. "The Generation of the 1790s and the Idea of Luso-Brazilian Empire." In *Colonial Roots of Modern Brazil: Papers of the Newberry Library Conference*, edited by Dauril Alden, 107–144. Berkeley and Los Angeles: University of California Press, 1973.

Metcalf, Alida C. *Family and Frontier in Colonial Brazil: Santana de Parnaíba, 1580–1822*. Berkeley: University of California Press, 1992.

Michelena y Rójas, Francisco. *Exploración oficial por la primera vez desde el norte de la America del Sur siempre por rios, entrando por las bocas del Orinóco, de los valles de este mismo y del Meta, Casiquiare, Rio-Negro ó Guaynia y Amazónas, hasta Nauta en el alto Marañon ó Amazónas, arriba de las bocas del Ucayali bajada del Amazónas hasta el Atlántico . . . Viaje a Rio de Janeiro desde Belen en el Gran Pará, por el Atlántico, tocando en las capitales de las principales provincias del imperio en los años, de 1855 hasta 1859*. Brussels: A. Locroix, Verboeckhoven, 1867.

Miller, Shawn William. *Fruitless Trees: Portuguese Conservation and Brazil's Colonial Timber*. Stanford, CA: Stanford University Press, 2000.

Mills, Kenneth, William B. Taylor, and Sandra Lauderdale Graham, eds. *Colonial Latin America: A Documentary History*. Wilmington, DE: Scholarly Resources, 2002.

Mintz, Sidney W. *Caribbean Transformations*. 1974. Reprint, Baltimore: Johns Hopkins University Press, 1984.

————. "The Role of the Middleman in the Internal Distribution System of a Caribbean Peasant Economy." *Human Organization* 15, no. 2 (Summer 1956): 18–23.

Monteiro, Joachim John. *Angola and the River Congo*. London: Macmillan, 1875.

Monteiro, Tobias. *História do Império: A elaboração da Independência*. 2nd ed. Reconquista do Brasil, n.s., no. 39–40. Belo Horizonte and São Paulo: Itatiaia and EDUSP, 1981.

Moraes [Pai], Alexandre José Mello, *Historia do Brasil-Reino e do Brasil-Imperio*. 2 vols. Rio de Janeiro: Typ. Pinheiro, 1871–1873.

————. *A independencia e o Imperio do Brazil [sic], ou A independencia comprada por dois milhões de libras sterlinas, e o Imperio do Brazil com dous imperadores no seu reconhecimento e cessão; seguido da historia da Constituição politica do patriarchado e da corrupção governamental, provado com documentos authenticos*. Rio de Janeiro: Typ. do Globo, 1877.

————. "Praças, largos, ruas, becos, travessas, templos, [e] edificios que contém as dez freguezias da cidade do Salvador, Bahia de Todos os Santos." In Alexandre José de Mello Moraes [Pai], ed., *Brasil historico*. Rio de Janeiro: Pinheiro, 1866. 2ª Serie, Tomo 1, pp. 257–282.

————, ed. *Brasil historico*. Rio de Janeiro: Pinheiro, 1866.

Morineau, Michel. "Rations militaires et rations moyennes en Holland au XVII siécles." *Annales: Economies, Sociétés, Civilisations* 18, no. 3 (May–June 1963): 521–531.

Morse, Richard M., Michael L. Conniff, and John Wibel, eds. *The Urban Development of Latin America, 1750–1920.* Stanford, CA: Stanford University Center for Latin American Studies, 1971.

Morton, F. W. O. "The Conservative Revolution of Independence: Economy, Society and Politics in Bahia, 1790–1840." Ph.D. diss., University of Oxford, 1974.

————. "The Military and Society in Bahia, 1800–1821." *Journal of Latin American Studies* 7, no. 2 (November 1975): 249–269.

Mosher, Jeffrey C. *Political Struggle, Ideology, and State Building: Pernambuco and the Construction of Brazil, 1817–1850.* Lincoln: University of Nebraska Press, 2008.

Mota, Carlos Guilherme, ed. *1822: Dimensões.* São Paulo: Perspectiva, 1972.

Mott, Luiz. "A escravatura: A propósito de uma representação a El-Rei sobre a escravatura no Brasil." *Revista do Instituto de Estudos Brasileiros* 14 (1973): 127–136.

————. "Subsídios à história do pequeno comércio no Brasil." *Revista de História*, no. 105 (1976): 81–106.

————, ed. and trans. "Um documento inédito para a história da Independência." In *1822: Dimensões*, edited by Carlos Guilherme Mota, 465–483. São Paulo: Perspectiva, 1972.

Muldrew, Craig. *The Economy of Obligation: The Culture of Credit and Social Relations in Early Modern England.* London and New York: Macmillan and St. Martin's, 1998.

Mulvey, Patricia Ann. "The Black Lay Brotherhoods of Colonial Brazil." Ph.D. diss., City University of New York, 1976.

Nascimento, Anna Amélia Vieira. *Dez freguesias da cidade do Salvador: Aspectos sociais e urbanos do século XIX.* Salvador: Fundação Cultural do Estado da Bahia, 1986.

Nazzari, Muriel. "Concubinage in Colonial Brazil: The Inequalities of Race, Class, and Gender." *Journal of Family History* 21, no. 2 (April 1996): 107–118.

Neves, Guilherme Pereira das. "As Máximas do Marquês: Moral e política na trajetória de Mariano José da Fonseca." In *Retratos do Império: Trajetórias individuais no mundo português nos séculos XVI a XIX*, edited by Ronaldo Vainfas, Georgina Silva dos Santos, and Guilherme Pereira das Neves, 297–321. Niterói: Editora da Universidade Federal Fluminense, 2006.

————. "O reverso do milagre: Ex-votos pintados e religiosidade em Angra dos Reis (RJ)." *Tempo* 7, no. 14 (January–June 2003): 27–50.

Neves, Lúcia Maria Bastos P[ereira das]. *Corcundas, constitucionais e pés-de-chumbo: A cultura política da Independência, 1820–1822.* Rio de Janeiro, 2002.

————. "Intelectuais brasileiros no oitocentos: A constituição de uma 'família' sob a proteção do poder imperial (1821–1838)." In *O estado como vocação: Idéias e práticas políticas no Brasil oitocentista*, edited by Maria Emília Prado, 9–32. Rio de Janeiro: Access, 1999.

Normano, J. F. *Brazil: A Study of Economic Types*. Chapel Hill: University of North Carolina Press, 1935.

Oberschall, Anthony, and Michael Seidman. "Food Coercion in Revolution and Civil War: Who Wins and How They Do It." *Comparative Studies in History and Society* 47, no. 2 (July 2005): 372–402.

Oliveira, Maria Inês Côrtes de. "Libertas da freguesia de Santana (1849): Ocupações e jornais." Paper distributed at a conference held at the Arquivo Público do Estado da Bahia, Salvador, July 1993 (courtesy of Alexandra Brown).

———. *O liberto: O seu mundo e os outros (Salvador, 1790–1890)*. São Paulo and Brasília: Corrupio and CNPq, 1988.

Ott, Carlos. *Formação e evolução étnica da cidade de Salvador: O folclore bahiano*. 2 vols. Salvador: Manú Editora, 1955–1957.

Paim, Antonio. *Cairu e o liberalismo econômico*. Rio de Janeiro: Tempo Brasileiro, 1968.

Paiva, Eduardo França. "Celebrando a alforria: Amuletos e práticas culturais entre as mulheres negras e mestiças do Brasil." In *Festa: Cultura e sociabilidade na América portuguesa*, edited by Ístvan Jancsó and Íris Kantor, 505–18. São Paulo: HUCITEC and EDUSP, 2001.

———. *Escravidão e universo cultural na colônia: Minas Gerais, 1716–1789*. Belo Horizonte: Editora UFMG, 2001.

Pang, Eul-Soo. *O Engenho Central do Bom Jardim na economia baiana: Alguns aspectos de sua história, 1875–1891*. Rio de Janeiro: Arquivo Nacional and Instituto Histórico e Geográfico Brasileiro, 1979.

———. *In Pursuit of Honor and Power: Noblemen of the Southern Cross in Nineteenth-Century Brazil*. Tuscaloosa: University of Alabama Press, 1988.

Pantoja, Selma. "A dimensão atlântica das quitandeiras." In *Diálogos oceânicos: Minas Gerais e as novas abordagens para uma história do império ultramarino português*, edited by Júnia Ferreira Furtado, 45–67. Belo Horizonte: Editora UFMG, 2001.

Parés, Luís Nicolau. "The 'Nagôization' Process in Bahian Candomblé." In *The Yoruba Diaspora in the Atlantic World*, edited by Toyin Falola and Matt Childs, 185–208. Bloomington: Indiana University Press, 2004.

Pereira, Hernani da Silva. *Considerações sobre a alimentação no Brazil: These para o doutoramento em medicina apresentada à Faculdade da Bahia*. Salvador: Imp. Popular, 1887.

Phillips, Carla Rahn. *Six Galleons for the King of Spain*. Baltimore: Johns Hopkins University Press, 1986.

Pinho [de Araújo], José Wanderley. "A abertura dos portos—Cairu." *Revista do Instituto Histórico e Geográfico Brasileiro* 243 (April–June 1959): 94–147.

———. "A Bahia, 1808–1856." In *História geral da civilização brasileira*, edited by Sérgio Buarque de Holanda, 242–311. São Paulo: Difusão Européia do Livro, 1964.

———. *Cotegipe e seu tempo: Primeira phase, 1815–1867*. São Paulo: Editora Nacional, 1937.

Pirenne, Henri. *Medieval Cities: Their Origin and the Revival of Trade*. Translated by Frank D. Halsey. Garden City, NY: Doubleday, 1925.

Pizarro e Araújo, José de Souza Azevedo. *Memórias históricas do Rio de Janeiro*

[1820–1822]. 2nd ed., 10 vols. Edited by Rubens Borba de Moraes. Rio de Janeiro: Instituto Nacional do Livro, 1945–1948.

Poppino, Rollie. "The Cattle Industry in Colonial Brazil." *Mid-America* 31, no. 4 (October 1949): 219–247.

———. *Feira de Santana*. Translated by Arquimedes Pereira Guimarães. Salvador: Itapuã, 1968.

Posthumus, Wilhelmus. *Inquiry into the History of Prices in Holland*. 2 vols. Leiden: Brill, 1946–1964.

Prior, James. *Voyage Along the Eastern Coast of Africa to Mosambique, Johanna, and Quiloa; to St. Helena; to Rio de Janeiro, Bahia, and Pernambuco in Brazil, in the Nisus Frigate*. London: Richard Phillips, 1819.

Proctor, Frank "Trey," III. "Gender and the Manumission of Slaves in New Spain." *Hispanic American Historical Review* 86, no. 2 (May 2006): 309–336.

Querino, Manuel. "Dos alimentos puramente africanos." In *Antologia do negro brasileiro*, comp. Edison [de Souza] Carneiro, 449–453. Rio de Janeiro: Edições de Ouro, 1967.

Ramos, Donald. "Marriage and the Family in Colonial Vila Rica." *Hispanic American Historical Review* 55, no. 2 (May 1975): 200–225.

Rebello, Domingos José Antonio. "Corographia, ou abreviada historia geographica do Imperio do Brasil [2nd ed.]." *Revista do Instituto Geográfico e Histórico da Bahia* 55 (1929): 5–235.

Reichert, Rolf, ed., trans., and comp. *Os documentos árabes do Arquivo do Estado da Bahia*. Publicações, no. 9. Salvador: Centro de Estudos Áfro-Orientais, Universidade Federal da Bahia, 1970.

Reis, Isabel Cristina Ferreira dos. *Histórias de vida familiar e afetiva de escravos na Bahia do século XIX*. Salvador: Centro de Estudos Baianos, 2001.

Reis, João José. "Candomblé in Nineteenth Century Bahia: Priests, Followers, Clients." *Slavery and Abolition* 22, no. 1 (2001): 116–134.

———. "Domingos Pereira Sodré: Um sacerdote africano na Bahia oitocentista." *Afro-Ásia*, no. 34 (2006): 237–313.

———. "A elite baiana face os movimentos sociais, Bahia: 1824–1840." *Revista de História* 54, no. 108 (December 1976): 341–384.

———. "A greve negra de 1857 na Bahia." *Revista USP*, no. 18 (June–August 1993): 6–29.

———. *A morte é uma festa: Ritos fúnebres e revolta popular no Brasil do século XIX*. São Paulo: Companhia das Letras, 1991.

———. "'Nos achamos em campo a tratar da liberdade': A resistência negra no Brasil oitocentista." In *Formação: Histórias*, vol. 1 of *Viagem incompleta: A experiência brasileira (1500–2000)*, edited by Carlos Guilherme Mota, 241–263. São Paulo: SENAC, 2000.

———. *Rebelião escrava no Brasil: A história do levante dos malês, 1835*. São Paulo: Brasiliense, 1986.

———. *Rebelião escrava no Brasil: A história do levante dos malês em 1835*. 2nd ed. São Paulo: Companhia das Letras, 2003.

———. *Slave Rebellion in Brazil: The Muslim Uprising of 1835 in Bahia*. Translated by Arthur Brakel. Baltimore: Johns Hopkins University Press, 1993.

———. "Slave Resistance in Brazil: Bahia, 1807–1835." *Luso-Brazilian Review* 25, no. 1 (Summer 1988): 111–144.

Reis, João José, and Márcia Gabriela D. de Aguiar. "'Carne sem osso e farinha sem caroço': O motim de 1858 contra a carestia na Bahia." *Revista de História*, no. 135 (2° semestre 1996): 133–159.

Reis, João José, and Beatriz Galloti Mamigonian. "Nagô and Mina: The Yoruba Diaspora in Brazil." In *The Yoruba Diaspora in the Atlantic World*, edited by Toyin Falola and Matt Childs, 77–110. Bloomington: Indiana University Press, 2004.

Reis, João José, and Eduardo Silva. *Negociação e conflito: A resistência negra no Brasil escravista.* São Paulo: Companhia das Letras, 1989.

Relatorio apresentado á Mesa e Junta da Casa da Santa Misericordia da Capital da Bahia pelo provedor Conde de Pereira Marinho por occasião da posse em 2 de julho de 1885. Salvador: Tourinho, 1885.

Ribeiro, Alexandre Vieira. "O comércio de escravos e a elite baiana no período colonial." In *Conquistadores e negociantes: Histórias de elites no Antigo Regime nos trópicos—América lusa, séculos XVI a XVIII*, edited by João Luís Ribeiro Fragoso, Carla Maria Carvalho de Almeida, and Antônio Carlos Jucá de Sampaio, 311–335. Rio de Janeiro: Civilização Brasileira, 2007.

Ribeiro, Ellen Melo dos Santos. "Abastecimento de farinha da cidade do Salvador, 1850–1870: Aspectos históricos." Unpublished master's thesis, Universidade Federal da Bahia, 1982.

Ribeyrolles, Charles. *Brasil pitoresco: História, descrições, viagens, colonização, intituitções, acompanhado de um álbum de vistas, panoramas, paisagens, costumes, etc. por Victor Frond.* 2nd ed. 2 vols. Translated by Gastão Penalva, with an introduction by Afonso d'E. Taunay. São Paulo and Brasília: Martins and Instituto Nacional do Livro, 1976.

Ridings, Eugene. *Business Interest Groups in Nineteenth-Century Brazil.* Cambridge, Eng.: Cambridge University Press, 1994.

Rocha, Antonio Penalves. "A economia política na desagregação do império português." In *A economia política e os dilemas do império Luso-Brasileiro (1790–1822)*, edited by José Luís Cardoso, 149–197. Lisbon: Comissão Nacional para as Comemorações dos Descobrimentos Portugueses, 2001.

Rodrigues, José Honório. *História da história do Brasil*, vol. 2, Tomo 1: *A historiografia conservadora.* Brasiliana, Grande Formato, no. 23. São Paulo and Brasília: Editora Nacional and Instituto Nacional do Livro, 1988.

———. *Independência: Revolução e contra-revolução.* 5 vols. Rio de Janeiro: Francisco Alves, 1975–1976.

Roosevelt, Anna Curtenius. *Parmana: Prehistoric Maize and Manioc Cultivation Along the Amazon and Orinoco.* New York: Academic Press, 1980.

Rose, Willie Lee, ed. *A Documentary History of Slavery in North America.* New York: Oxford University Press, 1976.

Rugendas, Johann Moritz. *Malerische Reise in Brasilien.* 1835. Facsim. ed., Stuttgart: Daco-Verlag, 1986.

Rugendas, Maurice [Johann Moritz]. *Voyage pittoresque dans le Brésil.* Translated by Marie de Golbery. Paris: Englemann, 1835.

Russell-Wood, A. J. R. "'Acts of Grace': Portuguese Monarchs and Their Subjects of African Descent in Eighteenth-Century Brazil." *Journal of Latin American Studies* 32, no. 2 (May 2000): 307–332.

———. "Black and Mulatto Brotherhoods in Colonial Brazil: A Study in Collective Behavior." *Hispanic American Historical Review* 54, no. 4 (November 1974): 567–602.

———. *The Black Man in Slavery and Freedom in Colonial Brazil.* New York: St. Martin's, 1982.

———. *Fidalgos and Philanthropists: The Santa Casa da Misericórdia of Bahia, 1550–1755.* Berkeley: University of California Press, 1968.

———. "Prestige, Power, and Piety in Colonial Brazil: The Third Orders of Salvador." *Hispanic American Historical Review* 69, no. 1 (February 1989): 61–89.

Ruy, Affonso. *História da Câmara Municipal da cidade do Salvador.* 2nd ed. Salvador: Câmara Municipal de Salvador, 1996.

"A Sabinada nas cartas de Barreto Pedroso a Rebouças." *ABNRJ* 88 (1968): 207–218.

Santos, Mario Augusto da Silva. "Sobrevivência e tensões sociais: Salvador (1890–1930)." Ph.D. diss., Universidade de São Paulo, 1982.

Saraiva, José Hermano. *História de Portugal.* Lisbon: Publicações Europa-América, 1993.

Sánchez-Albornoz, Nicolás. *The Population of Latin America.* Translated by W. A. R. Richardson. Berkeley: University of California Press, 1974.

Saunders, A. C. de C. M. *A Social History of Black Slaves and Freedmen in Portugal, 1441–1555.* Cambridge, Eng.: Cambridge University Press, 1982.

Scarano, Julita. "Black Brotherhoods: Integration or Contradiction?" *Luso-Brazilian Review* 16, no. 1 (Summer 1979): 1–17.

Schwartz, Stuart B. "The Formation of a Colonial Identity in Brazil." In *Colonial Identity in the Atlantic World, 1500–1800,* edited by Nicholas Canny and Anthony Pagden, 15–50. Princeton, NJ: Princeton University Press, 1987.

———. "'Gente da terra braziliense da nasção': Pensando o Brasil: A construção de um povo." In *Viagem incompleta: A experiência brasileira (1500–2000)—Formação, histórias,* edited by Carlos Guilherme Mota, 103–125. São Paulo: SENAC, 2000.

———. "The Manumission of Slaves in Colonial Brazil: Bahia, 1684–1745." *Hispanic American Historical Review* 54, no. 4 (November 1974): 603–635.

———. "Resistance and Accommodation in Eighteenth-Century Brazil: The Slaves' View of Slavery." *Hispanic American Historical Review* 57, no. 1 (February 1977): 69–81.

———. *Slaves, Peasants, and Rebels: Reconsidering Brazilian Slavery.* Urbana: University of Illinois Press, 1992.

———. *Sugar Plantations in the Formation of Brazilian Society: Bahia, 1550–1835.* Cambridge, Eng.: Cambridge University Press, 1985.

Scott, Julius Sherrard, III. "The Common Wind: Currents of Afro-American Communication in the Era of the Haitian Revolution." Ph.D. diss., Duke University, 1986.

Scully, William. *Brazil: Its Provinces and Chief Cities; the Manners and Customs of the People; Agricultural, Commercial and Other Statistics Taken from the Latest Official Documents; with a Variety of Useful and Entertaining Knowledge Both for the Merchant and the Emigrant.* London: Trübner, 1868.

Seidman, Michael. *Republic of Egos: A Social History of the Spanish Civil War.* Madison: University of Wisconsin Press, 2002.

Seligman, Linda J., ed. *Women Traders in Cross-Cultural Perspective: Mediating Identities, Marketing Wares.* Stanford, CA: Stanford University Press, 2001.

Selling Júnior, Theodor. *A Bahia e seus veleiros: Uma tradição que desapareceu.* Rio de Janeiro: Serviço de Documentação Geral da Marinha, 1976.

Serrão, Joel. *Dicionário de história de Portugal.* Porto: Iniciativas Editoriais, 1979.

Sierra y Mariscal, Francisco de. "Idéas geraes sobre a revolução do Brazil [sic] e suas consequencias." *ABNRJ* 43–44 (1920–21): 49–81.

Las siete partidas del sabio rey D. Alonso el IX con las variantes de más interés, y con la glosa del lic. Gregorio Lopez. Barcelona: Antonio Bergens, 1844.

Silva, Andrée Mansuy-Diniz. *Portrait d'un homme d'etat: D. Rodrigo de Souza Coutinho, Comte de Linhares, 1755–1812.* 2 vols. Lisbon and Paris: Fundação Calouste Gulbenkian and Centre Culturel Calouste Gulbenkian, 2003–2006.

Silva, Antonio Delgado da. *Collecção da legislação portuguesa desde a ultima compilação das ordenações . . .* 9 vols. Lisbon: Typ. Maigrense, 1825–1830.

———. *Collecção da legislação portuguesa desde a ultima compilação das ordenações . . .* 2nd ed. Lisbon: Typ. L. C. da Cunha and Typ. Maigrense, 1833–1858.

Silva, Antonio de Moraes. *Diccionario da lingua portugueza.* 8th ed. Rio de Janeiro: Empreza Litteraria Fluminense de A. A. da Silva Lobo, 1889.

Silva, Francisco Carlos Teixeira da. "Elevage et marché interne dans le Brésil de l'époque coloniale." In *Pour l'histoire du Brésil: Hommage à Kátia de Queirós Mattoso,* edited by François Crouzet, Philippe Bonnichon, and Denis Rolland, 321–330. Paris: L'Harmattan, 2000.

———. "A morfologia da escassez: Crises de subsistência e política econômica no Brasil colônia (Salvador e Rio de Janeiro, 1680–1790)." Ph.D. diss., Universidade Federal Fluminense, 1990.

Silva, Ignacio Accioli de Cerqueira e. *Memórias históricas e políticas da província da Bahia.* 2nd ed. 6 vols. Edited by Braz do Amaral. Salvador: Imprensa Official do Estado, 1919–1940.

Silva, Luiz Geraldo. *A faina, a festa e o rito: Uma etnografia histórica sobre as gentes do mar, sécs. XVII ao XIX.* Campinas: Papirus, 2001.

Silva, Maria Beatriz Nizza da. "Mulheres brancas no fim do período colonial." *Cadernos Pagu: Fazendo História das Mulheres,* no. 4 (1995).

———. "Mulheres e patrimônio familiar no Brasil no fim do período colonial." *Acervo* 9, no. 1–2 (December 1996): 85–98.

———. *A primeira gazeta da Bahia: "Idade d'Ouro do Brasil."* São Paulo and Brasília: Cultrix and Instituto Nacional do Livro, 1978.

———. *Sistema de casamento no Brasil colonial.* Coleção Coroa Vermelha, Estudos Brasileiros, no. 6. São Paulo: T. A. Queiroz and EDUSP, 1984.

Silva, Marilene Rosa Nogueira da. *Negro na rua: A nova face da escravidão.* São Paulo: HUCITEC, 1988.

Slemian, Andréa, and João Paulo G. Pimenta. *O "nascimento político" do Brasil: As origens do estado e da nação (1808–1825).* Rio de Janeiro: DP&A, 2003.

Slenes, Robert W. *Na senzala uma flor: Esperanças e recordações na formação da família escrava—Brasil sudeste, século XIX.* Rio de Janeiro: Nova Fronteira, 1999.

Smith, Adam. *An Inquiry Into the Nature and Causes of the Wealth of Nations.* 6th[?] ed. Edited by Edwin Cannan. Chicago: University of Chicago Press, 1976.

Smith, Robert. "The Canoe in West African History." *Journal of African History* 11, no. 4 (1970): 515–533.

Smith, Robert C. *Arquitetura colonial bahiana: Alguns aspectos de sua história.* Publicações do Museu do Estado, no. 14. Salvador: Secretaria de Educação e Cultura, 1951.

Soares, Carlos Eugênio Líbano. *A capoeira escrava e outras tradições rebeldes no Rio de Janeiro (1808–1850).* Campinas: Editora Unicamp, 2001.

Soares, Cecília Moreira. "As ganhadeiras: Mulher e resistência em Salvador no século XIX." *Afro-Ásia,* no. 17 (1996): 57–71.

Soares, Márcio Sousa. "Cirurgiões negros: Saberes africanos sobre o corpo e as doenças nas ruas do Rio de Janeiro durante a primeira metade do século XIX." *Locus: Revista de História* 8, no. 2 (2002): 43–58.

Soeiro, Susan A. "A Baroque Nunnery: The Economic and Social Role of a Colonial Convent—Santa Clara do Destêrro, Salvador, Bahia, 1677–1800." Ph.D. diss., New York University, 1974.

———. "The Social and Economic Role of the Convent: Women and Nuns in Colonial Bahia, 1677–1800." *Hispanic American Historical Review* 54, no. 2 (May 1974): 209–232.

Souza, Laura de Mello e. *Desclassificados do ouro: A pobreza mineira no século XVIII.* Rio de Janeiro: Graal, 1982.

———. *O diabo e a Terra de Santa Cruz: Feitiçaria e religiosidade popular no Brasil colonial.* São Paulo: Companhia das Letras, 1987.

Souza, Paulo César. *A Sabinada: A revolta separatista da Bahia.* São Paulo: Brasiliense, 1987.

Spix, Johann Baptist von, and Karl Friedrich Philipp von Martius. *Através da Bahia: Excerptos da obra "Reise in Brasilien".* 3rd ed. Translated by Manuel Augusto Pirajá da Silva and Paulo Wolf. São Paulo: Editora Nacional, 1938.

Stampp, Kenneth M. *The Peculiar Institution: Slavery in the Ante-Bellum South.* New York: Vintage, 1956.

Stein, Stanley J. *The Brazilian Cotton Manufacture: Textile Enterprise in an Underdeveloped Area, 1850–1950.* Cambridge, MA: Harvard University Press, 1957.

Sudarkasa, Niara. *Where Women Work: A Study of Yoruba Women in the Marketplace and in the Home.* Anthropological Papers, no. 53. Ann Arbor: Museum of Anthropology, University of Michigan, 1973.

Sullivan, Edward J., ed. *Brazil: Body and Soul.* New York: Guggenheim Museum, 2001.

Super, John C. *Food, Conquest, and Colonization in Sixteenth-Century Spanish America.* Albuquerque: University of New Mexico Press, 1988.

Suzannet, Conde de. *O Brasil em 1845 (Semelhanças e diferenças após um século).* Translated by Márcia de Moura Castro, with an introduction by Austregésilo de Athayde. Rio de Janeiro: Casa do Estudante do Brasil, 1957.

Sweigart, Joseph E. *Coffee Factorage and the Emergence of a Brazilian Capital Market, 1850–1888.* New York: Garland, 1987.

Taunay, Hippolyte, and Ferdinand Denis. *Le Brésil, ou histoire, moeurs, usages et coutumes des habitans de ce royaume.* 6 vols. Paris: Nepveu, 1822.

Tavares, Luís Henrique Dias. *História da sedição intentada na Bahia em 1798 ("A conspiração dos alfaiates").* São Paulo: Livraria Pioneira, 1975.

——. *A independência do Brasil na Bahia.* 3rd ed. Salvador: EDUFBA, 2005.

Terraciano, Kevin. "Native Expressions of Piety in Mextec Testaments." In *Dead Giveaways: Indigenous Testaments of Colonial Mesoamerica and the Andes,* edited by Susan Kellogg and Matthew Restall, 115–140. Salt Lake City: University of Utah Press, 1998.

Thompson, E. P. "The Moral Economy of the English Crowd in the Eighteenth Century." *Past & Present,* no. 50 (February 1971): 76–136.

Thornton, John. *Africa and Africans in the Making of the Atlantic World, 1400–1680.* Cambridge, Eng.: Cambridge University Press, 1992.

Tollenare, L. F. de. *Notas dominicais tomadas durante uma viagem em Portugal e no Brasil em 1816, 1817, e 1818.* Salvador: Progresso, 1956.

Turnbull, John. *A Voyage Round the World, in the Years 1800, 1801, 1802, 1803, and 1804 in Which the Author Visited Madeira, the Brazils, Cape of Good Hope, the English Settlements of Botany Bay and Norfolk Island; and the Principal Islands in the Pacific Ocean. With a Continuation of Their History to the Present Period.* London: Maxwell, 1813.

Vainfas, Ronaldo. "Moralidades brasílicas: Deleites sexuais e linguagem erótica na sociedade escravista." In *História da vida privada no Brasil,* vol. 1: *Cotidano e vida privada na América portuguesa,* edited by Laura de Mello e Souza (Fernando A. Novais, gen. ed.), 221–273. São Paulo: Companhia das Letras, 1997.

Vale, Brian. *Independence or Death! British Sailors and Brazilian Independence, 1822–1825.* London: British Academic Press/I.B. Taurus Publishers, 1996.

Van Young, Eric. *Hacienda and Market in Eighteenth-Century Mexico: The Rural Economy of the Guadalajara Region, 1675–1820.* Berkeley: University of California Press, 1981.

Vargas, Thomaz Tamayo de. "A restauração da cidade do Salvador, Bahia de Todos os Santos, na provincia do Brasil pelas armas de D. Felippe IV, rei catholico das hespanhas e indias, publicada em 1628." Translated and edited by Ignacio Accioli de Cerqueira e Silva. *Revista do Instituto Geográfico e Histórico da Bahia,* no. 56 (1930): 7–315.

Varnhagen, Francisco Adolfo de. *História da independência do Brasil até ao reconhecimento pela antiga metrópole, compreendendo, separadamente, a dos sucessos ocorridos em algumas províncias até essa data.* 3rd ed. Edited by Baron of Rio Branco and Hélio Vianna. São Paulo: Melhoramentos, 1957.

Vasquez de Warman, Irene. "El pósito y la ahóndiga en la Nueva España." *Historia Mexicana* 17, no. 3 (January–March 1968): 395-426.

Verger, Pierre. *Notícias da Bahia—1850.* Salvador: Corrupío, 1981.

——. *Trade Relations Between the Bight of Benin and Bahia from the 17th to 19th Century.* Translated by Evelyn Crawford. Ibadan: Ibadan University Press, 1976.

Versiani, Flávio Rabello. "Escravidão no Brasil: Uma análise econômica." *Revista Brasileira de Economia* 48, no. 4 (December 1994): 463–478.

Vide, Sebastião Monteiro da. *Constituições primeiras do arcebispado da Bahia, feitas e ordenadas pelo. . . 5º arcebispo do dito arcebispado . . . , propostas e aceitas em o synodo diocesano que o dito senhor celebrou em 12 de junho do anno de 1707.* São Paulo: Typographia "2 de Dezembro" de Antonio Louzada Antunes, 1853.

Vilhena, Luís dos Santos. *A Bahia no século XVIII.* 2nd ed. Edited by Braz do Amaral. With an introduction by Edison Carneiro. Salvador: Itapuã, 1969.

Walsh, Robert. *Notices of Brazil in 1828 and 1829.* 2 vols. Boston: Richardson, Lord, and Holbrook and Carvill, 1831.

Webb, Sidney, and Beatrice Webb. "The Assize of Bread." *Economic Journal* 14 (June 1904): 196–218.

Westphalen, Cecília Maria. *Porto de Paranaguá, um sedutor.* Curitiba: Secretaria de Estado da Cultura, 1998.

Wetherell, James. *Brazil: Stray Notes from Bahia, Being Extracts from Letters, Etc., During a Residence of Fifteen Years.* Liverpool: Webb and Hunt, 1860.

Willems, Emílio. *Latin American Culture: An Anthropological Synthesis.* New York: Harper and Row, 1975.

Zemella, Mafalda P. *O abastecimento da capitania das Minas Gerais no século XVIII.* 2nd ed. São Paulo: HUCITEC and EDUSP, 1990.

CREDITS FOR MAPS AND ILLUSTRATIONS

Map 1.1. The Recôncavo of Bahia. Derived, with some additions and alterations, from Bahia, Secretaria dos Transportes e Comunicações, Mapa do sistema de transportes, 1981, with additional information drawn from "Vista hydrographica do Recôncavo da Bahia," in Alexandre José Mello Moraes [Pai], *Historia do Brasil-Reino e do Brasil-Imperio*, 2 vols. (Rio de Janeiro: Typ. Pinheiro, 1871–1873), unpaged insert.

Maps 1.2 and 1.3. Salvador's bay shore, ca. 1847, and Salvador's center, ca. 1847. Based on Carlos Augusto Weyll, Mappa topographico da cidade de Salvador e seus suburbios, 1846, Arquivo Público do Estado da Bahia, Planta 32, copied courtesy of João José Reis.

Map. 4.1. The Bahian coast. Derived from "Estado da Bahia," in Rubens de Azevedo, comp., *Atlas geográfico Melhoramentos*, 28th ed. (São Paulo: Companhia Melhoramentos, 1968), p. 66.

Figure 1.1 and frontispiece. Panorama of the city, 1861. Lithograph made from photograph by Victor Frond, in Charles Ribeyrolles, *Brazil pitoresco . . .* (Paris: Lemercier, 1861), Plate 35. Copied courtesy of the Seção de Iconografia, Biblioteca Nacional do Rio de Janeiro.

Figure 1.2. The lower city as seen from above, 1860. Photograph by Benjamin R. Mulock, from Coleção Gilberto Ferrez, Acervo Instituto Moreira Salles.

Figure 2.1. Female street vendor, ca. 1776–1800. Watercolor by Carlos Julião, copied courtesy of the Seção de Iconografia, Biblioteca Nacional do Rio de Janeiro.

Figure 2.2. Male street vendor, 1960. Photograph by Richard Graham.

Figure 2.3. Corner grocery store and street vendors, 1835. Lithograph by Maurice [Johann Moritz] Rugendas, *Voyage Pittoresque dans le Brésil*, trans. from the German by Marie de Golbery (Paris: Englemann, 1835), p. 321.

Figure 3.1. Street vendors at Rosário church, with Carmo in the background, 1860. Photograph by Benjamin R. Mulock, from Coleção Gilberto Ferrez, Acervo Instituto Moreira Salles.

Figure 4.1. Sailboat with provisions, 1835. Lithograph by Maurice [Johann Moritz] Rugendas, *Voyage Pittoresque dans le Brésil*, trans. from the German by Marie de Golbery (Paris: Englemann, 1835), p. 306.

Figure 4.2. Sailboats docked in Nazaré before sailing to Salvador, 1860. Photograph by Camilo Vedani, 1860/65, from Coleção Gilberto Ferrez, Acervo Instituto Moreira Salles.

Figure 4.3. Sailboats unloading provisions at a Salvador beach, 1960. Photograph by Richard Graham.

Figure 11.1. City council chambers, Salvador, ca. 1860. Photograph by Benjamin R. Mulock, from Coleção Gilberto Ferrez, Acervo Instituto Moreira Salles.

Numbers in italics refer to maps.

CPSIA information can be obtained
at www.ICGtesting.com
Printed in the USA
BVHW071621110121
597452BV00002BA/67